Graham A. Reid

LONDON, 17th Dec., 2009.

FOUR WYCLIFFITE DIALOGUES

EARLY ENGLISH TEXT SOCIETY
O.S. 333
2009

OXFORD
UNIVERSITY PRESS

Great Clarendon Street, Oxford OX2 6DP

Oxford University Press is a department of the University of Oxford.
It furthers the University's objective of excellence in research, scholarship,
and education by publishing worldwide in

Oxford New York

Auckland Cape Town Dar es Salaam Hong Kong Karachi
Kuala Lumpur Madrid Melbourne Mexico City Nairobi
New Delhi Shanghai Taipei Toronto

With offices in

Argentina Austria Brazil Chile Czech Republic France Greece
Guatemala Hungary Italy Japan Poland Portugal Singapore
South Korea Switzerland Thailand Turkey Ukraine Vietnam

Oxford is a registered trade mark of Oxford University Press
in the UK and in certain other countries

Published in the United States
by Oxford University Press Inc., New York

First published 2009

British Library Cataloguing in Publication Data
Data available

Library of Congress Cataloging in Publication Data
Data applied for

ISBN 978-0-19-957848-1

1 3 5 7 9 10 8 6 4 2

Typeset by Anne Joshua, Oxford
Printed in Great Britain
on acid-free paper by
The Cromwell Press Group, Trowbridge, Wiltshire

FOUR WYCLIFF
DIALOGUES

Dialogue between Jon and Ri
Dialogue between a Friar and a
Dialogue between Reson and G
Dialogue between a Clerk and a

EDITED BY

FIONA SOMERSET

Published for
THE EARLY ENGLISH TEXT SOCI
by the
OXFORD UNIVERSITY PRESS
2009

PREFACE

Like many editions, this one has simmered for a long time, often on the back burner, while its editor became wiser. I am grateful to all those who have helped along the way. Anne Hudson's scholarly generosity towards a doctoral student visiting from the USA and wanting to learn to edit will never be forgotten. Norman Kretzmann provided the solid grounding in medieval philosophy that made this edition's Explanatory Notes possible. Early on Dr Briar Gordon, discovering that copyright law restricts the circulation of the deposited copy of her thesis 'Four Lollard Dialogues' to New Zealand, kindly sent me her personal copy on extended loan, thus making it possible for me to read the full text of RG even before visiting Trinity College; later, she arranged to have two copies of her thesis deposited in US libraries so that more students might consult them. The librarians of Trinity College, Cambridge, Trinity College Dublin, and Durham University Library welcomed visits, provided generous access, and quickly responded to microfilm orders.

The University of Western Ontario's Vice President's research fund paid for the purchase of a microfilm reader, while the Social Sciences and Humanities Research Council of Canada provided a three-year research grant and the assistance of David Watt, then a graduate student, now a valued colleague. More colleagues, including David Aers, Helen Barr, Sarah Beckwith, Mishtooni Bose, Andrew Cole, Mary Dove, Shannon Gayk, Richard Firth Green, Ralph Hanna, Jill C. Havens, J. Patrick Hornbeck, Simon Horobin, Anne Hudson, Maureen Jurkowski, Jim Knowles, Steve Lahey, Mary Raschko, Nicole Rice, John Scattergood, Alan Somerset, and Lawrence Warner, shared knowledge (and sometimes microfilms and articles too) to elucidate specific points. Nicholas Watson is famous for accidentally using the back of one early draft of the edition for scrap paper, but also for giving just the right sort of practical help, at several key points—not least, the advice to set the edition aside for a time and write some articles. Ian Doyle generously shared an excerpt from his and A. J. Piper's forthcoming catalogue of Durham University Library manuscripts, as well as other encouragement and advice. Alan Fletcher very kindly double-checked some details in the Irish manuscripts as the volume went to press.

Duke University has been generous with research funding. The National Humanities Center provided a year's fellowship that made possible the edition's completion uninterrupted by other commitments. Bob Manners and Thomas Nickles provided essential IT assistance, respectively at the beginning and end of the process. The Society's Editorial Secretary, Helen Spencer, the Society's anonymous reader, and the copy-editor Bonnie Blackburn gave very helpful advice. Will Revere and Hillary Eklund assisted with copy-editing and preparing the final draft for publication. Tim, Declan, Eoin, and Teagan have shown much forbearance during the many, sometimes weary, hours of separation brought by 'mummy's work'.

Permission from the Master and Fellows of Trinity College, Cambridge, the Board of Trinity College Dublin, and the University of Durham to print the texts and include the plates is gladly acknowledged.

F.S.

CONTENTS

LIST OF ILLUSTRATIONS

ABBREVIATIONS

The main manuscripts edited here are referred to under the following sigla:

B	Cambridge, Trinity College, MS B 14 50 [333]
C	Durham, University Library, MS Cosin V.III.6
F	Dublin, Trinity College, MS 244 [C 3 12]
R	Dublin, Trinity College, MS 245 [C 5 6]

However, since there is only one copy of each text, the contents of each dialogue will be referred to far more often by their abbreviated titles. The following table expands each abbreviated title in the order in which the texts appear in the volume, and assigns each text to its corresponding manuscript siglum:

JR	*Dialogue between Jon and Richard*	B
FS	*Dialogue between a Friar and a Secular*	F
RG	*Dialogue between Reson and Gabbyng*	R
CK	*Dialogue between a Clerk and a Knight*	C

All other non-standard abbreviations used in the Introduction, Explanatory Notes, and Glossary are included in the following list. For the symbols and abbreviations used in the edited texts and their apparatus, please consult the discussion of Editorial Method in the Introduction, pp. lv–lix.

37 Concl.	[Thirty-Seven Conclusions] *Remonstrance against Romish Corruptions in the Church*, ed. Josiah Forshall (London, 1851)
ALD	*Apology for Lollard Doctrines*, ed. James Henthorn Todd, Camden Society, 20 (London, 1842)
Arnold	*Select English Works of John Wyclif*, ed. Thomas Arnold, vol. iii (Oxford, 1871)
C. [etc.]	See 'canon law citations'
canon law citations	The different parts are cited in the Modern Form, explained in James A. Brundage, *Medieval Canon Law* (London and New York, 1995), Appendix 1, 190–201. The online, searchable editions of the *Decretum* and *Liber Extra* at ⟨http://mdz.bib-bvb.

	de/digbib/gratian> and <http://www.fh-augsburg.e/~harsch/Chronologia/Lspost13/GregoriusIX/gre_0000.htm> are used here.
CCC 296	Cambridge, Corpus Christi College MS 296
Chaucer	Geoffrey Chaucer, *The Riverside Chaucer*, gen. ed. Larry D. Benson (Boston, 1987). Canterbury Tales are cited by title, fragment, and line number within fragment.
CHLMP	*Cambridge History of Later Medieval Philosophy*, ed. Norman Kretzmann, Anthony Kenny, and Jan Pinborg (Cambridge, 1982)
Corpus of Middle English Prose and Verse	The online searchable database available as part of the website of the *Middle English Dictionary*: see *Middle English Dictionary*
D. [etc.]	See 'canon law citations'
Decretum	See 'canon law citations'
Dialogus	John Wyclif, *Dialogus sive speculum ecclesie militantis*, ed. Alfred W. Pollard, Wyclif Society (London, 1886)
EV	Earlier Version (see *Wycliffite Bible*)
EWS	*English Wycliffite Sermons*, ed. Anne Hudson and Pamela Gradon, 5 vols. (Oxford, 1983–96). Cited by volume and page number for introduction and commentary, and for text, sermon number, page number, and line number within sermon.
FD	*Friar Daw's Reply* (see *Upland series*)
FZ	*Fasciculi Zizaniorum*, ed. Walter W. Shirley (London, 1858).
Gower, *CA*	John Gower, *Confessio Amantis*, in *The Complete Works of John Gower*, ed. G. C. Macaulay (Oxford, 1899–1902), vols. ii–iii. Cited by volume, book, and line number.
IMEP	*Index of Middle English Prose*, gen. ed. A. S. G. Edwards (Woodbridge, Suffolk, 1984–). Cited by handlist number and page number.
IPMEP	*Index of Printed Middle English Prose*, ed. R. E. Lewis, N. F. Blake, and A. S. G. Edwards (New York and London, 1985). Cited by entry number.
JU	*Jack Upland* (see *Upland series*)
LALME	*A Linguistic Atlas of Late Mediaeval English*, ed.

	A. McIntosh, M. Samuels, and M. Benskin, 4 vols. (Aberdeen, 1986). Dot maps in vol. i are cited by dot map number, item maps from vol. ii by item map number, linguistic profiles from vol. iii by LP number (see also LP).
Liber Extra	See 'canon law citations'
Lindberg, i	*English Wyclif Tracts 1–3*, ed. Conrad Lindberg, Studia Anglistica Norvegica, 5 (Oslo, 1991)
Lindberg, ii	*English Wyclif Tracts 4–6*, ed. Conrad Lindberg, Studia Anglistica Norvegica, 11 (Oslo, 2000)
LP	Linguistic Profile (see *LALME*)
LV	Later Version (see *Wycliffite Bible*)
Matthew	*The English Works of Wyclif hitherto Unprinted*, ed. F. D. Matthew, EETS OS 74 (1880)
MED	*The Middle English Dictionary*, gen. eds. Hans Kurath, Sherman Kuhn, and Robert E. Lewis (Ann Arbor, 1952–2001). The online version available at <http://ets.umdl.umich.edu/m/med/> is used here.
NewIMEV	*A New Index of Middle English Verse,* ed. Julia Boffey and A. S. G. Edwards (London, 2005)
ODNB	*Oxford Dictionary of National Biography*, ed. Lawrence Goldman et al. (Oxford, 2004). The online edition available at <http://www.oxforddnb.com/> is used here.
OED	*Oxford English Dictionary*, gen. eds. J. A. Simpson and E. S. C. Weiner, 2nd edn., 20 vols. (Oxford, 1989). The online version available at <http://dictionary.oed.com/entrance.dtl> is used here.
PG	*Patrologia Graeca*
PL	*Patrologia Latina*
PP	*Piers Plowman* A, B, and C versions cited by passus number (or Prol. for prologue) and line number. The Athlone Press editions by George Kane (A, London, 1960), Kane and E. Talbot Donaldson (B, London, 1975), and Kane and G. H. Russell (C, London, 1997) have been used throughout.
PPC	*Piers the Plowman's Crede*. In *The Piers Plowman Tradition*, ed. Helen Barr (London, 1993)
PROME	*Parliament Rolls of Medieval England*, gen. ed.

	C. Given-Wilson, Scholarly Digital Editions, The National Archives, The History of Parliament Trust (Leicester, 2005); online at <http://www.sd-editions.com/PROME/home.html>. Cited by king, year and month of parliament, paragraph, and item numbers.
SEWW	*Selections from English Wycliffite Writings*, ed. Anne Hudson (Cambridge, 1978)
Thomson	Williell R. Thomson, *The Latin Writings of John Wyclif*, Subsidia Mediaevalia, 14 (Toronto, 1983). Cited by entry number in square brackets as well as page number.
Treatise on Penance	See 'canon law citations'
Upland series	*Jack Upland, Friar Daw's Reply, and Upland's Rejoinder*, ed. P. L. Heyworth (Oxford, 1968). See also *JU*; *FDR*; *UR*.
UR	*Upland's Rejoinder* (see *Upland series*)
Vae oct.	*Vae octuplex*, in *SEWW*, 75–83
Wycliffite Bible	*The Holy Bible, Containing the Old and New Testaments* . . ., ed. Josiah Forshall and Frederic Madden, 4 vols. (Oxford, 1850): in cases where the variation between what Forshall and Madden print as the EV and LV is merely orthographical, only the LV is given.
X [etc.]	See 'canon law citations'

INTRODUCTION

I. SCOPE OF THE EDITION

Each of the four texts included in this edition is a polemical prose dialogue extant in a single copy. None of the four dialogues has ever appeared in print, let alone in a published critical edition, even though three of the four are preserved in three of the best-known lollard compilations, heavily quarried by early editors and much studied by scholars.[1] Each dialogue was composed anew, or modified from previous sources, by a lollard writer committed (though perhaps not exclusively) to producing material in the vernacular, over the relatively short span of years between *c.*1380 and *c.*1420.[2] Yet the scope of this edition is wider than this description might suggest. Between them, the four dialogues draw upon a surprisingly broad sampling of the wide range of uses to which prose dialogue forms were turned in the later medieval period, as well as the literary devices by means of which these purposes were achieved. Their influences range from the literary products of quarrels within as well

[1] Arnold and Matthew between them put in print nearly all of the contents of F and R apart from one text previously edited by James H. Todd, but pass over the dialogues, in company with a few other short or fragmentary texts, in silence. Their omissions have previously been noted by Hudson, *Lollards and their Books*, 196 n. 2 (and see 183 n. 4). Deanesley, *Lollard Bible*, edits two texts from B; one was later edited again by Curt Bühler, 'A Lollard Tract', the other by Hudson in *SEWW*. Hudson includes an excerpt from C in *SEWW*. For details see the Descriptions of the Manuscripts, §2 below. For the manuscript sigla and abbreviated titles used throughout the volume, see the list and table at the beginning of the list of Abbreviations, p. ix. A brief guide to all other abbreviations used throughout the volume follows the list and table.

[2] The four dialogues as a group were first brought to the public eye in Anne Hudson's 'A Lollard Quaternion', an article centred on the Durham dialogue but briefly surveying the contents of all four: see Hudson, *Lollards and their Books*, 193–200. A previous thesis edition is by Briar Gordon, 'Four Lollard Dialogues: An Edition with Commentary', unfortunately unavailable for consultation through interlibrary loan owing to international copyright laws. A fifth anonymous prose dialogue associated with lollardy and extant in a single copy, that between a Wise Man and a Fool in Cambridge University Library Ii.6.26, is not included here since the manuscript in which it appears focuses over the course of twelve consecutive treatises on the issue of biblical translation. Thus its contents are better suited for publication as a whole, as in the thesis edition by Simon Hunt, 'An Edition of Tracts in Favour of Scriptural Translation and of Some Texts Connected with Lollard Biblical Scholarship'. Mary Dove is preparing an edition of the twelve tracts in CUL Ii.6.26, the Prologue to the Wycliffite Bible, and other texts advocating biblical translation for the University of Exeter Press.

as between fraternal and religious orders, to written renderings of the forms and idioms of oral academic disputation, to Wyclif's own *Dialogus* and *Trialogus*, to the literary efforts of publicists across Europe who engaged in arguments over papal authority in response to a series of crises including Philip IV of France's conflict with Boniface VIII in the first decade of the fourteenth century, Ludwig IV of Bavaria's dispute with John XXII in the 1320s and 1330s, and the Papal Schism of 1378–1417.

These four dialogues also bear witness to the variety of forms in which lollard writings were disseminated, recopied, and preserved across the span of years from the fourteenth through to the seventeenth centuries. B appears to be a university-trained preacher's two-part collection of useful materials in a working notebook. It was donated to Trinity College Cambridge (probably at his death in 1604, since his will bequeaths his parchment books to the college) by the prominent Calvinist John Whitgift, Master of the College 1567–77 and from 1583 to 1604 Archbishop of Canterbury.[3] F and R are two of the large anthologies produced by lollards: F's contents are for the most part strongly polemical and focused on abuses in the contemporary Church, while R seemingly aims to provide an alternative programme of religious instruction. Both were donated to Trinity College Dublin in 1661 as part of the library of the prodigiously learned James Ussher, archbishop of Armagh from 1625, who probably acquired them in the course of his many years of research on medieval heresies.[4] C is a single booklet or quaternion that appears to have circulated independently—as, indeed, other short texts may have done, whether in booklets or on individual leaves, before most of the writings that remain to us were recopied or rebound into larger anthologies.[5] Although not preserved more safely within a larger codex, C survived somehow until the early seventeenth century, when it was taken apart and interleaved with paper so that it could be supplied with a facing-page transcription. The transcription may have been prepared under the direction of the Puritan William Crashaw, another dedicated scholar of religious antiquities and a friend of Ussher's; it was Crashaw who supplied in his own hand a

[3] See *ODNB* s.v. 'John Whitgift'; James, *Western Manuscripts*, i, pp. vi–vii, 457.

[4] See *ODNB* s.v. 'James Ussher', and on the complexities of the donation of James Ussher's library, see Barnard, 'The Purchase of Archbishop Ussher's Library in 1657'.

[5] On the formats in which lollard writings circulated see further Hudson, *Lollards and their Books*; ead., 'Lollard Book-Production', esp. 135; Scase, '"Strange and Wonderful Bills"'.

title page and prefatory dedication to James I as well as extensive annotation of the original text, probably between 1605 and 1609.[6] Since Crashaw's annotations will be of interest to anyone investigating the seventeenth-century reception of lollard writings, they are reproduced in full (insofar as they are legible) in the textual apparatus.

There are, of course, also similarities between these works that justify bringing them together in a single volume, beyond their superficial commonality of form and genre, their common debt of survival to the scholarly activities of sixteenth- and seventeenth-century Protestants, and their shared neglect by early printers and editors. Most notable is the dialogues' common concern with staging a debate not only on the ostensible topic or topics under dispute, but on the issue of who has the right to speak and to be heard, and on what basis. A dialogue in which each disputant represents a type or class of person (as in JR, FS, and CK), or an aspect or quality of personhood (as in RG), is obviously an ideal arena for such debate. Thus, Reson evaluates the force of reasoned argument, while the Knight advocates lay criticism of the clergy, and Jon (a secular university clerk) defends the importance of fraternal correction through sharp speech. In addition, the dialogues have in common a concern not only with the representative or exemplary qualities of their disputants, but also of their arguments: the claims they make are, quite self-consciously, examples of how to make such claims. Arguments and argumentational methods treated allusively in any number of other polemical tracts are here given a comprehensive exposition, as for example in RG's detailed exposition of the attitudes believers ought to maintain towards various kinds of propositions (RG 262–75), or the Secular's explanation of the grounds of belief (FS 38–53). As a result these dialogues, like the already published *Testimony of William Thorpe* (itself, among other

[6] See *ODNB* s.v. 'William Crashaw'; P. J. Wallis, 'The Library of William Crashawe'; id., *William Crashawe: The Sheffield Puritan*; Hudson, *Lollards and their Books*, 193–200. I am most grateful to A. I. Doyle for sending me the latest revision of the description he and A. J. Piper have prepared in advance of the publication of their catalogue of the Durham University Library manuscripts. On the probable dating of the manuscript's putative presentation to James I (Doyle's conjecture) and its subsequent appearance in John Cosin's library and donation to the Durham library, see <http://www.dur.ac.uk/library/asc/theme/medmss/apviii6/>, accessed 12 Mar. 2009. It is unclear whether it was James himself, Charles I, or Charles II who passed the manuscript on to John Cosin, founder of the Durham library, but other books of Crashaw's seem to have passed directly to Cosin and thence to the library without any intermediary (see Wallis, *William Crashaw*, 34 n. 28).

things, a dialogue), are a good place for readers to start in learning about lollardy.[7]

The dialogues are arranged in a rough thematic order that follows their development of key ideas, from criticism of the fraternal orders, to debate on right living and its basis, to the proper constitution of the Church within England, to the relationship between the English Church and the larger Church hierarchy. This may also be their chronological order, although as with most lollard texts it is very difficult to be precise about dates. There are likewise no indications of authorship for any of these dialogues—nor any specific claims visible on the page about where they were copied and by whom, who owned them, and where they were kept, before the late sixteenth century. Nonetheless, there are some very suggestive similarities between JR and RG.[8] The attempt to assign authorial names to lollard writings has largely been abandoned for lack of evidence.[9] However, in our continuing study of lollard writings we may be able to cluster them into groups whose vocabulary, diction, sources, themes, translations of the Bible, and even overt cross-references seem to show especially close mutual influence. In her edition of *The Works of a Lollard Preacher* Anne Hudson has presented us with works that are very probably by the same author, while Hudson and Gradon in their edition of the *English Wycliffite Sermons* suggest that they are perhaps most likely the product of extended, intensive collaboration between a small group of authors.[10] JR and RG would seem likely to be either the works of a single author, or a by-product of the sort of close association that Hudson and Gradon describe.

[7] *Testimony of William Thorpe*; on the text's genre, see Hudson's Introduction, pp. liii–lix. For surveys of lollard prose writings geared to a reader new to the field, see Hudson, 'Wycliffite Prose'; ead., *Lollards and their Books*, esp. 1–12 and 249–52 (correcting and augmenting the list of lollard writings given in Talbert and Thomson, 'Wyclyf and his Followers'); Somerset, 'Wycliffite Prose'.

[8] See below, pp. l–li.

[9] See Hudson, *Lollards and their Books*, 110; *Premature Reformation*, 9–10; and a model for investigating possibilities for authorship as far as they can reasonably be pursued: *Works of a Lollard Preacher*, ed. Hudson, pp. lii–lxi.

[10] *The Works of a Lollard Preacher*, ed. Hudson, pp. lii–lxi; *EWS* iv. 32–7.

2. DESCRIPTIONS OF THE MANUSCRIPTS

JR: Cambridge, Trinity College MS B 14 50 [333] (B)

70 folios, parchment and paper, 144 mm × 104 mm; leaves are marginally taller in part I, which looks as though it had previously been bound in a slimmer volume.[11] Pricked and ruled, 25–6 lines to a page, single column throughout. In two parts: I (hand 1), ff. 1–25, paper and parchment, written area 110 mm × 75 mm; II (hand 2), ff. 26–70, parchment only, smaller hand, written area 105 mm × 80 mm (see Pl. 1). Collation ii, part I: 1^{12} paper with 1, 6, 7, 12 parchment; 2 single parchment leaf sewn in; 3^{12} paper with 1, 6, 7, 12 parchment; part II: 1^{10}, 2^{8}, 3^{4+5} (first leaf cut away), 4^{4+5} (first leaf cut away), 5^{4+5} (third leaf a stub). Quire signatures are provided consistently throughout parts I and II (and are correct except in quire I 3, and in that I 1 is labelled 'b' and I 3 is labelled 'a'), and catchwords used in quires I 1, II 1, 2, 3, and 4. Foliation is in pencil. Some damp stains in I (fos. 1–5, 20–5) do not affect legibility.

CONTENTS:[12]

I 1. Folios 1^r–7^v, Dominica 2^a mulier cum parit tristitiam habet Jo. 16. firste may be touchid here what þis womman bitokeneþ . . . here may be touchid of fyue loues and two fyschis wiþ þe wiche crist was þe puple fedyng. Amen. English (notes) and Latin (quotations): sermon notes on the Sunday gospels Dom. 2, 3, 4, Ascension, Trinity, Sundays 1–25 after Trinity.[13]

2. Folios 8^r–13^v, In die natalis sancti Johannis Baptiste. Johannes est nomen eius. Luc. 1° Here may be touchid þe forme þat Joon Baptist was born inne . . . sed futuram inquirimus. Ad quam aiutatem nos perducat Christus Iesus. Amen. English (notes) and Latin (quotations): sermon notes on saints' days John the Baptist, Mary Magdalene, Mary (assumption), Mary (birth), All Saints, Easter.

[11] For previous descriptions see James, *Western Manuscripts*, i. 457–9; *IMEP* xi. 13–15. Dated by James to s. xv; however, on the basis of content, an early 15th-c. date seems likely.

[12] Since B, F, and R each contain a large number of individual items, for reasons of space the descriptions of contents provide references to catalogues such as *IPMEP*, *IMEP*, and Thomson (updated as necessary, of course, from more recent findings) in place of comprehensive lists of other manuscripts and of editions of these items. Transcriptions of incipits and explicits retain manuscript spelling, word division, and capitalization and silently accept scribal corrections, but impose light punctuation for clarity and silently expand most abbreviations. Titles given to works in the manuscript are included in the incipit except when they are the same as the published titles.

[13] See Hudson, *Lollards and their Books*, 25–6.

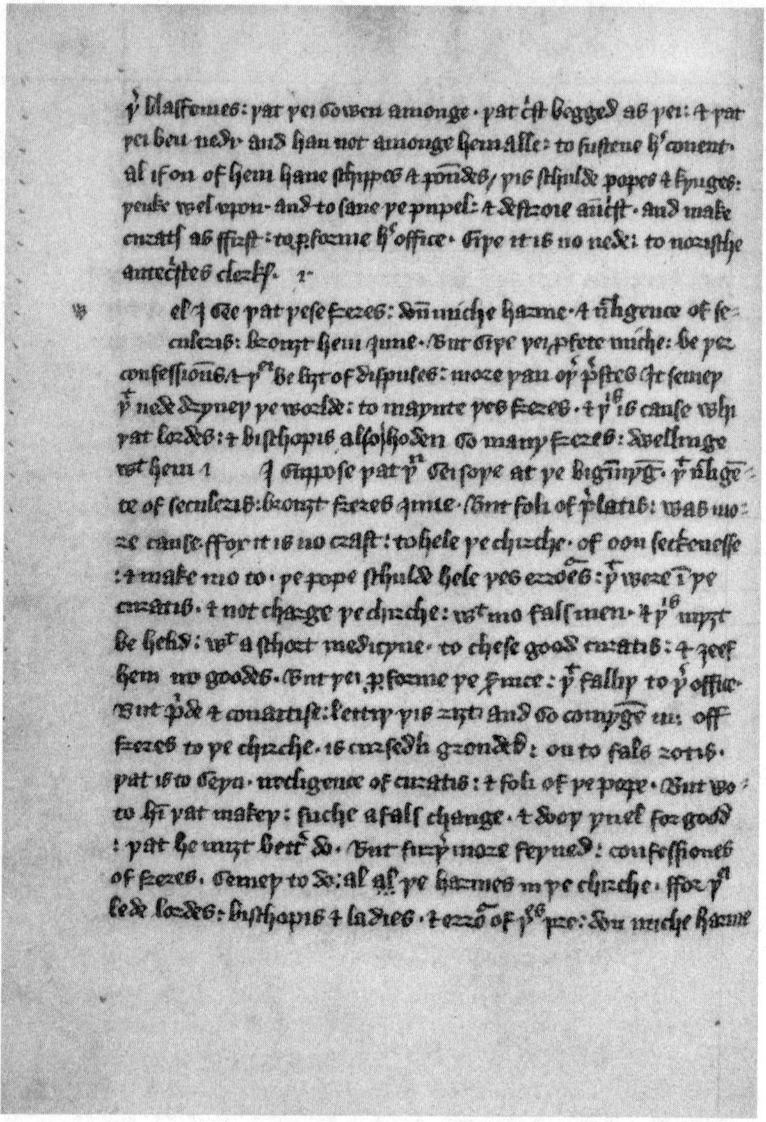

PLATE 1. Cambridge, Trinity College, MS B. 14.50, f. 45v, reproduced by permission of Trinity College, Cambridge

3. Folios 13^{v}/3–25^{v}, Notes in prose and verse, mostly Latin but some English, with a general focus on pastoral reform.

13^{v}/3–24, Nota quod in contricione deberent esse quattuor . . . peccator ingemuerit omnium iniquitatibus scilicet non re [*sic*]. On the four properties of contrition.

14^{r}–14^{v}/6, Nota quod gallus habet septem proprietates que pertinent cuilibet predicatori . . . a mortuis et illuminabit te Christus. On the seven properties of a cock (pertaining to preachers).

14^{v}/7–16, Diabolus cogitans quod si haberet filias multos [*sic*] . . . omnibus est communis et sic Auariciam. On the nine daughters of the devil.

14^{v}/17–24, 25–6, Sumptum non consumitur corpus saluatoris/ . . . Sicut vult huic tollitur datus vite donis; Verborum forma vinum cui mixta sit vnda/ Panis triteceus intencio presbiteratus. Two verses on the Eucharist, the first eight lines, the second two.

15^{r}–16/21, Quattuordecim Articuli. Sciendum est cuilibet fideli christiano quod tenetur . . . ita tunc erit iusticia sine misericordia liberante. Fourteen articles, seven on Christ's humanity, ff. 15^{r}/1–15^{v}/5, seven on his divinity (15^{v}/6–16^{r}/21).

16^{r}/22–4, Extendit manum et restituta est etc. . . . Frustra ergo manus ad dominum expandit qui has ad pauperes non extendit. On almsgiving.

16^{v}/1–20, septem sacramenta. Sacramentorum noue legis multiplex est . . . quidam recipiunt sacramentum et rem vt digne accedentes. Hec Thomas 'de veritate theo.' libro 6 capitulis 3 et 4. On the seven sacraments.

16^{v}/21–17^{r}/10, Bapteme is þe first sacrament þat makeþ . . . of synne in body and in soule. 'Seint edmund of ponteney seiþ þat' added interlin. after 16^{v}/20. Extract from an English version of the *Speculum Ecclesie* (similar to that found in Oxford, Bodleian Library MS Bodl. 416).[14]

17^{r}/11–17^{v}/13, Ponuntur autem hoc canone quare sabbatum

[14] Thanks to Jennifer Arch for providing this information in correspondence. On the *Speculum Ecclesie* see *IPMEP* 800 (though B is not mentioned there).

nostrum sit . . . prudenter et beneuolenter hoc die dominico sabbatizat. Reasons why the Sabbath has been moved to Sunday.

17^{v}/14–18^{r}/4, Oracio dominicalis debet fieri in ecclesia iuxta illud psalmi 67mi . . . significat presentis vite peregrinacionem. Reasons why Sunday prayer should happen in church.

18^{r}/5–18, Iratus deus peccatis hominum dixit 'Penitet me fecisse hominem . . . Fragilis est homo. Biblical quotation and gloss on the fall of man.

18^{r}/19–22, Notandum quod tribus de canonis . . . angelus peccauit in spiritum sanctum non homo, etc. Why God redeemed man, but not the fallen angels.

18^{r}/23–4, Nunc lege nunc ora nunc cum feruore labora/ Sic erit hora breuis et labor ille leuis. Verse on 'occupacio'(given in full).

18^{v}–20^{r} Latin sayings on priests, friars, and monks, ascribed in margins to Hugh of St Victor, Grosseteste, Isidore, pseudo-Chrysostom, Odo, Isidore, Gregory, Augustine, Wyclif, Jerome, Bernard. Wyclif's *Descriptio Fratris* is ascribed to 'doctor euangelicus' (20^{r}/11–13) and is followed directly by the altered quotation from Grosseteste used at the opening of JR.[15]

20^{v}–25^{v}/5, Mortuus viuet Jo. 2. Reuerendi secundum sentenciam beati Anselmi in de cura circa mortuos agenda. Inter omnia opera misericordie . . . et stelle in perpetuas eternitates. Dan. 12. hanc vitam nobis concedat. Amen. On burial of the dead.

25^{v}/6–12, Sacerdos debet esse sanctus, a peccatis segregatus . . . et securus in predicacione. On the qualities of a good priest.

25^{v}/13–23, Ve presbiteris qui tanto zelo et clamore decimas . . . et te ipsum custodire nescis. hec hampoll [i.e. Richard Rolle]. On tithes.

25^{v}/24–7, Pasce oues meas. Jo. 9. Pascere oues est credentes . . . Aduersariis obsistere, peccatores corrigere. Gloss on pastoral obligations.

[15] On the Wyclif text see Hudson, *Lollards and their Books*, 25; Thomson [433], 300.

II 1. Folios 26^{r}–30^{v}, Aȝens hem þat seyn þat hooli wriȝt schulde not or may not be drawun in to engliche . . . it hadde be þe lest sermoun þat euere þei herde. Defence of biblical translation: a translation and adaptation of a longer Latin debate on translation by Richard Ullerston.[16] *IPMEP* 37, add London, British Library MS Harley 425 (Bühler, 'A Lollard Tract', 167).

2. Folios 30^{v}–34^{r}, þes ben þe poyntis wiche ben putte be bischoppis ordinariis vp on men whiche þei clepen lollardis. þe first: þe brede or þe oost in þe auter . . . in hooly chirche alle þe wile we lyuen ben foule bigilid. *Sixteen points on which the bishops accuse Lollards*, *IPMEP* 676.

3. Folios 34^{r}–35^{r}, þes bene þe eiȝte condicions of mawmetrie þat men vsen abouȝte ymages . . . and setten þer glorie in her similacris. Treatise on image worship, also in Oxford, Bodleian Library MS Bodl. Eng. th. f 39.[17]

4. Folios 35^{r}–55^{v}, Jon and Richerd. Siþen crist biddiþ vs be war wiþ fals prophetis . . . suspecte of heresie as antecrist clerke. Explicet dialogus fratrum. Amen amen amen amen. *Dialogue between Jon and Richard*, edited in this volume as JR.

5. Folios 56^{r}–58^{r}, De fide sacramenti. Illa hostia alba et rotunda a sacerdote consecrata . . . in primo articulo fidei et in multis aliis. Identified as Wyclif's and printed in Thomson, 'John Wyclif's "Lost" *De Fide Sacramentorum*'.[18]

6. Folios 58^{r}–60^{r} Contra temporalia claricorum [*sic*]. Possessio duplex est scilicet secularis et spiritualis . . . Nemo si esset de numero saluandorum. Distinction on possession drawn from articles on 'possessio' and 'clericus' in the *Rosarium*.[19]

7. Folios 60^{v}–62^{v}, Contra mendicacionem fratrum. Mendicacio triplex est . . . unusquisque propriam mercedem accipiet secundum suum laborem. Cor. 3°. Distinction on begging drawn from articles on 'mendicacio' and 'labor' in the *Rosarium*, adding reference to friars.[20]

8. Folios 62^{v}–64^{v}, Contra edificaciones fratrum et aliorum. Si fratres et alii dicunt quod mendicant ad fabricandum . . . Omnis

[16] Hudson, *Lollards and their Books*, 67–84, 242–3.

[17] *IMEP* xii. 15. *IPMEP* 57 incorrectly identifies it with the treatise on images edited by Hudson in *SEWW*.

[18] Similar to the English confession on the Eucharist printed by Hudson from Bodley 647 in *SEWW*, 17–18: see Thomson [40], 71.

[19] *Rosarium*, ed. von Nolcken, 36–7.

[20] Ibid.

plantacio quae non plantauit pater meus celestis eradicabitur. Distinction on building drawn from article on 'edificacio' in the *Rosarium*, adding reference to friars.[21]

9. Folios 64^v–65^r, Nota quod homines non deberent elemosinas dare fratribus cum sint validi. Nunc patet per omnia ista predicta . . . post finem mundi in venies [*sic*] vitam eternam quia videbis multa perdita. Distinction on alms drawn from article on 'elemosina' in the *Rosarium*, adding reference to friars.[22]

10. Folios 65^v–66^r, Contra mendicacionem fratrum propter predicacionem verbi dei. Si fratres vel alii mendicant propter predicacionem verbi . . . non licet in ecclesiis parochialibus sine licencia rectorum. Et eadem patet 16 q. 2^a 'ad icimus'.[23] Distinction on preaching drawn from article on 'predicacio' in the *Rosarium*, adding reference to friars.[24]

11. Folios 66^r–67^r, Contra mendicacionem fratrum propter eorum suffragia scilicet oraciones etc. Siquidem fratres mendicent vel accipiant munera propter sua suffragia . . . et immo sunt maladicti et erunt distructi. Explanation of simony drawn from article on 'symonia' in the *Rosarium*.[25]

12. Folios 67^r–68^v, Nota de destruccione fratrum per propheciam. Beata virgo hildegaris turonice nacionis . . . et qui permittit eos et alios tales esse in tali ordine. Pseudo-Hildegard, *Insurgent gentes*, preceded by short introductory passage similar to those found in the other English manuscripts. Interpolated throughout; eight-line conclusion is added that asks who could fail to realize that these are the disciples of Antichrist.[26]

13. Folios 68^v–70^r, Contra [suplin.: id est modernam] adoracionem ymaginum Ymagines sanctorum non sunt contempnende . . . vela que contra religionem nostram veniunt non apendi hec ⟨d⟩. Against images, drawn from article on 'ymago' in the *Rosarium*; includes an excerpt from Wyclif's *De Mandatis* attributed there to 'd.e.' (i.e. 'Doctor Evangelius', Wyclif's usual designation); here, the attribution has been erased but the 'd' remains legible.[27]

[21] Ibid. [22] Ibid.

[23] The correct reference is C. 16 q. 1 c. 19; the reference given cites q. 2.

[24] *Rosarium*, ed. von Nolcken, 36–7. [25] Ibid.

[26] Edited (from six manuscripts not including B, and not witnessing the interpolations or conclusion found in B) by Kerby-Fulton, Hayton, and Olsen, 'Pseudo-Hildegardian Prophecy and Antimendicant Propaganda'.

[27] See von Nolcken, 'Notes on Lollard Citation', 417 and 430; Hudson, *Lollards and their Books*, 26.

Folio 70^{v} blank.

No decoration, and rubrication is sparse (some underlining and two-line capitals on ff. 62^{v}–68^{v}, a four-line capital on 30^{v} and on 68^{v}, first three speaker changes in dialogue marked on 35^{r} and 35^{v}) and sometimes not executed (e.g. space left for two-line capital on ff. 34^{r}, 35^{r}, 58^{r}, 60^{v}). Headings are set off from text, but except on 68^{v}, not underlined. Marginalia and titles of texts are contemporary with the manuscript's production and include corrections, divisions of texts into parts, numbered points, and a few sparse annotations.

Given to the library by John Whitgift, probably after his death in 1604: his will records the gift of his parchment books to Trinity College. On f. 1^{r} appears the early sixteenth-century annotation 'Quo quid antiquius eo melius G. Guggyn'—the same annotation appears on the verso of the third flyleaf in Cambridge, Trinity College MS B.14.38, and it may be presumed that both manuscripts belonged to the same otherwise unknown owner. There is no evidence about where the book was produced or who owned it before the sixteenth century.

FS: Dublin, Trinity College MS 244 [C 3 12] (F)

219 folios (includes missing f. 88; see below), parchment, to f. 91 of very poor quality, 208 mm × 140 mm (see Pl. 2).[28] Pricked from f. 155 onward. Ruled lightly in red (to f. 91) and in pen. Twenty-eight lines to a page for the most part except ff. 92–103, an inserted quire of twelve with 29 lines to a page and considerable textual compression in the final lines on f. 103^{v}. Single column throughout. Written area 158 mm × 100 mm. Two sheets of blue lined paper inserted before front flyleaves give a detailed description of the contents of the manuscript and its correspondences with CCC 296: these were very likely produced when the volume was rebacked (as noted in a different modern hand on the inside front pastedown) in 1951. Collation vi (one paper and five parchment flyleaves), 1–10^{8}, 11^{8} (final leaf, f. 88, missing but included in foliation), 12^{8} (lacks fourth leaf, 13^{12} inserted in place of fourth leaf as ff. 92–103, quire 12

[28] For previous descriptions see Abbott, *Catalogue*, 35–6; the description bound into the MS (see below); Hanna, 'Two Lollard Codices', 60–2. Dated by Hanna in the same article to early s. xv (52). Alan J. Fletcher suggests, on the basis of topical allusions in items 27 and 29, that it is likely that at least the latter part of the manuscript, perhaps the whole, was copied 'in 1389 or very shortly thereafter' ('The Criteria for Scribal Attribution', 628 n. 96). Of course, as he concedes, his remarks apply to the composition of these items, not necessarily to their copying here. Still, further investigation seems warranted.

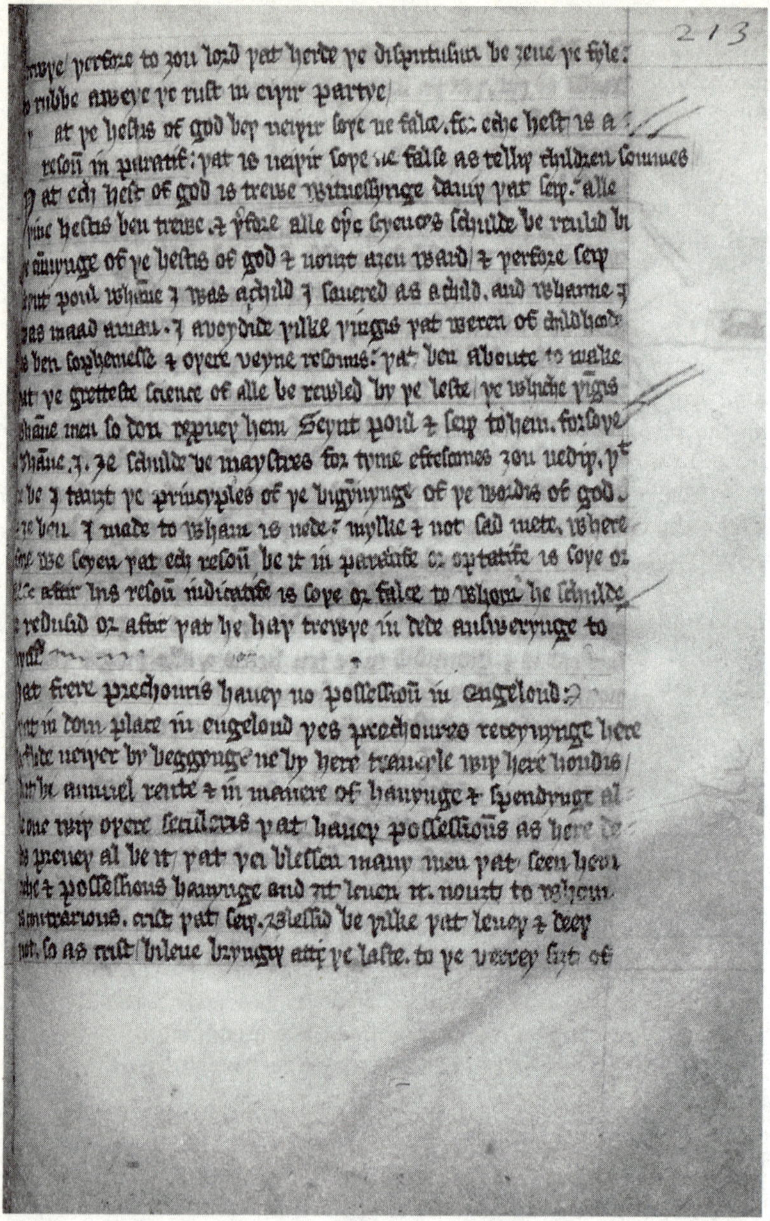

PLATE 2. Dublin, Trinity College, MS 244, f. 213r, reproduced by permission of Trinity College, Dublin

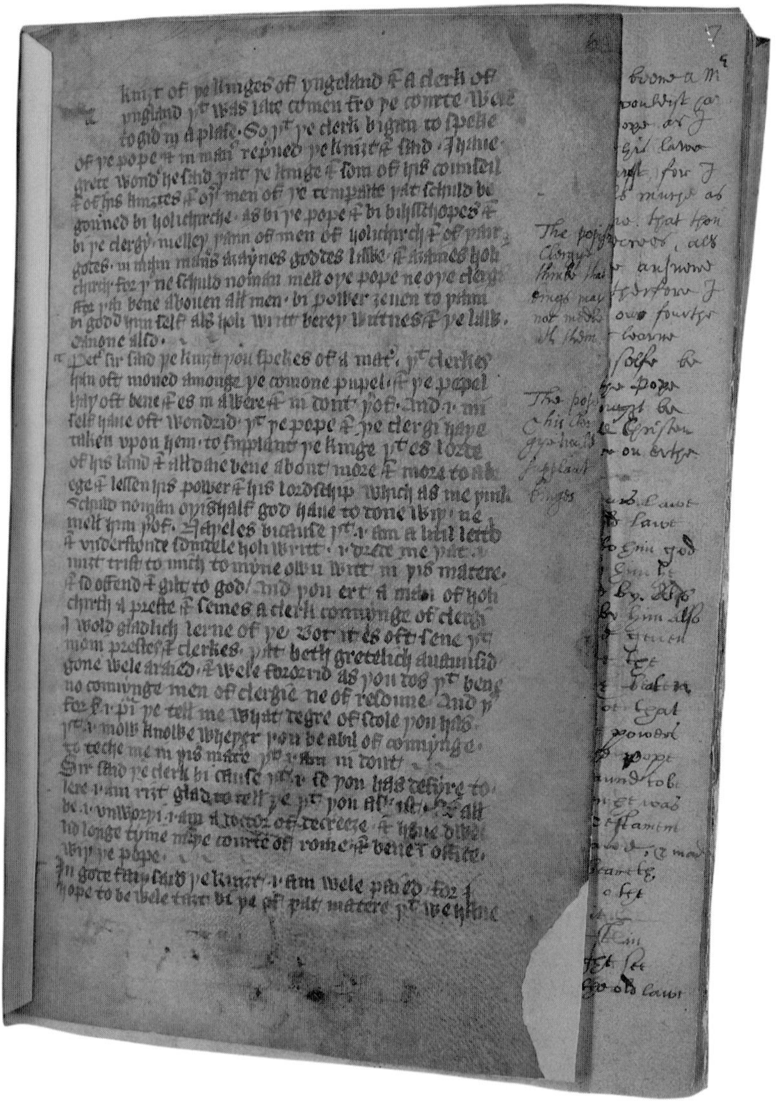

Durham University Library, MS Cosin V.III.6, f.6r

Folio 70^{v} blank.

No decoration, and rubrication is sparse (some underlining and two-line capitals on ff. 62^{v}–68^{v}, a four-line capital on 30^{v} and on 68^{v}, first three speaker changes in dialogue marked on 35^{r} and 35^{v}) and sometimes not executed (e.g. space left for two-line capital on ff. 34^{r}, 35^{r}, 58^{r}, 60^{v}). Headings are set off from text, but except on 68^{v}, not underlined. Marginalia and titles of texts are contemporary with the manuscript's production and include corrections, divisions of texts into parts, numbered points, and a few sparse annotations.

Given to the library by John Whitgift, probably after his death in 1604: his will records the gift of his parchment books to Trinity College. On f. 1^{r} appears the early sixteenth-century annotation 'Quo quid antiquius eo melius G. Guggyn'—the same annotation appears on the verso of the third flyleaf in Cambridge, Trinity College MS B.14.38, and it may be presumed that both manuscripts belonged to the same otherwise unknown owner. There is no evidence about where the book was produced or who owned it before the sixteenth century.

FS: Dublin, Trinity College MS 244 [C 3 12] (F)

219 folios (includes missing f. 88; see below), parchment, to f. 91 of very poor quality, 208 mm × 140 mm (see Pl. 2).[28] Pricked from f. 155 onward. Ruled lightly in red (to f. 91) and in pen. Twenty-eight lines to a page for the most part except ff. 92–103, an inserted quire of twelve with 29 lines to a page and considerable textual compression in the final lines on f. 103^{v}. Single column throughout. Written area 158 mm × 100 mm. Two sheets of blue lined paper inserted before front flyleaves give a detailed description of the contents of the manuscript and its correspondences with CCC 296: these were very likely produced when the volume was rebacked (as noted in a different modern hand on the inside front pastedown) in 1951. Collation vi (one paper and five parchment flyleaves), 1–10^{8}, 11^{8} (final leaf, f. 88, missing but included in foliation), 12^{8} (lacks fourth leaf, 13^{12} inserted in place of fourth leaf as ff. 92–103, quire 12

[28] For previous descriptions see Abbott, *Catalogue*, 35–6; the description bound into the MS (see below); Hanna, 'Two Lollard Codices', 60–2. Dated by Hanna in the same article to early s. xv (52). Alan J. Fletcher suggests, on the basis of topical allusions in items 27 and 29, that it is likely that at least the latter part of the manuscript, perhaps the whole, was copied 'in 1389 or very shortly thereafter' ('The Criteria for Scribal Attribution', 628 n. 96). Of course, as he concedes, his remarks apply to the composition of these items, not necessarily to their copying here. Still, further investigation seems warranted.

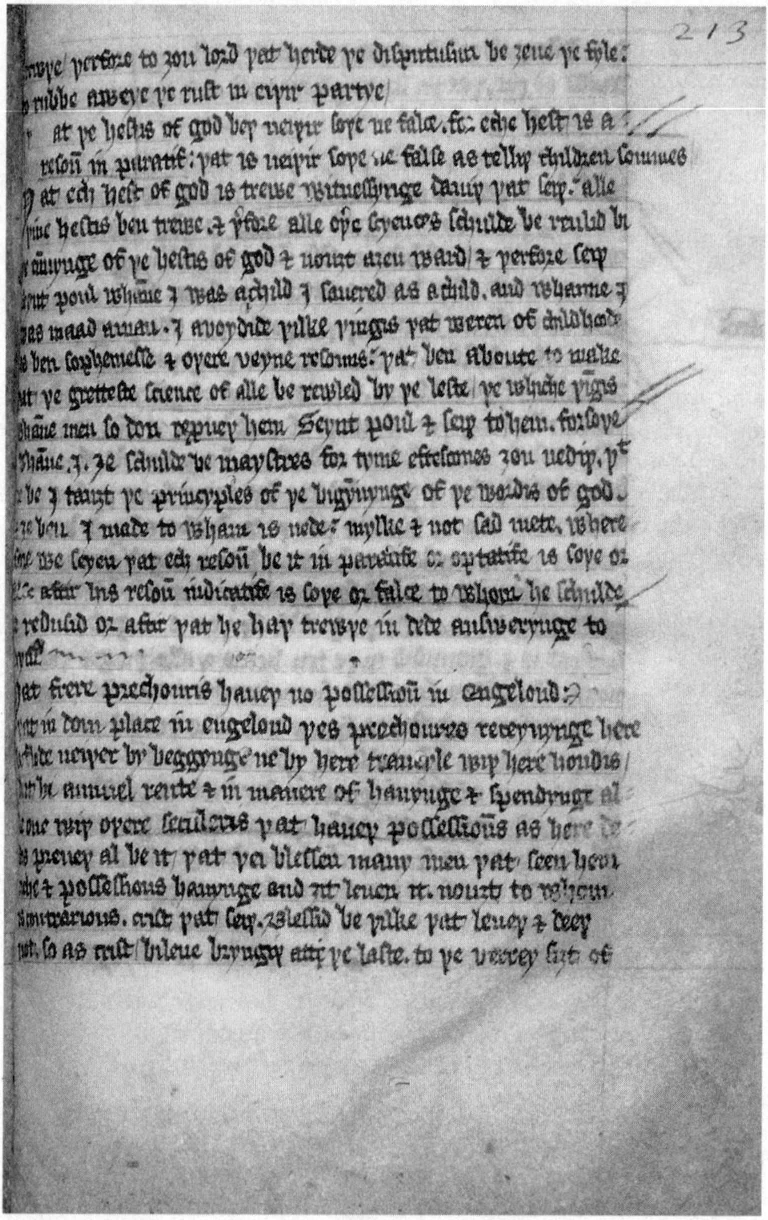
213
...nyþe / þerfore to ȝou lord þat herde þe disputisun be ȝeue þe sile:
...to wibbe answere þe trust in eiþir partye/
at þe hestis of god beþ neiþir soþe ne false. for eche hest is a
reson in preceptif: þat is neiþir soþe ne false as tellyþ children sommes
at eche hest of god is trewe witnessynge dauiþ þat seiþ. alle
þine hestis ben trewe. & þerfore alle oþer sciences schulde be reulid bi
kunnynge of þe hestis of god & nouȝt euen ward / & þerfore seiþ
seint poul whanne I was a child I sauered as a child. and whanne I
was maad a man. I avoydide þilke þingis þat weren of childhode
as ben sophemesse & oþere veyne resouns. þat ben aboute to make
þat þe grettest science of alle be reuled by þe leste / þe whiche þingis
whanne men so don repreueþ hem Seynt poul & seiþ to hem. for soþe
whanne I. ȝe schulde be maystres for tyme eftsones ȝou nediþ. þat
be I tauȝt þe principles of þe bigynnynge of þe wordis of god.
ȝe ben I made to wham is nede: mylke & not sad mete. where
fore we seyen þat eche reson be it in preceptif or optatif is soþe or
false after his reson indicatif is soþe or false to whom he schulde
reduid or after þat he haþ trewþe in dede answerynge to
wat
Þat frere prechouris haueþ no possessioun in engelond:
at in som place in engelond þes prechoures receyuynge here
lyflode neþer bi beggynge ne by here trauaile wiþ here hondis
wiþ annuel rente & in manere of hauynge & spendynge al
comun wiþ oþere seculeris þat haueþ possessiouns as here de
es preueþ al be it / þat þei blessen many men þat seen hem
riche & possessiouns hauynge and ȝit leuen it. nouȝt to whom
contrarious. and þat seiþ. blessid be þilke þat leueþ & deeþ
not. so as trist / bileue bryngiþ atte þe laste. to þe verrey lif of

PLATE 2. Dublin, Trinity College, MS 244, f. 213^{r}, reproduced by permission of Trinity College, Dublin

finishes as ff. 104–7), 14–16^{8}, 17^{8} (lacks third, fourth, fifth, and sixth leaves) 18^{8} (lacks first two leaves, stub after final leaf), 19^{8} (lacks final leaf), 20^{8} (quire lost), 21–4^{8}, 25^{8} (lacks seventh leaf, final leaf followed by stub), 26^{12}, 27–8^{8}, 29^{4}, vi (four parchment leaves, two paper); v recto has a list of missing leaves headed 'This MS imperfect', dated to 11 May 1835, and signed with the initials JHT (probably James H. Todd). iv and v are included in the foliation as ff. 220 and 221.

Quire signatures are regular and specify the order of the quires for quires 1–8. Quire 9 is unmarked, quire 10 is ordered and partly marked. Thereafter signatures appear intermittently with fair consistency but do not order the quires. Catchwords appear on ff. 1^{v}–11^{v}, 13^{r}, 14, 19^{v}, 21^{v}, and thereafter on the verso of the final folio of every quire except quires 11, 19, 25, and 29.

CONTENTS:

1. Folios 1^{r}–16^{v}, Attendite a fermento phariseorum quod est ypocrisie luc ii CRist comandiþ to his disciplis . . . falce lesynges of pharisees and her maynteneris. *Of the leaven of Pharisees*, *IPMEP* 94.

2. Folios 16^{v}–23^{r}, Hou men owen obesche to prelatis drede cures and kepe lawe. PRelatis sklaundren pore prestis and oþere cristene men . . . ȝif riȝt and resoun and charite be wel souȝt [next title intervenes] and considred. *How men ought to obey prelates*, *IPMEP* 549.

3. Folios 23^{r}–27^{r}, þis is þe rule of seynt fraunceis þat sueþ. The reule and lyuynge of frere menouris is þis . . . we han stedefastli bihiȝt or avowid bi professioun. *The rule and testament of St Francis*, *IPMEP* 698 (conflated with item 4).

4. Folios 27^{r}–32^{r}, Here endeþ þe reule of seynt fraunseis and here bigynneþ þe testament of seynt fraunseis. In þe name of þe fadir and sone and þe holi gost Amen . . . and most profitable to alle parties. Amen. Testament ends f. 29^{r}/9 and is followed by a list of counter-arguments against friars' modifications of the rule and testament. *The rule and testament of St Francis*, *IPMEP* 698 (see item 3); printed by Matthew as chapter 13 of item 3, followed by counter-arguments under the heading 'Comment'.

5. Folios 32^{r}–54^{v}, First freris seyn þat here religioun . . . wiþ owten errour of wrong bi lawis. Amen. *Fifty heresies and errors of friars*; follows items 3 and 4 in all three copies. *IPMEP* 187.

6. Folios 54^{v}–89^{r}, Here it telliþ of prelatis. That prelatis leuen prechynge of þe gospel . . . þise errours and oþere ȝif it be his wille.

Amen. *Of prelates*; Matthew 105/14–106/32 is missing on the lost f. 88. *IPMEP* 656.

7. Folios 89^{r}–92^{r}, Hou antecrist and his clerkis feren trewe prestis fro prechyng of cristis gospel bifoure disseytis. First þei seyn þat prechynge of þe gospel . . . to þat glorious blisse for his endeles mercy. Amen. *Speculum de antichristo*, *IPMEP* 200.

8. Folios 92^{r}–103^{v}, This is of clerkis poscessioneris. Clerkis possessioneris fordon presthod kny3thod and comuneris . . . and þe perfyt fredom of þe gospel. amen. *Of clerks possessioners*, *IPMEP* 133.

9. Folios 103^{v}–116^{r}, How þe office of curatis is ordeyned of god. In dei no mine [*sic*] Amen. For þe office of curatis is ordeyned of god . . . trewe techinge aftir crist and his apostlis. Amen. *Hou þe office of curatis is ordeyned of God.* Opening on f. 103^{v} highly compressed. *IPMEP* 216.

10. Folios 116^{r}–124^{r}, this is for þe ordre of presthod. For þe ordre of presthod is ordeyned of god . . . mercy and charite brynge þis holy ende. Amen. *Ordre of presthod*, *IPMEP* 217.

11. Folios 124^{v}–125^{r}, Ho⟨w⟩ men schulen fynde prestis. Thenkiþ wisly 3e men þat fynden prestis . . . as þe cronycle of sistrenþe telliþ. *De stipendiis ministrorum*. *IPMEP* 726.

12. Folios 125^{r}–131^{v}, How praiere of goode men helpiþ myche and praiere of synful men displesiþ god and harmeþ hem silf and oþer men. Oure lord Iesu crist techiþ vs to preie . . . as crist and his apostlis diden. Amen. *De precationibus sacris*, *IPMEP* 524.

13. Folios 131^{v}–133^{v}, Octo [written as vii^{to}] in quibus sed ucuntur [*sic*] simplices Christiani. There ben ei3tte thingis bi whiche . . . and pees and charite and to suffre gladly. . . . Incomplete at end, Arnold 450/33 'gladly'. *Octo in quibus seducuntur simplices Christiani*, *IPMEP* 710, add second copy in Dublin, Trinity College MS 246, pp. 68–73 of part 2.

14. Folios 134^{r}–136^{r}, . . . comunes for þei taken þe charge to hele alle men . . . in soule and in worldly goodis. Explicit. *Three things destroy this world*. Incomplete at start, beginning Matthew 181/2 'comunes'; and lacking pp. 184/4 'lordis'—186/30 'hem' because of lost leaves. *IPMEP* 170.

15. Folios 136^{r}–141^{v}, Of feynyd contemplatif liif of songe of þe ordynal of salelbury [*sic*] and of bodily almas and worldly bisynesse of prestis how by þese foure þe fend lettiþ hem fro prechynge of þe gospel. First whanne trewe men techen bi goddis lawe . . . be war of

sathanas disceytis. Amen. capitulum secundum. *Of feigned contemplative life*, *IPMEP* 204.

16. Folios 141^{v}–148^{v}, Plese it to oure most noble and most worthi kyng . . bi cursid ypocritis and erretikis and world. . . . *A petition to the king and parliament.* Untitled here, and marked as the second chapter of the previous work (see explicit to item 15 above). Incomplete at end, Arnold 520/17 'world-'. *IPMEP* 542.

17. Folios 149^{r}–152^{v}, . . . soulis is putt bihynde and conseil of þe world . . . vertuous liif and riȝtwisnesse and pees and charite. Amen. *How Satan and his children, etc.* Incomplete at start, beginning Matthew 213/20 'soulis'. *IPMEP* 182.

18. Folios 152^{v}–156^{r}, How men of priuat religioun schulden loue more þe gospel goddis heste and his ordynaunce þan ony newe lawis newe reulis and custumes and ordynauncis of synful men. Cristene men preien mekely and deuoutly . . . make lordis and comyns constreyne hem to this. Amen. *How religious men should keep certain articles*, *IPMEP* 130.

19. Folios 156^{v}–167^{v}, Of seruauntis and lordis how eche schal kepe his degre⟨e⟩. First seruauntis schulen trewly and gladly serue . . . of clerkis and alle þere sugetis. amen. *Of servants and lords*, *IPMEP* 193.

20. Folios 167^{v}–173^{r}, Whi pore prestis han none beneficis. Summe causis meuen summe pore prestis . . . þe riȝtte wey to heuene. Amen Iesu for þin endeles charite. *Why poor priests have no benefice*, *IPMEP* 612.

21. Folios 173^{r}–177^{v}, How antecrist and his clerkis trauailen to distroie holy writ and to make cristene men vnstable in þe feiþ and to sette here ground in deuelis of helle. As oure lord Iesu crist ordeyned to make his gospel . . . graunte to vs synful wretchis þis bone. amen. *How antichrist and his clerks travail to destroy holy writ*, *IPMEP* 77.

22. Folios 177^{v}–184^{r}, How sathanas and hise prestis and his feyned religious casten by þre cursid erresies to distroie alle good lyuyng and mayntene alle manere of synne. As almyȝtty god in trinite ordeyneþ men . . . Iesu crist for þin endeles mercy graunte vs þis ende. Amen. *How Satan and his priests, etc.*, *IPMEP* 72.

23. Folios 184^{r}–186^{v}, For þre skillis lordis schulden constreyne clerkis to lyue in mekenesse wilful pouert and discret penaunce and goostly trauaile. Opyn techinge in goddis lawe olde and newe . . . clene conscience to brynge clerkis to þis holy. . . . *Church temporalities.* Incomplete at end, Arnold 217/33 'holy'. *IPMEP* 511, delete San Marino, Huntington Library MS 503 (*IMEP* i. 32–3).

24. Folio 187^{rv}, þei and alle here meyne sterue for hunger and I lygge in prisoun . . . defautis of clerkis and brynge hem to þe meke lyuynge of Crist. And . . . Fragment of unidentified and apparently unique longer text, incomplete at both ends. The lower part of f. 187^{v} is ruled but left blank.

25. Folios 188^{r}–193^{v}, Siþ many falce gloseris maken goddis lawe derk . . . What euere comeþ to hem for so biddiþ charite. *Of dominion*, *IPMEP* 600, add ed. Lindberg, ii. 93–106.

26. Folios 193^{v}–208^{r}, FOr þis vnkouþe discenc`i´oun þat is bitwixe þes popes . . . But þei sendiþ soulis to helle and doiþ hem silf aftir. Explicut [*sic*] croyserrye. *De pontificum romanorum schismate*, *IPMEP* 218.

27. Folios 208^{r}–210^{v}, Alas forsorwe grete prestis sittinge in derkenessis . . . he graunte vs to see þat lyueþ and re⟨g⟩neþ wiþ [*sic*] eende. Amen. *The Last Age of the Church*, *IPMEP* 42.

28. Folios 210^{v}–211^{r}, The fend sekiþ many weyes to marre men in bileue . . . holy wryt on þe secunde manere may noȝt faile as crist seiþ. In dei nomine Amen. *On the sufficiency of Holy Scripture*, *IPMEP* 666.

29. Folios 211^{r}–212^{v}, Of feiþ of þe gospel gederen trewe men wiþ opyn counfessioun . . . þis cause but maynteyneþ falsehede aȝens truþe of crist. A series of short items, only the first published, as *De sacramento altaris*, *IPMEP* 501. This copy imperfect at end, Matthew 357/22 'þus'. The other unique, unpublished items are on the Papal Schism, followed by named witnesses to the first two items, then opposed descriptions of the beliefs of friars and true men on the Eucharist, a short description of the duties of bishops, and explanations of good and bad swearing and of lying.

30. Folios 212^{v}–219^{r}, Moost worschipfulleste and gentilleste lord duke . . . þe whiche blysse ȝow graunt crist Iesu. Amen. *Dialogue between a Friar and a Secular*. Edited in this volume as FS.

Folio 219^{v} blank apart from later jottings.

The ink foliation includes the missing f. 88 but not other missing leaves or quires; it also includes two final flyleaves, as specified above in the collation. Much discoloration is visible on f. 1^{r} and at the bottom right of the next two leaves, suggesting that the volume may have been stored unbound and much read at some stage. Extensive worming is visible from the end of the manuscript back to f. 187. Several leaves have been lost, and f. 71 is in peril of detaching. Apart from these problems the volume remains legible There are two and possibly three hands: Hanna designates ff. 1^{r}–91^{v} and part of the first line of f. 92^r as well as ff. 104^r–111^v/12 as the work of scribe 1; ff. 92^r–103^v and the first line of f. 104^r as well as ff. 188^r–219^r as the work of scribe 2; and ff. 111^v/12–187^v as the work of scribe 3, or possibly of scribe 2 in a more formal duct.[29] The mid-page personnel changes suggest that the scribes were deliberately collaborating in the production of a large volume, though whether in the same physical location or at some remove it is impossible to say. No decoration is provided, though titles, headings, paraphs, chapter divisions, and marginal citations are in red ink.

Medieval marginalia are mostly references to sources (mostly the Bible), though some also itemize points or chapters. The volume is extensively annotated in one or more secretary hands; enthusiastic underlining and double diagonal lines in the margin appear throughout as well. A later hand, perhaps that of 'JHT' as on the second-to-last flyleaf, marks the 'imperfect' sections noted on the flyleaf on the folios in question. Folio 1^r has the heading in a rather uneven hand with some italic features 'Anno 1308 Wicklif workes to the Duk of Lancaster' and in the same hand at the base of the page, 'Robert Cotton Bruceus' (Cotton's usual signature).[30] The volume comes from the library of Archbishop James Ussher, who is thought to have acquired it from Robert Cotton: it was donated to Trinity College Dublin in 1661. Nothing definite is known of its provenance before the sixteenth century. A large proportion of its contents correspond item for item with those of CCC 296, as discussed in detail in Hanna, 'Two Lollard Codices'.

RG: Dublin, Trinity College MS 245 [C.5.6] (R)

218 folios parchment (this including the blank ff. 7–8), 160 mm × 105 mm (see Pl. 3).[31] Pricked and ruled in ink, 32 lines to a page. Single column throughout. Written area 120 mm × 80 mm. Collation iii (paper; i is blank and conjugate with pastedown, ii and iii have on them a table of contents in pen, apparently in the same hand as the ink foliation, signed 'JHT' (probably James H. Todd) and dated 10 March 1836), $1–8^8$, 9^{10}, $10–27^8$, iii (paper; blank, iii conjugate with pastedown). There are no catchwords or

[29] Hanna, 'Two Lollard Codices', 59. See also below, p. xxxix–xl.

[30] O'Sullivan, 'Ussher as a Collector of Manuscripts', 36–7, where the relationship between Cotton and Ussher is discussed in more detail using Ussher's published letters.

[31] Previous descriptions Abbott, *Catalogue*, 36; *EWS*, ii, pp. xxi–xxiii; Jefferson, 'An Edition of the Ten Commandments Commentary', i, pp. xx–xxvii. Dated by Hudson and Gradon and by Jefferson to s. xv^I.

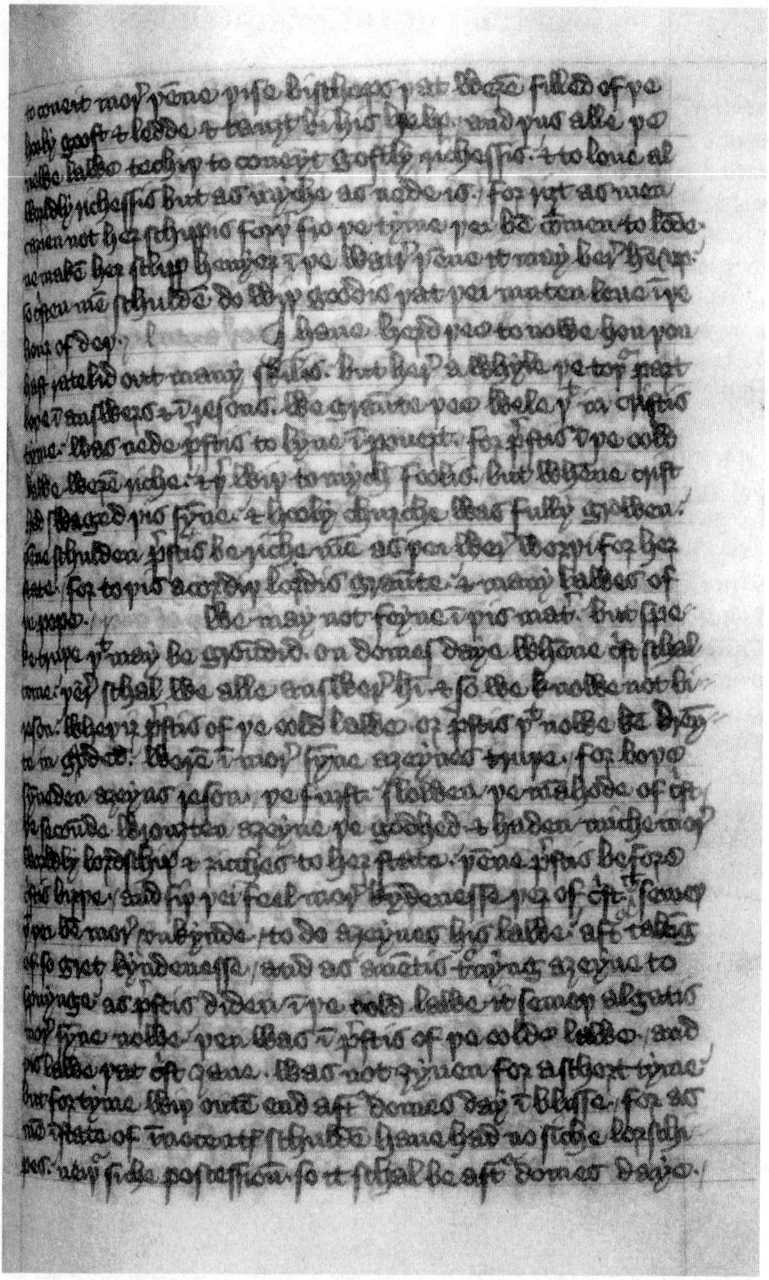

PLATE 3. Dublin, Trinity College, MS 245, f. 158r, reproduced by permission of Trinity College, Dublin.

signatures on the first quire. Given that ff. 7–8 are blank and that the only signatures in the volume, on quire 2, are ai–iiii, it seems likely that this first quire was added after some or all of the rest of the volume had been put together. Catchwords (but no further signatures) appear regularly on every quire from the second onward except for quire 20. The catchword on 218^{v} indicates that the manuscript is incomplete at the end.

CONTENTS:

1. Folios 1^{r}–2^{r}, Crede. It is sooþ þat bileue is grounde of alle vertues . . . wiþ glorie wiþ hem boþe and euere lyue in blisse. Explicit credo in deum patrem. *On the Apostle's Creed*, *IPMEP* 403, add Oxford, Bodleian Library MS Eng. th. e. 181.[32]

2. Folios 2^{r}–3^{v}, Pater noster. WE shal bileue þat þis Pater noster þat crist hymsilf techiþ . . . and þanne shal we haue euer lastyng fredom. Amen. Explicit pater noster. *The Pater Noster*. Incomplete at end, Arnold 96/19 'freedam'—as is every other copy apart from Arnold's base text.[33] *IPMEP* 810, add Oxford, Bodleian Library MS Eng. th. e. 181.[34]

3. Folios 3^{v}–4^{v}, Aue. Men greten comounly oure lady goddis moder, and we supposen . . . and worshipe we marie vp al oure myȝt. Explicit salutatio sancte marie virginis. *Ave Maria*, *IPMEP* 455, add Oxford, Bodleian Library MS Eng. th. e. 181.[35]

4. Folios 4^{v}–6^{v}, vii eresies. FOr false men multiplien bokis of þe chirche, now rendyng bileue . . . but neiþer is þis bileue ne groundid in resoun. Expliciunt vii hereses contra pater noster. Lacks final two Latin sentences of published edition, Arnold 446/3–5—though seven ruled lines are left blank following a Latin explicit separated from the text by a blank line. *Seven heresies*, *IPMEP* 208.[36]

Folios 7–8 blank.

5. Folios 9^{r}–26^{v}, Alle maner of men shulden holde goddis biddyngis . . . as he loueþ god or þe blisse of heuene. Expliciunt

[32] Hudson, 'New Look', 250; *IMEP* xii. 133. While James Simpson in *IMEP* vii. 22–5 claims that the versions of items 1, 2, and 6 in Bibliothèque Ste-Geneviève 3390 contain nothing 'specifically Wycliffite', the extent to which that manuscript's versions differ from those in R remains incompletely studied (though see Hudson, 'New Look', 256 and n. 63).

[33] Hudson, 'New Look', 251 n. 39.

[34] Ibid. 249–50; *IMEP* xii. 12.

[35] Hudson, 'New Look', 250, 257; *IMEP* xii. 12–13. On variation between the manuscript copies see also Peikola, '"And after all, myn Aue-Marie almost to the ende"'.

[36] See also Hudson, 'New Look', 251 n. 38; *IMEP* xii. 14.

Mandata. Amen. *þe ten comaundementis*, *IPMEP* 49, add Jefferson, 'Edition of the Ten Commandments', ii. 1–160 (from R).[37]

6. Folios 27^{r}–30^{v}, For it is seid in holdyng of oure haliday . . . he myȝt liȝtly come to heuene and wite who wente amys. Expliciunt Feiþ Hope and Charite. *Of faith, hope, and charity*, *IPMEP* 595, add London, British Library MS Harley 2385, ff. 7^{r}–8^{v} (extracts), Oxford, Bodleian Library MS Bodl. 938, ff. 56^{r}–58^{r} (extracts).[38]

7. Folios 30^{v}–35^{r}, 35^{r}–38^{r}, If a man were sure þat he shulde to morewe come bifore a iuge . . . and ellis as me þinkiþ vs failiþ riȝt to dymes. Expliciunt opera mercie corporalia. Siþ we shulden serue oure parishens in spiritual almes . . . as mede and nede and kynde techen cristen men. Expliciunt opera caritatiua etc. *þe seven werkys of mercy bodyly*, *þe seven werkys of mercy gostly*. Neither the bodily nor the spiritual works has a heading in R, but the two are presented as separate works, with the incipits and explicits given above. Arnold prints them as a single work, giving his second title as a subtitle to chapter 7 and following. *IPMEP* 331, note Cambridge, Mass., Harvard University English 738 is incomplete at end; add San Marino, Huntington Library MS HM 744 (first chapter only); delete New York H. P. Kraus MS.[39]

8. Folios 38^{r}–63^{r}, Siþ bileue techiþ vs þat euery yuel is oþer synne, or comeþ of synne . . . and faile not in þis trwe seruyce for sharp veniaunce takiþ god of siche. Expliciunt septem peccata capitalia. *On the seven deadly sins*, *IPMEP* 596.

9. Folios 63^{v}–75^{v}, Cristis chirche is his spouse, þat haþ þre partis . . . and to hate þat he hatiþ and þanne is his hiȝest vertu stablid. Explicit tractatus de ecclesia et membris eius. *The church and her members*, *IPMEP* 132, add ed. Lindberg, i. 106–70 (from Bodl. 788).

[37] Jefferson corrects and updates all previous attempts to catalogue this and similar Ten Commandments commentaries, determining that although some version of the same prologue, and thus the incipit, of item 5 is found in a much larger number of commentaries, nonetheless this specific commentary in 'two overlapping, but nevertheless very different versions' is found (version 1) in London, British Library MS Harley 2398, and (version 2) in R, in Cambridge, Mass., Harvard University MS English 738 and in York Minster Library MS XVI.L.12. See Jefferson, 'An Edition', i, pp. xxxiii–xxxiv and cxxx–cxciv for a detailed analysis of related versions with and without the shared prologue material. See also *IMEP* vi. 49. On the tract's citation of Wyclif see also von Nolcken, 'Notes on Lollard Citation', 420.

[38] *IMEP* viii. 72; see also *IMEP* vi. 50, both citing information from Anne Hudson. 'A slightly different version' (*IPMEP* 595) appears in Paris, Bibliothèque Ste-Geneviève MS 3390,ff. 30^{r}–37^{r}: the relationship awaits more detailed study (see also n. 32).

[39] *IMEP* vi. 52, citing corrections provided by Anne Hudson and in Voigts, *Handlist*, 27, and *IMEP* viii. 72, with further corrections.

10. Folios 76^{r}–80^{v} De apostasia cleri. Siþ ilche cristen man is holdon to sewe crist . . . þise cloþis ben of charite þat euere more shal last. And here is an ende. Explicit tractatus de apostasia et dotacione ecclesie. *Tractatus de apostasia cleri*, *IPMEP* 597.

11. Folios 81^{r}–95^{v}, For many beren heuy þat freris ben clepid pseudo or ypocritis . . . we wolden mekeliche a noon turne to treuþe when it were tauȝt. Amen. Explicit tractatus de pseudo freris. *Tractatus de pseudo-freris*, *IPMEP* 210, add ed. Lindberg, ii. 61–92.

12. Folios 96^{r}–101^{r}, Crist biddiþ vs be waar wiþ þes false prophetis þat comen in cloþing . . . and putte vs not in straunge perelis þat we han no nede to trete. Here enden þe eiȝte woos þat god wishid to freris. Amen. *Vae octuplex*, *IPMEP* 127, but see *EWS* ii. 366 for the most complete list of manuscripts, and add ed. *EWS* ii. 366–78.

13. Folios 101^{r}–116^{v}, Exposicio euangelii Matt. 24 Egressus Iesus de templo etc. þis gospel telliþ myche wisdom þat is hid to many men . . . but þe fend may dampne men but not rauyshe her hope in crist. Explicit Euangelium. *Of mynistris in þe chirche*, *IPMEP* 738, but see *EWS* ii. 328 for the most complete list of manuscripts, and add ed. *EWS* ii. 328–65.

14. Folios 117^{r}–124^{r}, Of antecrist and his meynee. Dauid seiþ, Lord sett þou a lawe maker vpon hem . . . Crist graunt vs grace þerto and heuen blisse. Amen. *Of antichrist and his meynee*, *IPMEP* 144.

15. Folios 124^{r}–126^{r}, Of antecristis songe in chirche. Also prelatis, prestis, and freres putten on symple men þat þei seyen . . . alle siche cerymoyns lest we taken þe grace of god in veyne. An excerpt from *On the twenty-five articles*, article 15, Arnold 479–82, ending at Arnold 482/36 'vayne'.[40]

16. Folios 126^{r}–127^{r}, Of praier a tretys. Also bischops and freres putten to pore men þat þei seyn . . . bishops mayntenyng it opynly and stidfastly ben cursud heretikes. Explicit tractatus de oracione. A second excerpt from *On the twenty-five articles* (see item 15 and n. 40), article 19, Arnold 486–8, ending at 488/35 'heretikis'.

17. Folios 127^{v}–137^{r}, Nota de confessione. Two vertues ben in mannes soule by whyche a man shuld be rewled . . . as þei waxen wiþout profit so þei han no grounde in god. Explicit etc. *Of confession*, *IPMEP* 790, add ed. Lindberg, ii. 33–60 (from Rylands 86).

18. Folios 137^{v}–143^{v}, Crist for soþe did al þat he couþe to obeye to lordis . . . Zacharie þe prophete seiþ þou shepherde and ydele

[40] Hudson, *Premature Reformation*, 210 n. 203.

forsakyng þi flok etc. Repudiation of the established sacrament of confession in favour of unmediated confession to God, developed as an ecclesiological implication of Christ's contrasting obedience to lords and sharp reproof of scribes and pharisees. Unique and unpublished.

19. Folios 144^{r}–145^{v}, ⟨Nota de sacramento altaris⟩ [blotted over with ink]. Cristen mennes bileeue tauȝt of Iesu crist, god and man . . . fro suche false prophetis and here sotile ypocrisie and fals heresye. Amen. *The Eucharist I*, *IPMEP* 131.

20. Folios 145^{v}–151^{r}, Crisostom seiþ þat fischers and buystouse men, makynge iche daye nettis . . . god for his endeles mercy to endure to þe last eende. Amen. A discussion of virtuous life in the world, touching on the conduct of priests, proper prayer, and worldly vs. spiritual wisdom. Unique and unpublished.

21. Folios 151^{r}–153^{v}, Seynt Barnard spekiþ þus to Eugenye þe pope. Supposest þou . . . neyþur he may þe fredam of goddis kunnyng fynde. Discussion of papal power, consisting of a brief synopsis of Bernard of Clairvaux's work of advice in five books to Pope Eugenius III, *De Consideratione*, followed by brief discussion of quotations from Grosseteste, Augustine, and Origen. Unique and unpublished.

22. Folios 153^{v}–160^{r}, GOd moueþ hooly chirche bi many maner of spechis to knowe þe treuþe . . . if þu wilt do þeis dedis seuen þu schalt haue þe blis of heuen, etc. Amen. *Dialogue between Reson and Gabbyng*, edited in this volume as RG.

23. Folios $160^{r–v}$, 160^{v}–161^{v}, And for noiþur men ne womman may perfitly do þe seuen werkis . . . wiþ him bi grace. And he in god be heuenly solace. Amen for charite. Two brief enumerated lists of the seven gifts of the Holy Spirit, the first making them a prerequisite for performance of the seven works of mercy through a brief architectural allegory, the second linking them to the beatitudes. The second ends (as do items 22 and 24) with a rhyming couplet. Unique and unpublished.

24. Folios 161^{v}–162^{v}, Clerkys knowen þat aman haþ fiue wittes outtward, and oþur fiue wittes inward . . . For god is good and ful of myȝt In tyme of nede to strengþ his knyȝt. Brief allegorical treatment of the five wits as five princes governing a kingdom. Unique and unpublished.

25. Folios 163^{r}–217^{r}, Here are questiouns and ansueris . . . and so I rede þeis beggars do bi tyme and come to crist. Amen Amen. *Apology for Lollard Doctrines*, *IPMEP* 188.

26. Folio 217^{r-v}, Hit is writen in þe first book of holy writ . . . To þis trinite joye and blis nowe and euer. Amen, etc. Brief exposition using Jacob's ladder as a mnemonic catechetical device.[41] Unique and unpublished.

27. Folios 217^{v}–218^{r} þeis ben þe nyne poyntis þat oure lord Iesu answerid . . . And þerfor loue god and þin euen cristen for goddis sake. Amen. Nine points of Christ's answer to a holy man, each correcting a popular form of piety; also preserved as an endpaper in Leicester, Wyggeston Hospital MS 10D 34/15.[42] Unpublished.

28. Folio 218^{r-v}, Of þe dedis of mercy god wille speke at þe dredful day . . . were clad wiþ seuen vertues, lowly knowing hemsilf ȝerþe and poudir, sewid. . . . Description of the works of mercy, numbered 1–7 in the margin and conflating the usual bodily and spiritual lists. Ends incomplete with the catchword 'in charite'. Unique and unpublished.

The corrected foliation is used (annotated 'Sept 1977 DAB', in pencil, and correcting the skip from f. 132 to f. 134 by subtracting one folio from the original, ink foliation from f. 133 onward).

Extensive worming of the final two leaves, especially on the outer edge of text, is less severe back to f. 199. The first ten folios also have minor worming. Otherwise the volume is well preserved and legible, although owing to the tight binding, text is lost in the inner margins on most pages of the microfilm. The full text may be read in the original manuscript. The volume is written in the same hand throughout, though production methods (e.g. ways of signalling the beginning of a new text and end of the previous, heading styles, decoration) shift markedly across the volume. Coupled with the displaced ai–aiiii quire signatures and missing catchword noted in the collation, and the changes in ink colour noted by Gradon, these variations suggest the scribe worked on the manuscript over an extended period of time, and may originally have conceived it as three or more separate units.[43] Red and blue ink are used for paraphs and headings as well as underlining of marginalia and some though not all biblical quotations, and running titles (which are used extensively, if not fully consistently). Decoration, while low-budget and tapering off somewhat as the volume progresses, is more elaborate

[41] Jolliffe, *Check-List*, M.7

[42] See *IMEP* xv. 36; Jolliffe, *Check-List*, I.12h.

[43] *EWS* ii, pp. xxiii, where Gradon similarly suggests, on the basis of the shifts in ink colour, that the manuscript was 'written at different times'. Gradon also suggests that a second scribe may be at work briefly on ff. 146^{v}–147^{r}.

than in the other manuscripts edited here: three-line and two-line capitals (and a few larger ones early in the volume) are executed throughout in blue, and many (especially at the beginnings of texts) have red flourishing extending over as much as a full folio. Marginalia that form part of the volume's production include annotations of authorities and enumerated points. There are also a few contemporary and later annotations drawing attention to specific passages. A sequence of annotations in a single, cramped cursive secretary hand, apparently of the late sixteenth century, is of special interest. The name 'Thomas Chamber' appears upside down in a sprawling secretary hand (not that of the extended series, but possibly that found on f. 75^{v}) at the bottom of f. 210^{v}. There are no other marks of ownership or provenance. Like F, R formed part of the library of Archbishop James Ussher. It has been suggested that F once belonged to John Bale, but Hudson and Gradon find no annotations by Bale.[44]

CK: Durham University Library MS Cosin V.III.6 (C)

Twenty-two folios. Eight-folio medieval parchment quire interleaved with ten-folio early modern paper quire; a four-folio early modern paper quire giving a title page and prefatory dedication has been added preceding the interleaved quire.[45] Pages measure 262 × 165 mm (parchment); 267 × 193 mm (paper). Single column throughout. Paper in first quire: ff. 2–3 of quire 1 are ruled in ink with written space 210 × 120 mm and up to nineteen lines to a page. Parchment of medieval quire shows traces of ruling but no pricking; written space 213 × 113 mm with forty lines to a page. Interleaved paper in this second quire shows pricking in inner margin, written space 225 × 140 mm with forty lines to a page (usually matching fairly closely with the facing-page lines they transcribe). Collation ii, 1^{4} (paper), 2^{18} (5 paper bifolia interleaving 6, 8, 10, 12, 15, 17, 19, 21 parchment), ii.

CONTENTS:

1(a). Folio 1^{r}, 'A/ Memorable Monument of/ Antiquitye/ Pro-

[44] *EWS* ii, p. xxiii and n. 52, citing McCusker, 'Books and Manuscripts', 163.

[45] Previous description by Hudson, *Lollards and their Books*, 193–4. I am grateful to Ian Doyle for sending me a copy of his most recent revised draft description in advance of the publication of the catalogue of Durham University Library manuscripts that he and A. J. Piper are preparing. The dating s.xiv ex. & xvi/xvii is Doyle's, and I have deferred to him on details of the measurements, page preparation, and scripts, and relied on his information about the manuscript's repair. To avoid any future confusion I have also adopted his numbering of the contents.

vinge/ The lawfull soveraigntye and supremacye/ of Christian kings and/ Defendinge/ it/ Against the vnlawfull and tiranicall Primacye/ of the Pope/ Written even in the midst of Popishe darkenesse/ And of late/ founde in an antient Manuscript transcribed/ verbatim and/ presented humbly to the veiue of his Highe/ Maiestye/ by/ W Crashawe Bachelour of Divinitye and preacher/ at[46] the Temple.' Title page.

Folio 1^{v} blank

1(b). Folios 2^{r}–3^{r}, To the greatest kinge on Earthe/ My graciouse Soverayne/ James . . . Your Ma. faithful subiecte/ W. Crashawe preacher of god's/ worde at the Temple. Dedicatory letter to James I.

Folios 3^{v}–4^{v} blank

2(a). Folios 5^{v}, 7^{rv}, 9^{rv}, 11^{rv}, 13^{r}, 14^{v}, 16^{rv}, 18^{rv}, 20^{r}. s.xvi/xvii transcription of 2(b). A knighte of the kinges of England and a clerk of England that was late . . . and god send grace that ther be a good end. Amen. Finis.

Folios 13^{v}–14^{r} blank

2(b). Folios 6^{rv}, 8^{rv}, 10^{rv}, 12^{rv}, 15^{rv}, 17^{rv}, 19^{rv}. A Kniȝt of þe kinges of Yngeland and a Clerk of Yngland þat was late . . . and God send grace þat þer be a gode ende. Amen. Finis. *Dialogue between a Clerk and a Knight*, edited in this volume as CK.

Folios 20^{v}–24^{v} blank, apart from pen trials, and annotation noted below, on f. 21^{v}.

Foliation in pencil includes two final flyleaves. The parchment leaves are stained and dirty, particularly towards the outer edges, which have also been partly eaten by rats (restorations are detailed by Doyle). Most of the parchment loss appears to precede Crashaw's annotation, and thus little of this is lost; however, some of the medieval marginalia are lost, and some of both the medieval and the added marginalia are illegible as a result of staining. The body of the text remains legible despite some dark patches. According to Doyle, Crashaw wrote ff. 1^{r} and 2^{r}–3^{r} himself and also made extensive annotations in the margins of the medieval text, 2(b): these annotations are included in full, wherever legible, in this edition (see below, Editorial Method). The transcribed pages of 2(a) are in another s. xvi/xvii hand, a rather inconsistent secretary variously current and perfused with italic letter forms. The final Gothic 'Finis' in the medieval text is also a later addition, probably by Crashaw or under

[46] at] *prec. by canc.* of

his direction. The transcription is mostly very faithful, correcting the original only rarely and modernizing its content quite sparingly. Space is left for a three-line decorated capital A on f. 6^{r} but the decoration was not executed. The text is written throughout in a legible textura hand. Few errors were made, and of those few, most are clearly corrected, apparently in the same hand. Some words spill into the margin slightly on the right side of the page. Medieval marginalia are few and are confined to the identification of sources. A few sources are indicated in the marginalia of the transcription, which also include corrections and inserted missing lines. The annotation 'Edward Robart sons Booke seruaunt to Sir Nicolas Shelley knight capten of' appears on f. 21^{v}; Doyle dates this hand s. xvi^{2}, and notes that C is entered in the 1669 manuscript catalogue of Cosin's Library, MS Cosin B.I.23, f. 94^{r}. On f. 3^{r} Thomas Rud (identified by Doyle) has written 'it seems scarce so old' beside Crashaw's claim in his dedicatory letter that the manuscript is more than 300 years old.

3. LANGUAGE OF THE TEXTS

JR

The hand in which JR is written is the second of two hands in B: *LALME* profiles the first text in this second hand, ff. 26^{r}–30^{r} (not ff. 26^{r}–34^{r} as stated), as LP 6680, placing its dialect in Buckinghamshire. There are some discrepancies between the linguistic profile of JR and that of the tract on biblical translation treated in *LALME*, though many of them are proportional (providing evidence of constrained selection of just the sort that might be expected in dialect translation) or clustered or isolated (in a way that is consistent with the skilled sloppiness this scribe otherwise displays; see below, pp. lvi–lvii).[47] However, the dialect can certainly be labelled as a

[47] Reversals of proportion: *LALME* 6680 has her (þer) in place of JR's overwhelming preponderance of þer; 6680 has þane (þan) while JR nearly always has þan; 6680 has mostly -liche with few -li or -ly while JR has very few -liche against many -li and two-thirds as many -ly. Clusters of variation suggesting dialectal drift include ȝif for if in the second quarter of JR, þanne instead of þan(e) for THEN in the third quarter of the text, and þeise in place of þes(e) for THESE in the first quarter. Isolated relicts or even errors include agayne for AGAIN, agene for AGAINST, firist for FIRST, nouȝt for NOT, þo for THE, þem for THEM. WITE is spelled in divergent ways in each of its three instances: wete, wiȝt, wite.

version of the central Midlands literary standard in which so many lollard writings are copied.[48] Overall, the orthography is highly consistent, though with a significant proportion of relicts, particularly for uncommon words, that suggests effort was applied to make it so.[49] Copying many central Midlands texts may have made the scribe tolerant of a wider range of forms than that typically found in a single county and its closest neighbours; thus, while Buckinghamshire is a possible location, various among the forms attested here might seem more likely to occur further east, or, on the other hand, further west.[50] In these circumstances, it is unlikely that any greater certainty about where the manuscript was copied or where its author might have lived can be achieved on the basis of dialect evidence alone.

FS

LALME locates the language of ff. 92^{r}–187^{v} in F to Buckinghamshire, noting (but not specifying how) that the language, 'but not, apparently, the hand' changes at f. 188^{r} (see LP 774; note that only ff. 92^{r}–104^{r} were analysed in detail). Hanna, however, suggests that two and possibly three scribes were involved in copying the range of pages described by *LALME*, with changes of scribe or at the very least of duct at ff. 104^{r}, line 2, 111^{v}, line 13, and 188^{r}.[51] It would be

[48] On the prevalence, frequent use in lollard texts, and difficulties of localizing his 'Type I', a standard literary language based on the dialects of central Midlands counties (especially Northamptonshire, Huntingdonshire, and Bedfordshire), see Samuels, 'Some Aspects of Middle English Dialectology', 84–7. Here and throughout this section, it should be understood that comments about the location of the dialect of the text do not necessarily imply that the text was copied there. The scribe might have lived there for an extended period, might have been trained there, or might even have been trained elsewhere to use this dialect, without necessarily having physically copied the manuscript in the given location. This proviso is important to keep in mind in the case of writings like those of the lollards; it is obviously of far less significance in the case of (for example) local records. On difficulties in using dialectal analysis to trace the origins and distribution of lollard texts, see Hudson, *Premature Reformation*, 19.

[49] For example, while WITE is spelt differently in each instance (see n. 47), the following spellings are used for every occurrence of these common words: 'aftur', 'any', 'before', 'chirche', 'hiȝe', 'schal', 'schul'.

[50] The preponderance of þer (but with ready tolerance of 'her') for THEIR, for example, suggests Huntingdonshire, while 'tuo' for TWO, nearly always used in JR, appears once each in Cambridgeshire and Middlesex but is common in the near-adjoining regions of Hereford/Worcester/Gloucester/Oxford. 'Wiche' for WHICH is found only in Worcestershire and Buckinghamshire. 'Wan' for WHEN, very common in JR, occurs nowhere in the east Midlands; yet it is fairly well attested in the same adjoining west Midlands area just noted.

[51] Hanna, 'Two Lollard Codices', 59.

odd if the language of two or possibly three scribes were so consistent, yet then the second scribe were to change abruptly at f. 188ʳ. Evidently the manuscript would repay closer investigation. The language of FS, on ff. 212ᵛ–219ʳ and in the hand of the second of two or possibly three scribes (the same scribe who copied at least ff. 92ʳ–103ᵛ and possibly f. 111ᵛ, line 13 to f. 188ʳ as well), is again a Midlands variety of the sort we expect to find in lollard manuscripts. While the language of this text varies in several small ways from that of RG (see below), it too may be located in Warwickshire, though a far more extended analysis is required in order to locate it firmly in a specific area owing to the broader distribution of most items in this sample. Among many items found across a swathe of Midlands counties, the combination of 'two' and 'twey(n)' for TWO (*LALME* item map 242) as well as 'eiȝen' and 'iȝen' for EYE, pl. (*LALME* item map 115), common in Warwickshire, seems particularly decisive. The linguistic profile is closely similar to that of San Marino, Huntington Library MS 502 (see LP 4675), a devotional miscellany that includes another lollard Pater Noster commentary (that printed by Arnold 98–110) in company with other texts of interest to lollards.[52]

THESE	þes	(*LALME* dot map 1)
SHE	sche	(*LALME* dot map 14)
IT	it	(*LALME* dot map 25)
THEY	þei	(*LALME* dot map 30)
THEM	hem	(*LALME* dot map 40)
THEIR	here	(*LALME* dot map 52)
EACH	eche	(*LALME* dot map 86)
MUCH	myche	(*LALME* dot map 102)
WERE	were, weren	(*LALME* dot map 132)
WAS	was	(*LALME* dot map 138)
THEN	þan	(*LALME* dot map 183)
IF	ȝif	(*LALME* dot map 212)
AGAINST	aȝens	(*LALME* dot maps 216, 222)
YET	ȝit	(*LALME* dot map 246)
BEFORE	bifore	(*LALME* dot map 361)
LESS	lasse	(*LALME* dot map 456)
SELF	silf	(*LALME* dot map 520)
WORSE	wers	(*LALME* dot map 594)
PRES.IND.PL. INFLEXION	-eþ as well as -en	(*LALME* dot map 654)

[52] See *IMEP* i. 30–2.

RG

LALME notes that the manuscript appears to be written in one hand throughout, but in several dialects (see LP 7990 of ff. 81r–95v, Warwickshire, as well as the annotation without further specification that ff. 127v–138r may be located in the south-east Soke of Peterborough or extreme North Huntingdonshire, and f. 164 and following to N Ely 'mixed with some other component(s)', *LALME* i. 77). The scribe's willingness to tolerate a variety of dialects is rather unusual.[53] Perhaps in this case all the dialects the scribe found in his copy texts were tolerable to him because they were mostly from the larger Midlands region within which most lollard manuscripts can be located. Regardless of the scribe's motivations, his unusual approach quite probably allows us to identify at the very least the previous layer of copying, if not the author's dialect. RG is not among the texts analysed in *LALME*, but its orthography is consistent and distinctive, and may be located with relative ease and certainty to the south-west Midlands, most probably south Worcestershire or Warwickshire. Within the broader pattern of the Midlands dialect laid out below, the distribution of 'furst', 'wurch', 'þen(ne)', 'þise', and 'ij' as in 'lijf' are especially revealing. Present tense verbal inflexions are in -iþ, eþ, plural in -en (see *LALME* dot maps 646, 652).

AGAINST	aȝeynes, aȝeyns, aȝeyne, aȝeyn	(*LALME* dot map 217)
CALL	clep-	(*LALME* dot map 378)
CHURCH	churche	(*LALME* dot map 386)
EACH	iche	(*LALME* dot map 87)
FIRST	furst	(*LALME* dot map 417)
LIFE	lijf	(*LALME* dot map 1163)
MUCH	myche, miche	(*LALME* dot map 102)
SINCE	siþ (siþe, siþen)	(*LALME* dot map 240
SUCH	siche	(*LALME* dot map 68)
THAN	þenne (þen)	(*LALME* dot map 189)
THEM	hem	(*LALME* dot map 40)
THEIR	her	(*LALME* dot map 52)
THEN	þenne (þen)	(*LALME* dot map 184)
THESE	þise (þese)	(*LALME* dot map 2)
THEY	þei	(*LALME* dot map 30)
TOGETHER	togidre	(*LALME* dot map 542)
WERE	were	(*LALME* dot map 132)

[53] As Benskin and Laing have noted elsewhere, it is far more typical for scribes to translate the texts they copy into the dialect they or their employers prefer ('Translations and *Mischsprachen* in Middle English Manuscripts').

WHEN	whenne	(*LALME* dot map 343)
WORK (v.)	wurch-	(*LALME* dot map 317)
YET	ȝitt	(*LALME* dot map 249)

CK

The medieval booklet that has been interleaved with seventeenth-century paper to form this manuscript has not been analysed by *LALME*. The dialect of its contents is not a version of the central Midlands literary standard found in most lollard manuscript books. However, this need not suggest that the manuscript is not lollard, or even that it was not at some stage copied by scribes involved in the production of lollard books—indeed, there are some indications that it may indeed have been copied in such a setting at an earlier stage. All that can firmly be said is that the consistency of orthography and the central Midlands standardization that is generally found in lollard codices does not appear to characterize this booklet, which seems to have circulated independently. Instead, while there are some notable inconsistencies of translation, and a significant admixture of forms that are not instanced in this area at all, the dialect on the whole is decidedly more northerly. It may be located fairly precisely to Derbyshire or eastern Staffordshire on the basis of the following:

THEY	þai	(*LALME* dot map 31)
THEM	hem (þaim twice early)	(*LALME* dot map 40)
THEIR	her (þair scattered through text)	(*LALME* dot map 52)
SUCH	siche	(*LALME* dot map 65, 68)
WHICH	whiche	(*LALME* dot map 82)
MANY	moni (mony, many)	(*LALME* dot map 91)
ANY	oni (ony)	(*LALME* dot maps 99, 100)
MUCH	miche	(*LALME* dot map 102)
IS	es	(*LALME* dot map 134)

These items map the text to northern Derbyshire. However, the following items either drag the location slightly southward, or complicate our understanding of the text's possible origins.

ANY	oni (ony)	(*LALME* item map 15)
BEFORE	tofore	(*LALME* dot map 362)
IF	ȝeue, ȝef (ȝiue, ȝif)	(*LALME* dot map 209, item map 33)
THEN	þo (3, against 26 þan)	(*LALME* dot map 185)
WORK (v.)	wirch-	(*LALME* dot map 313)

3SG.PRES.IND. AND PRES.IND.PL.	-eþ	(*LALME* dot maps 646, 654)
LY	lich, liche (li)	(*LALME* dot map 609, 606)

Many of the forms found in this text have a range of orthography that suggests production in a border region where a wide range of northern and southern forms occur together.[54] Another possible explanation would be that a southern text has been recopied, but inconsistently (and recopying in a border region may account for much of the inconsistency), into a more northern dialect. In this respect 'oni' and 'ȝeue' may be especially significant: *LALME*'s item map reveals that the 'oni' (as opposed to 'eni' or 'ani') spelling is only common in the east Midlands and adjoining areas of East Anglia: two instances appear as minority spellings in Gloucestershire, but five appear in Norfolk (four clustered on the west border), one in Cambridgeshire, two in Ely, and one in north Bedfordshire. 'Ȝeue' for IF, though strongly prevalent in CK, is even more unusual, over the whole country occurring only once each in Norfolk and Exeter. In addition, 'tofore', 'þo', 'wirch', and the less prevalent 'ȝef' all occur slightly south-west of north Derbyshire, but are very common in the east Midlands and East Anglian region centred near Cambridge as well as in the south-west Midlands and around London. This evidence suggests that CK may previously have been copied in a dialect whose usages cluster around north Cambridgeshire.

4. SOURCES, INFLUENCES, AND CIRCULATION OF TEXTS

As is typical for lollard writings, we know little about who wrote these dialogues and when, who owned the extant copies before the sixteenth century, or who read them. Clearly their writers were familiar with a range of other lollard writings: although the four dialogues are certainly not uniform in tone, content, and approach, all four do exhibit the 'certain sameness' often noted in lollard writings, where distinctive usages of terms, turns of phrase, and types of arguments tend to crop up over and over again.[55] While the

[54] In addition to the profile items listed, consider GIVE ȝaue, gaf, gafe, gaue; HAVE haue, pres. pl. habbeþ; HOLD hald, holde, hold; OWN own, owen, owne, awen, awne.

[55] The description is Matthew's (*English Works*, p. xlviii). For further analysis see Hudson, 'Some Problems of Identity and Identifications'; Peikola, *Congregation of the Elect*; von Nolcken, 'A "Certain Sameness"'.

citation or quotation of one Lollard work in another is frustratingly rare, as is any form of internal comment on the writer's expectations of his readers, between them (as explained below; see p. li on RG, p. xlvii on FS) these dialogues provide examples of both.[56] The inclusion of FS and RG in large anthologies suggests that they circulated among lollard readers. So, in a different way, does the layering of dialects in CK, and to a lesser extent in JR. Still, we have little direct evidence of reception in the fourteenth and fifteenth centuries: the manuscripts' medieval marginalia are chiefly confined to the citation of references, and the dialogues are not mentioned in the sorts of heresy trial proceedings that often give us some evidence (albeit coerced) of how lollards used their books.[57]

We know more about the reception of these dialogues in the sixteenth and seventeenth centuries, when literary dialogues like those edited here were popular among religious dissenters and Protestants. We know that these manuscripts passed through the hands of prominent scholars including Whitgift, Ussher, Crashaw, Cotton, and Cosin as well as lesser-known book collectors who have also signed their names or left their shelfmarks. We can glean information from the manuscripts' later annotations. And we have some evidence about how dialogues like these were used. A disputation between a friar and a clerk is mentioned in the trials of John Hacker, John Pykas, and John Tybal in London in 1528, as well as that of the Wily family in 1532. Hacker was apparently engaged in distributing books in London and Essex in the 1520s and admits owning the dialogue, Pykas admits having received the dialogue from his brother William, and Tybal reports having heard William Pykas recite the work.[58] The daughter of the Wily family reportedly could recite the same dialogue (or one with a similar title) from memory.[59] There is no firm evidence (though the corroborative detail is suggestive) that the dialogue in question is one of those included here.[60] Yet this example provides information on how dialogues were

[56] For another example of each see Hudson, *Works of a Lollard Preacher*, pp. xlviii and lii–liii.

[57] An early 15th-c. example would be the trial of John Claydon, centred on his possession and use of the *Lanterne of Li3t*. See Hudson, *Premature Reformation*, 13, 211–14.

[58] Ibid. 487.

[59] Ibid. 489.

[60] As Hudson points out, a similar incipit to that of FS is linked, but not identified, with the dialogue of similar title (*Premature Reformation*, 486). Of all known lollard works in dialogue or quasi-dialogue form, FS would seem an unlikely candidate for memorization owing to its difficult syntax and use of technical terms, yet the topics it debates certainly had lasting interest.

read and circulated, and the practices described may have a longer history.

JR

The manuscript in which our one copy of JR appears is closely relevant to the dialogue's circumstances of composition. The sermon notes and other short items in both part I and part II of B show the steps by which Wycliffites adapted previous anticlerical and antifraternal writings.[61] Thus, I item 3 quotes a sermon by Grosseteste critical of monks, adapted to refer to friars and frequently cited in this form in lollard writings (on f. 20^r; see p. xx), and II items 7–10 newly apply a series of quotations from the *Rosarium* describing abuses by the clergy to friars (see pp. xxi–xxii). Wycliffites also adapted previous antifraternal writings in order to generalize their claims from one order to all, or even to all clergy in general, or to adduce them as evidence of the coming of Antichrist, as in II item 12, an adapted version of pseudo-Hildegard's *Insurgent gentes* (see p. xxii). JR itself illustrates both these processes of Wycliffite adaptation, and cites both the Grosseteste passage and pseudo-Hildegard's *Insurgent gentes* (JR 9–12 and n., 1005 and n.).

The dialogue form was a popular means of publicizing the sometimes quite fractious debates within and among religious and fraternal orders. Several such dialogues from the fourteenth and fifteenth century are extant, though they vary both in format and in the specificity of their occasions. They are written in both Latin and the vernacular, prose and verse, as separate compositions that engage one another's arguments one by one (whether this exchange is genuine or fictional), as well as in dialogues like those edited in this volume, where the exchange (again, whether real or staged) is internal to a single composition. Despite the wide variation in their formats, these works tend to recycle the same claims and accusations over and over. While some of them, and some of their sources, have been well studied (for example Chaucer's altercation between a Friar and a Summoner in the *Canterbury Tales*, *Piers Plowman* (*PP*), *Piers the Plowman's Crede* (*PPC*), the Latin O and I poems edited by Rigg, and among sources, William of St Amour's *De periculis novissimorum temporum*, and Fitzralph's *Defensio Curatorum*), others have received less attention (for example, the works making up the *Upland series*, JR and FS, and among sources, John of Hildesheim's

[61] These processes have been well described by Scase, *'Piers Plowman' and the New Anti-clericalism*, and are described in more detail in the notes to JR.

Dialogus inter directorem et detractorem de ordine Carmelitarum (*c.*1370–4), and a public debate in Cambridge in 1374 between the Dominican John Stokes and the Carmelite John Hornby).[62] In naming its disputants 'Jon' and 'Richard' JR is probably paying homage to the prominent antifraternal writer Richard Fitzralph, whose *Summa in questionibus armenorum* and *De Pauperie Salvatoris* are dialogues between 'Johannes' and 'Richardus'.

There are three main Wycliffite examples of antifraternal literary dialogue: *PPC*, the *Upland series*, and JR. All recycle quite similar arguments, and all are self-consciously literary; all clearly rely closely on *PP*. This is a familiar claim in the case of the *Upland series* and of *PPC*, both of which have long been regarded as part of the *Piers Plowman* tradition.[63] While JR is a newcomer to the expanding *Piers Plowman* tradition, its aspirations in this direction are unmistakable, especially perhaps where Jon comments on how the friars 'galpe aftur gulles of grace' in a flight of prose alliteration (JR 47), or where he develops through allegory an alternative ecclesiology under threat from friars (JR 289–326), in a passage that more broadly recalls the final passus of *Piers Plowman* B/C.

An effort to gain greater precision in the dating of JR than can be derived from the evidence provided by its manuscript meets with little success. The tract on biblical translation that precedes it in the second part of B, II item 1, can be dated by means of its source and its references to Arundel between 1401 and 1414 (and probably before 1407 since it does not refer to Arundel's *Constitutions*, first formulated in Oxford in that year).[64] JR itself refers in veiled terms to the Papal Schism (JR 138 and n.), suggesting that it was written after 1378 (as we would have expected in any case) and before the schism was resolved in 1417. If the suggestion that JR refers to *Piers Plowman*'s final passus in the B or C version is correct, then JR must post-date the first composition and publication of some version of passus B 20/C 22. However, this is to raise all the debates over the dating of *Piers Plowman*: JR might be placed after any date in the range 1377–90.[65] If

[62] Chaucer, *Canterbury Tales*, *PP*, *PPC*; Rigg, 'Two Latin Poems against the Friars'; Szittya, '"Sedens super flumina"'; William of St Amour, *Opera Omnia*; Fitzralph, *Defensio Curatorum*; *Upland series*; JR, FS; and on the Hildesheim dialogue and Stokes/Hornby debate, Jotischky, *Carmelites and Antiquity*, 58–60, 168–80.

[63] On the long-standing members of the *Piers Plowman* tradition see *The Piers Plowman Tradition*, ed. Barr; Hudson, 'The Legacy of *Piers Plowman*'.

[64] See Hudson, *Lollards and their Books*, 81.

[65] On the dating of *Piers Plowman* B 20 see Barney, *The Penn Commentary on Piers Plowman*, v. 174–6. See also Warner, 'The Ending, and End, of *Piers Plowman* B'.

the cross-reference in RG does indeed refer to JR, perhaps among 'oþur places' (see below, p. li), then JR's composition may be tentatively fixed before that of RG.

FS

Of the four dialogues, FS is provided with the most circumstantial evidence. Not only is it the most plausible candidate for being the dialogue referred to in trials of the 1520s and 1530s, but it seems to have a specific occasion, an addressee who is expected to 'fulfillen in dede þe trewþe' once the dialogue has brought him to see it (see FS 359 and n.), and participants identified at the very least by their social status, if not by name. The Lord Duke of Gloucester to whom this dialogue is addressed may be Thomas Woodstock, 1355–97, youngest son of Edward III, one of the Lords Appellant in the Merciless Parliament of 1388 and convicted of treason and killed (or died by natural causes?) in Calais in 1397. An inventory of Woodstock's possessions reveals that he owned a copy of the Wycliffite Bible (now British Library Egerton MS 617–18, the earliest datable manuscript of the Earlier Version), among eighty-four books in his house and in addition to forty-two books in his chapel.[66] This evident interest in letters and in piety certainly makes Woodstock a plausible target of address, regardless of whether the claim that the addressee witnessed the dialogue is a fiction. Humphrey, Duke of Gloucester, 1390–1447, youngest son of Henry IV, may also be a possible recipient: Duke Humphrey was a well-known patron of letters and the patron or dedicatee of works by Lydgate, Upton, and Capgrave among others, as well as the recipient of a version of the Lollard Disendowment Bill in 1431 and of the presentation copy of the *Songe du Vergier* in 1427.[67] Duke Humphrey is also known to have owned a copy of Ockham's *Dialogus*, since he donated it to the University of Oxford in February 1443–4.[68]

[66] See *ODNB* s.v. 'Thomas Woodstock' and Hudson, *Premature Reformation*, 12, 112. Jenny Stratford adds weight to the possibility that Thomas commissioned this Bible: see '"La Somme Le Roi" (Reims, Bibliothèque Municipale, MS 570), the Manuscripts of Thomas of Woodstock, Duke of Gloucester, and the Scribe, John Upton'. Matti Peikola gives details of its polemical content: see 'The Sanctorale, Thomas of Woodstock's English Bible, and the Orthodox Appropriation of Wycliffite Tables of Lessons'.

[67] See *ODNB* s.v. 'Humphrey, duke of Gloucester' and Hudson, *Premature Reformation*, 340. For an edition of the Disendowment Bill see *SEWW*, 135–7, 203–7. On the *Songe du Vergier* see below, p. liii.

[68] Now London, British Library MS Harley 33. See A. C. de la Mare, 'Manuscripts Given to the University of Oxford by Humfrey, Duke of Gloucester', 40–2; Ockham, *Dialogus*, MSS, siglum Lb, for London, British Library MS Harley 33.

Of the two possible addressees, Thomas Woodstock would seem the more likely, if only because there are some hints that FS may be a product of early Wycliffism. The work's tone is speculative and exploratory rather than polemical: the writer seems to take delight in trying to render material from the university curriculum in arts into English, and in using these techniques to shed light on disputed matters of doctrine. While this rather unusual approach may be in part a product of the work's occasion and audience, it does give a sense that some issues have not yet become so polarized by contentious debate that downright assertion is required. Another hint is that the passages of biblical translation are clumsily done, and in some places very close to the wording of the Earlier Version of the Wycliffite Bible.[69] While this similarity may be coincidental, it remains suggestive: FS may have been composed, and the debate it records may have taken place, in the same time period when the earlier stages of the Wycliffite Bible translation were under way. While this period may not be fixed precisely, a date between *c.*1380 and 1397 seems likely.[70]

Special appeals to lords and to the king, of the kind made in such a pointed form in FS, are common in lollard writings, which typically treat the higher levels of the secular hierarchy as potential allies in their campaigns against the fraternal and other religious orders or against the ecclesiastical hierarchy. The *Thirty-Seven Conclusions* and the *Tractatus de regibus*, for example, are respectively examples of works that seem designed to appeal to lords and to the king. At least some works that make a special appeal to lords likely refer to relationships that may be aspirational rather than already firmly established: John Deveros's account of how he began writing in defence of images and pilgrimages prompted by the questions of an *armiger* and Richard Wyche's explanation of how a knight advised him during his trial are cases in point.[71] While FS may not be certain

[69] See, e.g., FS 20–3 and n., FS 61–2 and n.

[70] On the difficulties of dating the stages in the translation of the Wycliffite Bible, see Hudson, *Premature Reformation*, 238–47, esp. 246–7. Mary Dove suggests work on the translation began before the middle of the 1370s, and dates the Prologue (composed when work on the Later Version was largely complete) to 1387; *The First English Bible*, 80, 110–13.

[71] On Deveros see Hudson, *Premature Reformation*, 94: it is interesting that Lollard opponents, too, could see an advantage in claiming alliances with lords and knights. For Richard Wyche's letter see Matthew, 'The Trial of Richard Wyche'; on his relationship with the knight who participates in his trial, see von Nolcken, 'Richard Wyche, a Certain Knight'.

of its would-be patron's support, there is some corroborative evidence suggesting that the dialogue may indeed be an occasional piece, the product or at least the offshoot of a genuine disputation. The dialogue has the feel of a quodlibetal exercise, where topics follow one another in a loosely associated sequence rather than developing and pursuing a well-defined topic. The dialogue's language is dense with the idioms of academic disputation, and the syntax is extraordinarily Latinate: it seems quite likely that FS was written in Latin then translated, or perhaps that it was transcribed in English on the basis of a disputation staged in Latin.[72] A reference to the friar as a Dominican also has a circumstantial feel: Wycliffites more often lump all friars together rather than specifying the order to which they belong.[73] One detail that does not seem particularly realistic is that the friar comes off decidedly worse in every exchange: it seems clear that if a debate did take place, the friar did not have a hand in writing it down.

RG

RG is a free translation and adaptation of the first twelve chapters of Wyclif's *Dialogus*, also known as the *Speculum ecclesie militantis*. While the author of RG makes quite extensive changes to Wyclif's text, he engages closely with the *Dialogus* throughout, repeatedly using it as a point of departure for his own adaptations and working especially closely with Wyclif's chapter 12 as his own dialogue concludes, as detailed in the Explanatory Notes. Among all Wyclif's works, the *Dialogus* seems to have been especially popular. There are more extant manuscripts of the *Dialogus* than of any other work by Wyclif: twenty-two manuscripts contain all or part of the original Latin text, two more manuscripts contain a shorter Hussite redaction in five chapters known as the *De triplici ecclesia*, and one contains seventeenth-century extracts.[74] While such a popular work may be an unsurprising choice for translation into Middle English, the author of RG seems to have had some specific reasons for the selection he makes from Wyclif's text and the ways he modifies it.

Wyclif's two speakers are Veritas and Mendacium, rendered by RG's author as Reson and Gabbyng. Reason, of course, is not

[72] See FS 10–11, 20–3, 40–2, 61–2, 96–7, 98, 114, and nn.

[73] See FS 27 and n. *PPC* does of course provide a representative of each order in turn, but this too is rather unusual.

[74] See Thomson [408]. There is in addition an early 15th-c. translation (or better, adaptation and augmentation) into Czech by Jakoubek of Stříbro: see *Mistra Jakoubka ze Stříbra překlad Viklefova dialogu*, ed. Milan Svoboda (Prague, 1909).

identical with what would seem the most direct vernacular equivalent for 'veritas', that is, truth. But the relationship between reason and truth is what the author sets himself to explore and finally to anatomize, in the passage from Wyclif's chapter 12 with which he chooses to conclude. The author equates Reson with Christ and Gabbyng with the devil more bluntly than Wyclif, who had presented his personae as literary devices then linked them with Christ and the devil through exegesis (see RG 4 and n.). Throughout his adaptation of Wyclif's text, the author plays up the relationship between reason, truth, and authority, in preparation for his peroration about the judgement Reson/Christ will provide on Doomsday, as opposed to the attitudes we human beings should maintain, in the meantime, to the question of our own and others' salvation (see RG 1–2, 354–83). One result of this careful thematic development is that while the author, like Wyclif, is not concerned to give his participants equal billing, and allows Reson to dominate the conversation especially at the outset, nonetheless he is rather more careful than Wyclif to keep his speakers in character (see RG 7 n.).

Like Wyclif in his *Dialogus*, RG's author relies extensively on a three-estates model as his basis for an extended exposition on contemporary failings among the clergy. In contrast to Wyclif's, however, his model is less hierarchical: he develops an extended allegory of the three estates as sisters in order to emphasize their parity and their interdependence, and he repeatedly modifies Wyclif's contrasts between 'higher' and 'lower' (see RG 37 n.). In addition, RG's author eliminates Wyclif's abstract, largely theoretical discussions of the role of the pope and the pope's jurisdiction over England (issues that will, however, emerge in CK) in favour of a focus on more local issues. He is especially preoccupied with pastoral obligations, and adds a description of the duties in return for which priests in some circumstances may receive monetary support that is more detailed and practical than in any other lollard text I have examined; he also inserts several admonitions against covetousness.[75]

RG's author's most intriguing modification to Wyclif's text is an extended excursus (see RG 108–99) in which he gives his own concerns free rein. The content is thematically related to alterations to the *Dialogus* made elsewhere, for example in its concern with 'last things', death and 'domesday' (RG 112, 151–2, 157, 263, 273, 283), as

[75] See RG 17–32 and n. for the description of how priests should be supported; further references to covetousness and to pastoral obligations are cited in the following paragraph.

well as its concern with clerks' performance of pastoral duties and avoidance of covetousness (RG 17–32, 46–57, 106–12, 189–93, 210–37, 250–63). Departures from what is elsewhere or previously typical of RG include the switch here to direct address to the would-be right-living reader (RG 112–17, 185–8) and the abandonment of previous efforts to strengthen the characterization of the speakers (cf. RG 7 n.) evident in pervasive third-person reference to Christ, reference to reason (RG 112, 129, 131), and direct address to Christ (RG 145, 150, 159). The topics of the interpolated material do appear, most of them quite often, elsewhere in Wyclif's and Wycliffite writings; nevertheless, a surprising number of topics treated in JR recur here. The author is concerned, for example, to explain how to obey tyrannical rulers (RG 125–42 and n.; cf. JR 943–57 and n., 992–4 and n.). He rejects prayers at specific times and in specific forms, as for example those of books of hours, in favour of the Pater Noster (RG 172–81; cf. JR 748–69). He designates Christ as our true abbot and proponent of the rule of Christ (i.e. the gospels), in implicit contrast to the abbots of religious orders and their rules, in the same quite unusual way as JR (RG 168–97; cf. JR 336 n., RG 168 n.). He emphasizes that the failure to prevent a sin, whether by refusing a sinful order or request, or by chastising the sinful, is a form of consent to and thus implication in that sin (RG 122, 189–93, cf. *Dialogus*, 12/19–22, JR 404–6 and n., 817–20 and n., 990 and n.). In developing this argument, he gives a cross-reference to fuller treatment elsewhere of the damage done to both parties by auricular confession that may refer to JR: 'And here sculd men arunt feynt penytaunsers, confessours, and oþur prestis þat assoylen for mony. For boþe þe partis aftur þe scentence in Goddis lawe is fouler aftur fyȝelid in synne, whiche mater we han openly declared in oþur places' (RG 189–93). While complaints about confession as mandated by the Church do appear in other Wycliffite writings, JR contains an unusually extensive discussion of the topic (JR 550–85, esp. 567–8, 'boþe parties be þis fallen in many errours'). Both dialogues use the unusual conjunction 'al if', frequent in (if not entirely exclusive to) the *EWS* and a small number of other Wycliffite writings.[76] The cumulative evidence is rather suggestive: common authorship is plausible, if not proven.

Little may be specified about the date of RG, beyond that obviously it must post-date its source (Williel Thomson dates

[76] See Hudson, 'A Lollard Sect Vocabulary', 169 and nn. 24 and 25.

Wyclif's *Dialogus* to his final years, placing it tentatively in late 1379) and must post-date JR if the two works are indeed by the same author. Like JR, and following Wyclif, RG refers to the Papal Schism of 1378–1417 (RG 327–8 and n., JR 185–6 and n.): while it is not impossible that RG's author would have retained the reference even after the end of the schism, a date of composition before 1417 seems more likely.

CK

Conflicts over papal as opposed to imperial or regal power produced very much the same sort of profusion of works in dialogue form as the conflicts within and between religious and fraternal orders that influenced JR. However, in addition to a tendency to recycle similar arguments drawn from a range of key sources, the dialogues debating spiritual as opposed to temporal power show a greater tendency towards quotation, adaptation, and even wholesale incorporation of one another's contents. Across the course of the fourteenth century, writers produced dialogues in response to specific crises in the relation between Church and state. But writers also read dialogues produced in the context of earlier crises, and adapted these older materials to new purposes. For example, the anonymous *Disputacio inter militem et clericum* of *c.*1296–1302 was written in response to Philip the Fair's conflict with Boniface VIII.[77] This conflict had a wider international impact, and six extant manuscripts demonstrate the continuing popularity of the *Disputacio* in England in the fifteenth century.[78] So does a translation into English, and adaptation towards contemporary English concerns, made by John Trevisa some time in the 1370s or 1380s.[79] A generation later, William Ockham produced a lengthy *Dialogus* as part of his writings on behalf of

[77] See the critical edition and translation by Erickson, 'A Dispute between a Priest and a Knight'. For an analysis of the work's royalism and attempts to intimidate the French clergy see Renna, 'Kingship in the *Disputatio Inter Clericum et Militem*'.

[78] In one sense the impact of these events scarcely needs demonstration, since they led in 1303 to an attack on the pope, and a month later to his death. For an analysis of the more subtle effects in France and England of the propaganda campaign against the pope, see below at n. 82. On the English manuscripts see Erickson, 'A Dispute', 289–90 (lists five); Fowler, *The Life and Times of John Trevisa*, 153–63 (adds a sixth). There are no extant 14th-c. manuscripts, although Erickson points out that her stemma suggests that there must have been at least five (p. 289), and we know that Trevisa must have had access to an earlier copy.

[79] For analysis of how John Trevisa alters his translation to address English concerns see Somerset, *Clerical Discourse*, 78–93, esp. 79–81.

Ludwig IV of Bavaria in his conflict with Pope John XXII.[80] This work too was known in England: in addition to the manuscript owned by Humphrey Duke of Gloucester in the 1440s, there are two other known manuscripts with British connections before the mid-fifteenth century.[81] In the mid- to late 1370s, on the brink of the Papal Schism, both the *Disputacio* and Ockham's *Dialogus* were incorporated into the vast *Somnium viridarii* (1374–6) as well as its French translation and adaptation the *Songe du Vergier* (1376–8), by the author of both, Evrart de Trémaugon, who was writing for Charles V.[82] In 1425 the Duke of Bedford gave Charles V's own presentation copy of the *Songe* to his brother Humphrey Duke of Gloucester.

The author of CK, like Evrart de Trémaugon, was familiar with previous stages in the ongoing conflicts over papal authority. He mentions the tendency of cardinals to call the pope a tyrant when the pope withstands their will; this is very likely an allusion to the cardinals' accusation that Boniface VIII is a tyrant in the course of his posthumous trial of 1303–11 (CK 161–2 and n.). William Courtenay has suggested that the trial was notorious as a result of the propaganda campaign in its favour across France, and that the controversy drove some English scholars home from the University of Paris; this allusion may suggest that some of CK's sources have their origins in this earlier conflict.[83] The author of CK also refers to the claim, prominent in Ockham's *Dialogus*, that the pope can be accused of heresy because, after all, the correct faith might be preserved in any one person, as it was in Mary between the crucifixion and resurrection (CK 335–7 and n.). It is possible that the author of CK had read both the *Disputacio* and the *Dialogus*, though he does not incorporate their content directly as does Evrart.

Like Trevisa in his adaptation and translation of the *Disputatio*, the author of CK focuses on England. In the beginning he specifies that both speakers are 'of England', but that the Clerk has recently come

[80] Ockham, *Dialogus*. As the editors note, part I of Ockham's *Dialogus*, the part most relevant to the present discussion, was probably written shortly after Ockham's break with the pope in 1328.

[81] Ockham, *Dialogus*, MSS, sigla Lb and Lc (donated to British libraries by Englishmen in the 15th c.) as well as Mw, Mz (copied by a friar with an English name in the 14th c.). There are in addition several manuscripts whose provenance has not been traced.

[82] See *Somnium Viridarii*, ed. Schnerb-Lièvre, as well as the review by Howard Kaminsky, in *Speculum*, 71 (1996), 1015–19; *Le Songe du Vergier*, ed. Schnerb-Lièvre, 2 vols.

[83] Courtenay, 'Between Pope and King'.

from the papal court in Rome, in the process establishing an expectation both of where the speakers' loyalties should lie—and of where they in fact do, as their conflicting definitions of 'spiritual' power and possession make clear. Like Trevisa again, the author of CK plays on later fourteenth-century anxieties in England up until the deposition of Richard II in 1399, about who is loyal to the king, and who on the other hand is encroaching on the king's 'regalie' in a way that might be construed as treason.[84] These similarities support a date for CK before 1399, in conformity with Doyle's dating of the manuscript to before the end of the fourteenth century. The assertion that the clergy own a third of the property in the realm may support a date after 1380, when this claim was made in Parliament (CK 197–9 and n.); while the complaint may have already been conventional, we would expect a date after 1380 for a Wycliffite work in any case. The pope is always placed in Rome, and spoken of in the singular, but these details need not be incompatible with a dating of the work during the Papal Schism of 1378–1417 if by referring to one pope in Rome the author means to affirm England's partisan support of the Roman pope Urban VI or his successor Boniface IX, or even if the author is merely evading any engagement with this new complication as he adapts pre-1378 sources.[85]

Of course, it is unusual enough for any Wycliffite work to speak in favour of any pope: CK's qualified support of papal power limited to spiritual matters seems an oddity given that so many Wycliffite tracts label the pope as antichrist.[86] The Knight's position makes sense when we remember that the author is working within a tradition that labours to develop coherent theoretical accounts of papal and regal power, rather than to explain why a given pope's exercise of his power is evidently corrupt, and when we notice that the Knight's main concern is to characterize the pope when he exceeds these bounds not as antichrist, but as a traitor to the king. Other aspects of the author's exposition are characteristically lollard, for example the distinctive

[84] See CK 273–96; cf. Trevisa, *Dialogus*, 514/14–516/8. See also Somerset, *Clerical Discourse*, 80–1 (on Trevisa), 140–53 (on shifts in the definition of treason during Richard II's adult rule and after his deposition). There are a number of other resemblances between the two dialogues that may not be considered in detail here; some have previously been noted by Hudson, *Lollards and their Books*, 199.

[85] Hudson, *Lollards and their Books*, 195, instead suggests that the references to the pope in Rome 'indicate the theoretical nature of the argument'.

[86] See JR 249–52, where the pope is labelled antichrist; friars are called antichrist's clerks throughout this dialogue. For a very full development of antichrist arguments see 'De Papa', Matthew 460–82. See also CK 4–11, 12–19 and n.

claim that the king and his lords are responsible for taking away goods from corrupt clergy and bestowing them on those who will fulfil their office, if they do not themselves wish to be judged by God as responsible for clerical corruption (see CK 210–29 and nn.).[87]

5. EDITORIAL METHOD

Each text is printed from its single surviving manuscript; specific notes on individual texts follow this general description. Editorial emendations are enclosed in square brackets, while editorial omissions are recorded only in the apparatus. The one surviving witness to each text is inevitably flawed by human error, yet given that we have only one surviving witness to rely on, the approach to emendation is in general a conservative one. Scribal corrections are accepted and noted in the apparatus. Emendations are avoided where an unusual spelling or idiom is used consistently in the text, especially though not only if it is attested elsewhere in Middle English, above all if in other lollard texts or writings commonly read by lollards. Emendations are made where the manuscript is illegible, where scribal error or omission (e.g. due to eyeskip) has evidently occurred, and to supply deficient sense in other cases where corruption of the exemplar can reasonably be conjectured. The bases for emendation in order of preference are (1) usage in the text itself, (2) reference to the source if any, (3) usage in other lollard writings, writings known to have been read by lollards, or writings produced in response to lollardy, and (4) an attempt to reconstruct and reverse scribal error. Where the basis of an emendation (or, sometimes, of the decision not to emend) is not self-evident, it is briefly explained in the apparatus or Explanatory Notes.

Modern capitalization and punctuation are imposed in place of that used in the manuscripts, except that the capitalization used in sixteenth- and seventeenth-century marginalia is preserved as it appears. Modern word division is imposed except as noted below. Double *f* at the beginning of words is modified to *F* or *f* as appropriate. Manuscript *i/j* and *u/v* are retained. The designations for the participants in each dialogue are capitalized in the text whenever they clearly refer to the speakers, regardless of whether

[87] See Hudson, *Lollards and their Books*, 197–9, for further examples of CK's lollard claims.

these designations are proper or common nouns. Changes of speaker are indicated uniformly throughout, by a new paragraph headed by the name of the new speaker. The method used to distinguish speakers in the manuscript is noted in the specific notes below; any variations in practice, or editorial modifications to the scribe's designations of speaker, are noted in the apparatus. Marginal and interlinear additions are indicated in the text (see table below). Marginalia other than corrections or additions are noted in the apparatus, keyed to the reference to the source in the text (if any) or failing that the opening word of the passage they annotate. However, marginalia with a less specific referent are keyed to the word beside which they begin. On the treatment of marginal and interlinear additions, as well as conjectural reconstructions, see the table below.

Abbreviations in the text are silently expanded, using the most frequent unabbreviated spelling found in the manuscript, if any, or failing that, a form consistent with the text's dialect: special difficulties and their solutions are noted below. Abbreviated Latin references are minimally expanded for clarity; where they occur in marginalia they are recorded in the apparatus, and the full modern references supplied in the Explanatory Notes. Numbers written as arabic numerals are transcribed into their modern numeric equivalents, rather than as words. *Ihu* is transcribed as *Iesu*, and *an'crist* throughout as *antecrist*, in keeping with its written-out form in JR and CK.

JR

There are many supralinear corrections and words marked for reversal in this careless copy; on many more occasions it is clear that errors remain uncorrected. *W* with superscript *t* is transcribed as *wiþ* except on the one occasion when it is written out as *wit*. Macrons are used for non-standard purposes: often to expand *sent* to *seint*, and often apparently ornamentally, or perhaps to indicate final *-e*. Occasions where the macron or other abbreviation mark is treated as ornamental and not expanded are noted in the apparatus. The first three changes of speaker after the preamble are marked by the interposition of the name of the new speaker in red. Thereafter, most new speeches begin with a minuscule *i* (for Jon) or *r* (for Richard) followed by a word-sized blank space. One change of speaker, apparently carelessly omitted by the scribe but clearly required for the exchange between speakers to make sense, is added at JR 70, as noted in the apparatus.

FS

Apart from some notable instances of textual corruption (as at FS 6), and some more minor omissions apparently of single words, this is a fairly clean copy with few corrections. Changes of speaker are mostly marked by a partial blank line, usually decorated with a long jagged pen stroke, followed with a new line of text that begins with a two-line capital (though occasionally these are left unexecuted). On some occasions a text box in the partial blank line or the margin designates the speaker (as noted in the apparatus). The contents of f. 217 and f. 218 are reversed in the manuscript: together they form the innermost bifolium of a quire, inadvertently placed inside out. Their reversal into proper order is noted in the apparatus. The text of the dialogue may have been modified in this or a previous copy, as noted in the Explanatory Notes (see esp. FS 312 n.): the text is followed as given rather than emended. Extensive but evidently fairly slapdash underlining and use of enthusiastic accompanying diagonal lines in the margin to indicate items of interest has been ignored in the apparatus. A few words are hidden in the page gutter, as noted. Care has been taken to preserve the often heavily Latinate syntax as well as the academic idiom of this dialogue, which draws especially closely on the conventions of university disputation.

RG

Apart from a few uncorrected dittographs and other minor errors, this is a reliable copy with few scribal corrections. The foliation used is the more recent, corrected foliation. The manuscript is very tightly bound, and a portion of the text on each page is hidden in the gutter on microfilm; however, nearly all of the text (except as noted in the apparatus) can be read in the manuscript itself. Changes of speaker are marked with a minuscule *r* (for Reson) or *l* (for Gabbyng), followed by a word-sized space. This marker is used to indicate continuation as well: Gabbyng is given little to say except near the end, and the scribe's response to this violation of the more typical dialogue form is to remind us several times during Reson's initial speech that Reson is still speaking. Each of these internal divisions is marked in the edited text with a new paragraph headed with a similar reminder.

CK

The text is a clear copy with few corrections and fewer remaining errors; the facing-page seventeenth-century transcription is for the most part faithful, though it does modernize spellings. Changes of speaker are marked with unusual consistency: most speeches begin with a slightly enlarged majuscule letter, some with a symbol in the margin as well, while the end of nearly every speech is marked with a partial blank line, nearly always ornamented with two curved penstrokes descending to the right. The transcription is consulted directly only in the few cases where the original text is illegible: these are noted in the apparatus. The seventeenth-century annotations by William Crashaw are recorded in full in the apparatus, keyed to the word in the text adjacent to which they begin. *S* has been expanded as *sir* rather than *ser* (following the examples where the word is written out), *ꝑde* as *parde* rather than *perde* (in keeping with the text's dialect); *for to* is preferred to *forto* except to resolve ambiguity (as at CK 324).

The following conventions have been used in the text and apparatus:

]	Separates lemma from annotation (in italics) and/or manuscript reading (in roman)
/	Line break (usually only noted when it helps to explain scribal error)
//	Page break (usually only noted when it helps to explain scribal error)
⟨. . .⟩	Angle brackets enclose illegible material. At minimum the number of illegible letters is estimated, giving one full stop for each letter. Where possible some conjecture as to the content, or explanation of the reasons why the text cannot be read, are included.
[aaa]	Square brackets enclose emended text added to, or modified from, the manuscript reading, as explained in the apparatus
‵a′	Forward and reverse primes enclose supralinear or marginal insertions, as explained in the apparatus
a^1, a^2, a^3	For precision, superscript numbers specify which of multiple occurrences of a given letter, letter

	combination, or word within a word or a line of text is the referent
abbrev.	Abbreviation
canc.	Cancelled, either by subpunction or crossing out
cf.	Compare
corr.	Corrected in the manuscript (the annotation then specifies how)
corr. by canc.	Corrected by cancellation
interlin.	Designated text has been inserted between the two lines (interlinear)
marked for rev.	Written in order stated as manuscript reading, but marked for reversal as in the corrected text
subpunct.	Subpunction, or dots added under and sometimes over the text in order to cancel it
suplin.	Designated text is added above the line (supralinear)
twice	The scribe copied the same word twice in error

BIBLIOGRAPHY

MANUSCRIPTS CITED

Cambridge, Gonville and Caius College MS 354/581 (*Middle English Rosarium*).

Oxford, Bodleian Library MS Bodley 158 (William Rymington, *Tractatus*).

Oxford, Bodleian Library MS Bodley 703 (William Woodford, *72 Quaestiones de sacramento altaris*).

PRIMARY SOURCES

The Apocrypha and Pseudepigraphia of the Old Testament in English, gen. ed. and trans. R. H. Charles, 2 vols. (Oxford, 1913).

Aristotle, *Aristotle's Categories and On Interpretation*, trans. J. L. Ackrill (Oxford, 1963).

—— *Nicomachean Ethics*, trans. J. A. K. Thomson, rev. Hugh Tredennick, rev. edn. (London, 2004).

—— *Posterior Analytics*, trans. with commentary by Jonathan Barnes, 2nd edn. (Oxford, 1994).

Les Auctoritates Aristotelis: Un florilège médièval. Étude historique et édition critique, ed. J. Hamesse (Louvain and Paris, 1974).

Augustine, *De Doctrina Christiana*, ed. and trans. R. P. H. Green (Oxford, 1995); cited by book, chapter, and section followed by page numbers.

Bede, Venerable, *In Pentateuchum Commentarii*, in *PL* 91: 189–394.

Boniface VIII en Procès: Articles d'accusation et dépositions des témoins (1301–1311), ed. Jean Coste (Rome, 1995).

Book to a Mother, ed. Adrian J. McCarthy, Salzburg Studies in English Literature, Elizabethan and Renaissance Studies, 92; Studies in the English Mystics, 1 (Salzburg, 1981).

Bühler, Curt F., 'A Lollard Tract: On Translating the Bible into English', *Medium Aevum*, 7 (1938), 167–83.

Capgrave, John, *The Life of St Norbert by John Capgrave O.E.S.A. (1393–1464)*, ed. Cyril L. Smetana, OSA (Toronto, 1977).

Chronicles of Rome: An Edition of the Middle English Chronicle of Popes and Emperors and the Lollard Chronicle, ed. Dan Embree (Woodbridge, Suffolk and Rochester, NY, 1999).

Codex Regularum Monasticarum et Canonicarum, ed. L. Holstenius, 3 vols. (Graz, 1957–8).

Dives and Pauper, ed. Priscilla Heath Barnum, 2 vols. in 3, EETS 275, 280, 323 (1976–2004); cited by volume (i.i, i.ii, ii), as well as page and line number.

Dymmok, Roger, *Liber Contra Duodecim Errores et Hereses Lollardorum*, ed. H. S. Cronin, Wyclif Society (London, 1922).

The English Works of Wyclif hitherto Unprinted, ed. F. D. Matthew, EETS OS 74 (1880).

Erickson, Norma N., 'A Dispute between a Priest and a Knight', *Proceedings of the American Philosophical Society*, 111 (1967), 288–309.

Fasciculus Morum: A Fourteenth-Century Preacher's Handbook, ed. and trans. Siegfried Wenzel (University Park, Pa., 1989).

Fitzralph, *Defensio Curatorum*, in *Dialogus inter militem et clericem, Richard Fitzralph's Sermon 'Defensio curatorum' and Methodius* . . ., ed. Aaron J. Perry, EETS 167 (1925).

A Fourteenth-Century English Biblical Version, ed. Anna C. Paues (Cambridge, 1904).

The Fyve Wyttes: A Late Middle English Devotional Treatise, ed. R. H. Bremmer (Amsterdam, 1987).

Gordon, Briar, 'Four Lollard Dialogues: An Edition with Commentary' (Ph.D. thesis, Otago, 1983).

Gregory the Great, *Moralia in Iob*, ed. Marcus Adriaen, 3 vols., Corpus Christianorum Series Latina, 143, 143A, 143B (Turnhout, 1979–85).

Grosseteste, Robert, *Roberti Grosseteste quondam episcopi Lincolniensis epistolae*, ed. H. Luard, Rolls Series, 26 (London, 1861).

Higden, Ranulph, *Polychronicon . . . together with the English translations of John Trevisa and an unknown writer of the fifteenth century*, ed. Churchill Babington and Joseph R. Lumby, 9 vols., Rolls Series, 41 (London, 1865–86).

Hoccleve, Thomas, *Regiment of Princes*, ed. Charles Blyth (Kalamazoo, 1999).

—— *Selections from Hoccleve*, ed. M. C. Seymour (Oxford, 1981).

Hunt, Simon, 'An Edition of Tracts in Favour of Scriptural Translation and of Some Texts Connected with Lollard Biblical Scholarship' (D.Phil. thesis, Oxford University, 1994).

Iacopo da Varazze, *Legenda Aurea*, ed. Giovanni Paolo Maggioni, 2 vols. (Florence, 1998).

The Idea of the Vernacular, ed. Jocelyn Wogan-Browne et al. (University Park, Pa., 1999).

Jakoubek of Stříbro, *Mistra Jakoubka ze Stříbra překlad Viklefova dialogu*, ed. Milan Svoboda (Prague, 1909).

Jefferson, Judith Anne, 'An Edition of the Ten Commandments Commentary in BL Harley 2398 and the Related Version in Trinity College Dublin 245, York Minster XVI.L.12, and Harvard English 738 together with Discussion of Related Commentaries', 2 vols. (Ph.D. thesis, Bristol University, 1995).

Julian of Norwich, *The Writings of Julian of Norwich*, ed. Nicholas Watson and Jacqueline Jenkins (University Park, Pa., 2006).

Kerby-Fulton, Kathryn, Hayton, Magda, and Olsen, Kenna, 'Pseudo-Hildegardian Prophecy and Antimendicant Propaganda in Late Medieval England: An Edition of the Most Popular Insular Text of "Insurgent gentes"', in Nigel Morgan (ed.), *Prophecy, Apocalypse, and the Day of Doom: Proceedings of the 2000 Harlaxton Symposium*, Harlaxton Medieval Studies, 12 (Donington, 2004), 160–94.

The Lanterne of Liȝt, ed. Lilian M. Swinburn, EETS OS 151 (1917).

The Lay Folk's Catechism, ed. T. F. Simmons and H. E. Nolloth, EETS OS 118 (1901).

Lollard Sermons, ed. Gloria Cigman, EETS 294 (1989).

Lydgate, John, *A Critical Edition of John Lydgate's Life of our Lady*, ed. Joseph A. Lauritis, Duquesne Studies, Philological Series, 2 (Pittsburgh, Pa., 1961).

Matthew, F. D., 'The Trial of Richard Wyche', *English Historical Review*, 5 (1890), 53–44.

The Middle English Translation of the Rosarium Theologie, ed. Christina von Nolcken, Middle English Texts, 10 (Heidelberg, 1979).

The Middle English Verse Life of Edward the Confessor, ed. G. E. Moore (Philadelphia, 1942).

Minor Poems of the Vernon Manuscript, ed. F. J. Furnivall, EETS OS 117 (1901).

Mum and the Sothsegger, in *The Piers Plowman Tradition*, ed. Helen Barr (London, 1993).

Ockham, *Dialogus*. Online critical edition 'under the auspices of the Medieval Texts Editorial Committee of the British Academy': see <http://www.britac.ac.uk/pubS/dialogus/ockdial.html>, accessed 15 February 2007.

—— *Dialogus* MSS. The manuscripts used in the critical edition. Working list of sigla and short descriptions at <http://www.britac.ac.uk/pubs/dialogus/sigla.html#Sources>, accessed 15 February 2007.

Omnis Plantacio, in *The Works of a Lollard Preacher*, ed. Anne Hudson, EETS 317 (2001), 2–153.

Owen, Nancy H., 'Thomas Wimbledon's Sermon: "Redde racionem villicacionis tue"', *Mediaeval Studies*, 28 (1966), 176–97.

Peraldus, William, *Summae Virtutum ac Vitiorum*, 2 vols. (Paris, 1668–9).

Pecock, Reginald, *Folewer to the Donet*, ed. E. V. Hitchcock, EETS 164 (1924).

The Piers Plowman Tradition, ed. Helen Barr (Everyman's Library; London, 1993).

The Plowman's Tale, in *Six Ecclesiastical Satires*, ed. James M. Dean, TEAMS (Kalamazoo, Mich., 1991).

Political Poems and Songs Relating to English History . . ., ed. Thomas Wright, 2 vols., Rolls Series, 14 (London, 1859–61).

Rosarium, in *The Middle English Translation of the Rosarium Theologie*, ed. von Nolcken.

The Rule of St Albert: Latin Text Edited with an Introduction and English Translation, ed. and trans. Bede Edwards (Aylesford and London, 1973).

The Sarum Missal, ed. J. Wickham Legg (Oxford, 1916).

Secretum Secretorum, ed. Mahmoud Manzalaoui, EETS 276 (1977).

Select English Works of John Wyclif, ed. Thomas Arnold, vol. iii (Oxford, 1871).

Somnium Viridarii, ed. Marion Schnerb-Lièvre, 2 vols. (Paris, 1993).

Le Songe du Vergier, ed. Marion Schnerb-Lièvre, 2 vols. (Paris, 1982).

Supplementary Lives in Some Manuscripts of the Gilte Legende, ed. Richard Hamer and Vida Russell, EETS 315 (2000).

The Testimony of William Thorpe, in *Two Wycliffite Texts*, ed. Anne Hudson, EETS 301 (1993).

Thomas of Erfurt, *Grammatica Speculativa*, ed. and trans. G. L. Bursill-Hall (London, 1972).

The Three Kings of Cologne, ed. C. Horstmann, EETS OS 85 (1886).

Three Treatises by John Wycklyffe, D.D., ed. James H. Todd (Dublin, 1851).

Tractatus de regibus, in *Four English Political Tracts of the Later Middle Ages*, ed. Jean-Philippe Genet, Camden Society, 4th ser., 18 (London, 1977), 5–19.

Trevisa, *Dialogus*, in *Dialogus inter militem et clericem, Richard Fitzralph's Sermon 'Defensio curatorum' and Methodius . . .*, ed. Aaron J. Perry, EETS 167 (1925).

William of St Amour, *Opera Omnia* (Constance, 1632).

The Works of a Lollard Preacher, ed. Anne Hudson, EETS 317 (2001).

Wyclif, John *De Civili Dominio*, ed. Reginald Poole (vol. i) and Johann Loserth (vols. ii–iv), 4 vols., Wyclif Society (London, 1885–1904).

—— *De Ecclesia* = *Tractatus de ecclesia*, ed. Johann Loserth, Wyclif Society (London, 1886).

—— *De ordine Christiano*, in *Op. Min.*

—— *De Potestate Pape* = *Tractatus de potestate pape*, ed. Johann Loserth, Wyclif Society (London, 1907).

—— *De Veritate Sacre Scripture*, ed. Rudolph Buddenseig, 3 vols., Wyclif Society (London, 1905–7).

—— *Dialogus* = *Dialogus sive speculum ecclesie militantis*, ed. Alfred W. Pollard, Wyclif Society (London, 1886).

—— 'Exposicio textus Matthei XXIII', in *Op. Min.*

—— *Opus Evangelicum*, ed. Johann Loserth, 2 vols., Wyclif Society (London, 1895–6).

—— *Op. Min.* = *Opera minora*, ed. Johann Loserth, Wyclif Society (London, 1913).

—— *Pol. Wks.* = *Polemical Works in Latin*, ed. Rudolph Buddenseig, 2 vols., Wyclif Society (London, 1883).

—— *Sermones*, ed. Johann Loserth, 4 vols., Wyclif Society (London, 1887–90).

—— *Supp. Trial.* = *Supplementum trialogi*, in *Trialogus.*

—— *Tractatus de apostasia*, ed. Michael H. Dziewicki, Wyclif Society (London, 1889).

—— *Tractatus de officio pastorali*, ed. Gotthard Lechler (Leipzig, 1863).

—— *Tractatus de officio regis*, ed. Alfred W. Pollard and Charles Sayle, Wyclif Society (London, 1889).

—— *Tractatus de simonia*, ed. Sigmund Herzberg-Fränkel and Michael H. Dziewicki, Wyclif Society (London, 1886).

—— *Trialogus cum supplemento trialogi*, ed. Gotthard Lechler (Oxford, 1869).

SECONDARY SOURCES

Abbott, T. K., *Catalogue of the Manuscripts in the Library of Trinity College, Dublin* (Dublin, 1900).

Aers, David, *Sanctifying Signs: Making Christian Tradition in Late Medieval England* (Notre Dame, Ind., 2004).

Appleford, Amy, 'Learning to Die: Affectivity, Community, and Death in Late Medieval English Writing' (Ph.D. thesis, University of Western Ontario, 2004).

Aston, Margaret, '"Caim's Castles": Poverty, Politics, and Disendowment', in Barrie Dobson (ed.), *Church, Politics and Patronage in the Fifteenth Century* (New York, 1984), 45–81, repr. in Margaret Aston, *Faith and Fire: Popular and Unpopular Religion, 1350–1600* (London, 1993), 95–132.

—— 'The Impeachment of Bishop Despenser', *Bulletin of the Institute for Historical Research*, 38 (1965), 127–48.

Barnard, T. C., 'The Purchase of Archbishop Ussher's Library in 1657', *Long Room*, 4 (1971), 9–14.

Barney, Stephen A., *The Penn Commentary on Piers Plowman*, v (Philadelphia, 2006).

Benskin, Michael, and Laing, Margaret, 'Translations and *Mischsprachen* in Middle English Manuscripts', in Michael Benskin and M. L. Samuels (eds.), *So meny people longages and tonges: Philological Essays in Scots and Mediaeval English Presented to Angus McIntosh* (Edinburgh, 1981), 55–106.

Black, A., 'Church and State', in *Political Thought in Europe 1250–1450* (Cambridge, 1992), 42–84.

Bose, Mishtooni C. A., and Hornbeck, J. Patrick, II (eds.), *Wycliffite Controversies* (Turnhout, 2009).

Boyle, Leonard E., *Pastoral Care, Clerical Education, and Canon Law, 1200–1400* (London, 1981).

Broadie, Alexander, *Introduction to Medieval Logic*, 2nd edn. (Oxford, 1993).

Brooke, R. B., *The Coming of the Friars* (London, 1975).

Bruzelius, Caroline, 'The Dead Come to Town: Preaching, Burying, and Building in the Mendicant Orders', in Alexandra Gajewski and Zoë Opačič (eds.), *The Year 1300 and the Creation of a New European Architecture* (Turnhout, 2007), 203–24.

Burton, J., *Monastic and Religious Orders in Britain, 1000–1300* (Cambridge, 1994).

Catto, J. I., 'Wyclif and the Cult of the Eucharist', *Studies in Church History, Subsidia*, 4 (1985), 97–115.

Cole, Andrew W., 'Trifunctionality and the Tree of Charity: Literary and Social Practice in *Piers Plowman*', *English Literary History*, 62 (1995), 1–27.

Congar, Yves M.-J., 'Incidence ecclésiologique d'un thème de dévotion mariale', *Mélanges de Science Religieuse*, 8 (1951), 277–92.

Constable, G., 'The Interpretation of Mary and Martha', in *Three Studies in Medieval Religious and Social Thought* (Cambridge, 1995), 3–141.

Courtenay, William J., 'Between Pope and King: The Parisian Letters of Adhesion of 1303', *Speculum*, 71 (1996), 577–605.

Dawson, James D., 'Richard FitzRalph and the Fourteenth-Century Poverty Controversies', *Journal of Ecclesiastical History*, 34 (1983), 315–44.

Deanesly, Margaret, *The Lollard Bible and Other Medieval Biblical Versions* (Cambridge, 1920).

D'Evelyn, C., and Foster, F. A., 'V. Saints' Legends', in *A Manual of the Writings in Middle English, 1050–1500*, vol. ii, gen. ed. J. Burke Severs (New Haven, 1970).

Dove, Mary, *The First English Bible: The Text and Context of the Wycliffite Versions* (Cambridge, 2007).

Dupraz, L., *Les Passions de S Maurice d'Agaune*, Studia Friburgensia, 27 (Fribourg, 1961).

Edwards, A. S. G. (ed.), *A Companion to Middle English Prose* (Woodbridge, Suffolk, 2004).

Fletcher, Alan J., 'The Criteria for Scribal Attribution: Dublin, Trinity College, MS 244, Some Early Copies of the Works of Geoffrey Chaucer, and the Canon of Adam Pynkhurst Manuscripts', *Review of English Studies*, 58 (2007), 597–632.

Fletcher, J. M., 'Developments in the Faculty of Arts 1370–1520', in *The History of the University of Oxford*, ii: *Late Medieval Oxford*, ed. J. I. Catto and Ralph Evans (Oxford, 1992), 315–45.

Forrest, Ian, *The Detection of Heresy in Late Medieval England* (Oxford, 2005).

Fowler, David, *The Life and Times of John Trevisa, Medieval Scholar* (Seattle, 1995).

Ghosh, Kantik, 'Wycliffite Affiliations: Some Intellectual-Historical Perspectives', in Bose and Hornbeck (eds.), *Wycliffite Controversies*.

Gibbs, M. E., and Lang, J., *Bishops and Reform, 1215–1272, with Special Reference to the Lateran Council of 1215* (London, 1934).

Gillespie, Vincent, 'Thy will be done: *Piers Plowman* and the Pater Noster', in A. J. Minnis (ed.), *Late-Medieval Religious Texts and their Transmission: Essays in Honour of A. I. Doyle*, York Manuscripts Conferences: Proceedings Series, 3 (Cambridge, 1994), 95–119.

Given-Wilson, Chris, *The Royal Household and the King's Affinity* (New Haven, 1986).

Grant, James, *A Practical Treatise on the Law of Corporations in General, as well Aggregate as Sole: Including Municipal Corporations, Railway, Banking* . . . (Philadelphia, 1854).

Hanna, Ralph, III, 'Two Lollard Codices and Lollard Book-Production', *Studies in Bibliography*, 43 (1990), 49–62; this fuller version is used rather than the shorter one repr. in Ralph Hanna III, *Pursuing History: Middle English Manuscripts and their Texts* (Stanford, 1996), 48–59.

Harvey, M., *Solutions to the Schism: A Study of Some English Attitudes 1378–1409* (St. Ottilien, 1983).

Higgins, Iain, *Writing East: The 'Travels' of Sir John Mandeville* (Philadelphia, 1997).

Hudson, Anne, *Lollards and their Books* (London, 1985); previously published articles are cited in this edition, since many of the articles were revised and updated for their publication here.

—— 'Contributions to a Bibliography of Wycliffite Writings', *Notes and Queries*, 218 (1973), 443–53; repr. in *Lollards and their Books*, Essays 1 and 16.

—— 'The Debate on Bible Translation, Oxford 1401', *English Historical Review*, 90 (1975), 1–18; repr. in *Lollard and their Books*, Essay 5.

—— 'The Legacy of *Piers Plowman*', in John Alford (ed.), *A Companion to Piers Plowman* (Berkeley, 1998), 251–66.

—— 'Lollard Book-Production', in Jeremy Griffiths and Derek Pearsall (eds.), *Book Production and Publishing in Britain 1375–1475* (Cambridge, 1989), 125–42.

—— 'A Lollard Compilation and the Dissemination of Wycliffite Thought',

Journal of Theological Studies, NS 23 (1972), 65–81; repr. in *Lollards and their Books*, Essay 2.

—— 'A Lollard Quaternion', *Review of English Studies*, NS 22 (1971), 451–65; repr. in *Lollards and their Books*, Essay 12.

—— 'A Lollard Sect Vocabulary?', in Michael Benskin and M. L. Samuels (eds.), *So meny people longages and tonges: Philological Essays in Scots and Mediaeval English Presented to Angus McIntosh* (Edinburgh, 1981), 15–30; repr. in *Lollards and their Books*, Essay 10.

—— 'A New Look at the Lay Folks' Catechism', *Viator*, 16 (1985), 243–58.

—— *The Premature Reformation: Wycliffite Texts and Lollard History* (Oxford, 1988).

——'Some Aspects of Lollard Book Production', *Studies in Church History*, 9 (1972), 147–57; repr. in *Lollards and their Books*, Essay 11.

—— 'Some Problems of Identity and Identifications in Wycliffite Writings', in A. S. G. Edwards and Derek Pearsall (eds.), *Middle English Prose: Essays on Bibliographical Problems* (New York, 1981), 81–90.

—— 'Wycliffite Prose', in A. S. G. Edwards (ed.), *Middle English Prose: A Critical Guide to Major Authors and Genres* (New Brunswick, NJ, 1984), 249–70.

James, M. R., *The Western Manuscripts in the Library of Trinity College, Cambridge*, 4 vols. (Cambridge, 1900).

Jolliffe, P. S., *A Check-List of Middle English Prose Writings of Spiritual Guidance* (Toronto, 1974). Cited by class (A through O) and numbered entry.

Jotischky, Andrew, *The Carmelites and Antiquity* (Oxford, 2002).

Kantorowicz, Ernest H., 'Inalienability: A Note on Canonical Practice and the English Coronation Oath in the Thirteenth Century', *Speculum*, 29 (1954), 488–502.

Kenny, Anthony, *Wyclif* (Oxford, 1985).

Kerby-Fulton, Kathryn, 'Hildegard of Bingen and Anti-Mendicant Propaganda', *Traditio*, 43 (1987), 386–99.

—— 'Prophecy and Suspicion: Closet Radicalism, Reformist Politics, and the Vogue for Hildegardiana in Ricardian England', *Speculum*, 75 (2000), 318–41.

Knowles, Dom David, *The Religious Orders in England*, i (Cambridge, 1948).

Kellogg, A. L., and Talbert, Ernest W., 'The Wycliffite Pater Noster and Ten Commandments, with Special Reference to English MSS 85 and 90 in the John Rylands Library', *Bulletin of the John Rylands Library*, 42 (1960), 345–77.

Lamb, David, 'Service, Image, and Leadership: The First Century of the Franciscan Settlement in the West Midlands', *Midland History*, 27 (2002), 16–37.

Little, A. G., and Easterling, R., *The Franciscans and Dominicans of Exeter* (Exeter, 1927).

Loserth, J., 'Johann von Wiclif und Richard Grosseteste', *Sitzungsberichte*, Kaiser Akademie, 186 (Vienna, 1918), ii. 1–81.

McCusker, H., 'Books and Manuscripts Formerly in the Possession of John Bale', *The Library*, 4th ser., 16 (1935).

McGrade, A. S., 'Somersaulting Sovereignty: A Note on Reciprocal Lordship and Servitude in Wyclif', *Studies in Church History*, *Subsidia*, 9 (1991), 261–8.

Mann, Jill, *Chaucer and Medieval Estates Satire* (Cambridge, 1973).

Mare, A. C. de la, 'Manuscripts Given to the University of Oxford by Humfrey, Duke of Gloucester', *Bodleian Library* Record, 13 (1988), 30–51.

Martin, C. A., 'The Middle English Versions of the Ten Commandments, with Special Reference to Rylands English MS 85', *Bulletin of the John Rylands Library*, 64 (1981), 191–217.

Middleton, Anne, 'Acts of Vagrancy: The C Version "Autobiography" and the Statute of 1388', in Steven Justice and Kathryn Kerby-Fulton (eds.), *Written Work: Langland, Labor, and Authorship* (Philadelphia, 1997), 208–317.

O'Sullivan, William, 'Ussher as a Collector of Manuscripts', *Hermathena*, 88 (1956), 34–58.

Pantin, W. A., *The English Church in the Fourteenth Century*, MARTS (Toronto, 1980).

Peikola, Matti, ' "And after all, myn Aue-Marie almost to the ende": *Pierce the Ploughman's Crede* and Lollard Expositions of the Ave Maria', *English Studies* (2000), 273–92.

—— *Congregation of the Elect: Patterns of Self-Fashioning in Lollard Writings* (Turku, 2000).

—— 'The Sanctorale, Thomas of Woodstock's English Bible, and the Orthodox Appropriation of Wycliffite Tables of Lessons', in Bose and Hornbeck (eds.), *Wycliffite Controversies*.

Pennington, Kenneth, *Pope and Bishops: The Papal Monarchy in the Twelfth and Thirteenth Centuries* (Philadelphia, 1984).

Pickering, Oliver, 'Saints' Lives', in Edwards (ed.), *Companion*, 267–9.

Raban, Sandra, *Mortmain Legislation and the English Church, 1279–1500* (Cambridge, 1982).

Renna, Thomas J., 'Kingship in the *Disputatio Inter Clericum et Militem*', *Speculum*, 48 (1973), 675–93.

Rigg, A. G., 'Two Latin Poems against the Friars', *Mediaeval Studies*, 30 (1968), 106–18.

Samuels, M. L., 'Some Aspects of Middle English Dialectology', *English Studies*, 44 (1963), 81–94.

Scase, Wendy, *'Piers Plowman' and the New Anti-clericalism* (Cambridge, 1989).

—— '"Strange and Wonderful Bills": Bill-Casting and Political Discourse in Late Medieval England', *New Medieval Literatures*, 2 (1998), 225–47.

Somerset, Fiona, *Clerical Discourse and Lay Audience in Late Medieval England* (Cambridge, 1998).

—— 'Wycliffite Prose', in Edwards (ed.), *Companion*, 195–214.

Spencer, H. Leith, *English Preaching in the Late Middle Ages* (Oxford, 1993).

Stratford, Jenny, '"La Somme Le Roi" (Reims, Bibliothèque Municipale, MS 570), the Manuscripts of Thomas of Woodstock, Duke of Gloucester, and the Scribe, John Upton', in Marie-Clotilde Hubert, Emmanuel Poulle, and Marc H. Smith (eds.), *Le Statut du scripteur au Moyen Age* (Paris, 2000), 267–82.

Swanson, Robert N., *Church and Society in Late Medieval England* (Oxford, 1989).

Szittya, Penn R., *The Antifraternal Tradition in Medieval Literature* (Princeton, 1986).

—— '"Sedens super flumina": A Fourteenth-Century Poem against the Friars', *Mediaeval Studies*, 41 (1979), 30–43.

Talbert, Ernest W., and Thomson, S. Harrison, 'Wyclyf and his Followers', in J. Burke Severs (gen. ed.), *A Manual of the Writings in Middle English 1050–1500* (Hamden, Conn., 1970), ii. 354–80, 517–3.

Tatnall, E., 'John Wyclif and Ecclesia Anglicana', *Journal of Ecclesiastical History*, 20 (1969), 19–43.

Thomson, S. Harrison, 'John Wyclif's "Lost" *De Fide Sacramentorum*', *Journal of Theological Studies*, 33 (1932), 359–65.

Thomson, Williell R., *The Latin Writings of John Wyclif*, Subsidia Mediaevalia, 14 (Toronto, 1983).

Tierney, Brian, *Foundations of the Conciliar Theory*, enlarged new edn. (Leiden and New York, 1998).

—— *The Idea of Natural Rights: Studies on Natural Rights, Natural Law, and Church Law 1150–1625* (Atlanta, Ga., 1997).

Ullman, Walter, *The Growth of Papal Government in the Middle Ages: A Study of the Ideological Relation of Clerical to Lay Power*, 2nd edn. (London, 1962).

—— *The Origins of the Papal Schism* (London, 1948).

Voigts, Linda Ehrsam, *A Handlist of Middle English in Harvard Manuscripts*, special issue, *Harvard Library Bulletin*, 33/1 (1985).

Von Nolcken, Christina, 'A "Certain Sameness" and our Response to It in English Wycliffite Texts', in Richard Newhauser and John Alford (eds.), *Literature and Religion in the Later Middle Ages: Philological Studies in Honor of Siegfried Wenzel* (Binghamton, NY, 1995), 191–208.

—— 'Notes on Lollard Citation of John Wyclif's Writings', *Journal of Theological Studies*, NS 39 (1988), 411–37.

—— 'Richard Wyche, a Certain Knight, and the Beginning of the End', in Margaret Aston and Colin Richmond (eds.), *Lollardy and the Gentry* (New York, 1997), 127–54.

Wallis, P. J., 'The Library of William Crashawe', *Transactions of the Cambridge Bibliographical Society*, 2 (1956), 213–28.

—— *William Crashawe: The Sheffield Puritan*, repr. with addenda and index from *Transactions of the Hunter Archaeological Society*, 8/2–5 (1960–3) (Sheffield, 1963).

Warner, Lawrence, 'The Ending, and End, of *Piers Plowman* B: The C-Version Origins of the Final Two Passus', *Medium Aevum*, 76 (2007), 225–50.

Warr, Cordelia, 'Religious Habits and Visual Propaganda: The Vision of the Blessed Reginald of Orléans', *Journal of Medieval History*, 28 (2002), 43–72.

Watt, J. A., 'Spiritual and Temporal Powers', in *The Cambridge History of Medieval Political Thought*, ed. J. H. Burns (Cambridge, 1988), 367–423.

—— *The Theory of Papal Monarchy in the Thirteenth Century: The Contribution of the Canonists* (London, 1965).

Whitehead, Christiania, *Castles of the Mind: A Study of Medieval Architectural Allegory* (Cardiff, 2003).

Wilks, Michael, *The Problem of Sovereignty in the Later Middle Ages: The Papal Monarchy with Augustinus Triumphus and the Publicists* (Cambridge, 1964).

—— 'Roman Candle or Damned Squib: The English Crusade of 1383', in *Wyclif: Political Ideas and Practice: Papers By Michael Wilks*, ed. A. Hudson (Oxford, 2000), 253–72.

Wood, Diana, *Medieval Economic Thought* (Cambridge, 2002).

FOUR WYCLIFFITE DIALOGUES

DIALOGUE BETWEEN JON AND RICHARD

Cambridge, Trinity College B 14 50 [333]

Siþen Crist biddiþ vs be war wiþ fals prophetis, and techiþ vs be wat signes þat we schulden knowe hem, Cristen men schulden stodie to lerne þis lore of Crist and publiche þis lore for profiȝt of ho[li] chirche. And so tuo persones spoken be þer wiles, Jon and Richard, and treten þis maner mater.

JON Siþen þe most perel of hooly chirche standeþ in false freres, it were to bigynne atte hem and make hem more knowen. And for þe discriuynge of þings declareþ hem more, þerfore schulden we wete wat is suche a frere. Þe grette clerke Grostehed discriueþ hym þus: 'A fals frere þat wendeþ ouȝt of þe cloyster of his soule is a dede caren cropon ouȝt of his sepulcur, wappid in cloþes of deel and oþer fals signes, and dryuen ouȝt of þe deuel for to drecche men.' Þe cloister of soule schulde be þus schapen, as is þe bodili cloister: gostili to speike, so þat foure cardinal vertues schulde be þe foure wallis keping þe soule fro þe worlde and worldely þingis, and | so iche vice brekeþ þis f. 35v cloister.

RICHARD Þeise wordes may plese vertues men, but a sophester wolde schame for to speike hem, and þerfore, I preie þe, declare hem more.

JON Aftur þe elde of men and he`re´ res of wordis schulde a man ordeyne his speche in sentence and forme, and I am certeyn þat alle þe sophistris of freres cannot pinche at þese wordis, ne dispreue her sentence. Suche a frere is a dede careyne, as þeise clarkes seyn; for al if he be grett and fatte in his body, naþeles siþen hym wantiþ spirit of lijf, he is a deed body, stynkyng wiþ synne. He comeþ ouȝt of his cloister þat he clepiþ his sepulcrer, for he is biried from þe worlde wiþinne fowre wallis and only heuene and heuenly þings ben opyn to his wittis, and grene gresse of vertues and fowles of heuene teche hym to clymbe euene to heuenewarde. But he leueþ not his bodily

4 holi] ho   11 deel] *prec. by canc.* deuelt   17 þeise] þeises   20 hereres] re` *suplin., marked for insertion*

abite, for þat ipocrite may better þer[bi] gile fooles of þe worlde. þre colowres of þer abite betokenen þre vertues, þat is to seye, trauel and clennes and mornyng of synne, so þat alle þe freres ben claþid in tuo of þeise þre, tuo abouen and tuo beneiþe. þe schape of his cloþis, þat ben so deformed, betokene dispite of his owne schappe. His girdel betokeneþ scharpenesse of penance, and euery ri3te of þeise cloþes signifieþ vertues be þer owne ordinance in bigynnynge of þer order. Bot siþen alle þese signes croken from trewþe, þe fende be his ypocrisie deseyueþ þe puple. For amonge alle þe craftis þat þe fende haþ, noon is soteler to hym þan þeise newe orderis. And þerfore seiþ | [f. 36r] Crist in þe booke of his gospel þat kynrede of horedam secheþ suche signes, ne þe weddings wiþ hem profitiþ not to þe seruice of God, but stiriþ hem to pride and gregeþ her synne. But Crist to destrie þis wedding wiþ signes ordeyned on þe Friday þat he died one þat his abite schulde be schaunged þries wiþouten synne. O siþen þese blasfemes ben moost eretikis, and þei ben alle leprous as seint Bede techiþ, how many lordes and ladies ben smyten wiþ þis lepur. God wolde þei were heremites in desert wiþ seint Jon Baptist, and haunted not howses of lordes ne chamboris of ladies. For þe gospel seiþ þat leprosus schulde stande afer. þan þe breþ of her blasfeme schulde blemyche fewe folke. But antecriste hieþ hem, and putteþ hem in sitees. And 3ut many men þenken hem hi3ed inowe, for siþen it falleþ to þer craft on many gates to lyen, it semeþ þat þei ben worþi to comense in lesingis. For not al only þer signes ben bagged wiþ lesingis, but þeise apostataas moweþes, þat ben misturned, medelen lesings of mouþe wiþ lesynges of dede. Who schulde be crowned in þis craft but suche ly3eris. Ne it dispergeþ not Cristis religioun siþen þei ben founded in li3es contrary to trewþe, as ordour of worschipe is noþing fowled 3if þer ben kynges and bischopis of harlatis. But siþen þe charite of Crist caccheþ men to councel, and freres ben fisches wiþouten water þat dwellen ou3t of cloister, I wolde counsele hem come cleue to Cristis religion. þane my3te þei frely wander in cloyster of soule, and flodes of wateris of wisdam schulden renne of þer bodies, and þane nedid hem not þus be ded as to Crist, ne | [f. 36v] galpe aftur gulles of grace as fisses wiþou3ten watur. God saue his chirche wiþou3ten harme of antecristis clerkes, for of ei3te pereles þe moste is in false freres.

30 þerbi gile] þer bigile *word division modified for sense* 50 þe] *corr. by canc. from* þei 59 noþing] not þing

RICHARD I kan not pynche at þese wordes. But me þinkeþ hem to scharpe, liche gulardes wordes, and not of þe gospel.

JON O how scharpeli techeþ þe gospel to repreue pharesies þat contrarien þe treuþe, siþen Crist þat myȝt not synne spake himself scharpely to pharesies, so þat eiȝte siþes þe gospel techiþ þat he williþ woo to pharesies as he schulde do. And so Cristen men schulden nevere speike aȝens þes settes but wane þei spake scharpely to repreue þer vices. And so þer comens[ing]is schuld no man gr[aunt]e, þat þei ben founded on þe gospel, or ellis vpon reson. For before þat þei comense, þei casten many weies and spenden pore mennes godes in wast wiþ many lesings before þei ben amonge hem chosen to þe chaier, and so enuye is sowen and charite is exiled. But at þat tyme þat þei comense, þer rule is suspendid wane þei comense as lordes and not as pore beggeris. And siþen þe money þat þei disspenden comeþ not from heuene, for Criste toke of þe erþe þeise temperal goodis. And sciens of alkemie helpiþ hem not, for þei can not þeron, in speculatif ne practiffe, for þan þei were false: asaie if þou wilt. And so þe pore pupel mut make þer dispenses, boþe in þer comensing and oþer priuey festes. And siþ it is harde to gedere of þe pore pupel so myche money as freres here dispenden, how many lesings and flaterings bene souen before al þise money is gadered of þe puple. And siþen þat þe gospel forfendeþ bisinesse abowte fode or cloþyng, and þei do reuerse, it is opon þat freres contrarien þe gospel of Crist. And | [f. 37r] if þou wilt knowe wat fruȝte comeþ of al þis, certen but pride and worschipe of þe worlde, for þe frere aftur þat he comensed schal haue a chambor and a chapilen as a bischope and be serued costily as a lorde. But risinge at mydnyȝt is suspended from hym and oþer werkis of penance þat fel to a frere. If he preche or rede as þei late doun, he checiþ hym a tyme wanne moost þanke schulde falle him. And if he wandere in þe worlde and etiþ wiþ lordes, he lokiþ to be serued and sette as a bischope. Suche frutes comen of comensi[n]ge of freres. And so þei fallen alle in þe chapitre of pharesees to sitte in hiȝe chaieris and first at þe mete and be clepid maister of alle maner of men. For certes þis is contrari to þe biddyng of þe gospel. And siþen þat freres schulden coueite poyntis of mekenes and eschewe as venym henesse of þe worlde, it semeþ þei schulde not þus cast [for] suche degres.

70 *change of speaker not marked* 75 comensingis] comenseintis *with macron over* int
76 graunte] grounde 99 comensinge] comensige 104 for] fro

RICHARD þis sentence semeþ to be grounded on þe gospel. But o þing I haue to sei to þi self: þat þou and many seculeris ben in þe same caas. And so as ypocrite schalt þou be reproued of Crist, þat schal sei to þee as his traytour, 'Wicked seruant I þe iuge of þine owne mowþe'.

JON I graunte I haue done amysse in many dedes of my lijf, and if I wolde iustifie al þis þat I haue done, I were Goddis traitour, worþi to be dampned. But I knowe mekely synne þat I haue done and hope of Goddis mercy, for I wolde do no more. And o þing I am certen: If I hadde grace to kepe me fro ypocrisie of freres and not falle eft þerinne, f. 37v I schulde | sicurly be saued at þe dai of dome. But wel I wot þat I haue oft synned in ypocrisie, and specialy wanne I coueited to be hiȝe in scole. But now me þinkeþ if þis lijf were al to bygynne, I schulde go al be anoþer weye. For Crist and his apostilles comenseden not þus, ne martires, ne þese fowre dottouris þat ben now hiȝe in heuen. And for sekyng of þis blisse schulde we only trauel. And welle I wot þat þis degre com be an heþin costom. But God haþ ordeyned of his grace of þis com summe good, for he wille suffer no synne bot good cam þerof. But wel I wot þat þise wordes excusen not our synne. And it semeþ þat þe freres synnen more here, for þei oblychyn hem more to mekenes and to pouerte, and passen more here in excesse of spensis. And lickely þei gaderen as iuel þe goodis þat þei dispenden. But o þing I am certen: þat I wolde no more of þis if ȝowþe and tyme comen to me as þei sumtyme deden. And wolde God þat þese settis iwere stabeled in þis porpos. Many godes, I knowe, wolde com of þis costom, as bisines of scole and aschaping fro synne; scharping of wittis and knowyng of perellis; and redy arowes to antecristis clerkes. But al þis excusid not þat ne we schulde better disspende oure tyme as Goddis lawe techiþ. And so iche Cristen man schulde helpe to Cristis lawe and destroye þis paynem custummes and sewe Crist in maneres. For assentyng to þe contrarye accusiþ Cristen men.

RICHARD Telle ȝit grandely how þeise freres come and be wat autorite and how longe siþen.

JON In þis þat þou axist faylen me two þings: witnesse of hooly | f. 38r writ, felyng and resoun. And þerfore take þat I sei of noon autorite, but lesse þane beleue, as cronicles or fabellis tellen. Aȝenes al goode of

118 anoþer] *canc.* nere *between* a *and* noþer 121–2 of þis com summe good] of þis summe good com *marked for rev.* 137 and] *change of speaker indicated before* and *rather than before* Telle 140 or] *prec. by canc.* o *followed by descender*

kynde or vertues in freres, it is no drede þat it comiþ be autorite of God. Aȝens þer erroures and punisching of þe chirche, it þinkeþ me þat it come of fellenes of þe fende. For þe chirche was necligent in sewynge of Crist and ȝaf hem to þe worlde, slowe in Cristis lawe, and þus cam chanounus inne, wiþ mounkes and freres, and þer was medelynge goode puple and iuel. Good men hadden good purpose, but hem lacked prudence. Þei þouȝte to amende þe chirche and make it sewe Crist. But þei amended not þe fawttes of þe first clerkis, but brouȝten inne prowdely new sectis and lete olde vices regne. But þis eschewed Poule as priuey seed of errour, and so mai we see how þe freres com inne and be whos autorite. Vpon diuerse resouns: as to al þe good in þis priuate religiouns, þei comen inne be autorite of oure lorde Iesu Crist, and as to þer erroures and harmenge of Cristis order, þei camen inne be autorite of prince of þis worlde. As aȝens þe tyme þat freres comen inne to þe chirche, þei stryue amonge her self and grounden hem on lesings. Comune cronicles seyn þat aftur þe fende was losed come inne þe frere prechours, and sone aftur þe menoures. Þe prechours comen, as þei seyn, of þe rewle of Austin, for chanounus lyueden to wordely and held not his rewle. And boþe þese freres comen in pope Innocentis tyme, and þer capiteynes were Dominik and Fraunses. Afturwarde longe, frere Austynes comen inne, and seen þat oldenesse was myche tolde by in þe puple, and seide þei were six hundered ȝeer before þe frere prechours, but þei | [f. 38v] were vnknowen al þis tyme for þer wonyng in moores, as þese Austines were, but for Benet or Domynik. And confirmacioun of þis: þei seyn þat Austyn wrot many faire epistilis to his breþeren in deserte. Þane þe Carmes seen how oldnesse myȝt be falsely forged, and seiden þei were before al oþer, ȝ⟨h⟩e before þat Crist was bo`r´ne, for þei were in þe mount of Carmely vndur Heli þe prophete. But beholde þe erroures þat ben in þese orderes, and þane it semeþ to many men þat þese foure kynredes begane in Caymes tyme, and þan were figured in foure letteris of his name, and lasted euer syþen. But in popis Innocentis tyme were tuo knocked out, wane two mones appered in þe firma`me´nt. Tuo oþer ordres were aftur gederid togeder wane power of antecrist was more in þe chirche. And þis þing is certen, as Crisostomus seiþ, þat Caym was rote and fadur of al þat schul be dampned, and Abel was þe fadur and

149 sectis] *prec. by canc.* þouȝtis 156 grounden] *abbrev. macron over* en *ignored* cronicles] *abbrev. macron over* es *ignored* 168 ȝhe] *illegible: it appears a medial* e *was modified into an* h *without erasure* borne] r *suplin., marked for insertion* 170 and þane] *prec. by canc.* þat ben kynredes] *prec. by canc.* b *followed by minim* 173 firmament] me *suplin., marked for insertion*

figur of alle þat schul be saued, and from hem into þis day failed not þise tuo kynredes. But berkyng of stryues amonge þese foure freres schulde not be rehersed amonge Cristen men. But oo þinge me semeþ: þat it were good to þe chirche þat þese freres duelt in deserte, as frere Austynes seiden þei did wanne þei were most perfiȝt. But oo þing semeþ certen of cronycles: þat alle þese foure freres ben confermed of þe pope, and he chaunged boþe þer reule and þer abute and ȝeuen hem leue to begge as þei do. And þis is a gret cause whi þei magnifie þe pope and þei ben clouen in hemself, as þer hede is f. 39r clouen. And it semeþ to many | men þat title of lesings founded þese foure orderes as it founded her faderis. Þe first lesinge is of bygynnyng of þer orderes. Þe secunde lesing is blasfemie of beggyng of Crist. Þe þred lesinge is falsenesse of þer abite and þer howses. And þe fourte þat nappiþ not is lesinge of wordes þat freres sowen þicke wandryng in contres. And so þe first fader of þese freres semeþ þe fende, and þer last fader semeþ þe pope. But of al þat þei haue in kynde or vertues ouþer is God þer fadur and suffereþ hem to synne.

RICHARD Þis semeþ scharpily seid wiþouȝten fagyng. But þer semeþ perel [in] inpungnynge of þe pope; and siþen in hym liȝtt riȝt gouernance and lore of alle þe chirche þat fiȝteþ in erþe, it semeþ þis sentence is aȝens al holy chirche. But who schulde be brent but suche an heretike?

JON At þe bygynnynge of owre speche maden we a couenant þat we schulde speke for Crist, and worschipe trewþe, and spare no þing for fawour of þe worlde ne drede of bodily deþ ne oþer cowardise. For he is vntrewe knytte to Crist and his God þat lettiþ for any of þise to sei Cristis lawe. It semeþ me þe pope principaly erriþ for he seweþ not Crist ne makeþ not oþer to swe hym, and ȝit he seiþ þat he is ful Cristis vicarie in erþe and haþ power in erþe as miche as þe apostiles. For as glosatowres seyn, he is God in þe erþe. And so in þis mater ben blasfemes pondrede, and to fewe knyttis of Crist dar telle hem to þe pupel. But as blasfemes þese clerkes floreschon Cristis lawe, and seyn, of it sueþ þat iche bischope of Rome is suche a viker of Crist as we haue before seide. But for euery Iew or paynem and iche trewe Cristen man schulde scorne þis sentence be iugement of reson, þerfore me þenkeþ þat iche man in erþe schulde conseyue þe f. 39v trewþe of þis | mater for gretnesse of puple þat liggeþ þerinne. But

181 Austynes] *abbrev. macron over* y *ignored* 190 þicke] þricke 195 in inpungnynge] inpungnynge

no man can seey wy iche bischope of Rome schulde haue þis primacie, but if oon of þese causes moued þerto. First, for seint Peter died in Rome. But þis cause is to lewde, syþen Crist died in Ierusalem þat was more þan Peter, and as wicked men han ben bischoppis of Rome as w[ere] in Ierusalem siþen Crist died. Þe secunde cause þat moueþ to hiȝe þis bischoppe is multitude of martires þat weren dede in Rome. But in Ierusalem semeþ þat als many d[i]ede, and s`p´eciali Crist is hede of al martires. And it semeþ wonder þat sleyng of martires schal halow a place and abile it to popis, siþen suche sleing axiþ halowing of chirches. Þe þrede cause þat is feyned: it is þe wille of þe emperour þat as he is lorde of his empere, so his prest schulde rewle in God, al þe same lordschep. And þerfore he dowed þe chirche þat was worþi made. But it is knowen of beleue þat þe emperour is not God, and so he mai not abil a man to be Cristis vicary. And so it semeþ to many men þat dowyng of þe chirche made men `worþi´ to be rewarded wiþ þe peyne of helle. Þe fou`r´þe cause þat moueþ many men in þis mater is þat cardenalles chesen hym for to be pope, and þese cardenales haue vertu of al holy chirche. But þis is þe blyndest cause þat euer man founde. For name of cardenales is founden out of hooly write, and Crist ȝaf hem neuere power þus to lede his chirche. And siþen þei ben comonly foles and vicious in lijf, þei may liȝtli erre and che[se] a man vnabel. But where were more blasfemes þan sey þat Crist were nedid to stonde to her eleccioun and make þat man his vicarie, whomeuer þei chosen to be bischope of Rome. And þerfore seyn trewe men þat boþe Yndes and Grekes ben better Cristen men þan þise Westerne fooles. And so þe moost foly of al is | brouȝt in be þis errour, þat if þe f. 40r
bischope of Rome ȝif leue to any þing þan Crist and his lawe ȝeueþ leue to þe same. And so whoeuere most seweþ Crist in manere of lyuynge, Crist clepiþ hym to be his viker and profiȝt to his chirche, and is þat ilke þat lyueþ more pore lijf and profitiþ more to his chirche be his meke seruice. And it is perel if suche ben vnknowen þorow blowing of name to þe worlde, for þe worlde schendeþ many men. And alle schulde we trowe þat Crist lyueþ in heuene bischop of oure soules and wonderful pope. And so beleue of Cristes lawe nedi[þ] vs to trowe þat þe wille of God crokeþ not for chesing of men, but þan is þe chesyng good wane þei ben confermed to God. And so if þe p[ope]

218 were] was 220 diede] dede speciali] p *suplin.*, *marked for insertion* 228 worþi] *suplin.*, *marked for insertion* 229 fourþe] fourþee, r *suplin.*, *marked for insertion* 234 chese] che 238 þise] *prec. by canc.* we 240 þing] *corr. by canc. from* þings 246 And] *macron ignored* schulde] *prec. by canc.* suche we trowe] *prec. by canc.* be trewe 247 nediþ] nedid 249 pope] puple

lyue more pore lijf and lesse charge worschipis and riches of þe worlde, it is an euydence to men þat he more sueþ Crist; and if he do þe contrary, he is antecrist. And for to iuge who is suche, Crist left vs his lawe sufficient to gouerne his chirche wiþ in techinge of it. And so if þe freres haue no patroune but þis pope, þei lenen vpon a staaf of reedes and swen antecrist. I trowe þat he þat seiþ þis sentence and stondiþ þerby schal be don to deþ wiþ fire or wiþ oþer peyne, for þus was Crist martired be procuryng of false prestes. And it is likely þat þei schul resume þis power agayne, for þei haue distrowed in part þe emperoure and his knyttis.

RICHARD þis were a gret presumpcioun to þus renewe þe chirche, siþen a þowsand aȝens oon witnesse þe contrarye. And siþen Siluester tyme were many þousande sentis þat spake neuer of þis sentence, but worschipid þe popes, as þise foure docturis; and oon of hem was pope. Weþer schulde men trowe more al þese þan oo | foole?

f. 40ᵛ JON We schulden trowe more þe gospel þane alle þese seintis, and more Cristis lijf þan þe court of Rome. For þe first is beleue, and þe toþer naked cronicles. But note we wel þat þis chirche peyriþ in lyuynge, and goþ afer fro Crist and neiȝeþ antecrist, and so litel errour þ[at] was insensible first was gret and knowen errour aftur be processe of tyme. And cause of þis errour was departing from Crist. For we schulden beleue þat Crist myȝt not synne, but at poynt deuys he did al þat euer he did. But prelatis þat comen aftur hym variden more and more. And herfore seint Ciprian techiþ for a rewle þat men schulden here al only Crist in his membris; þat if so any seint sued Crist, we leue \`to´ here of þis sent, and here Crist in hym. For alle þese sentes erred oiþer more or lesse, and if þou sewe hem nakidly and leuen þe swete of Crist, þou must algatis erre and bowe from riȝwissenes. And so al þise sentis þat were fro þe tyme of Siluester come not to þe apostilis and sentis þat were before. And siþen þat alle þese sentis ben not for to preyse but in as myche as þei seued Crist, and Crist is more nyȝe and more opon to sue, whi schuld we swe þese seyntis and leue ledyng of Crist? And so we schal supposon þat þese sentis were gode and sued Crist ofte siþes, and often siþes erred; and in þer last daies be sorowe of þer synnes we[re] þei brouȝt to heuene be grace of Crist. And al ȝif þei grucched aȝens þis worldely lijf, naþeles to litel,

250 charge] chargen 262 many þousande sentis þat spake] many þousande þat spake sentis *marked for rev.* 268 errour] erroures 269 þat] þer 273 for] *prec. by canc.* fro 274 we] wel 275 to] *suplin., marked for insertion* 284 were] we/

and wordelynesse was lesse. But ȝif þei lyued today and see þe state of þe chirche, þei schulde repreue it, bodily for to suffer deþ. And þus haþe þe fende be litil and litil brouȝt clerkes from lesse errour to antecristis weye, as woso | tillid forþe a childe for forþe to depe f. 41r watur. And it is lickely þat nowe ben a þousande aȝens on to stonde for cause of antecrist and reuerse Crist, for bischoppis and freres and most parte of clerkis wolde sey today þat þe chirche were distroued ȝif it stode in pouerte, as Crist put it inne, and dampne hem as heretikis þat seid it schulde be so. But siþen þe gospel techiþ vs þe contrari of þis, and we schulde more trowe it þan al men of þe worlde and for to sustene it suffer scharpe deþe, we schulden leeue to trowe falsenes of þe worlde and take tristily þe trewþe of þe gospel. And before þat suche knyttis come wil þe chirche sinken. And so trowe þe gospel, and neþer Ieffe ne Ion, for neiþer seynt ne oþer schulde be trowed in þis mater but as myche as þei grunden hem in þe gospel. And so take we hede wat þe seyntis seide and how þat þei grounded hem in þe lawe of Crist, and so miche trowe hem, and leue þer errouris. For we schulde sue Peter in þat þat he sewed Crist, and in þat þat he forsoke Crist and synned in his lyuyng we schulde forsake hym and euer hate synnes. And so þese seyntis þat hadde dowing of þe chirche lyfed a pore lijf and dide þer office and hadden þer þouȝt on Crist and on his seruice, departed þer goodis to pore men; and leften a litel þer perfeccioun. But now haþ þe worlde drawen prestes to contrarie, as þer bisinesse of þe worlde and þer loue scheweþ; as if a prest be more bisie to serue þe worlde þane he is to serue Crist in his membris, and coueitiþ more wordeli goodes þane perfeccioun of vertues, who wolde seye þat suche a prest were | on Godes behalfe? But for it is ouer harde to be wedded wiþ þe f. 41v worlde, Criste wordeyned his prestis to forsake þe worlde. And þis wisdome may no man reuerse. And so schulden we trowen Crist in his seyntis in þat þat þei sued Crist. And þese, wit goode angelis, ben more in multitude and holynes of witnesse þan alle fals witnesse þat reuerse þis sentence. And siþen alle seyntis in heuene affermen þis gospel, he were ouer grett a foole þat wolde falle herfro. For alle antecriste clerkes or fendes in helle and false glosis þat ben feyned to þe gospel of Crist schulde not be trowed, for þei ben not groundid. For þe lijf of Crist and his more seyntis telleþ clereliche inowe how it schulde be vnderstanden. But God forbede any man to trowe antecrist so myche, þat Cristis lawe was good but for a litil tyme and afturwarde þe popes schuld euermore last.

RICHARD It semeþ þat þe freres swen most Crist. For þei ben most pore men, chaste, and obedient; and in þese þre poyntis standiþ Cristis religion.

JON Oure beleue techiþ vs þat oure rule is better, siþen it is þe gospel þat Iesu Crist made, and þei mot axe confirmacioun of þer clouted reule. But ȝif þe pope schal be saued, þe gospel mot conferme him. And as we falle fro þe gospel, so þe freres fallen fro þer clouted rewle. But we may not put fauȝte in þe gospel as þei putten fauȝte in þer new reule and purchasen dispensacioun to haue new reules. But God biddiþ þat we schal not put to ne take fro his wordes. Ouer þis our knyttis han ben þe best men of alle, and our abbot is þe best, siþen he is God and man. And so many cloutes ben added to freres reule þat f. 42^{r} ȝif þer bodily abite were varied as þer reule, no harlot | in þis londe schulde were more specked mantyl. But siþen he þat ȝiueþ most parte of þer reule and susteneþ and defendiþ perfeccioun of þer order schulde be clepid patroun of þe same ordere, it semeþ þat alle freres ben patrouned of þe pope. And so falsely þei clepen hem freres of Dominik or Frances or Austyn or Iacomynes, but [ben] freres of þe pope. But go we to resoun. And first, bileue we þat in pouert of spirit stondiþ Cristes ordere. Forsakyng of þe worldes good profiteþ sumtyme, but it profetiþ not wiþouten þe first pouerte. And if freres haue þis pouerte as beggaris, naþeles þer hiȝe houses and oþer goodis þat þei haue in comyne schewen oponli þat þei be not pore aftur Crist. For þe gospel telliþ þat Crist was so pore þat he hadde non house to reste hym inne and hes couent, but þe freres contrarien in costily houses. And so me þinkeþ þis ypocrites blasfemen in God, for þei puttyn vpon hym suche manere of lyuynge. But Crist dampned Scharioth for 30 penes; but many freres han propur miche more þan þis. So if iche frere þat þus hadde more were oon Scarioth, þes orderes of freres were ful of Scariothis þat slept not, but vaken niȝt and day be þer couoytise, how þei schul gete more and venge hem on membris of Crist. And if þei sue Crist, it semeþ to many men þat þei seue him in þes 3^{e} poyntis: in þer hiȝe houses, in excesse of þer ordere, and þat þei putte religion in þer bodily abites. And it semeþ, siþen Criste knewe none of þes 3^{e}, þat þei passen hym, but in an yuel manere. Siþen þei haue þus hiȝe houses and Crist hadde noon, it semeþ þat in þis þei contrarien Crist. Siþen Crist was

332 we] *corr. by canc. from* wele   340 and] *prec. by canc.* no   343 ben] *added for sense*

almiȝthi and þerto al witty was paied of tuelue and on Scarioth, it semeþ þat freres þat passen Crist in þis, | blasfemen in God be lewde f. 42v presumpcioun, and if þei hadde no couent ne non suche priour it were good to þe chirche. For so diden þe apostles wane þer abot Crist was went to heuene fro hem. But as þei leuen Cristis reule as insufficient, so þei passen Cristis couent. But certes in synne as to chasti`t´e, I make þese freres iuges weþer þei passen in chastite seculer prestis. But for to speke of gostily fornicacioun, þei passen in þer nouel[r]ies vnkyndely fro Crist. But as to obedience þat freres han feyned, it is knowen by beleue þat it is not worþe but in as miche as it techiþ obesche to Crist. And so siþen þei miȝten more do þis obediens to Crist wiþouten suche prelatis, as þe chirches dide before þat suche worderes were brouȝt inne be cautel of þe fende, it semeþ þat suche obbediens serueþ of nouȝth. And oo þing I knowe: þat suche feyned obedience doþ myche harme to couentes and cuntres. For be þer neuer so miche a foole priour in a place, ȝif þat he bidde þat þey iuge no synne, þei seyen þat þei schulde do þat be vertu of obedience. And so siþen þe holy gost schulde stirre men to goode, and freres leuen þis and taken hem to þer priour, it semeþ þat freres in þis aȝenstanden God. And so þe more part of hem semen antecristis clerkes.

RICHARD Siþen freres kepen alle þat we do, and ouer þis þei don many þings of perfeccioun, it semeþ þat þer reule and þer liif is better and more perfiȝt þane oure. For ellis it were vnleful for to be a frere, or for to change mennes lijf from oo ordere to anoþer. But þe pope and þe pupel aȝeneseyen þis.

JON | As freres in many þings contrarien Crist, so þei han brouȝt in f. 43r customes to manye þat ben contrarie to Godes maneres. Crist was man most pacient and mekest of alle, and suffered w`r´onges and venged hym not. For as man is more meke, he is more perfiȝt in Cristis religioun; and so as Crist is most lowe as mydel of þe erþe, so is he most perfiȝt in ordre þat God approueþ. But for þe loue of God, take heed to freres, and loke weþer þei be most meke in suffering of þer wronges. I trowe þat no men in þe worlde aftur þer power ben more vengabel for a þing of nouȝt. For men þat tellen þe defauȝtis of þer lijf and soþely schewen howe þei disceyue þe pupel, as Crist did scharpely of þe phariseus, þese men felen malis of freris. For it is

368 chastite] *incompletely corr. from* chastise: t^2 *suplin*, *marked for insertion*; s^2 *not canc.*
370 nouelries] noue lyies 377 obedience] *prec. by canc.* orderis 384 is] is/is
390 wronges] r *suplin.*, *marked for insertion*

knowen to þe worlde how freres han pursued hem, and ne helpe hadde be of seculer men þei wolde haue brent hem or don hem to deþ. And ȝit þei feynen falsely þat þei don þus be charite. But siþen boþe merite and synne standeþ in wille, and wille of þes freres was to sle Cristis lymes, it is open þat þe synne of wille of freres was as myche as þei hadde kylde þese prestis. And so be þe epistil of Jon, þei ben mansleres and reguler for to synge, alle þese persones þat assentid þerto, and þat were þei alle. Se how oponly þei lie in suying of Crist. And þerfore no drede þei parten hem fro Cristis children and schewen hem brolles of antecristis couent. And here Richard may þou see þat þou cakest false, for freres kepen not mekenesse as seculers done. And ouer, siþen God biddeþ men not adde to his wordis, and freres in þer reules don þe contrarie, it is open how inobedient freres ben to God. But seculer prestis synnen not þus. It is leueful to expowne þe lawe þat God ȝaf and seie out þe sentence þat þe lawe hidiþ. But freres f. 43v maken newe lawes besides þise boþe. And were in Goddes | lawe schulde any man fynde þese abitis of freres, or ellis þer rites by wiche þei varien fro þe apostilis and oþer goode men? And certes þeise reules expoune not holi wriȝt. And so it semeþ þat þese freres reuersen þe comandemente of God and maken hem a newe lawe, and putten Goddes lawe abak. And so, siþen foure cardenal vertues schulden be foure wallis to holde þese freres in cloyster of þer soule, and þei breke alle þese and turnen to vices, it is opon þat þei ben false in bodily cloysteris. Iusticie is þe first wal þat Cristes religion axiþ, þat techiþ Cristen men to obesche to mesure of Goddis lawe. But þis wal han þei broken and clumben þerouer. Þe secunde vertu is strengþe to stonde in þe limites þat Goddes lawe haþ sette wiþouȝt sclidyng awaye. But þis wal is broken, and new wal maked for to stonde stifely in þer owne ritis. Þe þred vertu is p[r]udence, þat þei han forsaken, siþen it is no prudence to drynke trubily and venemous watur and forsake water of wisdom of God. Þe fourte vertu of þis cloyster is clepid temperance, þat þese freres han broken in maner of þer lyuyng. For take heede to þe[r] numbre, and efte to þer houses, and eke to þer reules, and al þat þei vsen, and we may opinly see þat temperance faileþ. And þis erroure haþ brouȝt þe pope and þe pepul in more depe erroures be freres ypocricie. For þei iuge be þe face and not be þe werkes, and be cautelis of þe fende ofte ben deceyued. And so freres

405 mansleres] *corr. by canc. from* manseleres   427 prudence] pudence
428 watur] *prec. by canc.* vati   431 þer] þe   433 þis] *corr. by canc. from* þus
435 freres] *prec. by canc.* þe

taken falsely þe reson of glotounes, þat if a þing be good þat schulde be taken of man, euer þe more þat he takeþ, þe better it is. And herby freres failen in temperance and mesure. In þis mesure God ȝaf his lawe and his ordur | so þat eche miȝt frely and liȝtly holde it. But in f. 44r þis mesure failen þe freres more þan pharises in þe newe lawe þat wolde kepe þe rites of þe olde lawe, and þerwiþ þe fredom of þe lawe of Crist. But þei miȝt not do þis, as seint Poule techiþ.

RICHARD þis semeþ wel seide, woso vnderstande it. But ȝut þe freres semen passe seculer men, for þei prechyn ofter and þickelier in þe worlde, and preching maynteneþ most Cristis religion. And so ne were preching of freres, beleue of Crist were passed awey.

JON Soþe it is þat freres don sum good ; but not so miche as fendes and dampned men. And it is likly þat þei comen in for þe fauȝte of curatis, and so if alle curates dide al þat felle to hem, freres were superflu as buturflies in þe eir. But þe fende haþ founden more gamen in þer hode þane euer he dide in seculeres. For be þer ypocricie he deseyueþ þe puple, and makeþ hem to trist on þing þat is aȝens beleue. And in token `þer´of, siþen freres comen inne haþ ben more disturblaunce and lesynges in þe worlde. And þise men þat be more lede wit freres ben commynly more yuel in Cristes religioun. And so holi chirche is charged wiþ prestes, and frute of þer chargyng turneþ to harme. And so, as good preching is þe best werke þat prestes don to profite of men, so yuel preching noieþ more men, siþen euer þe better þat a þing be in his kynd, so werse it is wane it is turned to yuel. But techinge of freres faileþ many weyes, for þei preche | many tyme f. 44v lesings or troufulinges or cronicles of þe worlde to plese more þe puple, so þat wat þei trowe more to plese þe pupul and wynne more monei, al if it harme þe soule, þat þei chargen and leuen Cristis lawe. And so þei trespausen as traytourres aȝens God and man, for God biddiþ his prechours to teche his lawe and telle his pupel scharpily her synnes. And þan schuld þei plese God and dispisen þe world. þan schulde cristondom growe here in þe erþe and tirantrie of þe fende be chased awey. Summe freres schapen hem to begge feile siþe wane þat þei prechyn, neiþer wel nor yuel. And certes þis harlotes schame for to don, for harlotes axen not to haue of þe puple but if þei trauel first

437 takeþ] *extra pen stroke precedes following punctuation, perhaps to indicate proportionality* 438 mesure] mesu/ure 441 þis] to þis 447 þat freres don sum good] þat don freres sum good *marked for rev.* 453 þerof] þer *suplin., marked for insertion* 457 as] *prec. by canc.* þe 466 þan[2]] *prec. by canc.* and 467 cristondom growe] growe cristondom *marked for rev.*

in tonge be þer craft. But ofte is þer doumbenesse lesse yuel þan þer preching, for wane þei spitten on þe pepul wordes of venym, þan þei strangelen þer soules and maken hem die. And specialy if þes freres carpen for worldes wynnynge, for þane is þe stok cursed and þe fruȝte boþe, siþen order of charite schulde teche men to loue more sowles þan al þis wor`l´des good. And if þes freres don þe reuerse, þei ben cursed of God and þer preching boþe. But it is licly to manye þat þei reuersen þis order, and so þe ordere of God, siþen God is charite. For take awey fro freres hope of þer wynnyng, þei wil take from þee trauel of þer preching, and þis is þe cause whi þei prechin to þe pepul, and on þat wise, þat þei hopen þis wynnynge. And þat þes is soþe, examine þe freres be þer owne dedes, and wiþdrawinge of þer f. 45r prechinge: | of þis may we gedere þat preching of freres is cause of wynnyng, þat more loue. And it is no drede, if it be þus, þese apostatas ben cursed and heretikkes boþe. Also preching of freres is comonly ful of enuey and of sclander and of bacbitynge. And so þei make muk þer God, and sellen menes soules to Satanas for monei, and dampnen hemself for contrariouste þat þei beren vpon hem. And al þis reuerseþ þe dedes of Crist. But wat vertu comeþ comonly of suche mennes wordes? And þer lijf and þer wordes contrarien togeder, siþen þei prechin þat men schulde leue þe loue of þis worlde, and ȝif þer temperal godes to men þat ben nedy; but oponly þer lijf contrarieþ to þis, siþen þei begge gredily of men þat ben nedi and departen not to oþere wane [þei] haue nede. And so þei [trowe] þat perfeccioun stondeþ in þese goodes, and ȝit þei spoyle priuely men of þis perfeccioun aȝens þe wille of Crist, bi wiche he techiþ his chirche þat wat we wolde skylfully þat men dide to vs, schulde we do to hem for loue of first charite. But freres forgeten þis reule and glenen to hem wat þat þei may gete of þe puple. But it comeþ not aȝene, neiþer in lijf nor in deþ. For þe fendes dien not, ȝit þese riche men of þe worlde, if þei geder goodes be þer auarice and falssehed as þe fende hem techiþ, ȝit wane þei die, þer goodes ben schatered amonge men of þe worlde þat vsen hem welle. But wane þes goodes ben sunken amonge men of orderes, as þei were sunken into helle, þe[i] propheton not to þe worlde. Suche profetes comen of freres in preching and f. 45v beggynge, besides | þer blasfemes þat þei sowen amonge: þat Crist begged as þei, and þat þei ben nedi, and han not amonge hem alle to

476 worldes] l *suplin., marked for insertion* 481 þat þes is soþe] þat is þes soþe *marked for rev.* 491 þat] *twice* 494 þei] wane/haue trowe] *added for sense* 495 spoyle] *corr. by canc. from* spoylye 501 as] *prec. by canc. descender* 504 þei] þe

sustene her couent—al if on of hem haue schippes and poundes. þis schulde popes and kynges þenke wel vpon, and to saue þe pupel, and destroie antecrist, and make curatis as first to performe her office, siþe it is no nede to norische antecristes clerkes.

RICHARD Wel I see þat þese freres doun miche harme, and necligence of seculeris brouȝt hem inne. But siþe þei profete miche be þer confessiouns, and þei be liȝt of disp[e]nses more þan oþer prestes, it semeþ þat nede dryueþ þe worlde to maynte[ne] þes freres, and þis is cause whi þat lordes and bischopis also ho[l]den so many freres dwellinge wiþ hem.

JON I suppose þat þou sei soþe at þe biginnyng, þat necligence of seculeris brouȝt freres inne. But foli of prelatis was more cause. For it is no craft to hele þe chirche of oon seckenesse and make mo to. þe pope schulde hele þes erroures þat were in þe curatis, and not charge þe chirche wiþ mo fals men. And þis myȝt be helid wiþ a schort medicyne: to chese good curatis and ȝeef hem no goodes but þei performe þe seruice þat falliþ to þer office. But pride and couaitise lettiþ þis riȝt. And so comynge in off freres to þe chirche is corsedli gronded onto fals rotis; þat is to seyn, necligence of curatis and foli of þe pope. But wo to him þat makeþ suche a fals change, and dooþ yuel for good þat he miȝt better do. But furþermore, feyned confessiones of freres semeþ to do al þe harmes in þe chirche. For þei lede lordes, bischopis, and ladies, and errour of þes þre don miche harme. | þes f. 46r freres maken þes þre to beleue as feiþ þat leying of þer handes on hede on confessid doþ awaie þer synne and ȝeffeþ hem þe holi gost, and so is þer synne hidde more þan it was. And siþen disturbeling of remes comeþ of hiding of synne, it semeþ þat þese freres distourbelen most remes. þei schulde tele men confessed vnto hem þat contricioun and satisfaccioun boþe be þei nedeful if synne þat is doun schulde be remitted. And so confescioun maked to Joon Baptist of knyȝttes and pharezes was more worþe þan ȝif he had dwellid cont[i]nuely wiþ hem and þei had rouned in his ere as men nouȝ doun. For contricioun of hert and leuynge of synne be sufficient be hemself, wiþ þe grace of God. For þus were synnus forȝeuen in þe olde lawe, and also in þe newe lawe, til antecrist come.

514 dispenses] dispnses 515 mayntene] maynte 516 holden] hoden
525 riȝt] riȝti *the final i may be a smudged punctus elevatus* 529 al] *twice, 2nd canc.*
538 continuely] contnuely

RICHARD þis semeþ presumtuouse and perlouse in speche. For men miȝt liȝtli trowe be þis þat schrifte made to God were sufficient be itself wiþouȝt schrifte to man. But þat þe pope aȝeneseiþ wiþ expresse lawe, and seiþ þat euery man and woman þat comeþ to discrecioun mote ones in þe ȝeer be schryuen to his owne prest vpon þis maner. And be þis same skil, þat we schulde not kepe þis, we schulde kepe non vse þat holi chirche haþ ordeyned.

JON Here me þenkeþ þat men schulden kepe þis ordinance, for it, willi doun, profiteþ more þan any oþer þat I knowe made of þe pope. But we schul vnderstanden þat suche ordinaunce is not so nedeful þat ne Crist miȝte saue synful men wiþouten suche schrift, as if a man were so stede þat no prest were ny hym but Crist, þat seeþ contricioun of soule. Bot ouer þis schulde we wiȝt how þis schrift begane. And glose of decrees declariþ opinli þat þis maner of schrifte cam not into f. 46v þe chirche before pope Innocent. | Oþer maner of schrifte general made to God was before þis tyme, as general schrifte to men, and counsel of wise prestis was axed wan nede was. But so special schrifte and limitid to tyme was ordened of pope Innocent, as þis glose seiþ. And al if þis glose erred in many oþer þings, naþeles in þis poynt mote men trowe to it, for no man can telle wane þat, before þis, schrift begane. Suppose we þat þis schrifte be soþ, þat þis glose seiþ, and þat þis confessioun doþ miche good, and so þis confessioun is nedeful in manere. But ȝut we trowen þat it were profit to þe chirche þat þis lawe of confessioun hadde neuere be ordeyned, for hooli chirche profeted more before þat it began, and boþe parties be þis fallen in many errours. For we schul trowe þat asoiling of prest is noþing worþe but wane it is confermed to þe chirche of [soule], and þat þe prest knoweþ not, no more þan hi[s] heele. And also, be þis confessioun blasfemen þe prestes, for þe pope wil for mede limite pore prestes, and suche prestes willen axe mede for schriuynge of þer childeren. And it mai falle, because of suche rounyng, þat þe confessour schal synne wiþ his confessed. And herfore Job made couenant wiþ his wittis to þenke not on a virgyne: Lorde, whi schulde freres speke wiþ hir in preueie places, siþen þei mai be tempted as oþer men may? And so general schrefte were comounli more nedeful and ferþer fro simonie þat

554 stede] *corr. by canc. from* stedefast 557 Innocent] *abbrev. macron over* ent *ignored* 564 confessioun] *abbrev. macron over* con *ignored* 566 confessioun] *abbrev. macron over* con *ignored* 568 trowe] *corr. by canc. from* torowe asoiling] *abbrev. macron over* ng *ignored* 569 wane] *abbrev. mark over* an *ignored* soule] ⟨l⟩oue, ⟨o⟩one, *or perhaps* ⟨s⟩oul; *see note* 570 his] hi 576 siþen] *prec. by canc. illegible capital*

bleckeþ boþe parties. And herfore freres axen to ministren no sacrament but confessioun and sepulture, for her liȝt wynnyng. And so men schulde kepe good ordinaunce of þe chirche. But be ware þat men be not wedded wiþ hem, for ofte siþe more | medefully f. 47r seruen men God leuynge þe ordinaunce of þe chirche þan do it in dede. But here ware prudence is nedeful to men. And þus freres doun myche harme wiþ dwellinge wiþ lordes, and sumtyme sum good, þouȝ it be seldome.

RICHARD Whi mai not God ȝif vertue to abitis þat freres vsen, as to dede bodies? And siþen þat vsinge of hem vpon þe same witte betokeneþ stabulnesse of men and lasting in vertues, whi mai not freres perpetue suche abitis?

JON I graunt wele þei mai. But foly it is of hem, siþen þei ben not nowe confermed in vertues; and whane þei ben in vertues, þer colores skrieþ hem. But schame ȝou of þis resoun, þat if it mai be so, þan it is so, and schal be supposed. For be þe same skil, iche frere schulde be a fende and þer order schulde be dampned, for al þis mai be. But þenke wat good and wat ha[r]m mai com of þes abitis, and be wat autorite be þei brouȝt in. Good mai come of hem but accidentaliche. But myche more good schulde come of hem ȝif þei were appliede to oþer maner vse. Harme mot come of hem vpon many maneres, for þei be not grunded in Crist þat is vertu, siþen Crist vpon þe Fridaye þat he died on ordeyned þries for grete cause his abite to be chaunged. He hadde on first his iche daie cloþes, and siþen Heroude cloþid him in whitt as a foole, and siþen was he clede in cloþes of purpur. And al þis was doun at þe ordinaunce of Crist, and betokeneþ mo`re´ þan al þese freres abitis. And me þenkeþ it mot signifie þis: þat vertues | or f. 47v religioun þat God axeþ standeþ [not] in cloþes, but in clennes of soule. But blasfemye presumpcioun of antecristis clerkes wil putte hem in cloþes, and spoyle hem from þer soulis. But þis is an inpossible, ypocrit þouȝt, and herfore seiþ Crist þat kynrede of horedom sechiþ suche syngnes to be schewed to þe worlde. But of þis blasfem`i´e comen harmes inowe. Leue we wast of cloþ þat comeþ of mysschape, and speike we of gostili harme þat comeþ to þe soule. þei schewen frist þer vertues be suche dede singnes to knoweleche of

578 axen] *corr. by canc. from* axeden 587 vsinge] *abbrev. macron over* ng *ignored* 588 men] *prec. by canc.* vertu 595 harm] ham 598 for] *corr. by canc. from* foor 603 more] re *suplin., marked for insertion* þan] *twice* 605 not] *added for sense* 610 blasfemie] i *suplin., marked for insertion*

þe world, as hemself seiþ. But vertues schulden be preuey and hid vnto God, and schewed in werkis wiþouten any bost. But Lord, wat werkes of vertue myȝt not be don as wele or better wiþouten suche signes? And siþen wedding and keping of hem axeþ bisinesse in soule limited in power, [it] litt[l]eþ bisines to God þat alle suche haue. Furþermore, siþen suche freres ben not confermed of God, it falliþ many tyme þat þei fallen in synne, and seþen þei kepe þer abite to þe same entent, þei lie in þer signes, and maken hem more dampnabel. And ferþer, be occacioun taken of þes singnes þei fallen in many erroures reuersing beleue. þei seien first þat þer abite haþ vertue of God more þan Crist euer putte in his habite. And forþermore freres fagen þese ladies þat wat man or woman dieþ in þer abite schal neuere be dampned, be þe vertu þerof. And if no more heresye com of þese abites, it were worþi þat deuorse were made betuix hem. And þan were þese cumpanyes of antecrist dissolued. Lord, siþen synnes þat folowen þe sowles stonden in wille and not wiþouȝteforþe, but if it springe from | f. 48r inordinate wille, in hou vnclene places dwellen þese apostatas. And siþen suche synnes poluten þer places, how myche nede were it to halow hem. For siþen sleing of bodi is miche lesse synne þan sleing of a soule be bate and enuye, and þis is mansleing as sent Jon seeþ, wy schulde not þe place be polute and þe persones take? But þe fende techiþ men to charge þe lesse, and þe grete synne let freli be doun. And þus þe gospel seiþ þat þe pharesees fieþ þe gnatte and suelowen þe camele. And if witte of riche men þat dwellen in þis worlde weren liȝttid be feiþ and led be resoun, þei schulde not þus desire for to be biried amonge suche freres. For Goddes lawe seiþ þat he haloweþ not þe man for þe place, but aȝenwarde þe place for þe man. Forþermore, þes freres tellen so miche be þer abite þat if a frere leue it for resonable cause and cressing of vertues, as liȝtly mai falle, he is apostita repreued of God. And so freres ordinance schulde change Goddis wille and make him to hate a man for his vertues. And so it falliþ ofte þat freres presounen þer breþeren, and punyschen hem scharpeli, for þei do as þei schulde be þe lawe of God. And many suche heresies fallen þes freres for lesse erroure þat þei ben first wedded wiþ.

RICHARD It is harde to trowe þat of suche abites comen so many erroures as þou here rekenes, speciali siþen al men vsen suche

617 it littleþ] liiteþ haue] *abbrev. macron over* a *ignored* 620 signes] *corr. by canc. from* sigenes 623 freres] *twice, 2nd canc.* 636 camele] *abbrev. macron over* mel *ignored* 643 vertues] of vertues 648 comen so] so comen *marked for rev.*

customes, and if a more custome schulde geder more synne, þe lasse [s]iche costom schulde gader more synne. And siþe many sentis han kepte þes abites, it were agene resoun to destroie her ordinance. Whi schulde not freres be punysched for suche trespas, siþen be | continuaunce of it þer order were destroied? For if þer were no f. 48v suche distincioun of freres, þe worlde schulde not knowe hem amonge hemself, ne fro prestes and oþer comoun men.

JON Soþli, customes moten nedly be appreued, siþen þat vertues of men ben grunded in costomes. But þenke on þat temperance is þe ferþe wal þat schulde close a man in closter of soule, and so take hede þat þe customes be goode and temperali vsed, as menne of vertu axiþ, as men han custom to ete and trauele and slepe. But in suche customes many erroures bygynne, but if þei be reuled bi resoun of iustice. And so wane a man chargeþ to miche his costom and leueþ þerfore seruice þat he oweþ to God, þan þis costom in so miche is worþi to be dampnede. And so summe customes smachen euene vertues, and summe smacchen euene synne, and summe ner noiþer. þe first schulde be vsed be reuling of vertue; and þat oþer schulde be laft as venym of soule. But þe þrid costom schulde be euene taken in þat þat it helpiþ to seruice of God. And so a more costom smaccheþ oft synne wanne siche a lesse custom souneþ not in synne, as custom of cloþing of se[c]uler men telliþ not þer vertues as freres doun. And þerfore þer lesingis þat þei crien in þer cloþes smaccheþ ypocrisie, but seculeris not. And so seintis of þes priuate religiouns in þat þat þei synned not bisied hem not abouȝte suche rites, but bisied hem in Crist. And if þei synned sumwat in kepinge of þese customes, God forbede þat we | schulde take ensample of hem and sue hem in þis þat f. 49r þei synned inne. And so if frenes of Crist were kepte and þese orderis lessid, blessid were þe conclusioun þat sueþ heroffe. For þanne schulde we be ooned in Cristis religioun, and sectes of discencioun schulde be distried. For þre parties of þe chirche were sufficient, as prestes and knyttis wiþ þer comoun puple, and more changaunt diuisioun doþ miche harme, nameli in ordur of prestes þat schulde more be ooned. But antecrist bigynneþ his parting in prestis; but of his variaunce of abites is stiryng miche, boþe amonge freres and clerkis of scole. þe frere prechoures seien þat siþen þei mornen most; as blackenes of þer cope is ⟨schewed⟩ to þe puple, þei schal be most

651 siche] liche 653 be] be//be 669 smaccheþ] *prec. by canc.* schulde 671 seculer] seuler 673 religiouns] reli/giounse 680 sufficient] *abbrev. macron over* ent *ignored* 684 stiryng] *abbrev. macron over* ng *ignored*

counforted in þe blisse of heuene. Frere menoures seien siþen þer trauel is most schewed in russet of þer abite, þei schal be moste rewarded, as seint Poule seiþ. þe Austeynes seien siþe þei morne o[uer] prechoures, þei schal haue more mede at þe daie of dome. þe Carmes comen þane, and seien þat þei passe al þes oþer orderes as angelis in heuene, and for whiȝtnesse of þer copis scheweþ clennes of angelis, and russet of þer schapelarie scheueþ þer trauel. Suche schameful stryues schulde not be rehersed ne asoyled of men, for þei bynde not. But oon þing þei telle, al if it be fals: þat abite of freres wolde make an ape seint. And so þei stryue fast wiche of þise foure orderis is more holy, siþen eelde profitiþ nouȝt; and so as hores strof before Salamon, þus þis kynrede of horedom stryuen for her childeren. God wolde þat suche stryues were hide fro þe worlde, f. 49v but þat it knowe be dedus hiȝenesse of vertues. For | by suche feynyng þei deseyuen childeren, and seyn þat þei schal sitte wiþ Crist at þe daie of dome, and iuge men of þe worlde aftur þat hem likiþ, as þei prouen be Cristes worde[s] seide vnto Peter. But witte wel, þese ypocrites, siþen þei straungen fro þe apostilis more þan oþer men doun, þise wordes seide [vnto] Peter ben ful fer fro hem, siþen þei reuerse Crist. But more ben freres imingeled in mater of scole, wher þer religioun wiþ perfeccioun of þer ordere be grounded in þer habite or ellis in þer soule. Not onli in þer soules, as þe freres granten, for þanne were þer habite inpertinent to hem, and þei were[n] not apostatas [if] þei left it, and so þe capteynes of þer ordres diden al amys in prisonyng of þer breþeren for leuyng of suche signes. And so þei seyen þat aftur goodenes of þer habite is þer ordere good or werse as it weriþ; and wanne þei caste awey þer habite on niȝttes þei leue þer order and þer religioun. And so þei nede God to dippe in þer habites ȝeftis of grace þat passen al þis worlde; and non wondur if suche cloþes ben so precious. Suche folies of freres ben feyned in þe worlde, and disceyuen blynde men because of þer synne. And so freres schewen in þer maner of lyuynge þat þei principali worchen for þe worlde.

RICHARD þis semeþ seid to scharpli for abites of þes freres. But þou reherstes not werkes of deuocioun, as makyng of faire chirches, and our[n]ementis of hem, risynge at mydnyȝt wiþ fasting and preieris. þis schulde hiȝe þese freres, or Goddis lawe is fals.

690 ouer] os 703 wordes] worde 705 vnto] *added for sense* 709 weren] werer *final* r *not complete* 710 if] it 716 precious] *abbrev. macron over* ous *ignored* 722 ournementis] ourementis

JON þese ben fyue þingis þat most schuld prese þe freres. But as anemtes þe firist is making of chirchis. Many men ben mad ded be fabeles of freres, þat þei trowe þat þei mai not synne be dispending of chirches, so þe more þat þei dispende, þe more mede þei haue. | But (f. 50r) þis blynde resoun wolde mate þe freres, `for´ be þis blynde skille freres schulde haue non almes before þer chirche were hiȝed more þanne any mynster. And if þou sei þat almes stondeþ in ȝeuyng to oure mynster, who seiþ not þat suche freres ben not heretikes? Soþ it is þat men schulde helpe þer parische chirche, but in mesure and reson as God himself axeþ. For Crist preised not þe temple, but iuged it to be destroied. But in eche place a clene soule is acceptable to him; and more excesse of clennes is more accepted to God þanne excesse of cost of þe temple, be it neuer so coynte. For God wiþouȝte mesure preised more deuocioun of soule þane any erþely þing, be it neuer so costi, and herfore neiþer he ne his apostilis biside hem for makyng of bodili chirchis. Makynge of gostili chirches falleþ to Crist, and making of bodili chirches to lewed rewde men; so þat if chois of þese tuo were putte in a man, he schulde a þousandfolde more chese gostili chirches. For bodili chirche profitiþ not but in as myche as it serueþ and profitiþ to gostili chirche. And so he were a blynd man þat wolde denye þat ne almes dedes boþe spiritual and bodili weren more nedeful þan beldyng of houses. And so þe freres if þei hadde no chirches but bisied hem to preche þe lawe of þe gospel schulde profite more in chirche of þer soule þan þei nowe do wiþ al þer hiȝe howses. And þerfore Crist seiþ þat neiþer [in] hiȝe placis ne in solempne temples but in spirit and trewþe mot men preie God. As to þe secunde, þat ben ourenementis of | chirche, is þe same answere and (f. 50v) þe same resoun. For ournementis of vertues in a mannes soule ben more preciouse þane our[n]ementis of bodi. And þus Jon Baptiste wandred in deserte hadde more preciouse chirches wiþ his our[ne]-mentis þan was Salamounes temple wiþ alle þes freres houses. A mene of vertue schulde be holden in al suche þinges, for glorious houses and peynting of ymages fediþ of mennes eiȝen and spoules þer soules. And so schulde men bisie hemself bifore abouȝte gostili chirches and ourenementis of hem, and siþen aboute bodili þings, in caas þat þei profeten. As anemte þe þrid þing, þat is rising at mydnyȝt, schulde it be preised wan it is wel doun, siþen Dauid confessiþ þat he ros so. But

728 for] *suplin., marked for insertion* 748 in] neiþer /hiȝe 752 ournementis] ourementis 753–4 ournementis] ourmentis 756 peynting] *abbrev. macron over* in *ignored*

preier more deuoute plesiþ more God þan preier at mydniȝt þat is lesse deuowte. Crist preied al þe niȝt and in þe dai boþe, to teche vs þat tyme helpiþ litel preieres: he preied out of houses to teche vs preie so, and he is more þan Dauid or any oþer man. As anempte fasting, it is for to preise wane it is take discreteli and wiþ good wille, but þis is more amonge þe worlde þan amonge þe freres. And anempte þe fifte, þat is good preier, siþen it stondeþ in good lijf and fer fro ypocrites, it stondeþ more comounli in seculeres þan in freres, siþen þei blinden þer preeris wiþ ypocrite signes. Al þis schulde freres do hide from þe worlde, for wedding wiþ suche signes, sensibili don, litteliþ mede of freres and greueþ þer synnes. But siþen holdyng of Goddes lawe clene be hemself is most for to preise in alle suche lyues, loke we wher freres passen in þis lijf. Weddynge wiþ Goddes lawe is ful for to preise, |
f. 51r and daliance wiþ bilawes is for to repreue. But it semeþ to many men þat deuourse is maked betuix þe freres and clene Goddes lawe. But an hore and a begger of al mennes lawe is wedded wiþ freres, þat is, þer owne order, for þei telle more bi þat and sanctifie it more, and kepe it more trewly and punyschen þerfore þan þei do for þe lawe þat God himself ȝaf. And þis betokeneþ þat þei ben a kynrede of horedam, and diuided amonge hemself and parted fro God. For if þei louede Goddis lawe most of al oþer, þei wolde kepe it most tendurly and punysche most þerfore. But nowe a frere may trespas aȝens Goddis lawe as myche as he wole and be not clepid apostata ne punysched in prison. But for a litel trespas aȝens þis clouted begger he schal be prisouned and defamed as he hadde killed Crist. Who ne wolde seie þat freres ne were weddid wiþ þis beggerie, and partid be diuorse fro þe lawe of God? And suche putrie fordoþ religioun of Crist.

RICHARD It semeþ þou seist scharpeli as þou was wont to do, ne fagist not þese freres for wynnyng of þi name. But it semeþ þat þou passist charite and defamest þem alle. For if þis sentence were soþe, alle freres were apostatas, siþen þe[i] breken þe first and þe most mandement. For aftur þe first maundement, we schulde loue God ouer al oure herte, in al oure soule, and in al our mynde. Þe freres comen \`not´ þerto be reson þat þou madist, siþen þei loue not Goddis lawe ouer alle oþer þingis. And as þe gospel techiþ, louyng of God and louynge of his lawe answeren togeder boþe in more and lesse. And so as þei putten aback Goddis lawe in loue, so þei putten abak þer

789 wynnyng] *abbrev. macron over* y *ignored* 791 þei] þe 792 maundement] *abbrev. macron over* ent *ignored* 793 mynde] *abbrev. macron over* myn *ignored* 794 not] *suplin., marked for insertion*

God in loue; and if a corner of þer wittis were stopped wiþ Goddes loue, þer it is nowe stopped wiþ þer clouted reule, how | schulde þei f. 51v not so myche more loue God?

JON I were cursed of God if I faged freres, oþer afied me in þer helpe, to bere vp my name, siþen þei ben grounded in lesings and turnen as þe wederkoc. And þerfore triste we in God be oure goode werkis, for beleue techiþ vs aftur þat we werchen schal we take of hem ouþer good or yuell. And so we schul be charite talke to þes freres and telle hem þer fauȝtes, boþe for loue of hem and loue of þe puple. For God himself seiþ, 'þoo children þat I loue I snibbe and chastise as a good fadur schulde'. And weþer þei ben dampned or saued, be grace of God it schulde profite hem, for if þei go to helle þei schal more mekeli be dampned. And herfore Crist spake scharpeli to þe phareses, for he wiste be his reproue þei schulde lesse depli be dampned. And no Cristen man schulde drede vpon Crist, þat ne he dide vpon `charite´ al þat he dide. Wel I wot þat we faile in entent and maner, in reprouynge and sparing and al þat we do. But God helpe his seruauntis, as we haue entent to worche to worschipe of him and profite to his chirche. And if we coueite amys veniaunce of oure breþeren, we tristen on Godes mercy for oure good grounde. And it is licli to men þat mo schal be dampned for þer stille mouþe þan for þer scharpe speche, siþen God schal axe of Cristen men þe g`o´odes of þer breþeren þat þei myȝt do to hem and lettid be assent. But anemste [de]famynge, we schul vndurstande þat man, in þat he synneþ, defameþ himself. But anoþer þat seiþ of him þe soþe and on good maner doþ it as he schulde do to worschip of God. For hidinge of synne doþ myche harme. Anemtes þe apostasie of freres, I wolde it were aweye, for þei hemself schulden | be war of þis heresie, siþe þei f. 52r schal be dampned þerfore if þei laste þerinne. And so, as þou seide, al onli þe fauȝte of keping of þe first maundeme[n]t makeþ heretikes. And so wolde I concel al orderes of freres to gedere holly þer liȝf in þe lawe of Crist, and leue þer bagged beggerie of þer owne ordere. It is bagged and clouted be graunt of many popes; and so to summe it doþ good, and to many harmeþ.

RICHARD It semeþ þat þis biddyng of God mai not here be holden, siþen mannes lijf here in þis lijf is scatered aboute many þings

813 charite] *suplin., marked for insertion* 815 entent] *abbrev. macron over* ent *ignored*
819 goodes] o[1] *suplin., marked for insertion* 821 defamynge] þe famynge
823 hidinge] *abbrev. macron over* in *ignored* 827 maundement] maundemet

byside his God. And so noon schulde be weddid, ne vse no craft; for þe þing þat he vseþ lettiþ his loue. Whi mai not freres leue þer reule, as lewde men leuen þer wifes, and oþer craft?

JON Me þenkeþ þat þis biddinge of God schulde be kepte here in erþe, as it wel may, al if we synnen comounli in defauȝte of þis loue, and loue him not so holly as we schal in heuene. And herfore vnderstande þat loue of þi God be deppest in þi witte and hiȝest also, so þat `if´ þou loue any wordely þing, loue it in God; þat is to seie, in þat ordre and mesure þat it helpiþ to loue þi God more. And þe fauȝte of þis loue schendeþ most men. But þis we graunten, þat many men kepid here þis maundement, for elles þei were culpable of hem al ten, and Crist bad wiþouten cause men to kepe hem. But naþeles he biddeþ vs in lawe of his gospel, kepe al his maundementis if we wil come to blisse. And so it were an opon blasphemie to seie þat God biddiþ vs do more þanne we may. But diuerse men louen God on diuerse manere, for þes men þat lyuen clene contemplatiue lyue f. 52v gederen þer loue in oo þing, as Maudeleyne dide. But þese men | þat lyuen lijf of þe world be oft disturbeled and bisied in þer soule abowte many þings. þis lijf, [al if] it be perelouse, is preised of God, so þat men kepe w[e]ll þe grounde of þer loue. And so summe ben holden, and summe ben holden lesse, to loue þer God, aftur ȝiftis þat he ȝeueþ hem. And þus a man loueþ here God of al his herte, in al his soule, and al his mynde, as þe trinite axiþ. And if þou take any þing þat suche men loued, þei louen God in þat þing more [þan þat] same, for þei loued þat þing clenely in Good. And so bi al þe powers þat her soule haþ, þei loue God most, as iche man schu[l]de. But þat craft of loue is to litel knowen, for it is not clereli grounded in God. Wat man in þis lijf loueþ no þing but in order þat it profetiþ to þe loue of God? And Goddis lawe techiþ vs to kepe þis loue. And þus mai we loue iche creature in God, and so freres and þer reules; but not to kepe hem, siþen we myȝt liȝtlier serue God, and better also, to take cleneli his lawe and leue freres reulis. And so al if þat many men ben meued of God to take hem wifes and vse many craftis, naþeles it standeþ `not´ wiþ riȝtwyssenes of God þat he moueþ any manne to be wedded þus wiþ þese freres reules, and kepe hem in lyuyng more þan his owne. For þan hym failed witte in ȝeuyng of his reulis, and hiȝed þe freres

841 if] *suplin., marked for insertion* 842 And] loued And 843 most] *twice* 852 al if] *added [eyeskip?]* 853 well] wil þe] þer 857 þan þat] þat þan 859 man] *abbrev. macron over* n *ignored* schulde] schuhde 862 loue[2]] *prec. by canc.* kepe 866 not] *suplin., marked for insertion*

ouer himself. And if þat summe seyntis of freres ben not wedded þus wiþ þe frere reules, naþeles to many ben smyten wiþ Lucifers pride, and þis makeþ hem cowardly lette to blame men, and leue to stande be Goddis lawe, for drede of þer ordere. And so siþen God aproueþ matrimonie and craftis, and he approueþ now[h]er þat freres schulde lyue þus, þis apis argument þat freres | maken scheweþ þer foli and dampneþ hemself. If þei cowde schewe were Crist bad hem lyue þus, or theche be his wordis þat þis were leful, þane þei grunded þer order more þane þei can. Wat if þe pope or oþer foles approueþ þis doing? þat mot proue þat þise men synned not hereinne. But God haþ ȝeuen a sufficient reule, as oure feiþ techiþ, þat is more liȝt and more fre to iche Cristen man to holde. Whi schuld not Godes seruaunt be dampned for þis choise? And if þou seie þat seyntis, as Benet and Fraunces, Dominick, or Bernard, and many suche oþer, held holiche þis rewle, whi schulde not we, here freres taken on hem þat þei cannot proue. For as we supposen þat þise men ben seintis, so we supposen þat þei holdin þe goode of þis reule and left venym þat before and aftur was brouȝt inne. For þus mouȝte þei seie þat diuerse orderis holden þe good of þer order and leften þe wicked. For ellis Austines weren foles to parte from þis chanouns, or ellis white monkis to passe from þes blake. But soþli alle þese sectis ben dampnable foolis, siþen o reule of Crist sufficed for hem alle, and God axit of hem keping of þat reule, as he axiþ of vs, and þer wille excuseþ not. But we mai trowe þat many sorowed herfor in tyme of þer deþ.

f. 53r

RICHARD Lette telle me wat resoun may meue any man to kepe cloþing or mete for a certen while, þat ne þei may kep it euere be þe same skylle; and as þei mai for oon dai, so euermore aftur.

JON But schame þou for glotouns argument and of apis boþe. For þus glotouns arguen til þei be drounken, for if a pynt of vyne profitiþ to a man, a quart þat is to so gode wolde tuo so miche prophete, and so til þe glotoun haue to miche mette and drynke. Preie we þese ypocritis let God haue summe priuilage, siþen summe of his ȝeftis betoken his priuilegis. For | as vertues ben as þings þat no man mai mysvse, so þei ben þinges þat euere `þe´ more þe better. But it is not of þings þat God graunteþ man to make. And soþ it is of reules þat God himself haþ maded, þat euer þe lenger þat þei be kepid þe better þei ben. But mennes ordinaunce mot last for a tyme and faile in þe ende, siþen þei

f. 53v

874 nowher] no/wþer 888 þe[2]] þer 901 ȝeftis] *prec. by canc.* priuilegis 903 þe] *suplin., marked for insertion*

ben not lordes of tyme. Þus sermonies of freres ben good for sum men, and harmen many oþer, for þei ben not lorde of alle. God ordeyneþ to sum men chaunging of elde, diuersite of complexioun, and of power also. And so, þat freres reule þat wolde spede for a tyme, wolde noie for a more tyme, as Goddis mesure axiþ. And so, þat same reule þat were good for oon, were yuel for anoþer for variing of Goodis ȝifte. But herto þes folis take non hede in making of freres, but as blynde Baierd putteþ general statutes, and chalengiþ lorschip of comunite of þingis þat is propred to God, as blasfemes doun. And if þou seie here þat no frere reules bidden kepe þer statutes but it is best, certes þis hadde God ordeyned before þe freres come, and if þis were kept wel freres schulde be dissolued, and no frere be prisoned for he doþ þe better. And so þei prisoune Goddis lawe and magnifie þer ordere. And as þei glosen Goddis lawe be many fals castes, so þei don seint Austenes reule inprison hem togedere, as wane seint Austin biddeþ þat men þat contrarien þis reule be put ouȝt of his hous; þat is to seien, þe freres be closed in scharpe prison. And þus þei gile þe chirche of brede of þe auter, and aleggen grette docturis and þer straunge speche, and leuen holy writte þat God himself ȝaffe. And wane men aske hem wat is þat þat hemself sacreþ, and was before þe sacring ouþer bred or wynne, or ellis in þeise þings þat þei before offered, þei leuen al þis questioun and tellen a strange tale, or ellis þat f. 54r it is | an accident, or ellis noþing. And þus þese fals freres deceyuen þe puple.

RICHARD It semeþ be þis tale þat no man schulde be wedded wiþ noon vse of þis chirche, but lyue as we wolde. And so wolde iche obeidience to þe pope be dissolued, and Salusbiri vse and many oþer ordinaunce.

JON I preise not wedding wiþ no mannes ordinaunce, but only ordinance of God þat is oure bileue; and to defende þis ordinaunce schulde we putte our lijf. And so mannes ordinaunce, schulde we suppose, profetiþ for a tyme; and afturwarde, leue it wane þe reson axiþ and Goddis lawe techiþ. Men schulde obeische to alle men and more to þe pope, but for him do not but þat God biddeþ. And so to alle prelatis schulde we obeysche as to ministeris of God or to Goddes seruantis. If any man biddeþ þee do contrarie to Goddes lawe, fle þat as venym siþen ȝow art Goddes seruantis. And so to manere of

932 iche] þer iche (*perhaps an indication that text has been lost, but now redundant*)
939 obeische] obelische 940 pope] ppope

obedience schulde men wel marke; oon for to do þat þi prelate biddeþ wane it is confermed to mandement of God, and anoþer to forsake þat his voice mameliþ whan it is contrarie to þe wille of God. In boþe þeise obedience obeysche þou to God, and ellis schuldest þou not obeysche vnto man. And if þou seie þat þe secunde obedience is quoynte, siþ no man seiþ þat he obeyscheþ þat aȝenstandiþ, soþeli þis obedience, to aȝenstande, is to litil tauȝt and vsed þis daie. But þis tauȝt Grosteed, and seide to þe pope þat obedientli he aȝenstode þings þat þe pope bade. For euery man and iche þing seiþ Goddes welle and biddiþ kyndeli for to do it, and so wane þi prelate blaberiþ aȝenes God, he biddeþ þe kyndely to do Goddes welle. But þou were to myche a fole, to do his cursed bidding and leue þe holy bidding of God | and of hym, and so þou obeiest vnto him, leuyng his cursed f. 54v bidding. Þus schulde men obeische to popes and to prelatis, and neuer obeysche vnto hem but wane þei obeysched first vnto God. And þis wolde riȝt þese orderis aftur Goddes lawe. And so Salusbirie vse schulde be now performed, and nowe lefte for þe better þat Goddes lawe tauȝte. And if þou seiest þat þou must trowe al be iust and aftur Goddes wille þat þi prelate biddeþ þe do be obeidience, soþeli it falleþ ofte þat þi prelate is a fole, and reuersiþ Goddes wille in hym and in his subiectis. And how schulde [we] þis beleue, þat he we confermed ne miȝte not erre in his folis bidding? And so Gooddes lawe of riȝt obedience wolde dissolue errouris in þese false orderis.

RICHARD Þis sentence semeþ strett to seculer lordes, for þei comaunde oft þingis vngrounded in Goddis lawe, and be þis skile lordes schulde obeische to þer sugettis and serue hem as þei don hem, and oft siþus more.

JON Goddis lawe biddiþ oft obeische to seculer lordis, and he were a cursed preist þat wolde reuerse þis. But naþeles discression standeþ in þis obedience, so þat no sugett schulde obeysche to his lorde but in as miche as he sufferiþ obedience to God. But for bodely seruice and rauysching of goodes stondeþ wiþ obedience to God, as suffering of deþ, þerfore seint Poule techiþ to suffrin in al þis: If þei constreine þe to do þat Goddis lawe forbediþ, stonde stifly in wille to suffering of deþ. On þis wise dide Mauris and al his legioun, suffering Maximian

948 obedience] *abbrev. macron over* en *ignored* 951 aȝenstode] *corr. by canc. from* aȝenstonde 962 obeidience] *abbrev. macron over* en *ignored* 964 we] schulde /þis 966 obedience] *abbrev. macron over* en *ignored* 973 obedience] *abbrev. macron over* en *ignored* 974 obedience] *abbrev. macron over* en *ignored*

to sle þer bodies, for þei were sure of Goddis lawe þat Crist schulde saue þer soules and restore þer bodies. Þe cause of marturdom of þis hooli legioun stode in tuo þings, as her story telleþ: þat þei wolde not |
f. 55r pursue Cristen men, for þan þei pursued Crist; and for þei wolde not do sacrifice to his fals goddis. And suche a couent of freres was neuer non fondoun; ne, as I trowe, suche a legioun is not seyntes in heuene of al ordris of freres or mounkis or chanouns. And if þou put on hem cowardise þat þei wolde not fiȝte, certis þei ches þe better and more sure algatis, for in fiȝtting þei miȝt a died out of charite and haue nyed more þer killeris þan þei nowe dide. Þus schulde freres teche þese seculer lordes, and not counfort hem to fiȝt and bere hem companye, for 6^{e} maner of concense is most priuey synne þat antecrist haþ to disceyue Cristis seruantis. And so to speike of obedience: as Crist obeisched to Baptist, and to þe deuel Scharioth, as þe gospel seiþ, þe most lorde of þis worlde schulde obeie to his seruant; not be obedience of þe worlde but be obedience of heuene. And so iche worldely lorde is holden to his seruant defende him and mayntene him, and þat is miche more þan erþeli rentis þat þe seruant ȝiueþ aȝene. And þis is signe of lordeschepe, siþen þe lorde of alle lordis may not take seruice of man but if he be holden aȝene and do þe man more good þan he mai do to God. But antecrist clerkes wolen be free fro þis, and herfore be þei folk wiþouȝten hed, but if þei haue þese foure, Caym and Scariot and antecrist þe þride, and him þat next deceyued hem, þat þei clepen þer beupere. And siche a wounder aȝene kynde schendeþ Cristes kirke. And siþen þei ben þeues and robben commoon puple, and traituris to God, as seint Poule seiþ and Hildagar expowneþ oponly inow, it semeþ þat lordes schuld distroie þes traitours, boþe for loue of God and loue of þer sugg`e´tis. If we taken hede to rauisching of temperal goodis þat þei taken of tenauntes
f. 55v wiþouȝten autorite, it comeþ | to many þousand pounde in þe reme of Englond. And siþen þei medelen ypocricye and deseyuyng of þer soule, it is opon þat þis þefte is werst of al oþer. And if þou wilt wite how þes þefes mai liȝtli be stanched, telle comouns how þei schulde axe bisili of hem vndur þer comoun seel wat þer almes schal profite to oþer soules, siþen no man schulde chafer be beding and louyng but euery parti were serten of his chaffer. Teche seculer lordes to aske of þes freres whe[r] Crist begged so, and grounde hem on þe gospel and

980 soules] *prec. by canc.* bodies 998 þe] *twice* 1000 folk] *prec. by canc.* flock 1006 suggetis] e *suplin., marked for insertion* 1012 profite] propfite 1015 wher] whe

witnesse be þe comoun seel þat þis is þer sentence. Teche persouns and preistis to axe of þes freres wat þing þei sacred last wane þei sungoun masse, and weþer þei voidede anyþing þat before was brede, and wat ben þe ostis sacared þat be kept in þe chirche; for if þei ben wers in kynde þan any ereyne webbe, it were no religion to worschipe hem þus. For we trowe þat iche of hem is brede of Godis body, and for many freres varien in þis sentente, haue vndur þer comoun seel wat al þer secte seiþ. Siþen suche ben honeste axingis and of litel cost, and wolde purge freres of heresies þat nowe ben putte on hem, suspecte we þe freres þat wile denye þise charteris. And God schulde ordeyne clerkes to examyne hem, þat wiþinne litil wile schulde þer heresies be knowen, and on no wise schulde men ȝif hem of þer goodes before þei had þese answeris vndur þer comoun seel, for þat frere þat wolde for sixpens bring letter of fraternite, and wil not for miche more good þus his bileue, is suspecte of heresie as antecrist clerke.

Explicet dialogus fratrum. Amen amen amen am[en].

1019 þe[1]] *corr. by canc. from* þeise   1032 amen] am

DIALOGUE BETWEEN A FRIAR AND A SECULAR

Dublin, Trinity College MS 244 [C 3 12]

Moost worschipfulleste and gentilleste lord duke of Glowcestre, ȝoure seruaunt sendiþ ȝou [a] disputusun writen þat was bifore ȝow bytwixe a Frere and a Seculer ȝoure clerk, preiynge [ȝow] of boþe sidis to chese and apreue þe trewþe. For as seyeþ oure bileue, 'ouere alle þing vencuscheþ þe truþe'. And as seiþ Aristotle acordynge wiþ oure bileue, 'tweyn beynge frendis it is holy to b[i]for[e] honour þe | f. 213r trewþe'. Þerfore to ȝou, lord, þat herde þe disputusun be ȝeue þe fyle, to rubbe aweye þe rust in eiþir partye.

FRERE Þat þe hestis of God beþ neiþir soþe ne falce. For eche hest is a resoun inparatif þat is neiþir soþe ne false, as telliþ children sommes.

SECULER Þat ech hest of God is trewe, witnessynge Dauiþ þat seiþ 'alle þine hestis ben trewe'. And þerfore alle oþere scyences schulde be reulid bi þe cunnynge of þe hestis of God, and nouȝt aȝenward. And þerfore seiþ seynt Poul, 'whanne I was a child I sauered as a child, and whanne I was maad a man I avoydide þilke þingis þat weren of childhoode', as ben sophemesse and oþere veyne resouns þat ben aboute to make þat þe gretteste science of alle be rewled by þe leste—þe whiche þingis, whanne men so don, reproueþ hem. Seynt Poul [also] seiþ to hem 'Forsoþe, whanne ȝe schulde be maystres for tyme, eftesoones ȝou nediþ þat ȝe be itauȝt þe princyples of þe bigynnynge of þe wordis of God, and ȝe ben imade, to wham is nede, mylke and not sad mete'. Wherefore we seyen þat ech resoun, be it inparatife or optatife, is soþe or false aftir his resoun indicatife is soþe or falce to whom he schulde be redusid, or aftir þat he haþ trewþe in dede answerynge to hym.

FRERE Þat frere prechouris haueþ no possessioun in Engelond.

2 a] *added for sense* 3 ȝow] *added for sense* 6 bifore] be fore *see note*
20 also] *ampersand in MS; macron that would form* etiam/also *om. by scribe* ȝe] I ȝe

SECULER þat in dom place in Engelond, þes prechoures receyuynge here lyflode neiþer by beggynge ne by here traueyle wiþ here hondis, but bi annuel rente, and in manere of hauynge and spendynge alle one wiþ oþere seculeris þat haueþ possessiouns, [haueþ possessiouns], as here dedis preueþ—al be it þat þei blessen many men þat seen hem riche and possessions hauynge and ȝit leuen it nouȝt. To whom is contrarious Crist, þat seiþ 'Blessid be þilke þat leueþ and [s]eeþ not'. So, as Crist bileue bryngiþ atte þe laste to þe verrey siȝt of | here bileue, so þe bileue þat þes men techen bryngiþ to f. 213v
verrey blyndenesse of þat þat þei see wiþ here eiȝen. And so þei don þis myracl⟨is⟩ to make seynge men blynde.

FRERE It is nouȝt soþe þat alle þingis þat is nouȝt of þe bileue is synne, al be it þat þe Apostle seiþ so. þe which is vndirstonde, þat alle þing þat is nouȝt of good conscience is synne, and noȝt ech good conscience is not of bileue. Also, vnauysed rubbynge of a mannes berde is nouȝt of þe bileue and ȝit it is no synne, for it is neiþir good ne yuel.

SECULER We seyen wiþ þe Apostle þat alle þing þat is nouȝt of þe bileue is synne. For eche þing þat is nouȝt of þe ten hestis of God is synne, and þe ten hestis of God is oure bileue; þerfore alle þing þat is nouȝt of oure bileue is synne. And ȝif men asken what is oure bileue, and where in ony article of þe bileue ben þe ten hestis igroundid, we seyen wiþ seynt Austyn þat al holy wryt is oure bileue, and þat þe ten hestis of God ben vnderstonden in þis artycle of þe bileue: 'I bileue in God þat is.' 'I bileue þat alle þing þat God seiþ or biddiþ is trewe, and as þe hieȝeste goode I loue him ouer alle þing.' Also siþ þere is no good conscience but þat is igroundid in þe ten hestis, and alle þingis þat is nouȝt of goode conscience is synne, myche more alle þingis þat is noȝt of þe ten hestis is synne, and so alle þingis þat is noȝt of þe bileue is synne. Also, siþ God is oure bileue, and alle þingis þat is nouȝt of God is synne—as seiþ seynt Jon, þat 'wiþouten him is made nouȝt', þat is, synne—þanne alle þingis þat is nouȝt of oure bileue is synne. þerfore, wondringe of þes men þat seyen þe reuerse, seynt Ieremye seyþ into þe confusioun of hem 'What is he þis þat seyde, þat þeere schule be don ony þing þe lord not comaundynge'. þat þerefore

31–2 haueþ possessiouns, haueþ possessiouns] haueþ possessiouns *see note* 35 seeþ] deeþ 38 myraclis] myracl⟨..⟩ *end of word obscured by binding* 45 þe clerk *marks change of speaker: appears in box drawn in margin, linked with a line drawn to vertical line division just before* We

f. 214r þe rubynge of a mannes | berd, whanne it is don wiþ cause approued of God, it is good; and whanne it is ellis, it is veyn and yuel. And þerfore, al be it þat þis rubbynge of berd in his kynde be neiþer good of vertu ne yuel of vyce, neuere þe lattere wiþ good circumstaunce it is good, and wiþ yuel circumstaunce yuel.

FRERE No man synneþ but of bifore deliberacioun. And þerfore children, to þe tyme þat þei haueþ discrecioun of resoun, synneþ not, as bifore þat tyme þei [n]aueþ deliberacioun. And a man þat bygynnyþ to slepe of charite, he synneþ nouȝt aftirward in his slepynge.

SECULER þat þere is twey manere of synnes. Oon is clepid synne of leeuynge þat a man schulde doo, and anoþer is synne of doynge aȝens þat þat a man schulde do. Riȝt as in þe weye of vertu first is fleynge of synne and aftirward is doinge of good, as seiþ Dauiþ, 'bowe fro yuel and do good', riȝt so in þe weye of vyce is first omyssioun þat is leeuynge of þat þat a man schulde do, and aftirward synne of comyssioun þat is doynge þat þat a man schulde not do. þanne siþ bifore þe synne of omyssioun ofte goiþ no deliberacioun, ofte siþes a man synneþ wiþouten ony delyberacioun bifore. For ofte siþes men so uereylyche doiþ here yuel dedes þat þei abide nouȝt so longe to make of deliberacioun. And also ofte siþes whanne a man synneþ, þe wyl of him gooþ bifore ony resoun, good or yuel, and delyberacioun is but of resoun. Also, in yuel delyberacioun a man synneþ, bifore whiche delyberacioun goþ non oþir delyberacioun. þerfore riȝt as þe first yuel delyberacioun of a man is synne, riȝt so a man synneþ wiþouten ony delyberacioun bifore. Also, a man makiþ ofte good delyberacioun, and ȝit aftir of forȝe[tyng]nesse synneþ aȝenst þilke delyberacioun, and so f. 214v he synneþ, and nouȝt of delybera | cioun bifore, but raþer aȝenst, as a monk þat bifore he slepiþ makiþ his delyberacioun to rise at myddenyȝt as he were holde, and ȝit in tyme whanne he scholde rise of forȝetynge lieþ stille and sleepiþ. And as seynt Gregorie ensaumpliþ, a man, bifore he sittiþ at þe mete, he makiþ his delyberacioun for to ete no more but þat þat is nedful to him, and ȝit aftir of vndelyberacioun he etiþ or drynkiþ to myche, no delyberacioun goinge bifore oþere þan goode. And þerfore I wot

68 + seiþ *marks change of speaker: appears in box at end of half blank line, after several short pen strokes, before* No 70 naueþ] haueþ 71 slepe] *prec. by canc.* clepe 73 þat] *prec. by* he seiþ *to mark change of speaker, in text, but marked off from text with two vertical lines before and behind* 89 forȝetyngnesse] forȝeuenesse

neiþer whi men schulde seie þat þere is no synne but of delyberacioun bifore, but for þei wolde nouȝt be atteynte in þe malice þat Dauiþ spekiþ of whanne he seiþ 'þe yuel man wolde not vndirstonde þat he schulde do good'; þat is, he schulde leeue delyberacioun to do good, þat he myȝte be excusid by noon-delyberacioun of doynge of yuel. And for children beþ nou`ȝ´tt excusid by non-delyberacioun, seiþ þe wise man þat þe turnynge awey of children, þat is here synne of omyssioun wiþouten any delyberacioun, schal sclee hem.

FRERE A child synneþ not in his modir wombe, al be it þat it be in origynal synne in his modir wombe, þat is þe synne of his forme fadir Adam. þerfore riȝt as wiþouten his desertis þe grace of Crist purgeþ him fro þilke synne, so bifore þat grace of Crist he is in synne of Adam, al be it þat þan he synneþ nouȝt hymsilf.

SECULER We seyen wiþ þe Apostle in his epistle to þe Romayns þat alle men synnede but þilke þat weren halwid in here modir wombe. For siþ eche child haþ his body in obeyschaunce to his sprite, and þe sprite more folwynge þe body þan þe hestis of God, he synneþ (be he neuere so ȝonge) so þat he be noȝt halowed in his modir wombe. þan eche suche child, anoon as his sprit is wiþ |inne his body, f. 215r
synneþ. And þerfore seiþ þe Apostle þat þo`r´uȝ kynde we ben þe sones of wreþ alle. And as it is but a foly to seie þat a child is in defaute and ȝit defauteþ not ne neuere dide, riȝt so it is but a folye to seie þat a child is in synne and synneþ nouȝt. For þere is no child now, be it neuere so ȝonge, þat is in þe personel synne of Adam, siþ Adam is in heuene and haþ now no synne. þerfore siþ a childe, anoon as he is quick, he is in synne, and in non oþer synguler synne but in his owne, so þanne he synneþ himsilf. For in eche synne somme þing [is]; þanne in þe orygynal synne of þis child synneþ sum þing; and noon oþer but þilke child himsilf. þerfore riȝt as þe child is in þat synne, so he synneþ in þat synne. And þerfore holy wryt neuere more settiþ dyfferrence bytwixe þes two, but haþ hem for alle oone, 'þis man is in synne' and 'þis man synneþ'; as it is alle one 'þis man is in his rennynge' and 'þis man renneþ'. And þerfore seiþ holy wryt þat þe sone schal nouȝt bere þe wickidnesse of [þe] fadir; þat is, þe sone schal not be in þe wickidnes of his fadir but for he is wickid himsilf. And þat is þe cause whi God cursid Canaan þe sone of Cam, and not Cam, þat

103 nouȝtt] ȝ *suplin., not marked for insertion* 117 þo`r´uȝ] r *suplin., marked for insertion* 123 he] as he 124 þing is] þingis *with* is *canc. by subpunct.* 131 þe fadir] fadir, *prec. by insertion mark, but no insertion given*

couered not þe preuye harneyes of his fadir, for his sone schulde be more wickid in þat synne þanne was Cam his fadir. And þerfore þat cursynge was nouȝt cursynge of demynge, but cursynge of prophecye, þe `whiche´ schewiþ þe comynge of goostlyche synne aftir þe comynge of bodilyche synne. And for God is so good þat in eche goodnesse he is bifore and in eche yuel he comeþ aftir in effecte, demynge him in þat synne þat synneþ þerinne, þerfore al be it þat wiþouten oure desertis God sendiþ vs his grace of forȝeuenesse of oure synnes, ȝit he demeþ vs nouȝt in no synne but aftir þat we haue synned þereinne. þerfore it may not be þat a man be in synne raþere þanne he synneþ, as God may not demen him in synne raþer þanne he synneþ.

f. 215v FRERE | þe children þat dien in orygynal synne, lackynge of þe siȝt of God and of þe blesse of heuene is to hem no peyne, for þei haue no felynge ne knowynge of it.

SECULER We seyen, as þe siȝt of God and his blisse of heuene is þe grettest lykynge mede þat may be to hem þat ben in heuene, as it is þe grounde of alle oþere ioye in hem, so to þilke þat ben in helle þe grettest peyne of alle oþere and þe ground is þe pryuacioun of þe siȝt of God and of þe blisse of heuene. And riȝt as alle þe spirites in helle, as þei of children or of oþere, knowen þat þei ben idampned and why þei ben idampned, so þei knowen þat þei lacken þe siȝt of God and þe blisse of heuene, to þe whiche in kynde þei were imarkid. As a blynde man in birþe and contynuellyche aftirward knowiþ þat he is blynde, and þat þat blyndnesse is peyne to him, so boþe þe seyntis in heuene and alle þe yuel spiritis in helle knowen þat þe lackynge of þe siȝt of God and of his blisse is to hem þe grettest peyne.

FRERE Sum men dwellen longe in deedly synne, and ȝit while þei contynuen in þat synne þei synnen not in noon oþere synne. For ȝif as longe as a man dwelliþ in dedely synne he synneþ euere more newe synne and newe, þan ȝif a man cried God mercy in dedelyche synne, he synned þerinne. And ȝif þat lassid his synne, newe synnynge lassid þe synne.

SECULER We seyen þat alle þe while a man is in deedely synne, whateuere he do, he synneþ contynuellyche newe synne and newe, as þe lengere he contynueþ in his synne, þe grettere is his synne. For alle

137 whiche] *marked for insertion from margin* 164 synne[2]] *abbrev. macron over* y *ignored*

þe while he dwelliþ in deedly synne, he spendiþ contynuellyche amys þree newe graces of God, þat ben þe grace of God of his bodily durynge alyue, þe grace of his tyme, and þe grace of þe seruyce of Goddis creaturis to him; þe whiche as þei ben euere more newe and newe, so þei ben euere more newe and newe spende amys, for þei ben ispende | wiþoute charite aȝenst þis hest of God, 'alle ȝoure þingis be doon in charite'. f. 216^{r} þanne alle þe while a man is in deedely synne, he synneþ contynuelyche newe, whateuere he do. þerfore seiþ þe Apostle 'alle þingis is clene to clene men; to þilk þat beþ defouled and vntrewe þere is no þing clene'. But here þouȝt and here conscience beþ defoulid; þei knowleche þat þei knowen God, but in dedis þei deny`e´n him, siþ þei ben abhomynable and vnable to good bileue and reproued to alle goode werkis. And riȝt `as´ a seruaunte þat haþ trespassid greuoslyche to his lord, in wyl to contynuen his trespase or a werse, in biddynge his lord mercy nys but a trayterouse faytour, as gregynge his olde trespase or a werse, so a man in deedly synne biddinge God merci wiþouten good wille to leeuen al deedely synne is but a trayterouse faytour of God, and so in þat biddynge of mercy synneþ greuouselokere þanne he dide bifore. And ȝif wiþ good wil to leeue his synne he biddiþ Goddis mercy, þan he is sory for his synne and in good wille to do þat þat he may as God wole and holy chirche to haue remyssioun of it, þanne in þat crienge of mercy is a spar[c]he of charite. And so in þat cryynge of mercy is no deedly synne, but as it is doon in charite, for in good wille to leeue his synne, so it is not idon in deedelyche synne, ne wiþ deedly synne, and ȝif men aske wheþir a man schulde cry God mercy while he is in dedelyche synne, I seie 'ȝee'. But ȝit he schulde nouȝt wiþ dedelyche synne crie God mercy, as he schulde neuere more be wiþ deedely synne, but oute of dedely synne.

FRERE Summe men fulfillen more þan þe hestis of God, as þe religious þat fulfillen þe hestis of God and Cristis counseyles.

SECULER We seyen þat þere may no man fulfille more þan þes tweyn hestis of God: 'loue þi God ouere alle þing' and 'þi neiȝbore as þisilf', | as þere is no doynge more þan to loue God ouer alle þingis f. 216^{v} and to loue þi neiȝbore. And þerfore seiþ Crist þat in hem two hangeþ alle þe lawe and þe profetis, to þe whiche whoso addiþ or lassiþ, he is acursid of God. And þerefore may no man wel fulfille more ne lasse

177–8 ad ty/tu[m] 1° *in margin; see note* 181 denyen] e^{2} *suplin., marked for insertion* 182 as] *suplin., marked for insertion* 192 sparche] sparthe þan þe hestis of God, and þerfore whoso fulfilliþ oon of hem, fulfilliþ hem alle. For alle þe hestis of God biddiþ no more but 'loue wel', wiþouten whiche loue forþere is noo hest fulfullid. Seiþ seynt James þat whoso offendiþ in oon offendiþ in alle. þerfore ri3t as he þat kepiþ ten hestis kepiþ no more ne lasse þan oon, ri3t so þei þat kepen þe hestis of God and Cristis counseylis kepen no more þan þe ten hestis.

FRERE Freris ben excusid fro trauaylynge wiþ here hondis, for here studi[y]nge and prechinge of þe word of God, and for here risynge att mydny3t, and for here masses seiynge, and for oþere seruyce of God.

SECULER We seyen þat siþ biggynge wiþouten nede, as is stronge bigginge, is ensaumple and mayntenynge of þeues, as it is open wrongful coueytynge of oþere mennes þingis, and so it is þe brekynge of þe tenþe heste of God. So, stronge biggynge may for no se[r]uice of God be excusid. For whanne it is so, it is but feyned equyte, and so double schrewednesse, as doynge of a good dede to maynteyne a schrewed. þerfore þes stronge biggers þat excusen hemsilf by here fastynge and wakynge and preyer ben ifigured bi þe farisee, þat preyinge in þe temple lyft vp his i3en to heuen and seyde 'Lord I þanke þee I am nou3t as oþir men beþ, but I faste twey as in þe woke, and 3eue tyþis of alle þat I haue'. So þes stronge beggeris li3ften vp here i3en to heuene, | (f. 218r) in as myche as þei wenen þat þei lyuen so heuenelyche þat þei schulde not traueyle wiþ here hondis. And þerfore þei seyen þat þei be not as oþere men, but in fastynge, preyinge, and prechinge passen alle oþere. And so here mouþ þei putten into heuene, but here tunge passiþ into erþe, in as myche as wiþ here feyned beggynge þei licken þe temparal goodis of þe erþe. And þerfore þe pupplican þat wolde not heue vp his i3en, as beþ þe lewid peple þat holden hem not worþi to þe office of presthode and þerfore trauayliþ wiþ here hondis, knowlechinge here synnes and biddinge mercy, passen [iustified] fro þes beggeris þat ben as wolues, 3ollynge a3ens heuene and lyuynge in raveyne of symple bestis.

FRERE Seynt Johun come to seynt Edward in lickenesse of a pilgrime and beggynge of him. Whi may not þan freris begge as he dide?

214 studiynge] studinge 220 seruice] seuice 228 f. 218r] *contents of ff. 217 and 218 transposed in MS* 237 iustified] I in stysied *see note, and cf. Luke 18:14*

SECULER We seyen þat no seynt in heuene while he is in blisse neuere ȝit begged of man here in erþe, as no seynt in heuene may be nedy to himsilf of mannes helpe here in erþe, ne don ony schamefast dede as is beggynge. And þerfore I am in certeyn þat seynt Johun begged not of seynt Edward. But ȝif þat visyoun of seynt Edward be soþ, it mote nede be vndirstonde acordauntlyche wiþ oure bileue; þat is, þat þe grace of God come to seynt Edward in þe lickenesse of seynt Johun, biddinge him in fygure þes almes-dede, þat he schulde not be here as a kyng of þis world, but as a pilgryme þat haþ no dwellynge cite here but sekiþ his dwellynge and his restynge in þe kyndom of heuene, as biddiþ seynt Petir and seynt Poul. And þerfore seynt Johun appered in lickenesse of a pilgryme, and in token þat seynt Edward wolde so don, settynge nouȝt bi þis erþelyche diuite in | comparisoun to þe blisse of heuene, he took him þe rynge of his f. 218v fynger, willynge to be iweddid to þe king of heuene and not to þe erþely kyngdom. And of þis men may se þat þes þat aleggen seynt Johun a begger faren as a man in þe jawnes to whom alle colouris semeþ ȝelowe: so [to] a stronge begger alle askynge semeþ beggynge.

FRERE þe apostle begged of þe Corinthes to þe seyntis in Ierusalem and ordeyned collectis to be imaad for hem. Whi þanne nowe [may] not freris so begge, as þei do, to here felawis þat stodyen at home?

SECULER Here we seyen þat þere is greet differrence bitwixe þe freris beggynge and þes collectis makynge of seynt Poul to þe seyntis in Ierusalem. Firste, for among freris þouȝ oon begge for alle, it schal not be departid among alle to eche as it were nede, as it was amonge þe seyntis in Ierusalem, and þerfore þer beþ inedide bisidis þe comoun beggynge eche to begge for himsilf; and so was it nouȝt amonge þe seyntes in Ierusalem to whom alle here goodis was comoune. Anoþere is þis: þat þe seyntis þat were in Ierusalem were alle of oon religioun wiþ þe seyntis in Greces and þe Corynthees, and vndir apostle Poul as vndir here abbote. And þerfore þat biddinge þat Poul bede, collectis to be imaad to þe seyntes in Ierusalem, was not biddyng of beggynge but biddinge of autorite, as biddinge of an abbote to his monke; ne ȝeuynge of þe Corynthees was not pure almesse-dede, but more dette þan almesse-dede. For siþ þe seyntis in Ierusalem weren of oon religioun wiþ þe seyntis of Corynthees, þei hadden here goode

259 so to] so   262 may] *added for sense*   263 at] *corr. by canc. from* atte
268 þe] *corr. by canc. from* þei

comoune; and þerfore þe Corynthees sendinge of here goodis to þe seyntis in Ierusalem þe whiche were nedye was but ȝildynge of here dette.

FRERE þis biddinge of God 'Algatis be þere no beggere among f. 217r ȝow', | is vndirstonde on þis wise, 'þat men be so almasful to þe pore þat þer be not ifounde noon nedful man beggyng amonge ȝow'.

SECULER Siþ charite bigynneþ at himsilf, and a man þat is of power is holde to be so almesful to his neiȝbore þat he haue no nede to begge, miche more a man þat is of power, as ferforþ as he can and may, is holde to be so trauaylous þat he haue no nede to begge. And siþ lordis han charge to reule þe comunte þat þere be no begger among hem, and specially no stronge begger, and þerfore seiþ seynt Poul 'who þat will not trauayle he schal not ete', þanne þis hest of God, 'be þere no begger amonge ȝou', bynddiþ men to almess-dede to here neiȝbores, but more men hemsilf þat þei raþer trauaylle wiþ here hondis as ferforþ as þei connen and mowe, þan þei goon and begge. For boþe ˋkyndeˊ and resoun aschameþ of beggynge. But moste þat hest byndeþ lordis—þat as þei most plenteuouslyche lyuen by trauaile of þe cominalte, so þei beþ moste iholde to constryne men to trauayle, þat þere be plente of alle Goddis goodis in þere peple; and to lette þat þere be no stronge begger among hem, þe whiche is a wede þat distroyeþ þe goode herbis of traueyloures bi whom alle men lyuen. Forsoþe, berynge out of money oute of þe rewme to plees to bigge benefices to meden enemyes of þe realme myche febliþ þe rewme, but certis myche more stronge beggeris þat lassen þe laboreres of þe rewme þat ben rote of alle money in þe rewme. þerfore as he þat distroyeþ þe rotis of þer herbis in a gardeyn more distroyeþ þe gardeyn þa[n] he þat distroyeþ þe leefes, so stronge beggeris [more] distroyen þe rewme þan bereres of þe money oute of þe rewme. þerfore þe lawe syuyl comaundiþ, and þe lawe of Yngelond, þat f. 217v stronge beg | geris be putt in prisoun for þe[r] yuel ensaumple to þe peple þat wolde raþere begge þan lyue by here trauayle. And þerfore bidiþ seynt Poul þat men schulde not comoune wiþ stronge beggeris þat beggen vndir colour of holynes, as ben freris and thrilleris.

282 þe frere *marks change of speaker: appears in margin beside start of Friar*'s *speech* 283 f. 217r] *contents of ff. 217 and 218 transposed in MS* 285 þe seculer *marks change of speaker: appears in box after pen stroke on ¾ blank line* bigynneþ] *corr. by canc. from* bigynyneþ 295 kynde] *marked for insertion from margin* 306 þan] þat more] *added for sense* 309 þer] þe 311 2a ad thes' ult' *in margin*; *see note*

FRERE It is semeful to begge for to ensaumple mekenesse to þe peple and to styre men to þe werkis of mercy.

SECULER Siþ Crist neuere ensaumplid begging wiþouten nede, but þe mekenesse of traueylynge Crist ensaumpled boþe in word and in dede, as techeþ seynt Poul, and þerfore Crist in þe gospel is clepid a carpenter for he trauaylde wiþ his fadir, helpinge him to here boþe lyflode, and oure lady for sche wolde not gon on beggynge trauaylede wiþ here hondis; freris, siþ þei wolden ensaumple mekenesse, whi wole þei not ensaumple þe mekenesse of trauaylynge wiþ here hondis þat is so groundid in oure bileue and in þe werkis of Crist? And beggynge is nouȝt groundid, but myche lettiþ þe seruyce of God, as it is wrongful coueytynge of oure neiȝbores goodis. And so lettiþ not þe seruyce of God trauayle wiþ hondis, for þanne wolde not þe Holy Goost haue diden it, ne Crist and oure lady haue don it. But siþ þe freris ben aschamed to trauayle, þei ben aschamed to folwe Crist. And þan þei sample pride, and not mekenesse, and þerfore seiþ Dauiþ in þe sauter, 'þei ben not in þe trauayle of men and wiþ men þei schulle not be schourged'. And þerfore wiþholdiþ hem pride. And siþ þe beste styrynge to almesse-dede is wiþ trauellynge of hondis to ȝeuen almesse-dede boþe bodily and goostly, as dide seynt Poul, þan siþ freris letyn hemsilf most parfyt, þei schulde traueyle wiþ here hondis to ȝeue almesse-dede boþe bodily and goostly. And siþ beggynge is nouȝt irekened in noon of alle þe werkis of mercy, þan beggynge is no good styrynge to almesse-dede, but yuel, as synne styreþ to sorowe; ne good mekenesse but yuel, as is | ⟨low⟩tynge to þe mawmet of f. 219r
schrewednesse þat is richesse. And so beggynge is seruyce to þe fend, and so myche werse þat it is colour⟨id⟩ wiþ þe seruyce of God.

FRERE þe more a man ȝeueþ for Goddis loue, þe more almes-dede he doþ. þan ȝif a man ȝeue al þat he haþ for Goddis loue, and goþ himsilf a-beggynge, he doþ moste almesse-dede, namelyche ȝif he putt hym in þe ordre of beggeris. For as seiþ seynt Aus⟨tyn himsi⟩lf, þat 'he ȝeueþ more þat ȝeueþ þe tree wiþ þe fruyt [þ]an he þat ȝeueþ þe fruyte one'.

313 ensaumple] ensaumple of *see note* 317 act' 20° *in margin*; *see note* 329 trauayle] trauayle⟨.⟩ *final character illegible*, *perhaps canc.* 337 lowtynge] ⟨..⟩wtynge *illegible*; *obscured by binding* 339 colourid] colour/⟨..⟩ *illegible*; *obscured by binding* 341 doþ¹] *corr by canc. from* doiþ 343 Austyn himsilf] Aus/⟨.........⟩lf *illegible*; *obscured by binding* 344 þan] han

SECULER þe mychelnesse of almese-dede is not aftir þe quantyte of bodily goodis ȝeuen, but aftir þe quantyte of charite of þe whiche men ȝeuen here goodis. And þerfore seiþ Crist in þe gospel þat þe widewe þat ȝaf but a ferthyn ȝaf more into þe tresoure of God þanne alle þe toþere þat ȝeuen more of bodily goodis; and ȝit sche went not o-beggynge. For so gret charite wil not be ydil. And siþ þat tyme þat sche offrede weren many riche farisees þat ȝeuen myche richesse into þe tresoure of God whom in almesse-dede ȝeuynge passiþ þe wydewe, and ȝit sche was of no religioun but of þe comoune religioun of God. And siþ sche was in more charite þan þe farisees þat weren priuat religious, sche more verrylykere ȝaf þe tree of here wille wiþ þe fruytis of here werkis to God þan many of þe priuat religious.

þes þingis seiþ and sendiþ ȝoure seruaunte wiþ þe mendynge of ȝow, þat ȝe fulfillen in dede þe trewþe whanne ȝe se ȝoure tyme. For Dauiþ seiþ þat blessid be þei þat don doome and riȝtwisnesse eche tyme, þe whiche blysse ȝow graunt Crist Iesu. Amen.

DIALOGUE BETWEEN RESON AND GABBYNG

Dublin, Trinity College MS 245 [C 5 6]

God moueþ hooly churche bi many maner of spechis to knowe þe treuþe of his lawe and þerbi to come to blisse. And þus God spekiþ bi summe men as if two persones dispitiden togidre, þe whiche we clepyn Reson and Gabbyng, wheche ben Crist and þe fende.

RESON Siþ I am God þat schal iuge men, summe to joye and summe to peyne, alle men schulden þenc on me and be reuled bi me in þere conscience. An for þis I cam dawen fro heuene and lyued man here more þenne þritty ȝere, so þat bi my dedis and by my wordis my breþeren schulden hoomly knowe me. For alle þe werkis I did in erþe weren done euen aftur þe biddyng of my fadur. Wherfore I bad þe Iewis þat þei schuld | not trowe to me but if I did þe werkis of him þat f. 154r sent me. I departid my churche in þre parties: in lordis, prestis, and comyns. þe furst part schuld be lordis, þat schuld be vikers of my godhed and bi strengþe medelid wiþ resoun defende my lawe aȝens þe fende. And bi þis seruis þei hold of me and han lordschip of þis world. þe secound part schuld be my clerkis, þat schuld sue me next in lijf and lyue on almes as I did. For oft tymes whenne I began to teche my fadur lawe to þe peple, men cleped me home to her housis, ȝyuyng me bodily sustynaunce, alþouȝ I were myȝty bi my godhed, to ȝyue ensaumple vnto preestis to fleȝe richesse in þis lijf. True preestis þat prechen þo gospel, if þei ben beden of þe peple, may leuefully for her traueil, for þe tyme þei teche þe puple, take of þem her sustynaunce. Ȝea, if a prest for his perfeccioun were required of oo person or of many to abide wiþ hem in amendyng of her soulis, so þat he were for þe moost part ocupied in techyng of Goddis lawe, he myȝt for his goostly traueil resceyue of hem bodily foode. And if a preest of lytle letturer had wille to teche Goddis lawe truly, and nedid for wantyng of scharpnesse of witt to bisi him eueriche werkday aboute þe telling of Goddis lawe of þe gospel on þe haliday, for siche goostly traueil þat

1 G *of* God *is two-line decorated capital followed by word-sized space before* Siþ
5 *beginning of Reson's speech marked by* r
6 þenc] *abbrev. macron over* e *ignored*
19 alþouȝ] for alþouȝ

souneþ to þe comoun profit siche a prest myȝt leuefully, of siche a man þat myȝt bere it, take his sustynaunce in mesure. But looke he wele he passe not þat. Þe þridde part of my churche ben commouns, ground to þise two, þe wheche bi her bodily traueile sustenen boþe lordis and clerkis. But I wil þat charite knytt þise þre parties togidre. But `my´ clerkis schulun be liȝt to þise oþur and teche freely þe lawe of God boþe in dede and worde and meue hem þus to heuenward. True lordis schal bi charite help þise two sistris to lyue and mayntene hem bi wey of resoun to serue God and to comme to heuen. Comouns schulen wiþ good wille serue to lordis and help clerkis. For iche treue membre of þise þre schal help oþur in al his lijf be charite. And þus | f. 154v haue I ordeyned lijf to alle þre parties of þe churche. My clerkis þat suen me here schulen moost goostly lyue and next to heuen, þorouȝ ensaumple of whom þe peple ben drawyn from vices to vertues, to whom I forbed worldly wurschip. For þei schulen lyue in pouert as I did here, and teche þe peple to leue worldlynesse boþe bi lijf and bi word. For [bi] couetise of worldly good⟨is⟩ ben many men departid from God. And for mennes hertis ben here most enclinyng to siche couetyses, þe wheche willen not be remeuyd but bi þe contrarie, prestis schulun haue no more þen her nedful necessaries; þat is, mete and drinke mesurably and cloþis to couer þe body from colde and schame. Whenne Adam had synned in paradise he was aschamed of himsilf, for and he had neuer synned þere, man sculd neuer haue nedid cloþis. For he was clad in feirenesse, þe whiche he lost þoruȝ synne. And so for schame of himsilf men nedid cloþis aftur þat time. But synne is nowe so custumable þat men ben proude of her cloþis, and þerinne is grete lechorie. Wherfore my prestis moten wake bisily to repreue þis synne þat departis þe puple and me. Þe secound part of my churche, þat ben lordis, schulun haue worldly goodis and hool lordschip, for þat is nedful to her office þat I haue lymyt to her state. But herfore þei han no leue to passe þe bondis of myn heestis, but hem owen bisily to seke my lawe and kepe it, rulyng her sugettis aftur my lawe in perfit loue and charite. Þe þrid part of my churche, I wole þat it leue in bodily traueil. And þis part is clepid commyns, for bi þer commyn traueile ben þese þre sistris susteyned. And þouȝ þise true laborers for her traueil wanten worschip and eese, neþeles her wonyng stid is mad in blisse wiþouten eende. For what man þat makiþ a castel

31 in] in/in 35 my] *prec. by canc.* in; *marked for insertion from margin* 39 schulen] schulden 40 in] 'ri' *abbrev. over* n *ignored* 46 bi] *added for sense* goodis] good⟨..⟩ *end of word obscured by binding* 60 leue] leuee

and laiþ stonys deepe in þe erþe, he loueþ as wele þe castel grounde as he doiþ þe werke þat is leid abouen. And þus alle þise þree sistris of my spouse, I wil þei haue worldly goodis in mesure as myche as is nedeful to hem to do þe seruice þat I ax. And I wil þat noo | part of (f. 155r) my spouse be contrariouse to anoþur, ne lett anoþur to serue me, ne take no þinge proprid to anoþur. For as hiȝest acorde is in þe trinyte, so I wil þat þer be in þis churche.

RESON And for I wold þat þis lawe were more in mynde of Cristen men, I haue made to write it in þe oolde lawe and in þe newe. And as no man may be excusid þat ne he mot nedis kunne Goddis lawe and hou þat he schal serue God, but summe more and summe lesse, s[o] no man may be excusid þat ne he sculd know þe body of hooly churche, to do hir worschip and hoold hir hele, iche `of´ þise þre sistris in her degree, aftur þe ordynaunse of God. If presthod be wele rulid, þise oþur two sistris schulun haue good hele. And [her]for[e] I began [wiþ] þe reule of prestis: I wold þat lordis knewe my lawe, þat prestis passe not her boundis þat I haue lymyt to her state. For in þe fourþe boke of Goddis lawe it telliþ hou God seid to A`a´ron: 'In her londe schal ȝee not haue noo part among hem. I am part and þin eritage in þe myddle of þe children of Israel, but to þe children of Leuy ȝaue I alle þe tyþes of Israel in pocession, for her true seruice þat þei serueden me in þe tabernacle of couenaunt. I wol þat þei haue not ellis, but be payde wiþ offringis of tiþis.' Lord, siþ þis is Goddis word, and his lawe ȝouen to his churche, and þe witt is opyn inow, as þe bokis ben commyn to men, what þing meuiþ Cristen men to leue þis lawe so cowardly? þat þing þat souniþ to prestis wynnyng, as tiþis and offringis þat þei forȝeten not, alþouȝ þei forȝeten to serue God. And certis resoun at domesdaye wil not excuse þis necligens, nouþur in prestis þat done þus folily, ne in lordis þat suffren þis synne to regne. þe secounde witnesse of þe oold lawe is writen in þe fyueþ boke. Preestis and dekenys schulun not haue, and alle men of þe same kynreden, neiþer part ne eritage wiþ oþur children of Israel. For þei schulun ete sacrifice of þe Lord, and offryngis, and þei schal take noon oþur þingis of poscessioun of her breþeren. For þe Lord himself is here heritage, as he haþ seid to hem. þise wordis passen mannes lawe,

74 *continuing speech by Reson marked by* r *followed by word-sized space before* And 77 so] se *likely a slip of the pen, as for the ligature connecting* e *with the following* n 79 of] *suplin., marked for insertion* 82 herfore] for 83 wiþ] *added for sense* 84 Num. 18° *in margin; see note* Aaron] a^2 *suplin., marked for insertion* 96 oold] *corr. by canc. from* woold Deut. 18° *in margin; see note*

f. 155v for þei ben hestis of God hymsilf. | And prestis schuld not passe hem now if þei ben on Goddis parte. Þe þridde lawe is tauȝt of God bi his prophete Ezechiel. To prestis schal be non eritage, for I am eritage of hem. And ȝe schulden ȝyue to hem no poscessioun in Israel, for I am þeire possession. And noo glose excuseþ nowe prestis þat ne þei schulden holde nowe þise hestis, but if God be not nowe possessioun of hem, but þe feende. And to conferme alle þise lawe of prestis, Crist helde alle þise lawes sufficiently, boþe in himsilf and in hise apostlis. Lord, whi schuld not prestis nowe do so? Wheþur þat antecrist haue dispensid wiþ hem to do aȝeynes Crist? Suche false wordis wolun not excuse hem before resoun at domysday. Rede þe byleue þat God haþ ȝouen and stonde þerbi, puttyng awey al couetise, þorouȝ whiche prestis ben made blynd. And seke grace and þou schalt fynde, if þou perseuer in þin askyng. And þenke hou God is vnchaungeable, and his law is sufficient, and þenne beleue schal teche þee þat his ordynaunce mot nedis stonde. For he is now þat same God þat was and is and aye schal be. And no Cristen man awe to accepte no mannes biddyng but in as myche as it acordiþe to þe biddyng of God almyȝty. And here þise new ordris mowen be aschamed, þe wheche dreden more þe offense of men þenne þei done þe offens of God. But Goddis lawe forbediþ man to consent to eny synne; and þise apostatase of þe irreligiouse of antecrist, þorouȝ her false obedience done to here souereyns, ben made þer þoruȝ vnable to drawe vndur þe ȝoc of Iesu Crist. And ȝitt þe fend haþ tauȝ[t] hise children to alege here for hem hooly writt, s[ei]yng þat Goddis lawe biddiþ nat oonly to obeies to good men, but also vnto triuauntis. Here we answere to þise foolis þat ben blynde þoruȝ her owne foly þat þise wordis þat þei seie ben soþe, for Goddis lawe and resoun seiþ so. But þei vndurstonden hem amysse; and so þei blynden þe peple, but myche more þei harmen hemsilf. Soþe it is, and resoun techiþ, þat iche creature þat doiþ wele and seiþe eke schuld be accept to þe herers, for siche auditours ben f. 156r clepid obeysers to good men; and on þe toþur | syde þat siche men seyne þat men owen to obeise to tyrauntis þe wheche ben wickud men. We graunte wel þat þis is soþe. But þis biddiþ no Cristen man þe wheche is made free bi þe reule of Crist: from daye to daye to stonde wilfully vndur þe obediens of a false prelat. For iche man may suppose or knowe wheþer his obediens be good or noon. And if he feele it harmeþ himsilf and profiteþ not to him þat takiþ it, what foly

104 Ezek. 44° *in margin; see note* 125 tauȝt] tauȝ 126 seiyng] sauyng
133–4 men seyne þat] *twice*

obligacioun schulde bynde a man to siche a fleschely feende? O he þat were a kny3t of God and durst telle siche a feende his defaute, he schuld knowe truly obediaunce done to tyrauntis. For siche oon schuld for his treuþe be pursued, cursid, and clepid apostata. But al siche persecusioun, mekly suffrid wiþoute grucching for þe loue of Iesu Crist, is clepid of true men obedience done to tyrauntis. O Iesu, what may amende þis erroure þat so longe haþ growyn, wher we ben so fer fro grace þorou3 þe begilyng of þe feende and oure wi[l]ful assent in bidding us to siche obseruaunce? Wheþur we schal now lyue in dispeire, for þis synne haþe regned so longe? Iesu betokeniþ sauiour, and þat name þou chese before alle oþur, and þou was, is, and aye schal be iust in al þi wirchyng. For ri3twise dome askiþ þat a man be dampned taken oute of charite in þe last houre. Þou3 al he had lyued al his lijf before in keping of þe hestis, ri3tful dome askiþ for his wilful errour euerlastyng dampnacioun. And so, þorou3 ri3twisnesse of þe, we ben counfortid in oure bileue. Þow we han lyued al þe most part of oure lijf þoru3 ignoraunce, necligence, or wilfulnesse a3[e]yns þi heestis, if we duely repente vs at þe last eende of our lijf, forsakyng oure synne whiles we mowe do synne, þou3 þe tyme be neuer so schort, þoru3 ri3twisnesse of þi hooli name, Iesu, oure beleue counfortiþ vs to trist to þi mercy and so to haue for3yuenesse of oure longe trespasse. And herfore true men þenkyn þat þise irreligiouse, þe which haþ long a3eyne þe rule of Crist þus wickudly fou3ten, schuld not put her hoolynes in vtward signes, as in cloþing, eting, or fasting, or wakyng at oonis togidre | and aftur oo reule. For f. 156^v true men knowen wele þat þe habit makiþ not þe monke, chanoun, frere, ne prest. But as prestis mown best wiþouten charge of þe peple cume to pore cloþing to hil hem wiþal, charge þei no colour þat pertenyth to presthod. In etyng and drinkynge oure hooly abbot made hise postles free, and so alle prestis of his religiouse þat schal comme aftur, to ete and drinke in mesour if þat hem nediþ, siche as commeþ before hem. In wakinge or fasting oure hooly abbot Crist haþ comaundid his couent to prey specialy þe Pater Noster. For þerinne is contenyd as myche as is nedeful to bodi and soule of eueriche creature. And siþe noo preier auailiþ no but if Crist here it, and oure beleeue techis vs þat Crist heriþ no preiers gladlyer, it is good counseil þat we sett oure moost trust in þe Pater Noster. And charge we not tyme lymytid in certeyne, as mydny3t and kockis crowe, prime or vndorne, ne hou many we schal sey on þe day and þe

147 wilful] wiful   156 a3eyns] a3yns   162 þe] *twice*

ny3t, but loke we be war in al oure dedis þat we be not founden wurchyng þer-a3eyn. And so þoru3 þinkyng, wurching, and biddyng stynt we neuer in preyng þe Pater Noster, if þis reule of Crist schal make vs ay hungri to 3erne aftur ritwisnesse and fle vices, and þis bringiþ inne fastyng fro sinne þoru3 whiche our abbot is plesid. O siþ Iesu our sauyour is þus curteis and wilful to for3yue synne, who schuld be in eny dispeir, þou3 þis synne haue regned longe? Cumme we nowe freely and wilfuly to þe free reule of Iesu Crist, beseeching him þat he wil vouchesaaf to be oure ruly abbot, and of his ri3twisnesse he may not denye vs his mercy. For he biddiþ euery man þat þristiþ cumme to him and drinke wiþouten eny money. And here sculd men arunt feynt penytaunsers, confessours, and oþur prestis þat assoylen for mony. For boþe þe partis aftur þe scentence in Goddis lawe is fouler aftur fy3elid in synne, whiche mater we han openly declared in oþur places. Iche Cristen man loke wele if God wol 3yue him grace to see þis feiþ and to stonde þerwiþ, for þat is a tokyn þat God wole saue him. þise ben not feyned wordis, ne brou3t in f. 157r customes bi þe feend, but lawe 3yuen | of God of heuen, confermed of oure abbot Iesu Crist, bi streit keping here in erþe to 3yue ensaumple to flee þis world þe whiche is ful of synne and so to come to heuen blisse, euer to wone þere wiþouten ende Amen.

RESON Siþ þre witnessis of Cristis word, aftur his lijf þat he had tau3t. Men may witt of þe newe lawe þat Goddis wille was þat hise prestis schulden kepe his lawe as he himsilf did. For now is a pleyn resoun: for Crist seiþ in Markis gospel þat more heed of prestis and worldly lordis schuld be of diuers condiciouns, as it is saumplid of Crist himsilf. '3e witen', seiþ Crist, 'þat þei þat semen to be princes of folke ben lordis to hem; but it schal not be so in 3ou. But whoeuer wil be made more schal be 3oure master, and whoeuer wil be þe furst of 3ou, he schal be seruaunt of alle.' And [þis] prouiþ Crist bi a blessid cause; for mannes sone come not to take seruise, but þat he schuld serue to his breþeren and 3yue his lijf, a3eynby3ing for many. þis word of Crist schuld stir Cristen men to holde þis lawe as Crist did, boþ bi lyif and bi word, as oþur apostles tauten aftur. And þus Petur prince of apostles techiþ prestis in his epistle þat þei schuld feede her flok, purueying for hem not wiþ striuyng but wiþ wille bi fourme of God; ne for loue of foul wynnyng, but wilfully; ne as beyng lordis in

200 *continuing speech by Reson marked by* r *followed by word-sized space before* Siþ
203 Mark 10 *in margin; see note* 208 þis] *added for sense*

clergie, but be ȝe made fourme of folke of mekenesse. And wolde God þat alle decretals were suspendid for þis word, þat prestis knewe it cleerely and kepid it in her lijf. þenne þei schulden wel wit hou þei schulden goostly feede her f[lok], boþe by ensaumple of hooly lijf and by word of Goddis lawe. And þenne þei schulden puruey for hem not bi bodily confermyng, but goostly help to wynne hem heuen; not aftur þe world, but aftur God; not for getyng of foul wynnyng, as is dritt of worldly g`o´odis, but for wille to wynne hem to heuen. Lord, wheþur prelatis coueiten nowe to kepe her flok bi þis entent, and not for worschipes of þe world ne for wynnyng of worldly goodis? Her disposing in her soule and her wurchyng in her fourme techyn | þat f. 157^{v} þei louyn þe world and worldly goodis more þenne soule helþe; and if her entent be þus enfecte, al her lijf mot nedis roote þeraftur. And if þei wole `be´ lordis among clerkis and coueiten herfore suche dignitees, þe feende haþ venymyd furst þe roote and siþ þe frute þat schulde cumme þerof. þenne þei ben not fourme to her flocke in pouert and in mekenesse, but ryche and lusty to þe world, and yuel ensaumple to go fro Crist. In þis lawe schuld prelatis studie, and not in decretals of þe pope but if þei techen bettur Goddis lawe. For ellis it were a foolis chaunge. þis lawe of Crist schuld prestis teche, þat is better þenne alle þise popis. In dede and word preestis schuld it teche, and leue mennes lawis of lesse value.

RESON And ȝitt beleeue of þe gospel telliþ to alle Cristen men hou þei moten nede sue Crist if þei wolun eny tyme be saued. But þe gospel telliþ pleynly hou Crist fro his begynnyng to his deþ was þe porest man of alle, and tauȝt his pouert on many maneres. For Crist seid in Mathews gospel to hem þat sue him for wynnyng: 'Foxes han hoolis and briddis of heuen han nestis in þe eire, but mannes sone haþ not þus wherin to rest his heued.' And so men schuld not þus sue Crist, to gete hem here richessis and lordschip. But many ben marchaundis as foxes, and han moche of worldly goodis. Summe ben lordis as foulis of heuen, and han myche lordschip of þis erþe. But Crist þat is mannes sone haþ not þus to reste on his heued. Also Crist spake in his apostle, whenne Poule ȝaue a rule to Thymoþe, 'Haue we hillynge and foode and be we payȝed of þise'. Here biddiþ not Crist to bischops to take worldly lordschipes to hem. For þenne þei were not

219 flok] folke 223 goodis] o^{1} *suplin., not marked for insertion* 229 be] *suplin., marked for insertion* 238 *continuing speech by Reson marked by* r *followed by word-sized space before* And 241 many] *twice; first canc.* 242 Matt. 8° *in margin; see note* 249 1^{a} Tim. 6° *in margin; see note*

payed of foode and hylyng, but grucchen aftur worldly lordschipe; but þis is aȝeynes Crist and þe state of treue bischops. For þei ben lettid of oþur offises inowe, al if þe world lett hem nouȝt þus. For þus þouȝten þe chosen vessells of God, as Petur and Poule and oþur apostles. f. 158r What spirit schuld make þise foolis so hardy | to coueit more þenne þise bischops þat weren filled of þe Hooly Goost and ledde and tauȝt bi his help? And þus alle þe newe lawe techiþ to coueyt gostly richessis, and to leue al worldly richessis but as myche as nede is. For riȝt as men carien not her schippis forþer fro þe tyme þei ben commen to londe, ne maken her sc[h]ipp heuyer in þe watre þenne it may bere hem vp, so Cristen men schulden do wiþ goodis þat þei muten leue in þe hour of deþ.

GABBYNG I haue herd þee to nowe hou þou hast ratelid out many skilis. But here a whyle þe toþur part, boþe in answers and in resons. We graunte þee wele þat in Cristis tyme was nede prestis to lyue in pouert. For prestis in þe oold lawe weren riche, and þerwiþ to myche foolis. But whenne Crist had swaged þis synne, and hooly churche was fully growen, þenne schulden prestis be riche men as þei were worþi for her state. For to þis acordiþ lordis graunte and many lawes of þe pope.

RESON We may not feyne in þis mater, but speke truþe þat may be groundid on domesdaye whenne Crist schal come þere schal we alle answere him. And so we knowe not bi reson wheþir prestis of þe oold lawe or prestis þat nowe ben dreynte in g`o´odes weren in more synne aȝeynes truþe, for boþe synneden aȝeyns reson. Þe furst slowen þe manhode of Crist. Þe secounde wrouȝten aȝeyne þe godhed, and haden miche more worldly lordschip and ricches to her state þenne prestis before Cristis birþe. And siþ þei feel more kyndenesse þer of Crist, `it´ semeþ þat þei ben more vnkynde to do aȝeynes his lawe aftur taking of so gret kyndenesse. And as anentis turnyng aȝeyne to spuynge, as prestis diden in þe oold lawe, it semeþ algatis more synne nowe þen was in prestis of þe oolde lawe. And þis lawe þat Crist ȝaue was not ȝyuen for a schort tyme, but for tyme wiþouten end aftur domesday in blisse. For as men in state of innocentis schulden haue had no siche lorschipes neiþur siche poscessioun, so it schal be aftur

261 schipp] sclipp 264 *beginning of Gabbyng's speech marked by* l *followed by word-sized space before* I 272 *beginning of Reson's speech marked by* r *followed by word-sized space before* We 275 goodes] o[1] *suplin., marked for insertion* 280 it] *suplin., marked for insertion*

domesdaye. | In blisse men han none siche lordschip, as Crist had not, f. 158v ne hise apostlis. And siþ þe world in his elde is more erþely and coueitouse, and þe fend tempteþ fastre men to brynge hem into couetyse, it semiþ þat prestis were more nedid nowe to hold þis lawe þat Crist haþ ȝeuen. And þus þe fend ouȝt to schame to seie þat Cristis lawe schal last but schort tyme, as aboute þre hundrid ȝer, and an antecristis lawe for euermore. Ȝif autorite be souȝt, we han more autorite bi Crist þat is boþe God and man þen antecrist bi ony man. If þat resoun be chargid here, certis þe law þat Crist haþ ȝeuen acordiþ more to state of blisse and to state of innocens and makiþ men to sauer heuenly þingis and to leue foule erþely þingis. And as anentis þe graunte of lordis, it is seid oft þat þe feend disceyued hem and made hem to do aȝeyns þe ordynaunce of Crist. And siþen bileeue nediþ vs to graunt þat Crist is heiȝest lord, we schulden bi scyle acorde to Crist and crie him mercy of oure trespassis. For Crist is oure cheef lord þat mute ȝyue leue if þe graunt be ouȝt. And here schul men arunte þe feend þat stiriþ men to last in þis erroure, for he wold stire men to þis synne til þei be endurid as he is. And as anentis þe popis lawe, it is nouȝt but if þat God conferme it. And so reson wiþ Goddis lawe schuld oonly be acceptid here.

GABBYNG Hit semiþ a presumpcioun þat men schulden telle siche nouelrie. But oolde custome of many seyntis schulden be holden as Goddis lawe, siþ a þousand men wolen witnesse aȝeins a fewe eritikis.

RESON þese wordis ben not of resoun but `of´ chidyng wiþoute witt. And þerfore schulden men mekely, clerly, and softly sey to hem, 'It is seid oft tyme þat we coueyten not þat men trowe vs but if we grounden vs in þe beleeue or in reson of Goddis lawe; and þen beleeuen men vs not for þat we seyne þat þing, but for þat God seiþ it. And woo is him þat þenne trowiþ it not.' And it nys no presumpcion | to telle þis truþe in his fourme, for neiþer men done þis for pride, ne f. 159r for couetise of worldly goodis, but for loue of truþe of God and for worschip of his lawe. And þis lawe haþ longe slepte for cowardise of worldly prestis. And al if God waken it nowe, it is not newe, but in mannys knowyng. And as anentis many seyntis þat ben canonysid of þe pope þat helden boþ in lijf and word þat þis dowyng was nedeful,

307 *beginning of Gabbyng's speech marked by* l *followed by word-sized space before* Hit
311 *beginning of Reson's speech marked by* r *followed by word-sized space before* þese of^{2}] *suplin., marked for insertion*

here is a poynt of falshed þat begyleþ many men: þat if þe pope seye eny þing, and witnesse hit bi hise bullis, þenne men schulden trow it as bileue. But God forbede þat it were so, for þenne þe pope were neuer begiled in siche dedis for coueitise, but made oft a newe beleeue. And so he myȝt chaunge oft þe oolde beleue. And if two popis diffyneden contraries, God mote falle to hem boþe. But God forbede þat Cristen men trowe in siche heresyes. If resoun proue, or hooly writt, þat eny siche þing be soþe, assente þerto for loue of truþe. And ellis dwelle beneþe beleue: neiþer a man mot beleeue þis, ne beleeue þat þis is fals, but trowe it not wiþouten skil þat sculd meue men to trowe it. Men heren many seche talis, and men þat wolen may trowe hem. But it is a grete foly to trowe hem to lyȝtly. For truþe of man is litle inouȝ to be prented wiþ Goddis lawe. Whi schuld man made to mannes ymage charge his soule wiþ siche vncerteyne þinge? Man may haue opynyoun more or lesse bi opyn euydensis; but be he war þat þis turne not into beleeue but if Goddis lawe teche it. And as [anentis] witnesse of myche peple, þis is a skil of þe fend, siþ Salamon seiþ þat þe noumbre of foolis is wiþouten ende, and þise resoun had non ende but to proue þat þese two prestis þat dampneden Suzanne for feyned synne dampneden wele and lawfuly, and þat foure hundreþ of prestis of Bale witnessid wele aȝeyne Helye. And as anentis [heresye] þat is putt on seche men, þei schulden lerne of Cristis paciens, hou he was ledde oft to be stoned as blasfeme and heritykе,
f. 159v and at | þe last deed. Bi þis colour acorde a man wiþ Goddis lawe, and arme hym wiþ paciens and charite, and put he mekely in Goddis hond his lijf for þe loue of truþe.

GABBYNG þou spekist aȝeyn þe courte of Rome, and so aȝeyns Crist and his lawe. For if men schuld not trowe þat þat is seide in hooly writt, men schuld not trowe þat þat þe pope seiþ in hise bullis, ne many lettris of true men. But who schuld þenne trowe his broþur bi wordis þat he spake to hym?

RESON þou farest as þe fend did, temptyng Eue oure furst modre. He asseyed freiltee of þe womman, and whenne he fonde hir feynte in feiþ, he made to hir an opyn gabbyng and þus he disceyued

330 assente] and assente 339 anentis] *added for sense* 339–40 Eccl. I *in margin*; *see note* 345 heresye] Helye *probably an inadvertent repetition of* Helye *in the previous sentence*; *emended for sense and by comparison with* *Wyclif*'s *Dialogus* 22/4–10 349 *beginning of Gabbyng*'s *speech marked by* l *followed by word-sized space before* þou 354 *beginning of Reson*'s *speech marked by* r *followed by word-sized space before* þou

mankynde. Þou vndurstondest not hou þer ben foure answeris to spechis. Summe wordes men graunten, for þei witen þat it is soþe before God, as ben poyntis of beleeue and oþur treuþis þat we seene. Summe wordis men denyen, for þei witen þat þei ben false, as ben wordis contrarie to truþe þat we han grauntid for þe first truþe. Þer ben on þe þrid maner summe wordis þat we douten wheþer þei ben soþe or false for contrarie euydens þat we han. But þere ben on þe fourt maner summe wordis þat we supposen to be soþe or ellis false aftur þe euydens þat we han. As, I haue herd of a prelate moche truþe and Goddis werkis. I suppose þat he is a good preest and Goddis childe. But ȝitt I beleeue not þis. For I beleeue not ȝitt of my silf þat I schal come to blisse. But I hope þis surely, and of oþur men I suppose. Summe I suppose schal be dampned, for her wickud lijf þat I knowe; and of oþur I suppose þat þei schulun be saued, for her good lijf. And ȝitt I beleeue neiþur of þise, for if God wole þei may falle or fayle. But beleeue is so certeyne þat it may not fayle on no maner. Bi þis may Cristen men see and answere to wordes feyned aȝeynes truþe. A man may wele and medefuly speke aȝeyns þe courte of Rome if he wit wele þat it synneþ aȝeyns Goddis lawe and harmeþ his churche. And þus he schuld do bi charite for loue of þe churche— | in charite þat, as f. 160r
seynt Jame seiþ, heliþ þe multitude of synnes, witouten wiche charite neyþer man ne womman may plese God. And þanne Crist wil seie to hem on his left side: 'Departe fro me, ȝe cursud folc, into euerlasting peyne of helle þat is bifor ordeynid to þe deuel and his aungels and to alle þat kepid not myn hestis nor diden not þe seuen warkes of mercy after þe fourme of Godis law, neiþer bodily ne gostly.' Man if þu wilt do þeis dedis seuen þu schalt haue þe blis of heuen, etc. Amen.

357 *the four answers that follow are numbered* 1, 2, 3, 4 *in margin* 383 *after blank half-line, tract on seven works of mercy immediately follows, with no indication that a new text has begun*

DIALOGUE BETWEEN A CLERK AND A KNIGHT

Durham, University Library MS Cosin V.III.6

A Kniȝt of þe kinges of Yngeland and a Clerk of Yngland þat was late comen fro þe courte were togider in a plase, so þat þe Clerk bigan to speke of þe pope, and in maner repreued þe Kniȝt, and said,

CLERK I haue grete wonder, he said, þat þe kinge and som of his counseil and of his kniȝtes and oþer men of þe temperalte þat schuld be gouerned bi holi chirche, as bi þe pope and bi bihsschopes and bi þe clergy, melleþ þaim of men of holi chirch and of þair godes in mani maners aȝaynes Goddes lawe and aȝaines holi chirch. For þer ne schuld no man mell o þe pope ne o þe clergi. For þai bene abouen all men bi power ȝeuen to þaim bi Godd himself, als holi writt bereþ wittnes, and þe law canone also.

KNIGHT Peter! sir, said þe Kniȝt, þou spekes of a mater þat clerkes han oft moued amonge þe comone pupel, and þe pepel haþ oft bene and es in a were and in dout þerof. And I miself haue oft wondrid þat þe pope and þe clergi haþe taken vpon hem to supplant þe kinge þat es lorde of his land, and all daie bene about more and more to abrege and lessen his power and his lordschip, which as me þink schuld no man o þis half God haue to done wiþ, ne mell him þerof. Naþeles, bicause þat I am a litil lettrid and vnderstonde somdele holi writt, I drede me þat I miȝt trist to mich to myne own witt in þis matere, and so offend and gilt to God. And þou ert a man of holi chirch, a preste, and semes a clerk connynge of clergi: I wold gladlich lerne of þe. Bot it es oft sene þat moni prestes and clerkes þat beth gretelich auaunsid gone wele araied and wele fororrid, as þou dos, þat bene no connynge men of clergie ne of resoune. And þerfor,

1 A] *space left for three-line decorated capital* 7 þair] *in margin, 17th-c. hand*: The popish Clergye thinke that kings may not medle with them. 11 also] *end of speech marked by partial blank line, two curved pen strokes descending to right (similarly for all following speeches unless otherwise noted)* 11 Peter!] *beginning of speech marked by slightly enlarged and ornamented majuscule letter as well as symbol in margin (similarly for following speeches, with or without symbol, unless noted)* 14 miself] *in margin, 17th-c. hand*: The pope and his Clergye would supplant kinges.

sir, I prai þe tell me what degre of scole þou has, þat I mow knowe wheþer þou be abil of connynge to teche me in þis matere þat I am in dout.

CLERK Sir, said þe Clerk, bicause þat I se þou has desyre to lere, I am riȝt glad to tell þe þat þou askist, for all be I vnworþi. I am a doctor of decreeȝe and haue dwellid longe tyme in þe courte of Rome and bene in office wiþ þe pope.

KNIGHT In gode faiþ, said þe Kniȝt, I am wele paied, for I hope to be wele taȝt bi þe of þat matere þat we haue | spoken of. f. 6^{v} Neuerþeles, I had hopid þat þou haddest bene a maistere o diuinite connynge of Goddes lawe, for þan þou woldist haue said þe soþe and bene noȝt so fauorabil to þe pope as I suppose þou wolt be now, for þou art a doctor of his lawe. Naþeles, tell me and teche me als wele als þou canst, for I mene to mayntene þe kinge and his powere in als miche as I can, bi resone and none oþer wise. Bot I drede me þat þow will be wroþe, for it es þe maner of clerkes o decrees, als þou art, for to be riȝt vnpacient when þai bene answered be resoune oþerwise þan þai wold be. And þerfore I praie þe at our beginnynge, kepe wele paciens in oure forþ goynge, for þan schalltow þe better tech and I þe better lerne.

CLERK Sir Kniȝt, þou saist wele, and þerfor ȝeue þou will þiself be pacient, I hope I schall schewe þe openliche þat þe pope and þe clergi han siche powere þat it mai noȝt be wiþsaid bi no resoune. For þow wost wele, and all Cristen men aȝt to wit, þat þe pope es Cristes vikere here on erþ, and his powere es oneliche of God, ȝeuen to him boþe bi þe olde lawe and bi þe newe lawe. And bi þe emperoures law, Moyses was he[u]ed and leder of Goddes folk in þe olde lawe, and was figure o þe pope in þe newe lawe. And to him God ȝaue grete power in ledinge of þe folk, and to him he toke his ten comaundmentes þat þe pepil schuld be led bi. Also, God gafe to Jeremie þe prophete grete power, and bi him also es vnderstonde þe pope. 'Lo', said God to him, 'I haue ȝeuen mi wordes in þi mouþe. I haue ordayned and made þe abouen kingdomes and aboue þe folk to destroy and betene doune and to make edificacione and sett plantes'. So þat þou miȝt wele se, sir Kniȝt,

35 maistere] *extends into right margin* 44 lerne] *extends into right margin*
50 Moyses] *in margin, scribal hand*: Deut^{o} 5to 51 heued] heyed and^{2}] *in margin, 17th-c. hand*: See here the same places of scripture and argumentes abused in elder times for the Pope as nowe: so threedbare and old nowe are the shifts devised to vpholde his pride. Now, as good evidences and argumentes the elder the better, so shiftes and fallacyes the elder the worse. And that these be no better the answere will declare.

þat þis grete powers were ȝeuen to no kinges, ne to none emperoure, bot to þe pope, þat he schulld be souerayne and teche forþe and comaund to be kept in all þe world. Also, oure lord Iesu Crist, when he was commen here on erd, he ȝaue and ordained a newe testament and newe lawe, noȝt in vndoynge o þe olde lawe, and made saynt Peter heued þerof and souerayne, as þe gospell bereþ witnes. And said to him þus: 'To þe I schall ȝeue þe kaies o þe kingdome of heuene, and all þat þou bindest vpon erde it schall be bounden in heuen, and all þat þou vnbyndest in erde schall be vnbounden in heuene.' Lo, sir, þou miȝt se þat þe powere þat was grauntid to þe pope in þe olde law | f. 8r ne es noȝt chaungid bot openliche declared in þe newe lawe. Wherfor men mow know openlich þat þe pope es abouen all maner men. And þerfor it es wonder þat þe kinge or þe emperoure dar wiþstonde him or mell of him or of his clergie which þat schuld be vnder þe pope and vnder no man elles, as it es openlich schewid tofore.

KNIGHT Sir Clerk, said þe Kniȝt, þan þou hast wele said. And þerfore I praie þe þat þou take mi wordes pacientliche, for I mene wiþ all mi hert to saie noþinge aȝaynes þe bileue of holi chirche ne aȝeynes þe pope ne his skilfull power, bot wiþ all mi connynge mayntene þe pope and his skillfull powere, for þat es noȝt aȝeynes oure kinges power. And þerfor in his name, þat aȝaines kynde gaue miȝt to an asse, to speke and reprefe and vndernym his maister þat satt vpon him and vnriȝtfullich bett and prikid him wiþ his spores, for he ne wold noȝt bere his maister ne folowe his will aȝaynes Goddes will, I will speke and answere þe. Tristinge to God þat he will als wele ȝeue me miȝt and grace, to speke and wiþstonde þe vnriȝtfull betinge and prikkynge þat we suffer of þe pope and of þe clergi þat sitteþ vpon vs, for we ne will noȝt folow her will aȝeynes Goddes will, als he ȝaue to þe asse þat was an vnskilfull beste. And þerfore as to þat þat þou hast said, þat be þat miȝt and power þat God gaf to Moyses and to Jeremye in þe olde lawe es figured and betokned þe pope miȝt and his powere, in gode faiþ þou saist soþe. Loke þan wheþere þat power streche to temperalte or to spiritualte. And as it semeþ, and soþe it es, þat it ne streccheþ noȝt bot all oneli to spiritualte. And to no maner lordschip o þe world, bot all to be Goddes seruauntes, to dele þe sacramentes of

69 newe] *in margin, 17th-c. hand*: Popishe Clergye be not vnder kings but onely the Pope: See how longe they have labored to bringe this to passe. 81 wiþ] *in margin, 17th-c. hand*: Note well here how the best subiect to as⟨.⟩ is also the best subiect to his prince. 90 wheþere] *in margin, 17th-c. hand*: See how the temporaltye have of olde complayned that they have beene vniustly oppressed and vexed by the Pope and his courses.

holi chirche and techen and prechen to þe pupil, ȝeuynge and delinge seuen dedes of merci to Goddes pupil to help and helþ of mannes soule. As it es openlich schewid in þat þat he said to Moyses, when he bitoke him þe ten commaundmentes and bad him teche hem and tell hem forþe to Goddes pepil. Also bi þat þat God said to Jeremye, þat he schuld distroye and edifie and plante, es schewed þat he schuld distroye vices and plante gode vertues. For þat es þe office of þe pope and of all oþer prelates, to distroye bi gode liuynge and soþe prechinge vices and synnes, and plante vertues and gode liuinge. | And f. 8^{v} touchinge þat Criste ȝaue to Peter power to bynde and vnbynde, it es also to vnderstonde to bynde man be waye o schrift, to do penaunce for his synne and will to synne no more. And ȝeue a man wold in no maner amend him of his synne, þat he schuld bynde him bi corsynge, and elles noȝt. Bot now it es oþerwise: a man schall be for he will noȝt come to hem atte first somounynge, or for he wold noȝt paie þat þat þai wold aske him. For ȝeue he will paye a certaine bi ȝere, he schall be atte large to do and vse his synne longe ynoȝe. Also, þai schuld vnbynde a man, þat es to say, when a man es sori for his synn and es schriuen þerof þan þai schuld assoile him bi þair powere þat þai haue of God. Bot now it es sene þat men weneþ þat þai be assoyled when þai haue offrid at oni place þer pardoune es grauntid to. And ȝit in soþenes no pardoun mai auaile bot a man be sori for his synne and in will neuer to syn more. For þat was þe penaunce and absolucioune þat God ȝaue to Mari Mawdelayne, and to oþer þat þe gospell spekeþ of. And saynt Poule saiþ, spekinge to men of holi chirch, 'ȝe schuld be' he saiþ 'Goddes ministers, and dispendores of his godes in gode administracione'. And Crist himself in þe gospell of saynt Mathewe and in þe gospel of saynt Luke forbet to all prestes all maner lordschip, and said þat þai schuld be seruauntes and ministres to Goddes pepel in spiritualte. Herebi ȝe mow se þan þat ȝe ne haue no power of God, bi þe olde lawe ne be þe new lawe, to no maner worldlich þinge, bot all to gosteli þinge.

CLERK Ȝis, parde, sir, said þe Clerk. How it be of þe power ȝeuen bi God, þe emperoure Constantyne ȝaue to saynt Siluester when he

102 liuinge] *word spills into margin* And] *in margin, 17th-c. hand*: a true exposition of those places of scripture abused by the pope and his vassails to maintane his proude primacye 114 es] *in margin, 17th-c. hand*: See the abuse of popishe confession and excomunication in those elder times. 118 And] *in margin, scribal hand*: Cor' q^{to} 125 þinge] *speech runs to end of line; usual blank space and pen strokes missing* 126 Ȝis] *slightly enlarged initial majuscule is only marker of beginning of speech* 127 bi] *in margin, 17th-c. hand*: The vaine allegation of Constantines donation

was pope, and to his successores efter him, half his empyre, wiþ all þe worschip and lordschip þat longeþ þerto, as it es wele knawen to hem þat han sene or red þe charter þerof. þerbi ȝe mowe witt þat þe pope haþ grete and mich lordschip `ouer´ þe emperoure himself, and oure all oþer kinges and all Cristen men.

KNIGHT Sir Clerk, said þe Kniȝt þan, me wondreþ gretelich þat þou miȝt for schame alege for þe pope þat his lordschip schuld come of þe emperoure. For all þe lordschip he schuld haue schuld come of God, be þin awen tale. And parde, as it es openlich schewid tofore, þe f. 10r pope nes | noȝt abile to take none siche lordschip vpon him, bot all as Goddes minister in spiritualte. And þof it were so þat he miȝt and were able to haue sich lordschip, ȝit it semeþ bi all þe wordes of þe charter þat Constantyne ȝaue to saint Siluester þat he ne ment neuer þat þe pope schuld haue temperale lordschip. Bot in worschip of God þat had helid him of his meselrie, he ȝaue him þat to liue bi honestliche, and chargid him þat he schuld be euer after a gode mene for him to God, wenynge to haue done grete worschip to God bi þat gift. Naþeles it was venyme broȝt into holi chirche, as an aungel said þat self daie: 'Venyme', he said, 'es todaie sched in Goddes chirche.' And þof þat it were so þat þe pope had sich lordschip bi þe emperours ȝeft, ȝet ne had he no ferþer lordschip þan þe emperoure powere strecheþe. And parde þan schuld he haue no power ne no lordschip in Yngeland. For Yngland was neuer soget to þe emperoure, bot euer it haþ bene led bi himself and vsed his owen lawes, and no man haþe bene abouen him in temperalte. Wherfor, sir, siþen þe popes powere es all ȝeuene bi God in spiritualte, as it es openli schewed be þin owne allegeaunce, it es wonder þat þe pope and þe clergi holdeþ hem noȝt paied wiþ his power, bot aȝaine Goddes will and moni lawes of diuers popes es about to supplant and benyme oure kinge real power þat es ȝeuene to him be God himself. For ȝef þe kinge wold benym þe pope or þe clergie oni maner power þat he haþe or aȝt to haue bi þe gift of God, ȝe wold sai þat he were a tyraunt. And þat semeþ wele, for as it es said of clerkes þat haue bene at þe courte o Rome, þe cardinales clepes þe pope a tyraunt when he wiþstondes somdele of her will þat es wrongfull aȝeynes goddes will. And naþeles it were wele worþi þat men clepid hem tyrauntes when þai desire and

131 ouer] *corr. by canc. from* of; ouer *marked for insertion from margin* 133 Sir] *in margin, 17th-c. hand*: The popes power proved not to be of god 141 schuld] *in margin, 17th-c. hand*: Hodie venenum irropsit in Ecclysiam 149 powere] *in margin, 17th-c. hand*: nota Englande never subiect to any other prince 163 when þai] when þai/when þai; *first canc.*

be maistri bene about to abrege or to sopplaunt þe kinge of ony poynte of his reale power, which es ȝeuen to him bi God himself, as it es writen in þe first boke of kinges, and as it es writen in þe decreeȝ.

CLERK Me þink, said þe Clerk þan, þat ȝe ne holde noȝt of þe popes power ne of þe clergie, bot as it semeþe, ȝe wold be all aboue þe clergie and holi chirch. And parde, ȝe | witen wele þat þe pope es f. 10v
Goddes vikere here on erþe, and es heued of all Cristen men, as I haue schewed þe here openliche, bi þe olde lawe and bi þe newe lawe also. And moni gode men of holi chirch haue bene payntes, and bene saintes in heuene, boþe popes and bihsschopes and oþer gode prestes; and all þai in her liues vsid her power þat God had ȝeuen hem. And þat tyme þe kinge and þe lordes weren in prosperite, and þe comone pepel also, more þan þai han bene now moni daie, and was bicause þat þan was holi chirch noȝt so born doune, and her power wiþstonde, as it has bene now longe tyme. Wherfor in certayne þer schall neuer be gode pes amonge þe pepel to holi chirche be gouerned as it schuld be, to Goddes worschip, and peysibilliche mowe vse þe power þat God haþ ȝeuen þerto.

KNIGHT In gode faiþ, said þe Kniȝt þan, it es noȝt all soþe þat þou saist. For in certaine, I wote wele þat þe kinge and his counsel and þe lordes and þe comone pepill also hold riȝt miche of þe popes power, and wittnessen wele þat he es heued of all holi chirch and Goddes viker. And þat moni gode men of holi chirch vsing her power and her offices habbeþ and beþ sayntes in heuen, and þat was whiles þai vsid wele and trewliche her powere, and did her offices to God ward and to þe pupel in spiritualte, and ne mellid noȝt wiþ þe world. And þat tyme þe kinge and þe lordes vsed her power in temperalte as God had ordayned, wiþouten lettinge of þe clergie. And þo was þe kinge and þe lordes and þe comone pepil in prosperite, for eueri man held him payed wiþ his state. And þo þai did to holi chirch all þat þai aȝt to done, and þe clergi held hem paied wiþ her state and diden to þe pepel þat þai aȝt to done. Bot siþen þat clergie was so greteli dowid and englaymed with temperall possessions, þai bene so fallen in couetise to haue more and more þan þai haue. Now þe þrid dele o þe land es in her handes, and bene waxen worldliche lordes þat þe

166 writen] *in margin, scribal hand*: reg' ?6' 2a ex/q 170 heued] *in margin, 17th-c. hand*: See what an old cavill it is to complaine that the present times are evill and the former better. 189 wiþ] *in margin, 17th-c. hand*: note Against the exorbitant riches and power of the Romishe Clergye 191 clergie] *the following line of text is canc.*: and moni gode men of holi chirch haue bene sayntes and bene *note*: *repeats with same spellings line 172 above*

comone popil es greteli anentisid þerbi. So ferforþ þat when þe kinge had nede to be holpen of his popel of taxes and oþer tallyages, þai bene no3t of mi3t to help þe kinge. And þe clergi saiþ þat all þat þai haue es 3euen to holi chirche, and þerfor þe temperalte ne haþe no3t to done wiþ hem. And so bi coloure of holi chirche, þai þat ne schuld haue no possessiones bot in almess and vnder þe gouernaile of þe kynge, boþe her bodies and her godes, þai blyndeþ þe | f. 12r kynge wiþ a feyned pite, and all þe temperalte, and sayne þat holi chirch schuld be fre from all worldlich power. And þerof þai sayen soþe. Bot þai dissaiue þe pepel in þat þat þai beren hem on hand þat þai done a3aines holi chirch when þai wiþstonde þe clergi in wronges þat þai wold do, oþerwise þan þair power streccheþ. And 3it naþeles 3ef þe kinge were wele enfourmed, he schuld wele witt þat he mi3t no more help holi chirch þan to wiþstonde þe clergie when þai take vpon hem worldliche doynges and worldlich lordschip. For þat es forboden hem be Crist himself in þe gospell in dyuers places, and be saint Peter and bi saint Poule in diuers plases, and in þe bibel and bi þe popes lawes in decrees and decretales in moni places, so þat in þat maner þai schuld torne agayne to þe first state of pouerte and meke liuynge þat Crist taght his dissipills to liue. And þan were holi chirche as it schuld be. And whoso mayntenеþ hem in ricchesse and in worldliche lordschipes, he distroyes holi chirch in als mikel as in him es. And þerfor schuld euerich a man bi his power, bot principallich þe kinge, take awaie her worldliche godes fro hem, and giue hem to oþer gode men, þat wold serue God and holi chirch þerwiþ in þe maner þat Crist himself ordained. For in gode faiþe, bot 3eue he do so, me þink he ne schall neuer redress holi chirche, ne wele defend it fro antecrist disciples. After þat he es bounden be Goddes lawe, and after þat he schall 3eue straite reknynge how he haþ kept and defendid Cristes chirche þat he haþe take in his bonde to defende and kepe, as it es writen in þe boke of decrees. And herfor it semeþ þat þe pope, in þat þat he es about to lett þe kinge, bi oni wai, þat he ne mai no3t kepe and defend holi chirch as es his charge of God, he ne es no gode gosteliche fader, bot es about to distroie his sone gostelich. And is more perile þan 3eue he slowe or in his faute lete sle an hondreþ men bodeliche. And ri3t so it es of all bihsschopes and oþer clerkes of þis land þat

213 forboden] *in margin, scribal hand*: [iia] [q] 1a si t'on Mt 2[ ]o luc' 21 Pet' 4to cor 4 and q 1a s't in ecc et capitulo sequent' 222 giue] *in margin, 17th-c. hand*: A reproofe of the disorder treason and pride of the Pope and his Clergye as sharpe as if it had bene written in these dayes 229 boke] *illegible reference to canon law in margin*

bene his legemen, þat so lettiþ þe kinge. And namelich freres, þat bene confessoures and prechoures þat schuld in schrift tell and teche þe kinge what his powere es and his charge to God ward, and in predicacions preche and teche þe kinge and þe lordes to kepe and to do wele her office. It semeþ þat þai bene verrai traitors to þair kinge, more þan ȝeue þai slowe þe kinge bodelich. For it es mich more peryle, wiþout | comparisoune, to sle a mannes soule þan his bodie. f. 12v And ȝit as men sayen, sich freres for flaterynge of bihsschopes and oþer clergie, for þai ne schuld noȝt wiþdrawe fro hem her grete giftes of worldlich gode and be putt out of her office of confessioune, conceleþ all sich doynges, and wiþ lesinges and flateringes dessaiueþ þe kinge and oþer lordes, in destruccione and peryle of her own soules and of þe lord als. So ȝiue it be soþe, as it semeþ þat it es, þat þai do so, as tofor es said, God amend it when his will es. Amen.

CLERK A, sir, said þe Clerk, þou goste hard to me. Bot it semeþ þat þou spekest more of will and of maistrie þan bi reson. For it semeþ be þi wordes þat þe pope and þe clergie ne haue no maner power. But þai miȝt haue and kepe þe godes of holi chirche þat es ȝeuen for remedi of mannes sine, and no help of mennes soules. And parde bi þe lawe of holi chirch it es forboden þat no man schuld torn no such godes into no noþer doynge, bot to be dispendid in gode men of holi chirch þat loueþ and dredeþ God. And þerfor sir þou miȝt se what perile it es to take awai or benym men of holi chirche þe godes þat bene ȝeuene to hem to lif bi, to worschip of God and to help of mennes soules.

KNIGHT Sir Clerke, I said þe at our beginnynge þat þe clerkes of þe decrees and of þe popes lawe wolden sone be wroþe when þai had made all þair skilles. And it semeþ now þat it es soþe, for now þou ⟨ne⟩ canst noȝt answere me bi resone, þou berest me on hand þat I ne tell noȝt of þe pope, bot speke all of maistrie wiþouten resoune. And all it es þat for þou nill noȝt assent þat þe clergie misseoccupie and missespend þe godes þat bene ȝeuen in almes to holi chirch; and þat, þorȝe Goddes grace, euery Cristen man schuld help to distroye wiþ all his miȝt. Bot I ne said noȝt þat þe kinge ne none oþer man schuld benyme þe godes of holi chirch fro no gode preste, ne none oþer gode man. But I said þat þo godes schuld be taken awaie fro euyl liuynge

241 comparisoune] *in margin, 17th-c. hand*: The abuse of friars and confessors 248 Amen] *ends line; no other marker of end of speech* 263 ne] *from transcription; original badly smudged and illegible*

prestes, and ȝeuen to oþer þat wolde serue God þerwiþ in gode liuynge. For bi þe popes lawe, no man schuld here a prestes messe þat he wist had a lemman or a woman taken into his howse be wai of syn. | f. 15r Ne no suche preste schuld synge no messe, ne rede no gospell ne no pistel at messe, ne dwell amonge clerkes. And ȝit more, he ne schuld take no parte of holi chirche godes. And bi þe self skill, a preste schuld haue all sich vengeaunce for all dedeli synnes. Or elles ȝe mot sai þat liccherie es gretter dedeli synne þan ony oþer synne. And þat nis noȝt soþe. For it semeþ wele more synne for a preste þat es a parsone and haþe cure of mennes soules to leeue his schepe þat he haþ token of God to kepe—and þat he schall ȝeue hard answere of at þe daye o dome—and go and serue a bihsschope or anoþer lord in temperele office, as to be his steward or his countrollore or clerke of his kicchen or his tresorere or ony oþer seculere office. For þat es forboden bi saint Poule and bi þe popes lawe in mony sondri places, and þe gospell saiþ þat no man mai wele serue Godd and þe world attones. And also resoune scheweþ openlich þat no lord schuld hald ne haue no preste ne clerk þat had cure of mennes soules in no worldli[ch]e office. For ȝeue a lorde bayle had hyred men wiþ his lordes tresore for to wirch in his lordes werk to make a castell or anoþer grete werk, and þan toke þe same werkmen fro his lordes werk and putt hem in his own werk, to grete harme of his lord, were noȝt sich a baile a fals seruaunte? More skilfulli were a worldlich lord a fals seruaunte to God þat had auansid prestes wiþ Goddes tresore—þat es to sai, þe godes of holi chirche—and putt him in Goddes werk to wirche and trauaile in kepinge of Goddes pepel out of þe deueles mouþe, and þa[n] toke sich one fro Goddes seruyse and putte him in his own temperall seruice. And þerfor, whateuer excusacions þat ȝe make in þis mater, ȝe ne mow noȝt bene excusid. For all sich seruys and mellinge wiþ worldlich nedes es forboden to all prestes in diuers places in holi writ and in þe popes lawes, as I said tofore.

CLERK A, leue sir, said þe Clerk, þou hast said moni skilles. And as it semeþ be þi wordes, þe pope and þe clergie schuld be suggetes to

273 lemman] *in margin, scribal hand: illegible reference to canon law* 274 gospell] *in margin, 17th-c. hand*: a reproofe of popishe preists that havinge Cure of souls, do leave them and serve Bishops or other lords 288 worldliche] worldlic⟨*pen stroke apparently to convert first* c *to* h⟩ce 290 werk[1]] *the following line of text is canc.*; *obviously an eyeskip to* werk[2]: and þan toke þe same werkmen fro his lordes werk 296 þan] þai 301 tofore] *in margin, 17th-c. hand*: See here one of the manie foundations and true secrets of Popishe pollicye: as good no pope as to have no temporall power. Answer that if there were no pope there can be no Cherche, no religion, no Christianitye.

all worldli lordes and haue no power our hem, ne of no worldliche gode. Ȝeue þat were soþe, me þink it were als gode þat þer were no pope ne preste as elles, and þan were holi chirch distroyed, and Goddes lawe schuld be forȝeten amonge þe Cristen pepel, and þe bileue | of holi chirche also. Lo, sir Kniȝt, what mischeue schuld fall, f. 15v bot ȝeue þe pope and þe clergie were miȝti bi Goddes power, after þe gospell and þe lawes of holi chirche, to gouerne þe pepil to helþe of soule. And þerfor, sir, be wele war þat þou ne speke no more aȝaines holi chirch. For in gode faiþ it ne was neuer meri siþen þat a borell clerk, þat had lerned a littel to vnderstonde Latyn, schuld mell him of holi writt and of þe decrees and decretalles and þe popes lawe and his power. For þerwiþ ne haue ȝe noȝt to done. And þerfor ȝe ne schuld noȝt mell ȝow of men of holi chirch, bot liuen and kepe ȝoure degre and done als men of holi chirch teche ȝow. For þai be ordained of God to teche and preche þe pupel, as Goddes lawe bereþ wittnes, and als þu hast said þiself þat it schulld be so.

KNIGHT Lo, said þe Kniȝt, how wonderfullich þou answerest to mi spech. Þat þou saist, þat it semeþ þat þe pope and þe clergie schuld be suggetes to all worldlich lordes, in certaine þat es soþe. For þat saint Poule chargeþe ȝou straitliche, and saiþ þat her power es noȝt bot of God. And þerfor do wele and drede hem noȝt, for forto chastise misdoers þai bere þe swerde. And þer þat þou sai[s]t it were als gode þan þat þer were no pope ne preste, Peter! þou saist soþe, ȝeue it were so þat all prestes misleued. But I hope þat schall neuer be. For Criste will kepe allgate som gode prestes to hold vp his chirch, so þat þe bileue of holi chirch schall neuer faile. For Criste himself said to saint Peter, als saint Luke saiþ in his gospell. Also wher þou saist þat þe bileue schuld þan faile, parde sir, þof it were so þat all prestes and þe pope were out of þe bileue, as it neuer schall be ȝif God will, ȝit ne miȝt ne schuld þe bileue neuer faile. For after þat Crist had stabled þe bileue, he said to sainte Peter: 'I haue biden for þe þat þi bileue faile noȝt.' Ȝit þe þre daies þat Cristes bodi was dede and laie in þe sepulcre, all þe bileue of holi chirch failid in all þe apostils and all oþer men, saue onelich in oure ladi saint Mari, and ȝit was scho no preste. Also, þer þou saist þat holi chirche schuld be distroyed bot if þe clergi miȝt vse her power after Goddes lawe to help and helþ of mennes

308 of] *in margin, 17th-c. hand*: Poperye would not that lay men nor ordinary Clarks and preists should be cunninge in the scriptures nor the popes lawe. 323 saiþ] *in margin, scribal hand*: 3º 325 saist] sait 326 were] *in margin, 17th-c. hand*: Christian faith shall holde tho there were no pope. 331 þan] *in margin, scribal hand*: luc' 22º

soules, parde þou woste wele þat I ne said neuer þe contrarie. Bot I f. 17r said þat no preste mai haue no maner worldli | power, bot all spirituele powere, as I haue openli schewid tofore bi mani diuers places in holi writ and in þe popes lawe. And þer as þou saist þat a borell clerk schuld noȝt mell him of þe popes lawes ne of men of holi chirch, I wote wele þat ȝe bene wroþe þerwiþ. For moni of ȝow con litel of Goddes lawe ne of þe popes lawe neiþer, and þerfor ȝe wold þat borell clerkes couþ no more þan ȝe, for þan miȝt blynde Baiard be þe boldest hors in þe cart. And sir, me wondreþ mich of þe þat þou schuldest sai so. For all be it þat þou ne can, or elles fewe of þi degre conne, bot litel of þe gospel wherbi all holi chirch schuld be skill be reulid and gouernid, ȝit þou art a doctore of decrees and of þe popes lawes. And I ne haue bot litile said þat I ne haue schewid als wele be þe popes lawe as be Goddes lawe. It semeþ þan þat ȝe be suspect of all euil doynge þat es reknid and spoken tofor, siþen þat ȝe will noȝt þat ȝoure awne lawe be aleggid aȝayne ȝowe. And parde, as þou woste wele, I ne haue noþinge said in abreggynge of ȝoure gostli powere, bot vndernymmynge of þat, þat ȝe mell ȝow wiþ worldliche doynges and wiþ worliche powere, in lessinge and for to abrege þe kinges power, which I will wiþstonde wiþ all mi hert and all mi connynge. For als me þink, ȝeue ȝe miȝt haue ȝour will wiþouten wiþstondinge, in a schorte tyme ȝe schuld haue supplauntid michel of þe kinges power, a⟨ȝ⟩eines Goddes forbot.

CLERK Parde, sir, said þe Clerk þan, I am þe kinges legeman als wele as þiself, and als loþe me were þat his powere were abreggid of þat him aȝt to haue. Bot wele I wote þat be all lawes, riȝt as þe kinge es lord and souerayne of all temperaltes and temperal gode, riȝt so es þe pope lord and souerayne of spiritualte and spirituale gode and godes of holi chirch. For what gode euer þat es ȝeuen to holi chirche, it es holi and longeþ riȝtfulliche to prestes, as þe popes lawe bereþ wittnes in þe decrees. And þerfor it es wonder þat ȝe will mell ȝow wiþ ony þinge þat es ȝeuen to holi chirche. For all maner sich godes es holi and mai neuer after be torned into worldlich mannes power, as þe lawe of holi chirch bereþ wittnes. |

340 parde] *badly faded 17th-c. comment in margin is just visible, approx. 15 words*
344 noȝt] *in margin, 17th-c. hand*: the great Ignorance of popishe doctors in those dayes
365 Bot] *in margin, 17th-c. hand*: A notable shift to deprive kings of the substance and leave them nothinge but a shadowe of temperall power; but see the answere afterwarde.

KNIGHT Leue sir, I wote wele þat þou art þe kinges legeman and f. 17v aȝtest to maintene him and his reale powere als wele as oni man of his reume, boþ þou and all oþer prestes, bihsschopes, and oþer. Bot it semeþ þat ȝe sai one wiþ ȝour mouþ and anoþer wiþ ȝour hert, and for ȝe wolde be sotilte encroche to ȝou lordschipe of temperale godes. And þat es forboden to all clerkes, as I haue schewid openli tofore. And þat, me þinkeþ, þou scheweþ openliche in þat þat þou saist, þat þe kinge ne haþ no power of no worldlich gode after þat it es ȝeuen to holi chirch. For als þou saist, all [þis es] holi and mai noȝt be put in no temperal mannes possessioun. Lo, how openliche men mow se þat ȝe mene noȝt oneliche to abrege þe kinges powere bot to distroye holli his regalte. For ȝe haue þe þridd parte of þis land in ȝour handes, and ȝit ȝe beþe about to purchase and amortaise euer more and more, so þat ȝeue ȝe had ȝour will, in processe of tyme ȝe schuld haue all þe possessiouns of þis land in ȝour handes. And þan, als ȝe sayne, þe kinge had no more to done þerwiþ. And þan had he lost all his souerainte and gouernaile of his land. For ȝeue he wold þan hold oni land, him most hold it of þe clergie, and so ⟨b⟩e vnder þe soueraynte and þe gouernaile of þe clergie. And þan were he no kinge, bot as kinge in a somer game, or elles as a kinge paintid on a wall. God ȝeue him grace to be war and wiþstonde sich tresoune of þe clergie or it be wers þan it es. Also, ȝeue þat noþinge þat es ones in þe clergie hondes ȝeuen to holi chirche, als þou saist, miȝt neuer be affter in temperall mannes power, ne no temperall man haue power ne lordschip þerof, how schulld þan oni clerk bi him mete or drink, or ony oþer þinge þat him nedede, or sell to oni temperall oni maner gode þat þai had? For no man wold sell hem his gode, ne bigge noȝt of hem for mone, bot he miȝt be maister after of þat mone þat was erst a prestes mone, þat he had solde his gode fore. And also, bot he miȝt be maister of oni gode þat he boȝt of a preste and putt it in worldlich doynge riȝt als him likid. And also in processe of tyme all þe mone of þis land schuld be holi, and no man mell him þerof, bot all be in prestes handes. Lo, sir, sich abusiounes foloweþ of þat þat ȝe ask, oþerwise þan Goddes will es, and aȝaynes Goddes lawe. And ȝit for feynid pite | and coloure of holi chirch, and f. 19r semynge holines, nouþer þe kinge ne pepil wollen ne dar noȝt wiþstonde ȝour priue dissaites till þat þorȝe Goddes grace þai haue gode knowynge of ȝoure corsid malice, þat God graunt be tyme. Amen

376 boþ] *corr. from* bot 377 wiþ[2]] By popishe doctrine and practise the kinge might in a short time lose all his temporall Power and soveraigntye and be onely a kinge in bare name and shadowe. 382 þis es] his *cf lines 368–9; eyeskip* 391 be] *seems to be corr. from* ȝe 393 and] *twice; 2nd canc.* 395 miȝt] *prec. by canc.* b

CLERK Wele, sir Kniȝt, said þe Clerk, I se wele þat ȝe will haue ȝour will, what be maistrie and elles. Wherfor it semeþ þat holi chirch schall be born doune, and so þai þat schuld be soueraynes schull be suggetes, and þai þat schuld be suggetes schull be soueraines. And þerfor I can no forþer, bot God leue and ȝeue grace þat it wele be to Goddes worschip. For als me þinkeþ holi chirche es in poynte to be lost and distroyed.

KNIGHT Ow, sir Clerk, now I se wele þat þou art at þi wittes ende. For be þin own wordes it semeþ þat þou ne canst no resoune ne skill for to defend þi cause. Bot riȝt als Iak Roker or a lewd preste answereþ, riȝt so dostow. For it es þe maner of all sich lewde iauels when þai ne conne no forþer, þan þai concluden all þair mater wiþ 'God leue it wele be and God ȝeue grace to make a gode ende'. And all sich wordes semen holinesse when ȝe mene moste venyme in ȝoure hert. For whoso can oni resoune, he mai wele wit þat I ne haue noȝt said in distruccioune of holi chirch, ne in abreggynge of þe lawes ne þe power þerof. Bot als ferforþ als I mai or can, I haue forþerd and mayntened all þe clergie as mich as Goddes lawe will, in so mich þat me þinkeþ, and so it es, þat men of holi chirch aȝt to be soueraynes ouer all kinges and oþer men in spiritualte. Which soueraynte es a seruis þat þai aȝt to do to þe pepil, als I haue oft said, be Goddes lawe. Þat es to saie, to minister þe sacramentes, to schriue and assoile þe pepil, to prech and teche þe pepil, and ȝeuen hem ensaumpil of gode. But in all þinge þat longeþ to temperalte, þai schuld be suggetes to þe kinge and to oþer lordes temperales. And ȝeue þai wiþstonde þe temperale power, þe kinge and þe lordes temperals schuld chastise hem and constreyne hem. For þerto þai bereþ þe swerd, as it es said tofore be autorite of saynte Poule.

f. 19v CLERK Sir Kniȝt, þou ne takes none hede how Peter said to | Crist when he bad his disciples to sell her cote and bige hem swordes. 'Lord', said Peter, 'here bene two swerdes.' And Criste answerd and said 'þat es ynoȝe', in tokene þat Peter schuld haue boþ þe swerde of temperalte and þe swerde of spiritualte, þat es to mene, boþe spirituale powere and temperal powere, so þat þerbi ȝe mow se þat þe kinge ne haþe no power ouer þe pope ne of þe clergie, bot all schuld be suggetes to him bi þe gospell.

419 preste] *prec. by canc.* pre 432 gode] *single minim follows*; *transcription adds* lif *after* goode 441 Peter] Cri Peter

KNIGHT Saynte Mari! said þe Kniȝt. It es litel wonder þof ȝe ouerlede þe comone lewde pepil wiþ sich fals exsposiciones of holi writt. Parde, þou wost wele þat when þat Crist schuld be take, Peter drowe his swerde for to fiȝt and smote of Malkus here. And onone Crist repreued him and bad him putt vp his swerd, in token þat þe temperale swerde langid noȝt to him, ne to none oþer preste, for to fiȝt ne smyte wiþ no temperall swerd. But þe swerde þat he schuld smyte wiþ schuld be þe swerde of þe goste, þat es Goddes worde, as saynte Poule saiþ. And temperall men schulde chastise men bodelich wiþ temperall power. And þat bitokneþ þat þai bere þe swerde, as saint Poule saiþ. So þat þe pope and þe clergi mai noȝt do bot wiþ þe swerde of gode techinge and prechinge, and þe kinge and oþer lordes schuld constreyne wiþ þe swerde of temperall powere, as þe pope saiþ in his lawe, and es acordinge to þe gospell and to saint Poule boþ. And þerfor, sir Clerk, ȝeu[e] it vp, and late þe kinge and oþer lordes vse her powere in temperalte, and þe pope and þe clergie vse her power in spiritu⟨a⟩lte. For þan schall holi chirch stonde wele boþe in temperalte and in spiritualte, and þan schall þou haue þat þou askist of God when all resoune fayleþ þe, þat es, when þou biddist 'God leue it wele be and God send grace þat þer be a gode ende'. Amen. Finis

460 ȝeue] ȝeu/ 462 spiritualte] a(?) *incomplete*

EXPLANATORY NOTES

DIALOGUE BETWEEN JON AND RICHARD

1–2 Matt. 7: 15 warns that false prophets are wolves in sheep's clothing; 7: 16–20 goes on to describe ways one can recognize them.

9–12 Grosseteste is one of the authorities Wycliffites frequently invoke; they especially approve his defiance of the pope (see JR 943–58 and n.) and cite the resulting difficulties with his canonization as evidence of the unreliability of the Church's designations of sainthood (see e.g. Arnold 467/17). Grosseteste compares with a dead body the member of a religious order who leaves the cloister out of ambition and love of the world, however much that member may cite the pretext of engaging in necessary worldly administration. (Dictum 135: see the online edition of the *Dicta* transcribed from Oxford, Bodleian Library MS Bodley 798 at <http://www.grosseteste.com/cgi-bin/dicta-display.cgi?dictum=135>, accessed 8 Nov. 2005.) However, Grosseteste allows that members of a religious order may leave the cloister in body if they maintain their mind and will within the cloister; Wycliffites never make any such concession. For a comparison of Dictum 135 with its use in Wyclif's *De Civili Dominio* see Loserth, 'Johann von Wiclif und Richard Grosseteste', 31–2.

Wyclif and Wycliffites frequently use the passage: it appears in Latin at the head of the English tract 'Lincolniensis': 'talis est cadaver mortuum de sepulchro egressum pannis funebribus involutum a diabolo inter homines agitatum'(Arnold, 230). It appears in part I of this same manuscript, on f. 20^{r}, just after Wyclif's own *Descriptio Fratris* (see Introduction, p. xx). See also Arnold 60/20–3; Matthew 123/31; and *ALD* 105/2–5, as well as Wyclif, *Sermones*, iv. 270/9–12; *De Civili Dominio*, ii. 19/24–20/7; *Trialogus*, 336/23–338/18; *Supp. Trial.*, 433/28–435/33.

12–16 Very similar brief allegories of the soul as a cloister whose four walls are the four cardinal virtues appear in Wyclif, *Opus Evangelicum*, ii. 221/11–26 and *Book to a Mother*, 120/25–121/20. Comparisons between the soul and a building are common in Latin and vernacular medieval writings: for a wide-ranging study see Whitehead, *Castles of the Mind*. If not drawn directly from Wyclif or *Book to a Mother*, the dialogue's comparison to a cloister could simply have been drawn from the Grosseteste passage the writer is citing (see previous note) but might also have been influenced by the *De Claustro Animae* attributed to Hugh of Folieto, a work cited in the Middle English translation of the Wycliffite reference work the *Rosarium* and until recently attributed to Hugh of St Victor (See *The Middle English Translation of the Rosarium Theologie*, ed. von Nolcken, 79/5 and n.). Hugh's treatise includes an elaborate and detailed comparison between the individual soul and a properly conducted monastery or convent, as well as a section detailing monastic and fraternal abuses to be avoided in a well-run religious house (see *PL* 176: 1018–1184).

17 *sophester* In late medieval Oxford a student who has finished the first stage of his study in arts becomes a *sophista generalis*. (See Fletcher, 'Developments in the Faculty of Arts 1370–1520', 325.) In late medieval vernacular contexts, 'sophester' is typically a pejorative term for someone who brings much technical expertise to bear on matters not susceptible to proof by argument.

29–38 Both monastic and mendicant orders were much concerned with establishing and regulating the habit as a means of establishing and regulating the communal identity and behaviour of their members. This preoccupation may arise from Cassian's *Institutes*, where monastic dress, the topic of the whole of Book 1, is both foundational and symbolic (see *Codex Regularum*, ii. 6–9). Each of the orders of friars attaches symbolic significance to details of their habit such as its colour, its shape, and its component parts. These explanations come in for ridicule in both inter- and anti-fraternal satire; for a more elaborate example and further references see JR 683–719 and n. For an analysis, centred on Dominicans, of visual and written evidence for the perceived significance of fraternal habits, see Warr, 'Religious Habits and Visual Propaganda'. For a survey of late medieval controversies over habits, centred on Carmelites, see Jotischky, *Carmelites and Antiquity*, 45–78.

40–3 Matt. 12: 39, 16: 4; Mark 8: 12 (omits the reference to 'whoredom' or *adultera*); Luke 11: 29.

43–5 For more extensive treatment of the comparison between friars' habits and Christ's changes of clothes see Jon's later elaboration of this point, JR 599–606 and n.

45–6 Bede's *In Pentateuchum Commentarii* develops an extended comparison between lepers and heretics in its commentary on Lev. 13; see *PL* 91: 346–8.

48–9 It is sometimes suggested that friars prey especially on the poor, and particularly on poor women, whereas 'possessioners' (i.e. monks, bishops, and other high-ranking ecclesiasts) prey on the rich. See e.g. *37 Concl.*, 97/2–9, Matthew 14/8–30. But some complaints about clerics in the service of lords do mention friars (see Matthew 449/18–19 'þou mayst se in lordis housis persouns or munkis or chanouns and algatis freris to lede þer meyne', *PPC* 768–74, *Mum and the Sothsegger* 461–5, *Vae oct.* 75/30–76/42). And friars, especially Dominicans, did serve in the households of lords and the king in both temporal and spiritual capacities. On the diplomatic and spiritual service provided by Dominicans especially see Knowles, *Religious*

Orders, i. 166–8: the post of confessor to the king, for example, was held by a Dominican throughout most of the period from the reign of Henry III to that of Richard II, and again during the reigns of Henry V and VI. On service by clerics in Richard II's household in particular see Given-Wilson, *The Royal Household and the King's Affinity*, 175–83. In *Piers Plowman*, Mede's confessor in the king's court is 'coped as a frere' (*PP* B 3.35, see also A 3.34, C 3.38).

49–50 Luke 17: 12.

51 There is an extensive tradition of criticizing monks for dwelling in cities. It was, however, unexceptional for friars to live in cities and towns: in England the convents of Franciscan and Dominican friars were located in cities from the beginning as a matter of course, the Carmelite rule was mitigated to allow city dwelling in 1247, and Austin friars became urban by the late thirteenth century. See Knowles, *Religious Orders*, 131–9, 163–70, 197–9, 200–1, and Lamb, 'Service, Image, and Leadership'. Thus criticism of fraternal dwellings more typically centres on their size and sumptuousness rather than their location.

Scase suggests that in late medieval England the tradition of anti-urban satire merged with contemporary anxieties about lay vagrants, who were censured for living in urban areas and especially for moving from one to another; see Scase, *New Anti-clericalism*, 71–2, 127–9, 144.

54 *bagged* A satirically freighted term: see JR 829–31 and n.

60–1 On the commonplace of monastic satire that a monk out of the cloister is like a fish out of water, see Mann, *Medieval Estates Satire*, 29–31. As was the case for complaints about city dwelling (see JR 51 n.) this satiric topos applies to friars less naturally than to monks, since friars were not cloistered; but similarly it is employed against friars by those who object to the very institution of the fraternal orders. In 'De officio pastorali' (Matthew 449/25–30), the topos is applied to monks, but friars are mentioned as well, as a yet 'more vnkyndly wondir'. Cf. JR 9–12 n.

66 *eiȝte pereles* See JR 70–5 n.

69 *gulardes wordes*: 'words of goliards/buffoons'. Yet 'gulardes' also recalls the gulping after 'gulles' of JR 65, as well as Latin *gula* or 'gluttony'. Cf. *PP* B Prol.139, where goliard activity is similarly linked to gluttony, and gluttony is explicitly connected with intemperate use of language: 'a Goliardeis, a gloton of wordes'.

70–5 Matt. 23: 13–29; Luke 11: 42–56.

The polemic exegetical strategy of transferring Christ's criticisms of the Pharisees to the friars dates back at least to William of St Amour's attacks on the friars in the 1250s. For an introduction to this material and its influence see Szittya, *Antifraternal Tradition*, 11–61. Wyclif and Wycliffites often connect the eight woes to complaints about the contemporary clergy; see

Vae oct. 75–83, as well as Wyclif, 'Exposicio textus Matthei XXIII', 313–53 *passim*, *Opus Evangelicum*, ii. 36/1–14, and *Sermones*, ii. 314/20–322/10.

76 *founded on þe gospel, or ellis vpon reson* That Wycliffites insist on scriptural grounding for their own arguments and those of their opponents has been noted in the past; it is less often remarked that Wycliffites typically pair Scripture with reason, as here, when explaining what grounds they consider authoritative. See Somerset, *Clerical Discourse*, 180–3 for further discussion and examples. See also Ghosh, 'Wycliffite Affiliations'.

89–91 Matt. 6: 25, 28, 31, 34. Cf. *PP* A 8.112–17/B 7.129–35, B 14.29–33a.

99–101 Matt. 23: 6–7, Luke 11: 43 (on taking high chairs).

106 *seculeris* Confusingly, 'seculer' can be used as a noun designating the secular clergy (as opposed to the regular clergy who live according to a particular rule), as an adjective describing or associated with the same group, or on the other hand as an adjective describing or associated with lay persons whose life is not primarily associated with spiritual pursuits. Here the reference is to secular clergy; see the Glossary for the full range of meanings in this and the other dialogues.

107–9 Luke 19: 22. Only this version of the parable of the talents includes the point about self-condemnation. For another version of the parable see Matt. 25: 26.

110–33 Sorrow over one's wasted youth is a well-established literary convention; even the regret for having wished to do well in school (which functions as a kind of backhanded guarantee of the writer's erudition) has a long history, perhaps most familiarly instanced in Augustine's *Confessions*. For the *heu mihi sterilem* topos in Middle English, see *PP* B 1.141/C 1.140, B 5.440/C 7.54.

135 *assentyng to þe contrarye accusiþ Cristen men* See JR 404–6 n.

138–40 Wycliffites often carefully distinguish, as Jon does here, matters that may be taken as belief from matters that may be supposed or hoped to be true, and subjects that may only be discussed in general terms from those that may be referred to particular cases. Here Jon asserts that the matter Richard has raised does not require belief because there is evidence for it neither from Scripture nor from reasoning based in experience (cf. JR 76 n.). Instead it is, in the fullest sense, anecdotal evidence. See the full explanation of this topic in RG 329–38, which contains (adapting Wyclif's Latin) the fullest exposition of the subject I have yet found in any vernacular text. On the unreliability of chronicle evidence cf. Matthew 468/30–3.

145–6 *þer was medelynge goode puple and iuel*: 'good and evil people were mixed together'.

149–50 *þis eschewed Poule as priuey seed of errour* Gal. *passim*; Acts 20: 28–32.

154–69 For similar complaints that the fraternal orders argue among themselves and manufacture lies about which order was founded earliest, see 'On the Council of London', in *Political Poems and Songs Relating to English History*, ed. Wright, i. 262/7–18; *PPC* 32–419; see also Wyclif, *Sermones*, ii. 56/17–25, iii. 126/10–127/6; *Trialogus*, 361/1–362/25; *Pol. Wks.*, i. 24/20–5, 274/5–19. For a sketch of the development of each order's claims for its founding and history, as well as the internal and external pressures that shaped these and the controversies between orders, see Jotischky, *Carmelites and Antiquity*, 106–260 (Carmelites) 261–330 (other orders in comparison with Carmelites). See also JR 29–38 n.

156–7 *aftur þe fende was losed* The notion that Satan was unbound 1,000 years after the crucifixion has its scriptural basis in Rev. 20: 1–7. Satan's unbinding is linked to the advent of the fraternal orders, and also to controversies over private confession and the Eucharist in which friars were involved. See Szittya, *Antifraternal Tradition*, 161–7 for discussion, and for examples see Matthew 48/27–49/2, Arnold 449/10–11, *Vae oct.* 80/230–81/249, as well as Wyclif, *Trialogus*, 249/25–250/3; *Pol. Wks.*, i. 68/13–15; *Sermones*, iii. 279/2–6; *Tractatus de apostasia*, 46/1–16.

170–2 The letters C A I M (the normal late medieval spelling for 'Cain') with a little ingenuity can be made to spell out the first initials of the four orders of friars: Carmelites, Austins, Jacobins (or Dominicans) and Minorites (or Franciscans). See *Mum and the Sothsegger*, 493–4; *PPC* 486, as well as Wyclif, *Trialogus*, 362/13–25; *Sermones*, ii. 85/1–7. On the arguments for disendowment in which this point is usually made, see Aston, '"Caim's Castles"'.

172–5 Cf. Wyclif, *Supp. Trial.* 409/2–3, 'et tempore Innocenti III, sub quo duo ordines fratrum inceperant, apparuerunt duae lunae . . .'. This cryptic reference seems to have more to do with satiric tradition than chronicle evidence, and the two instances vary: for Wyclif, the moons mark the monstrosity of the foundation of the fraternal orders of Francis and Dominic, while here they herald the only temporary disappearance of two of four orders persisting since Cain.

175–8 See pseudo-Chrysostom, *Opus imperfectum*, in *PG* 56: 892 and 894. The dialogue writer may be drawing on another Wycliffite paraphrase of this passage in the *Opus imperfectum* such as that in *Lollard Sermons*, 29/691–30/705, which closely parallels the reference here. Wyclif develops the theme in in *Opus Evangelicum*, ii. 79/9–25, and in *De Ecclesia*, 70/8–71/9; see also *De Potestate Pape*, 148/4–17.

185–6 *þer hede is clouen* The cloven head refers to the Papal Schism of 1378–1417, which began with the election of Urban VI in Rome (where Gregory XI had recently transferred the papal curia from Avignon) and closely subsequent election of Clement VII as a rival pope who returned to Avignon. Allegiance to one or the other pope quickly divided along national lines: England followed Urban, while France followed Clement. The schism ended with the election of Martin V in 1417, but not before the efforts of various general councils to depose or elect popes had briefly increased the total number of popes to three. For further information see Ullman, *The Origins of the Papal Schism*, and Harvey, *Solutions to the Schism*.

191 *wandryng in contres* The tradition of satire against members of religious orders who wander, or gyrovagues, goes back to the *Benedictine Rule* (in *Codex Regularum*, i. 114–36: see 115–16). On this tradition and its adaptation to refer to friars from the thirteenth century onward see Scase, *New Anti-clericalism*, 128–33; Szittya, *Antifraternal Tradition*, 100, 104, 185, 228 n. 124.

196 *chirche þat fi3teþ in erþe*, that is, the *ecclesia militans*. The designation of the church on earth as the church militant is commonly part of a classification of the church into categories. The traditional Catholic division would be (1) church militant (on earth), (2) church triumphant (in heaven), and (3) church expectant (in purgatory). For a Wycliffite variant, dividing the church into (1) the 'litil flok' or congregation of the faithful; (2) the material church or church building and people gathered therein, who belong variously to Christ's church and the devil's church; and (3) the devil's church, see the *Lanterne of Li3t*, 22–137.

206 *God in þe erþe* The tendentious claim is that if the pope could dispense the spiritual treasure of heaven as his bestowal of indulgences seems to imply, then he would be God on earth. See Wyclif, 'Exposicio textus Matthei XXIII', 322/34–6, *Supp. Trial.*, 423/15–18.

220–1 *But in Ierusalem semeþ þat als many d[i]ede, and s`p´eciali Crist is hede of al martires*: 'But it seems that as many died in Jerusalem, and especially Christ, who is head of all martyrs.'

238-9 Greeks and Indians are similarly referred to in connection with schism in Wyclif, *Sermones*, iii. 275/8–12. *Mandeville's Travels*, too, pays special attention to Greek and 'Indian' Christians as mirrors for Latin Christendom's reform: for discussion see Higgins, *Writing East*, esp. 79–83, 108.

241-4 If spiritual leaders should be followed only insofar as they follow Christ (as Jon will soon argue; see JR 273–4 and n.), then the most worthy spiritual leader will be whoever follows Christ's example best. Langland's 'lewed vicory' claims on this basis that Piers Plowman would make a better pope than the cardinals' choice: see *PP* B 19/C 21.409–50 For similar arguments see Arnold 250/7–18; *Tractatus de regibus*, 7/6–14; Wyclif's letter to pope Urban, in Latin in *Op. Min.*, 1–2 and in English in Arnold 504–6, and Wyclif, *De ordine Christiano*, 135/29–136/14.

261–2 *Siluester tyme* On Constantine's donation of part of the Roman empire to Sylvester see CK 120–3 n. and Wyclif, *Supp. Trial.*, a work devoted throughout to arguing that the donation should be rescinded and the church returned to a state consistent with Christ's instructions to his apostles.

263 The four doctors are Ambrose, Augustine, Gregory, and Jerome. Gregory was pope 590–604. Wycliffites use these four doctors extensively in their own writings, and on occasion remark that older doctors are more trustworthy than new ones (see e.g. *The Testimony of William Thorpe*, 51/912–13; Wyclif, *Sermones*, i. 376–7, iii. 278; and Hudson, *Premature Reformation*, 274–5, 377–82).

273–4 *seint Ciprian techiþ for a rewle þat men schulden here al only Crist in his membris*: 'Saint Cyprian teaches as a general precept that men should attend only to Christ in [what] his members [enjoin]' translates Cyprian as quoted in the *Decretum*, D. 8 c. 9, where the sense is that we need follow the directives of subsequent leaders only if they are confirmed by what Christ did. Wyclif and Wycliffites frequently say we should follow saints only insofar as they follow Christ. See Matthew 381/12–32, 451/18–3/12, and *37 Concl.*, 47/16–50/13, as well as Wyclif, *Dialogus*, 19/24–21/11; *Sermones*, ii. 15/24–16/6, 33/26–36, iii. 154/6–24, iv: 66/1–15.

282 *supposon* A technical term for Wycliffites: it refers to a mental attitude short of full belief, but based on the assumption that whatever is being supposed is nonetheless a reasonable hypothesis. See RG 357–75 and n. for a detailed explanation. Use of the term in Wycliffite writings is remarkably consistent: see Somerset, *Clerical Discourse*, 205–8 for some examples, and cf. JR 938.

289–90 *as woso tillid forþe a childe for forþe to deþe watur*: 'as if someone enticed a child onward into deep water'.

311 *Crist in his membris* The church as a whole is frequently described as the body of Christ: therefore Christ's 'membris' are members of the church. Describing them in this way heightens the priests' delinquence. See also JR 273–5 and 403.

326–8 The Franciscan Rule's three main precepts, announced in its first sentence, are poverty, chastity, and obedience. For a sense of this Rule's importance elsewhere for Wycliffites see 'The Rule and Testament of St Francis' (Matthew 39–51), a translation of the 1223 Franciscan rule and the appended *Testament* that Francis wrote some time before his death in 1226, together with a Wycliffite or Wycliffite-adapted commentary on how friars fall short of Francis's expectations. See *Codex Regularum*, iii. 22–33 for the 1221 and 1223 Franciscan rules: on versions of the Franciscan rule, and for a translation of the 1223 rule, see Brooke, *The Coming of the Friars*, 33–5, 120–5). In the rules of the other orders these three precepts are not as prominent. The Austin friars and Dominicans based the constitutions of their orders on the Augustinian rule: see *Codex Regularum*, ii. 123–7 or *PL* 32: 1377–84, and for a modern English translation, <http: //ccat.sas.upenn.edu/jod/augustine/ruleaug.html>, accessed 16 March 2006. For the Carmelite *Rule of St Albert*, see *The Rule of St Albert*, ed. and trans. Edwards.

335 Rev. 22: 18–19. On not adding to God's words cf. Matthew 37/6–8, and also Wyclif, *De Veritate Sacre Scripture*, ed. Buddenseig, i. 384/2–385/1, ii. 131/19–23, and Wyclif, *Supp. Trial.*, 429/12–18.

336 *our abbot is þe best* This dialogue seems concerned to elaborate an alternative ecclesiology, as we see elsewhere, in its designation of Christ as bishop and wonderful pope (JR 246–7) and in its many references to Christ's law (JR 133–4, 144, 203, etc.) and to the knights of Christ (JR 202, 207). But this alternative ecclesiology is most elaborately worked out, beginning explicitly here, with a cluster of terms that develop an alternative to the supposed life of perfection available to those following a religious rule. Christ is an abbot (see also JR 366); Christ has his own 'couent' (JR 368), and Christ's order (JR 153, 345) follows Christ's religion (i.e. religious order) (JR 57, 62, 328, etc.) using Christ's rule, the gospels, which is better than any monastic or fraternal rule (JR 329–30, 880). References to Christ's religion, order, and rule are common enough elsewhere in anticlerical lollard writings, but calling Christ an abbot with a convent is more unusual. The terms 'abbot' and 'couent' are used together as part of a similar cluster of terms, and for remarkably similar purposes, in the long interpolation into RG (see RG 108–99 and n., esp. RG 168–97, 168 n.), as well as in *Book to a Mother*, 122–5. The similarity is suggestive. Elsewhere in the online *Corpus of Middle English Prose and Verse* Christ is called an abbot only in two of the *English Wycliffite Sermons*, *EWS* i. sermon 31, 354/94 and *EWS* ii. sermon 87, 188/68, and Christ's 'couent' is the apostles in the Wycliffite 'Tractatus de Pseudo-Freris', Matthew 318/34; there are no similar references anywhere else in the *Corpus*. Wyclif describes Christ as an abbot, though he does not develop the idea (see, e.g., *De Civili Dominio*, ii. 166/2, iii. 5/5, *Trialogus*, 263/3, 364/13).

337–9 Wycliffites consider fraternal rules to be 'clouted' or 'patched' (like their clothing: see 'Rule and Testament', Matthew 41/7–9) because they alter or palliate Christ's rule, the unadulterated gospel. See e.g. Arnold 448/19–32.

353 In Matt. 26: 15–16 Judas asks thirty pieces of silver from the priests for delivering Christ to them; in Matt. 27: 3 he returns the money. See also Mark 14: 10–11, Luke 22: 3–6.

362–3 *Siþen Crist was almiȝthi and þerto al witty was paied of tuelue and on Scarioth*: 'Since Christ who was almighty and also all-knowing was satisfied with twelve (disciples) and one Iscariot'.

397–8 Christ's sharpest criticism of the Pharisees of course appears in the 'eight woes' of Matt. 23: 13–24. See JR 70–5 n.

404–6 1 John 3: 10–15 argues that ill will towards another is tantamount to manslaughter, but does not mention assent. While 'assent' is used here in place of 'consent' (as later at JR 817–20), this is clearly a reference to the Wycliffite theory of consent cited explicitly at JR 990 (see note). See Wyclif, *Sermones*, iv. 312/31–313/10 for similar use of 1 John 3: 15.

428–9 Jer. 2: 13, 18.

434–5 *iuge be þe face and not be þe werkes* John 7: 24. This text is the basis of Fitzralph's influential and widely disseminated sermon the *Defensio Curatorum*, translated into English late in the fourteenth century by John Trevisa. Frequently in Wycliffite writings John 7: 24 is invoked (as it is in Fitzralph's sermon) where lay persons are exhorted to judge some group within the established church; see Matthew 84/20–2, 158/18–20, 291/30–1, 314/4–7; *37 Concl.*, 76/19–20.

439–42 Acts 15: 5–21, Rom. 7: 4–7, Phil. 3, Gal. 4, 5.

444 *seculer men* Here the meaning is probably 'secular priests'; yet the ambiguity about whether these preachers have lay or clerical status (cf. JR 400) may well be deliberate.

450–1 *þe fende haþ founden . . . gamen in þer hode*: 'the devil has made a jest of them' Proverbial: see Whiting G25, *MED* s.v. 'game', 6b.

464–6 Preaching injunctions may be found at Matt. 5: 19, 10, 28: 19; Mark 3: 14, 16: 15–18; Luke 9: 1–6.

472 The comparison of a preacher with a serpent has its basis in Matt. 10: 16: 'Ecce ego mitto vos sicut oves in medio luporum; estote ergo prudentes sicut serpentes et simplices sicut columbae.' For a very similar use see Chaucer, *Pardoner's Prologue*, 6. 412–22. The statute promulgated by William Courtenay on 30 May 1382 introduces this comparison into the earliest stages of the controversy over preaching associated with Wycliffism: those listening to an unlicensed preacher 'statim tanquam serpentem venenum pestiferum emittentem fugiat et euitet sub pena excommunicacionis maioris' (quoted in Forrest, *The Detection of Heresy*, 64 n. 17). Wyclif develops the implications of comparing the wise to serpents in *Sermones*, iv. 340/11–33, but does not mention the spitting of venom. The pseudo-Chrysostom *Opus imperfectum* comes close, mentioning that serpents pour out venom against others and suggesting that this is appropriate behaviour for Christians when they are speaking to non-believers, but that towards their fellow Christians, Christians should behave as doves (*PG* 56: 757/40–63).

496–8 This statement combines different teachings. Christ's two commandments of charity ('for loue of first charite') are to love God and to love one's neighbour as oneself: see FS 201–6 n. For Christ's injunction that we should do as we would be done by ('þat wat we wolde skylfully þat men dide to vs, schulde we do to hem'), see Matt. 7: 12, Luke 6: 31. See also Rev. 2: 4's reference to 'first charite'.

506–7 *Crist begged as þei* If it could be proven that Christ begged even though he was healthy and able to work, then it could be suggested that Christ's begging should be a model for that of mendicants. If on the other hand it could be shown that Christ begged otherwise than a particular order might intend him as a model (without keeping a reserve of money or food in a bag, for example—cf. JR 829–31 n.) or did not beg at all, then that would damage the mendicant claim that their way of life follows Christ's. Hence arguments over whether Christ begged were central to the mendicant's self-justifications, and to the rebuttals of their critics. For a helpful introduction to the whole course of the mendicancy controversy, and its development by Fitzralph in particular, see Dawson, 'Poverty Controversies'. See also Wyclif, *Sermones*, iii. 107/28–114/15.

528–9 For the tradition of satire on the friars' administration of the sacrament of confession see Mann, *Medieval Estates Satire*, 47–9. On the newer arguments see Scase, *New Anti-clericalism*, 16–21, and Szittya, *Antifraternal Tradition*, 124–32, 158–9, 282–6. See Fitzralph, *Defensio Curatorum*, 41–55, Matthew 181–2/15, *PP* B 3. 35–63 (cf. A 3. 34/C 3. 38), B 20/C 22. 309–79, as well as Wyclif, *Op. Min.*, 316/28–319/21. See also below, JR 578–9 n.

531–2 Wycliffite insistence that laying of hands on the head of those being absolved cannot confer grace may allude to Simon Magus's attempt in Acts 8: 18–24 to pay money so that he might obtain grace through a laying on of hands. For other examples see *PPC* 135; *Tractatus de regibus* 19/7–11; Wyclif, *Trialogus*, 331/17–27.

537–8 See Matt. 3: 5–9 (the only gospel to call those coming to see John Pharisees and Sadducees) and Luke 3: 14 (who mentions soldiers).

546–8 *Omnis utriusque sexus*, the twenty-first decree of the Second Lateran Council in 1215, laid down that every man and woman having arrived at the age of discretion must confess once each year to his or her own priest: see X 5. 38. 12. On the effects of this decree in England, see Gibbs and Lang, *Bishops and Reform, 1215–1272*; Boyle, *Pastoral Care*.

556 *glose of decrees* Precise source not traced. The reference is apparently to the *Glossa Ordinaria* on canon law; if not to the gloss on the decretal cited in the previous note, then probably to the glosses on C 33 q 3 in Part II of the *Decretum*, also known as the *Treatise on Penance*. The *Glossa Ordinaria* is incorporated into early printed editions of the *Decretum*, but not into more recent critical editions.

557–60 The term 'general' in association with confession typically refers to the recitation of the 'Confiteor' during Mass. But the reference here seems deliberately vague, in a way that might allow the author to include other informal and non-liturgical kinds of confession, both public or private. In contrast, 'special schrifte . . . limitid to tyme' refers to the private, auricular confession to a priest mandated by *Omnis utriusque sexus* (cf. JR 546–8 n.).

569 *soule* The first letter is incompletely formed, resembling a blotted l with a curved b lobe at the base, or else a blotted o or up-curving s. The final e is elongated. The scribe's uncertainty about the writer's tone and meaning may have contributed to miscopying. But it seems clear that 'we believe' in the validity of absolution only when it conforms to a state of affairs unknown to the priest performing it. The most likely referent for this state of affairs would seem to be the inward state of the person receiving absolution, as above at JR 554-5: hence 'chirche of soule' – an unusual phrase, but in keeping with this dialogue's sustained development of an inward-looking ecclesiology: cf the many repetitions of 'cloister of soul', as well as 'chirche of þer soule', below at JR 747.

574–5 Job 31: 1; cf. *Fyve Wyttes* 4/30–6; Wyclif, *Sermones*, i. 145/33–6.

578–9 It is often wryly noted that friars take interest in only the two most lucrative of sacraments, confessions and burials. See, for example, *Upland series JU* 220–5, *FD* 590–9; Arnold 374/14–375/6, Fitzralph, *Defensio Curatorum* 46/5–26. Burial is not of course a sacrament, but it is one of the seven works of mercy (see RG 381–2 n.), and this satirical pairing of burial with confession may in part emerge from commentaries on the seven works of mercy in which it is shown how friars or other clergy fail to accomplish the duties required of them. For a brief introduction to friars' conflicts with the secular clergy over parochial work, confessions and burials in particular, see Burton, *Monastic and Religious Orders in Britain, 1000–1300*, 126–8. On friars' burial of laymen within their churches see Bruzelius, 'The Dead Come to Town'.

592–4 Jon is mocking Richard's method of argument. On the technical meaning of 'supposed', see JR 138–40 n.

599–606 The gist of the argument here is that the friars' stubborn adherence to one manner of dress does not constitute an imitation of Christ because Christ changed his clothes. Christ's changes of clothing during his trial and crucifixion are recounted in the gospels at Matt. 27: 28–31, 35, 59; Mark 15: 17–20, 24, 46; Luke 23: 34, 53; John 19: 2, 23–4, 40. See also Arnold 389/15–33; Matthew 301/27–302/6; and in addition, Wyclif, *Pol. Wks.*, i. 27/19–28/4. Cf. JR 43–5.

608 *inpossible* During elementary training in logic students would be taught how to determine whether a sentence is capable in any circumstances of being true—is 'possible'—or is 'inpossible'. This determination is far from simple, for whether the semantic content of one or more elements of the sentence describes a state of affairs that can be true is only a starting point: the kind of conjunction or disjunction between the elements of the sentence and the potential for contradiction or contrariety between those elements must also be carefully analysed. The word 'inpossible' therefore associates its speaker with a particular kind of training; it connotes emphatic expert denial. Other vernacular works that exploit the associations of 'inpossible' include Chaucer, *Summoner's Tale* 3.2231, Matthew 126/18–19.

608–9 See JR 29–38 n.

622–3 See JR 683–719 n.

631–3 1 John 3: 15. See JR 404–6 n.

633 *wy schulde not þe place be polute and þe persones take*?: 'why should the place not be desecrated, and the persons apprehended?'. These deliberately vague terms knit together two biblical quotations. 'Place' refers forward to the singular use of 'place' in the quotation from Maccabees given below at JR 638–40, where 'hallow' is chosen as the antonym of 'polute' here, and links that quotation to the 'places', or religious foundations, just mentioned in JR 629 and 630. 'Persones' refers back to JR 404–6, just recalled by 'as sent Jon seeþ'. The suggestion is that since the friars are guilty of spiritual murder, their foundations have been profaned and they should be arrested.

634–5 *þe grete synne let freli be doun*: 'allow great sin to be done without constraint'.

635–6 Matt. 23: 24.

638–40 2 Macc. 5: 19–20; the word the dialogue writer translates as 'hallow' is given in the Vulgate as 'eligit' (which might be more closely translated as 'choose'—as indeed it is in the *Wycliffite Bible*'s 'chees'). See Arnold 487/14–16, where the same verse is cited, similarly translating 'eligit' as 'hallow'.

683–719 Much ingenuity was brought to bear on mocking friars' insistence on wearing of the habit, the symbolic significance they attach to its components, and the claim frequently imputed to them, that the habit has some intrinsic virtue. See, for example, *PPC* 227–30, 243–4, 291–301, and also in the *Upland series JU* 140–3, *FDR* 358–85, and *UR* 193–6, Arnold 372/24–373/19, 382/28–383/3, 389/15–32; Matthew 316/7–15, 352/3–21, and Bodley 806, quoted in H. Leith Spencer, *English Preaching in the Late Middle Ages*, 285; as well as Wyclif, *Pol. Wks.*, i. 26/21–28/4, 35/7–10, *Supp. Trial.*, 435/14–26, *Op. Min.*, 322/11–13. See also JR 29–38, 622–3, 695–6.

685–7 A satirical reference to the Beatitudes, where the kind of jostling sanctimoniousness rehearsed here is condemned: cf. Matt. 5: 5. See also JR 687–9.

687–9 1 Cor. 3: 8, 14; 1 Tim. 5: 17–18.

695–6 The notion that a habit might be able to cover or compensate for the easily discerned differences between ape and man is patently absurd; only slightly more absurd, it is implied, than the notion that a habit might conceal or improve its wearer's vices. The possibility that a habit might make an ape a saint is similarly satirically entertained in *UR* 182. Pseudo-Chrysostom bases a discussion of how heretics may be distinguished from true believers around the ease with which an ape may be distinguished from a man even though it has the same members and imitates the man's behaviour (*Opus imperfectum*, *PG* 56: 736–7); the anti-Wycliffite Roger Dymmok incorporates a large section of this discussion into his explanation of how to tell lollards from genuine priests (*Liber Contra Duodecim Errores et Hereses Lollardorum*, ed. Cronin, 307–8). The writer Wyclif cites as 'Parisiencis', William Peraldus (*c.*1200–71), compares heretics to apes in his *Summae Virtutum ac Vitiorum* (*c.*1236), ii. 264; cf. Wyclif, *Sermones*, i. 364–5.

697–8 3 Kings 3: 16–28.

703 Matt. 16: 16–19.

707 *perfeccioun of þer ordere* A sarcastic reference to religious perfection, or a vow to adhere not only to Christ's precepts, which apply to all, but his counsels of perfection, which apply only to those who make a special vow to adhere to them in addition. The traditional counsels of perfection appear in Matt. 19: 21, where a young man is enjoined to sell all he has and give it to the poor if he wishes to be perfect; and 1 Cor. 7 *passim*, where Paul counsels perfect chastity (advice in keeping with Christ's reference to the eunuchs for the kingdom of heaven in Matt. 19: 12).

733–4 Matt. 26: 61, Mark 14: 58, John 2: 19.

748–9 Christ does not say precisely this anywhere in the gospel, but it may be regarded as a summary and paraphrase of Matt. 6: 5–8, Mark 11: 24–5, Luke 11: 1–13.

752–3 *And þus Jon Baptiste wandred in deserte hadde more preciouse chirches*: 'and thus John the Baptist [while] wandering in the desert had more precious churches'.

752–4 On John's and Solomon's circumstances compare Matt. 3: 4 and Mark 1: 6 with 3 Kings 4.

760 *Dauid confessiþ þat he ros so* Ps. 118: 62.

762–4 References to Christ's prayer appear in the gospels at Matt. 14: 23, 26: 36–44; Mark 1: 35, 6: 46, 14: 32–9; Luke 6: 12, 9: 18–29, 11: 1, 22: 40–6.

777–9 It is a frequent, even pervasive, complaint that friars care more about their own rule than God's. See JR 915–19 n. for another version and references.

792–3 See Matt. 22: 37–40, Deut. 6: 5. Lollards frequently conflate Christ's two commandments or precepts with commandments 1–3 and 4–10 of the Ten Commandments (see Exod. 20: 1–17 and Deut. 5: 6–21), commenting on both together. For the most comprehensive and detailed account of these see Jefferson, 'An Edition of the Ten Commandments Commentary'. Jefferson's analysis responds to earlier work by Kellogg and Talbert, as well as Martin. See also *Lay Folks' Catechism*, 31–63; Arnold 82–92.

807–8 Prov. 3: 12.

810–11 See JR 70–5 n., 397–8 n.

817–20 *lettid by assent*: 'refrained by assenting'. Silence gives consent here, and this is a reference (even if the word 'consent' is not used) to the sixth kind of sinful consent commonly discussed by Wycliffites (see JR 990 and n).

829–31 On friars' 'clouted' rules see JR 337–9 and n. 'Bagged beggarie' is begging using a bag in which surplus money or food can be stored up against future need; it contrasts with the sort of begging where only the minimum required to serve immediate pressing needs is accepted. St Francis had ruled that his friars should not use bags, since that would constitute a kind of possession; thus 'bag-begging' is viewed as an illicit activity in which friars ought not to engage if they are genuine mendicants begging out of need. For the development of arguments over possession and mendicancy on the basis of Christ and his apostles' use of a bag, see Dawson, 'Richard FitzRalph and the Fourteenth-Century Poverty Controversies', 318–29. For the vernacular elaboration of these arguments in late medieval England, see Scase, *New Anti-clericalism*, 137 and n. 64; in addition to her references, see *JU* 275–81, *FD* 727–38. Heyworth's emendation of *FD* 362 to remove a reference to bags should be disregarded. See also JR 54.

836 *and oþer craft* This could roughly mean 'and others leave their craft'; or wives could be sloppily equated with 'other crafts' so that the translation would be 'as lay men leave their wives and (other) professions'; the sense is not much different.

841 That we should love earthly things in God is a late medieval commonplace much used in vernacular devotional writing. Its most important source is Augustine's explanation of how earthly things should be loved in *De Doctrina Christiana* 1.22.20–1, pp. 28–31.

849–50 Medieval commentators typically equate Mary Magdalene with Mary the sister of Martha, and the sisters Mary and Martha are often contrasted as models of the contemplative and active life respectively. See Constable, 'The Interpretation of Mary and Martha'. The most important biblical reference is Luke 10: 39–42. On Mary and Martha see also John 11: 1–45, 12: 1–3: 12: 2 equates Mary sister of Martha with the woman who pours ointment on Christ, mentioned also in Luke 7: 37–8, Matt. 26: 7, Mark 14: 3. See Matthew 189/19–34 for another Wycliffite reference, and see Wyclif, *Sermones*, ii. 147/1–27, iv. 387/23–32.

875 *apis argument* See JR 897 n., 695–6 n.

878–9 *Wat if þe pope or oþer foles approueþ þis doing? þat mot proue þat þise men synned not hereinne*. Dialogue is subsumed into monologue for a moment here as Jon anticipates a possible objection by Richard—yet 'foles' demonstrates that it is still Jon who is speaking.

897 *schame þou for glotouns argument and of apis boþe* Wyclif and his followers frequently label their opponents' arguments as those of gluttons or apes. These are not mere blanket terms of abuse: 'Of Prelates' explains that a glutton's argument proceeds from the fact that a small amount of something is good to the false conclusion that more of it is better, whereas an ape's argument concludes from the resemblance between one object or person and another that the two are in all respects the same and ought to be treated in the same way. (Matthew 96/8–97/22); see also Matthew 412/8–10 (ape) and 454/28–33 (glutton), and also Wyclif, *Pol. Wks*., i. 97/16; *Sermones*, ii. 43–4, 56, 101/5–25, 110/16–18, iii. 274/27–36; 'Exposicio textus Matthei XXIII', 338/30–5. See JR 695–6 n. for another, more general, kind of satire on apes, and JR 69 n. on a different kind of gluttonous speech.

914–15 This is a glancing reference to debates on dominion and common ownership—debates that were particularly pointed in the controversies over mendicancy. While monks renounced private property in favour of common ownership, the mendicant orders wished (initially at any rate) to renounce even common ownership, sparking heated debates over just what relationship friars then had to the goods that they used. For an introduction to these issues and their broader implications see Wood, *Medieval Economic Thought*, 17–41, and, for more detail, Tierney, *The Idea of Natural Rights*.

915–19 This argument disputes the concept of religious perfection (cf. JR 707 n.): God had already ordained the best way of living before the friars came, so injunctions to the best manner of living in the friars' rules are at best superfluous and at worst wrong and therefore misleading. For similar claims see Arnold 513/23–514/10, 444/18–445/10; Matthew 51/15–30, as well as Wyclif, *Pol. Wks*., i. 34/10–16, 26/15–20, 96/16–20; *Sermones*, ii. 101/5–25.

920–1 *þei don seint Austenes reule inprison hem togedere*: 'they make the rule of St Augustine imprison them together'.

921–2 On the Augustinian Rule see JR 326–8 n. The rule stipulates that those who refuse punishment or continue in their sin despite it are to be ejected (see *PL* 32: 1381/47–1382/3).

923–9 Vernacular Wycliffite materials typically take friars as their opponents on the sacrament of the altar—perhaps unsurprisingly, since it was mainly friars who determined against Wyclif at the Blackfriars council in 1382, and friars who wrote against Wyclif's writings. The key point at issue here is what happens to the bread and wine once it is consecrated: friars are accused either of evading this question, or of asserting that only the accidents (or non-essential properties, i.e. roundness, whiteness) of bread and wine remain, while the substance (or essence) of bread and wine is gone (an explanation Wyclif and his followers thought was impossible). For a clear introduction to the background to the issue, see Kenny, *Wyclif*, 80–90, and Catto, 'Wyclif and the Cult of the Eucharist', 97–115. For the Blackfriars council's condemned propositions on the Eucharist, see *FZ* 277–8. For important rebuttals of Wyclif's arguments see William Rymington, *Tractatus*, Oxford, Bodleian Library, MS Bodley 158, ff. 199–217, 188–97, and William Woodford, *72 Quaestiones de sacramento altaris*, Oxford, Bodleian Library, MS Bodley 703, ff. 102–183^{v}. For vernacular parallels to the accusations against friars given here see *Upland series JU* 390–400, *FD* 838–71, *UR* 380–93.

933 *Salusbiri vse* The order of services laid down in the Sarum Missal and other associated service books, including everything that is to be sung and said on all ecclesiastical occasions throughout the year. See *The Sarum Missal*, ed. J. Wickham Legg (Oxford, 1916). This version of the liturgy was widely used throughout most of England by the end of the medieval period; where Wycliffites complain about it, their objection is usually centred on the distraction from biblical study encouraged by the excesses of liturgical reading and performance more generally, rather than on this version in particular. See Matthew 170/8–16, 192/33–5, Arnold 202/17.

943–58 Jon is referring to Grosseteste's famous letter to Innocent IV, in which Grosseteste roundly declares that he 'filialiter et obedienter non obedio, contradico, et rebello' against Innocent in order to preserve his obedience to Christ. The letter is no. 128 in *Roberti Grosseteste quondam episcopi Lincolniensis epistolae*, ed. Luard, 432/1–437/5; see especially 436/19–437/5. See Higden, *Polychronicon*, vii. 240–4 for a fourteenth-century account of the surrounding circumstances, and Boyle, 'Robert Grosseteste and the Pastoral Care', in *Pastoral Care*, 3–51, repr. with orig. pag. from *MRS* 8 (1979), for a recent interpretation of them. Wyclif terms the sort of obedience where an earthly spiritual lord is flouted in favour of obedience to Christ *obedientia resistiva*, and cites the letter several times. See especially *De Ordine Christiano*, 137/28–138/28. This work, or another that interprets the letter's import similarly, may well be the dialogue writer's source rather than Grosseteste's letter itself: Wyclif like the dialogue writer explains that 'illam obedienciam vocat Lincolniensis obedienciam resistivam vel obedienciam indirectam, quia, ut ipse declarat, quelibet creatura dicit usque ad mortem generaliter Dei voluntatem, et ut sic obediendum est illi creature sed principaliter Domini suo' (138/13–17). See also Wyclif, *Sermones*, ii. 311/15–312/2, iii. 492/38–40; *De Civili Dominio*, i. 290/13–17, 384/26–394/22; *Pol. Wks.*, i. 301/17; *Op. Min.*, 137/29–138/2. For references in Wycliffite works see Arnold 278/16–20; *Chronicles of Rome*, ed. Embree, 138/11–19 and 243.

969 *as þei don hem*: 'as they (subjects) do (serve) them (lords)'. Opponents of Wycliffites often extend the implications of the Wycliffite claim that spiritual lords need not be obeyed where their commands contravene Christ's to accuse the Wycliffites of wanting to destabilize temporal power too, by urging the people not to obey temporal lords. Typically such arguments aim to counter Wycliffite appeals to secular power. For similar attempts to limit the temporal implications of the Wycliffite argument on spiritual power see Arnold 145/9–148/24, Matthew 412/4–33. See also Wyclif, *Sermones*, ii. 237/21–240/30, iii. 162/1–163/8. For Jon's counter-argument see JR 992–4 and n.

971 The most important biblical passages cited in support of obedience to lords are Eph. 6: 5, Col. 3: 22, Tit. 2: 9, Heb. 13: 17, and 1 Pet. 2: 18. For Wycliffite exhortations to obedience see e.g. Arnold 147/7, Matthew 227/1–230/14, 371/10–20.

978–83 The story of Maurice and the Theban legion is included in the *Legenda Aurea*: see Iacopo da Varazze, *Legenda Aurea*, ed. Maggioni, ii. 965–70. In *c.* AD 288 the Christian Theban legion under Maurice's command were asked by the emperor Maximian to sacrifice to idols. They all refused, so he decimated them twice then killed all the rest—though some versions of the story suggest that some escaped to tell the tale. For the versions of this story available in medieval England and their manuscripts see D'Evelyn and Foster, 'Saints' Legends', 613. For some conveniently edited early Latin versions, see the appendices to Dupraz, *Les Passions de S Maurice d'Agaune*. Maurice's defiance of Maximian is mentioned in Wycliffite writings on other occasions where there is a special appeal to the virtue of lords and knights: see e.g. Arnold 232/3, 264/37, *Plowman's Tale*, 293–6.

984–5 *suche a legioun is not seyntes in heuene of al ordris of freres or mounkis or chanouns*: 'there is not such a legion of saints in heaven from all the orders of friars, monks, or canons'.

988–9 For similar accusations see Matthew 9/27–32, where friars are accused of 'comforting' men to slay their brethren in false wars, and Arnold 348/28–349/9, 386/12–387/3, where they are in addition accused of taking part. See also Wyclif, *Sermones*, iii. 39/20–6, iv. 111/15–41, 118/7–119/7. Wycliffites commonly link this accusation to references to the Despenser crusade of 1383, in which Bishop Henry Despenser waged war in Flanders supposedly on behalf of Pope Urban VI, but actually in pursuit of English interests, and was thoroughly beaten by the French then impeached in the English Parliament. On the Despenser crusade's importance to English politics see Aston, 'The Impeachment of Bishop Despenser', and Wilks, 'Roman Candle or Damned Squib'.

990 *6^e^ maner of concense* Wyclif and Wycliffites use an elaborate theory of sin through consent to the sin of another to justify, and even to exhort, unorthodox actions: along with blaming preachers who fail to reprove their audiences (as here), this theory is also used to urge lords to reform the clergy unless they wish to be guilty by consent of clerical wrongdoings (as at JR 404–6) and to vindicate sharp speech against sinful clergy (as at JR 810–20). The biblical reference most commonly mentioned when one group is urged to censure or prevent the sin of another is Rom. 1: 32; see e.g. Wyclif, 'De Pauperie Christi' in *Op. Min.*, 26/4–9, and Arnold 214/22–4. See also 2 Thess. 2: 11. The mnemonic verse used for the six types of consent for which one can be guilty of the sin of consent is as follows: 'Consentit cooperans, defendens, consilium dans, / Ac autorisans, non iuvans nec reprehendens'; in this case the person who fails to speak sharply would be guilty of the sixth and last kind of consent. For quotation of this verse see Arnold 87/3–10, 141/3–10, 152/5–10, 232/13–15, 349/9–13; Matthew 372/4–8, 417/29–31; as well as Wyclif, *Tractatus de officio pastorali*, ed. Lechler, 15/4–9, 16/13–16; *Tractatus de simonia*, ed. Herzberg-Fränkel and Dziewicki, 98/8–99/8; *Pol. Wks.*, i. 19/6–10, 308/27–309/2; *Sermones*, i. 77/34–78/1, 279/10–34, 284/5–8, 321/10–324/14, iii. 482/29–40, iv. 359/14–22; *Trialogus*, 173/26–9, 307/25–308/30.

992–4 When accused of attempting to destabilize temporal hierarchy Wycliffites usually do just what Jon does here: they cite biblical references to show that servants are obliged to obey even tyrannical lords, and then they turn to advise lords that they too have obligations to their servants. Cf. JR 788 n., and for another example see Matthew 229/1–11. See also McGrade, 'Somersaulting Sovereignty'.

994–6 *iche worldely lorde is holden to his seruant defende him and mayntene him*: 'each secular lord is required to defend and maintain his servant'.

1002 *þer beupere* Presumably Satan.

1004–5 For Paul see 2 Tim. 3: 1–5. Hildegard of Bingen (1098–1179), abbess of Rupertsburg and writer of the prophetic visions *Scivias* as well as a number of other works, is often cited by critics of the religious orders. See e.g. Arnold 413/3–6, 421/27–9; Matthew 11/20–1; as well as Wyclif, *Trialogus*, 338/17–18; *Op. Min.*, 169/10–12; and and see Kerby-Fulton, 'Hildegard of Bingen and Anti-Mendicant Propaganda'. Here the reference is probably (especially given that there is a copy of it in this manuscript on ff. 67^r–68^v (see Introduction, p. xxii, item 12)) to the work attributed to Hildegard known as 'insurgent gentes quae comedent peccata populi', which accuses friars or encouraging or participating in a whole catalogue of crimes. On 'Insurgent gentes' see the new edition cited on the same page, as well as Kerby-Fulton, 'Prophecy and Suspicion'; Szittya, *Antifraternal Tradition*, 220 and nn. 102–3; and Little and Easterling, *The Franciscans and Dominicans of Exeter*, 60–1.

1012 The repeated insistence that friars should swear under their common seal emphasizes their legal status as a corporation, collectively bound, as well as enabled to act, by their common seal. English common law establishes the powers and obligations of corporations and the conditions for their formation and collective action using the common seal: for further details see Grant, *A Practical Treatise on the Law of Corporations*, esp. 55–66.

DIALOGUE BETWEEN A FRIAR AND A SECULAR

1 On Gloucester see the Introduction, pp. xlvii–xlviii.

4–5 3 Esdr. 3: 12, printed as 1 Esdras in *The Apocrypha and Pseudepigraphia of the Old Testament in English*, ed. and trans. Charles, i. 30. On the availability of this apocryphal book to Wycliffites see Hudson, *Premature Reformation*, 230 and n. 14. Contestation of the content and sufficient grounds for 'oure bileue' is one of the themes running through this dialogue: cf. FS 10–11 n., 39–40 n., 51–3 n., 53–7 n., 246–7 n.

5–7 It is significant, probably deliberate, that Aristotle is endorsed as an authority in accord with 'oure bileue' at the beginning of a dialogue that makes extensive use of argumentative techniques developed out of the study of Aristotle's works. The quotation being translated here is drawn from a common medieval collection of sayings from Aristotle: 'Duobus existentibus amicis sanctum est praehonorare veritatem, quamvis, secundum Stratium, justum sit honorare amicum' (see *Les Auctoritates Aristotelis*, ed. Hamesse, 233). This is a version of Aristotle, *Nicomachean Ethics* A4 $1096^{a}16$–17, where Aristotle is commenting that his commitment to pursuing truth outweighs his friendship with Plato. Thanks to Bonnie Blackburn for the suggestion that led to this reference. Unsurprisingly, this scribe or a previous copyist did not understand 'to befor(e) honour' in his copy-text as an attempt to translate 'praehonorare' (even though he does correctly render a similar usage of 'bifore' as prefix in 'bifore deliberacioun' below, at FS 68). Thus, he substituted 'be for' for 'befor(e)'. My reconstruction restores the conjectured original 'befor(e)', at the same time substituting the present scribe's spelling of 'bifore'.

9 *þat þe hestis of God beþ neiþir soþe ne falce*: 'That God's commandments are neither true nor false.' Notice the structure of this dialogue: the Friar makes a propositional assertion and sometimes provides a short argument to back it up, the Secular makes a contrary assertion and backs it up with extended argument, then the Friar (defeated, it seems) moves on to a different though usually related topic. Their exchanges are a simplified form of academic disputation.

9–11 This question seems to stage a sort of showdown between grammar and logic: the Friar is suggesting that one group of statements, those where grammatical analysis tells us the verb is in the imperative mood, are not accessible to logical analysis aiming to determine their truth or falsity. On medieval theories of verbal mood the fundamental textbooks are those by Donatus and Priscian, and by Peter Helias (extensively used by later grammarians). For a sophisticated discussion summarizing earlier theories, see the modistic grammarian Thomas of Erfurt's *Grammatica Speculativa*, ed. and trans. Bursill-Hall. The verbal moods, or *modi*, generally recognized are the indicative, imperative, optative, subjunctive, and infinitive . See further FS 23–6 n.

10–11 *as tellip children sommes* 'as/in the way that children add up sums' (*MED* s.v. 'tellen', v. 17e), or possibly 'as children recite sums' (*MED* s.v. 'tellen', v. 1a), if the emphasis is on the mode of the statement being made. Evidently the Friar is offhandedly adducing another example of a kind of statement not accessible to logical analysis (see previous note). It is not explained just why statements made by children learning arithmetic are not classifiable as true or false, though mathematical truths are a popular medieval example of statements not subject to disproof, probably thanks to Aristotle's similar citation of them in writings that were part of the university arts curriculum in logic (see e.g. *Posterior Analytics*, trans. with commentary by Jonathan Barnes, Book alpha, especially chs. 1–4). In the Wycliffite tract 'De Papa', 'bileue' and sums are similarly placed beyond the reach of experiential verification: 'bileue is insensible and more trewe þan siche signes; as þis treuþe is insensible þat two and þre maken fyue, and ȝit it is more certeyn þan ony sensible þing heere' (Matthew 469/15–18).

13 Ps. 32: 4, 118: 160.

15–17 1 Cor. 13: 11. 'Sauered' is apparently the dialogue writer's summary rendition of the Vulgate's 'loquebar . . . sapiebam . . . cogitabam', focused on the second of these three terms. The *Wycliffite Bible* instead has more precisely 'spak . . . vndurstood . . . thouȝte'.

17 *sophemesse* That is, the sort of false statements used in the university exercise described below at FS 68–72; see note below.

20–3 *Forsoþe, whanne ȝe schulde be maystres for tyme, eftesoones ȝou nediþ þat ȝe be itauȝt þe princyples of þe bigynnynge of þe wordis of God, and ȝe ben imade, to wham is nede, mylke and not sad mete*: 'Indeed, when you should be masters for the time [i.e. according to your seniority], again it is needful for you that you should be taught the principles of the beginning of the words of God, and for you is prepared, for whom there is the need, milk and not solid food.' Heb. 5: 12, cf. 1 Cor. 3: 2. This rendering of Paul is an especially good example of the sort of translation heavily influenced by Latin syntax that this writer favours—and of the difficulties in understanding it can produce. Richard Rolle, John Trevisa, and the Wycliffite Bible translators produced very much this sort of English prose in their first attempts or first drafts, though the frankness with which they acknowledge the difficulties varies: see the prologue to Rolle's *English Psalter* in *Idea of the Vernacular*, 246/62–9; Trevisa, *Dialogue between the Lord and the Clerk on Translation*, ibid. 134/142–135/3; and the *Prologue* to the *Wycliffite Bible*, i. 56/31–60/14; also in *SEWW* 68/36–66, 71/173–72/194.

23–6 The Secular contends in response to the Friar that the mood of the verb in a statement has no bearing on its accessibility to logical analysis: imperative and optative statements can be 'redusid' to the indicative mood as part of the process of linguistic analysis involved in their evaluation, and it is possible to compare them to external states of affairs, 'trewþe in dede'. Exactly what 'reducing' a statement might entail is not clear here since the writer does not give an example. But 'reduction' was a fairly common synonym for what was more usually called 'resolution'. Thomas of Erfurt, after explaining that verbal mood represents different dispositions of mind in the speaker or subject, uses what he calls 'resolution' to show how any verbal mood can be resolved to the infinitive: 'Dicitur autem infinitivus, quia omnibus communis est, cum omnes modi in ipsum resolvantur: ut dicendo, *lego*, id est, *indico me legere*; *lege*, id est, *impero te legere*, et sic de aliis' (*Grammatica Speculativa*, 224/19–22). The Secular may have in mind a similar process, where an optative 'legat librum' might become 'spero quod X leget librum', for example.

27 Monks possess property; friars technically do not, though the distinction becomes strained in practice, as the Secular points out (FS 28–38). The appelation 'frere prechouris' typically refers to Dominicans; an unusual specificity for lollards, who typically condemn all friars, whether order by order or in an undifferentiated mass. The friar who engaged in disputation before Gloucester may have been a Dominican, or the author may have invented this specificity for greater verisimilitude.

28 *dom place*: 'forum for holding court' (see *MED* s.v. 'dom', n. 8). The term suggests, though without specifying its source, that the preachers in question are or should be subject to some kind of legal judgement.

32 *haueþ possessiouns* The second repetition (and the sentence's verb) was probably omitted through eyeskip or a scribal attempt to correct a supposed dittograph.

34–5 *Blessid be þilke þat leueþ and [s]eeþ not*: 'Blessed are those who believe and do not see'. John 20: 29. (Seeing and believing are transposed here in FS.)

39–40 *alle þingis þat is nouȝt of þe bileue is synne* Rom. 14: 23. The Friar is rather clumsily logic-chopping in an attempt to show that the face value of Paul's statement is untrue. In his insistence that he is 'wiþ þe Apostle' (FS 45) the Secular will refuse to accept this interpretation of Paul's words (see

FS 53–7 n.). 'Of (þe) bileue' is the Friar's translation of Paul's 'ex fide', or the *Wycliffite Bible*'s 'of feith': the Friar deliberately exploits the ambiguity of the phrase.

40 *þe whiche is vndirstonde* Again, a word-for-word rendering of Latinate syntax, in this case an expository phrase common in philosophical writings: 'intelligendum est'.

46–7 Mainstream writers as much as Wycliffites regarded the Ten Commandments as central to a programme of vernacular teaching about belief: priests were required to instruct parishioners about the Ten Commandments as well as other topics by both Pecham's Constitutions of 1281 and Thoresby's of 1357 (see *Lay Folk's Catechism*, foot of facing pages, for a convenient edition of both). Wycliffites found ways to incorporate instruction about certain key Wycliffite tenets and complaints into commentary upon the Ten Commandments, often adapting previous commentaries for their own use. For further details see JR 792–3 n. For a detailed explanation of how friars transgress the Ten Commandments incorporated into a Wycliffite tract, see 'Of the Leaven of Pharisees' chapter 3, Matthew 7–13. See FS 213–16 and n.

50 See *De Doctrina Christiana*, 2.42.151, pp. 128/25–130/3. Of course the statements 'all truth may be found in the Bible' (as in Augustine) and 'all holy writ is our belief' (as here) are not equivalent, but they are closely aligned in lollard polemic on whether the Bible alone is an adequate guide to conduct (the topic the Secular and Friar are currently debating), and it is likely that this attribution to Augustine is produced second- or third-hand. For a similar lollard use of Augustine see the 'Prologue' to the *Wycliffite Bible*, i. 49.

51–3 The dialogue writer is apparently drawing on commentary on the Creed to produce an amplified version of its first article. The same three-part expansion of the Creed's first article (though in reverse order) appears in a Wycliffite commentary on the Apostle's Creed: 'Trow in God, and to God, and trow God; þat is þe leste. þat man levys in God þat clevys to hym be charite; and þus eche man þat ys in hed synne is owt of his beleve. That man trowys to God, þat belevyþ þat he is trewe and ryȝtful in al þynge þat he seyþ; and þus do unkende men, þat trow not in hym. þat man trowys God, þat trowys þat he ys; and so do develys þat trow not in hym' (Arnold 115/1–7).

53–7 The Friar had attempted simply to replace the Apostle's 'belief' with 'good conscience', without acknowledging how these concepts differ. In reply the Secular produces an a fortiori argument where a middle term—the Ten Commandments—highlights the difference between good conscience and belief through their differing relations to it: the Ten Commandments are our belief; good conscience is grounded in the Ten Commandments.

58–9 John 1: 3.

61–2 Lam. 3: 37. The phrase 'þe lord not comaundynge' is a word-for-word translation of the Vulgate's Latin ablative absolute 'Domino non iubente'—another example of this dialogue's predilection for Latinate syntax (cf. FS 10–11, 20–23, 40, 96–7, 98, 114). The phrase is more idiomatically rendered in the *Wycliffite Bible* as 'whanne the Lord comaundide not' (LV; EV has the similarly Latinate 'the Lord not comaundende').

66–7 According to penitential doctrine, the 'circumstances' of an action must be examined in order to determine whether it is sinful or not and if it is, how grave the sin is. The *Fasciculus Morum* gives the rhyme that helps confessors remember the standard list of circumstances that need to be considered: 'Quis, quid , ubi, quibus auxiliis, cur, quomodo, quando, / Quilibet observet anime medicamina dando' (478–9).

68–72 The Friar's final conclusion is obviously false—who could accept that once a man has begun to sin he can sin no more?—and the challenge for the Secular is to show the flaw in reasoning that leads to the false conclusion. The exchange between Friar and Secular has the character, though not the precise form, of the university exercise where students would resolve *sophismata*, or patently false yet seemingly flawlessly constructed statements. For an introductory discussion see Norman Kretzmann, 'Syncatoremata, exponibilia, sophismata' in *CHLMP*, 211–45. For discussion of another Wycliffite example in the *Testimony of William Thorpe*, and further references, see Somerset, *Clerical Discourse*, 187–88 and n. 24. For a similar proposition by the Friar see FS 161–6 and n.

73 Scholastic procedure is especially evident in the Secular's reply here as well the Friar's question (cf. previous note). The Secular begins with a distinction ('þere is twey manere of synnes') then lists one after another in a loose series all the counter-arguments he can produce.

76–7 Ps. 36: 27.

93–7 The dialogue writer appears to be paraphrasing Gregory's reference to unpremeditated gluttony in the last chapter of his *Moralia*: 'Sic etenim saepe intentionem nostram, dum ante Dei oculos recte incipitur, occulte subiuncta, et eam uelut in itinere comprehendens, intentio humanae laudis assequitur, sicut pro necessitate quidem cibus sumitur, sed in ipso esu, dum furtim gula subrepit, edendi delectatio permiscetur. Unde plerumque contingit ut refectionem corporis, quam salutis causa coepimus, causa uoluptatis expleamus.' Gregory the Great, *Moralia in Job*, 35.20.49. See *Moralia in Iob*, ed. Adriaen, iii. 1810/98–104.

96–7 *no delyberacioun goinge bifore oþere þan goode* Another ablative absolute; cf. FS 61–2 and n.

98 The adverbial use of 'neiþer' without an accompanying 'nor' or 'not', apparently under the influence of Latin 'nec', is fairly common in Wycliffite texts, especially those associated with the Bible translation, though not elsewhere in Middle English: see *MED* s.v. 'neither', adv.

100–1 Ps. 35: 4.

102 *þat he myȝte be excusid by noon-delyberacioun of doynge of yuel*: 'so that he might be excused for doing evil by his lack of any deliberation'.

104–5 Prov. 1: 32. *Dives and Pauper* uses the same example in its discussion of homicide (i. ii. 27/1–5).

106–8 According to the doctrine of original sin, all human beings are tainted by the sin of Adam and Eve. This is an example of the kind of test case that can arise from considering in what sense and to what extent humans may be viewed as individually guilty of that sin in person.

111–13 Only the statement that all men sin is Paul's (Rom. 3: 9–28, esp. 23–8). The exception 'but þilke þat weren halwid in here modir wombe' is required by God's statement to Jeremiah that he was hallowed in his mother's womb (Jer. 1: 5, Ecclus. 49: 9). This counter-example appears elsewhere in Wycliffite argument, as for example in the tract 'On Feigned Contemplative Life' (Matthew 188/22–6); see also *Fyve Wyttes*, 2/12–14.

114 *þe sprite more folwynge þe body þan þe hestis of God*. Another ablative absolute; cf. FS 61–2 and n.

117–18 Eph. 2: 3.

118–30 The Secular's argument that 'this man is in sin' and 'this man sins' are equivalent derives its force from discussions by logicians of the status of the copula 'est': the running man is a popular example in this context, and it is generally accepted in logical textbooks that the two statements 'Sortes est currens' and 'Sortes currit' are equivalent. For an explanation of the issues see Broadie, *Introduction to Medieval Logic*, 12, 23. Whether the Secular's argument that original sin is an act of the unborn child in whom it inheres may be considered proven by the resemblance between 'this man is in sin' and 'this man sins' is doubtful.

122–3 *anoon as he is quick*: 'as soon as he is alive', that is, from the moment of quickening or first noticeable movement in the womb.

130–1 Ezek. 18: 14–20.

132–5 The Secular is attempting to explain the notoriously troublesome passage Gen. 9: 20–7, which recounts the failure of Noah's son Ham to cover his nakedness when he was drunk. The difficulty is that it is Canaan, Ham's son, not Ham, whom Noah curses when he wakes: this would seem to be an example of just the sort of punishing of children for their fathers' sins that the Secular has just denied, but no explanation is given, nor is Noah blamed for this behaviour. The Secular explains that Noah's is a prophetic curse rather than a curse that judges Canaan's past behaviour.

146–8 *þe children þat dien in orygynal synne, lackynge of þe siȝt of God and of þe blesse of heuene is to hem no peyne, for þei haue no felynge ne knowynge of it*: 'Lack of the sight of God and bliss of heaven brings the children who die in original sin no pain, because they have neither feeling nor knowledge about it.'

153–6 Against the Friar's contention that children who die before baptism feel no pain at what they lack (i.e. the sight of God and joys of heaven), the Secular responds by explaining that such children can have propositional knowledge—'knowledge that'—even though they lack experiential knowledge. His analogy to a blind man underscores that this kind of propositional knowledge need not be explicitly taught: because humans are naturally suited for heavenly bliss, as a blind man is to see, they can be aware that they are not exercising a latent capacity even in the absence of any experience of using it. Even if it elides difficulties of acquisition and of degree, the Secular's reply shows interest in the various types of knowledge of a kind common in late fourteenth-century Oxford, and exhibited also in RG (see esp. RG 329–38, 357–75). For another example of Wycliffite analysis of mental acts and further references see Somerset, *Clerical Discourse*, 188–90.

161–6 Again (cf. FS 68–72 and n.) the Friar's argument resembles a *sophisma*: of course new sin cannot lessen an existing sin, but neither can it be true to say that a man in deadly sin sins in asking God's mercy.

175–6 1 Cor. 16: 14.

178–9 Tit. 1: 15.

182 *reproued to alle goode werkis*: 'given reproof by all good works'.

188–98 The crucial point of the Secular's solution is that what determines the sinful character of the sinful man's actions is the mental disposition with which they are performed. If goodwill and charity accompany the act of crying mercy, then the well-disposed act of crying mercy breaks the continuum of deadly sin. On interest in the analysis of mental acts in contemporary Oxford and in the writing of an Oxford-affiliated Wycliffite, cf. FS 153–6 n. This analysis also draws upon contemporary interest in continua and their division: see John E. Murdoch, 'Infinity and Continuity', *CHLMP*, 564–91. Note that the Secular's reply describes confession without any priestly intermediary, and constitutes a theological justification for confession without any resort to a priest, though the Secular does not press either point. For a similar set of claims by Wyclif, see *Trialogus*, 326–33, esp. 327/3–328/4.

190–1 *in good wille to do þat þat he may as God wole and holy chirche to haue remyssioun of it*. Taking 'God . . . and holy chirche' as a compound subject, 'in good will to do what he may, as God and holy church wish, in order to have remission of it'. 'Remission' refers to pardon or forgiveness, though not necessarily of an institutional sort, and the role attributed to 'holy chirche' in this phrase bears crucially on the question of what sort of confession the Secular means to describe (see previous note). So does what the author may mean by 'holy chirche', a term Wycliffites commonly use equivocally in order to give the impression of compliance, while they instead mean compliance with what they consider true. For an example see *The Testimony of William Thorpe*, 51/891–52/917.

199–200 For a similar exchange on who should follow Christ's counsels, see Wyclif, *Sermones*, iii. 233/3–238/34. Some late medieval English advocates of living 'parfitly' would claim that Christ's counsels were not intended as advice for all, but only for a few very dedicated souls who would strive beyond following the commandments towards the sort of perfection Christ recommends, for example, in Matt. 19 and 1 Cor. 7, where poverty and chastity are advised (cf. JR 707 n.). As the Friar notes, this sort of attempt at perfection is associated especially with adherents to religious rules. Others who aim at 'parfit' life stress that perfection is a goal for all Christians, though a difficult one, and can be aspired to by other means as well. The debate, of course, has a wider context. But it should be noted that all medieval English writers who produce precepts or rules of life or forms of living in the vernacular that make religious life more accessible to lay readers subscribe, at the very least implicitly, to the idea that lay people may aspire to perfection: this is by no means a view associated exclusively with lollardy.

201–6 Christ gives his two commandments and comments on their relation to the law and the prophets at Matt. 22: 37–40; cf. Luke 10: 27, Mark 12: 29–31. For a more detailed explanation of the relationship between these two commandments and the Ten Commandments see Rom. 13: 9–10: the first three commandments amplify 'love God' while the final seven detail 'love your neighbour as yourself'. For the requirement that nothing be added or taken away from God's law see Rev. 22: 18–19.

210 James 2: 10.

213–16 None of the four orders of friars categorically rejected manual labour and embraced mendicancy as its sole source of support from its inception. The Dominicans were the earliest to do so, becoming mendicant and rejecting manual labour in favour of study and preaching in 1220 (Knowles, *Religious Orders*, 149–51). The Carmelites adopted a rule closely based on that of the Dominicans in 1247, moving at that point from partial reliance on mendicancy to a way of life much like that of the Dominicans (Jotischky, *Carmelites and Antiquity*, 14–16), while the Augustinian Hermits made a similar shift: in 1290 they adopted constitutions modelled on those of the Dominicans (Knowles, *Religious Orders*, 200–1). The Franciscans in the beginning relied on manual labour as well as mendicancy, but had abandoned manual labour by *c.*1260 (ibid. 175–7).

As the friars came to reject manual labour, earlier polemic and satire that had been directed against monks who refused to work was turned on them. In mid- to late fourteenth-century England a more general anxiety about labour resulting from a shortage of workers after the Black Death in 1348–50 converged with this tradition of attack on the friars. On this more local development and its satirical implications see Scase, *New Anti-clericalism*, 71–2, 127–9, 144.

223–38 See Luke 18: 10–14 for the Pharisee/publican comparison.

231–2 Ps. 72: 9; cf. *Fyve Wyttes* 10/4–21.

239–41 In the legendary life of Edward the Confessor, St John in the guise of a beggar asks Edward for alms. Edward has no money with him, so he gives the beggar his ring. Later, St John appears to two English pilgrims who have lost their way on the way to the Holy Land, makes sure that they find their way safely, and asks them to convey to Edward both his ring, and the news that Edward will die within six months, but John will see his way safely into heaven. For three Middle English versions, see Moore, *The Middle English Verse Life of Edward the Confessor*; Moore also describes earlier Latin versions. For a fifteenth-century prose version of the story see *Supplementary Lives in Some Manuscripts of the Gilte* Legende, ed. Hamer and Russell, 22/762–23/809. See also D'Evelyn and Foster, 'Saints' Legends', 581 and Pickering, 'Saints' Lives'.

246–7 Notice how the Secular interprets the legend figurally so that it accords with belief: the pilgrimage, and the begging, and the marriage, are all figural rather than literal.

252 2 Pet. 1: 11; Heb. 11: 10, 16, 12: 22, 13: 14.

258–9 Proverbial. Again, as in the example of the blind man (cf. FS 153–6 and n.), the author shows an interest in perception and forms of knowledge.

260–1 1 Cor. 16. Cf. *Omnis Plantacio* 131/2747–132/2775.

282–3 Deut. 15: 4.

285–300 The Secular's reply separates 'strong beggars' from those beggars who are truly needy, but it also singles out lords as those to whom God's command is especially directed. It is lords who are responsible for ensuring that the truly needy are provided for and that 'strong beggars'—a category that by implication lumps together lay idlers and vagrants with mendicants—are put to work. It is a characteristically Wycliffite strategy to insist on the special obligation of secular lords to reform abuses in ecclesiastical as well as temporal affairs; cf. FS 359 n.

291 2 Thess. 3: 10.

297–300 Evidence of concern to enforce labour and prevent vagrancy in late medieval England is visible not only in the social commentary of literary and religious writers (on which see Scase, *New Anti-clericalism*, 70–3) but in the multiple re-enactments of the Statute of Labourers: see Middleton, 'Acts of Vagrancy'.

301–2 At issue is the holding of benefices by aliens, or those not resident in England. For an introduction to the concerns raised by alien benefices see Pantin, *The English Church in the Fourteenth Century*, 82–7. For the first treatment of these concerns in Parliament see *PROME*, Edward III 1346 September, paragraph 7 of the 'Introduction', and items 31–2, nos. XX–XXI.

308 Why civil law, that is, Justinian's *Corpus Iuris Civilis*, should be invoked alongside the common law of the realm is not entirely clear, unless the intention is to bolster the authority of the common law through reference to another widely used secular law code. On the citation of civil law by Wycliffites as well as earlier anti-mendicant writers, see Scase, *New Anti-clericalism*, 72 and n. 110. For criticism of civil law as 'heþene mennes lawe', on the other hand, see Matthew 184/23–27. Hoccleve cites Justinian against Oldcastle: see 'The Remonstrance against Oldcastle', in *Selections from Hoccleve*, ed. Seymour, 61–74, lines 185–92.

311–12 2 Thess. 3: 6–12.

312 *thrilleris* The word is not attested elsewhere. The Glossary's speculation that *thrilleris* may be a metathesized form of 'thirlers', i.e. 'penetrators', is one possibility, but deliberate substitution for another plural noun denoting a way of life associated with bold begging seems equally likely. Possibilities include 'faitours' (similarly paired with friars in *Piers Plowman*), 'spilleris' (unusual, but requires the smallest change), and (most intriguingly) 'lolleris'.

313 *ensaumple* The process of scribal corruption to 'ensaumple of' is not obvious. Yet 'ensaumple' as verb without 'of' (the idiom with 'of' is in any case unrecorded in the *MED*) is very likely to be the original reading, since the convention of academic or quasi-academic debates such as this one is to refute the opponent's exact words, rather than to oppose a different form of words without comment.

316–17 Acts 20: 33–6. For an introduction to the most relevant arguments on Christ's begging and labour, see Dawson, 'Between Pope and King'.

323–4 Wrongful coveting of one's neighbour's goods contravenes the ninth and tenth commandments. See the versions of the commandments and the commentaries cited in JR 792–3 n.

329–30 Ps. 72: 5.

331–2 2 Thess. 3: 8–12.

344–5 Although Augustine comments extensively on the fig tree cursed by Christ of Matt. 21: 19, and on the good trees bearing good fruits and evil trees bearing evil fruits of Matt. 7: 17–18 and Matt. 12: 33, none of his authentic works contrast 'he . . . þat ȝeueþ þe tree wiþ þe fruyt' with 'he þat ȝeueþ þe fruyte one'. The source may, instead, be proverbial.

348–51 Mark 12: 42–4, Luke 21: 1–4.

359 The exhortation to its noble audience implicit in this envoy is veiled as an appeal for just judgement, but remains easy to discern. Having been provided with the necessary information in a form he is competent to judge, Gloucester is now expected to 'fulfil in deed the truth' when the appropriate time comes: that is, to act on the dialogue's recommendations about the obligations of lords, expressed most directly at FS 285–300.

360 Ps. 105: 3.

DIALOGUE BETWEEN RESON AND GABBYNG

1–4 A shortened, simplified version of the preface to Wyclif's *Dialogus* (cf. *Dialogus*, 1/1–12), omitting Wyclif's announcement that catholic wisdom collected from the faithful in the vernacular will here be made more widely available in Latin (*Dialogus*, 1/3–4). For RG's author, we *call* the speakers Reason and Falsehood, but they *are* Christ and the devil. Wyclif's explanation of his chosen literary form similarly stresses God's role in its production, but names the persons of his dialogue Veritas and Mendacium, then asserts their identity with Christ and the devil more obliquely through exegesis: 'quia multi delectantur in loquela dialogi, moventur a deo duas personas adducere, scil. veritatem atque mendacium . . . Et quia veritas est Christus, ut patet jo 14°, et diabolus ipsum mendacium, ut patet jo 8°, racionabile videtur veritatem proponere et sermonem istum' (*Dialogus*, 1/6–12).Wyclif's efforts to keep Veritas in character as Christ will be inconsistent from the beginning and will disappear entirely after chapter 3 (see Pollard's Introduction, p. vi, for further comment), while RG's author will try harder, at least for a time (see RG 7 n.).

7 *for þis I cam dawen fro heuene*. RG's author has made some efforts to modify Wyclif's voicing to suit his own designation of the speakers: here he substitutes a first-person pronoun for Wyclif's 'Christus', then in what follows he removes two third-person references to 'racio' in the first speech made by Wyclif's Veritas (*Dialogus*, 1/15, 1/18). These efforts will not last long (see below, RG 145–61 and n., 200 and n., 354–7 and n.).

9 *hoomly*. Replaces Wyclif's emphasis on Christ's mildness: 'ut sermonibus suis mansuetis veritas catholica plus lucescat' (*Dialogus*, 1/19–2/1). As Watson and Jenkins note, 'homlye' is a keyword used by Julian of Norwich to describe God's wish for intimacy with mankind, used for the first time in her *Revelation* at chapter 4, line 15 and repeatedly thereafter (*The Writings of Julian of Norwich*, ed. Watson and Jenkins, *A Revelation of Love*, 137/1 and n.). The word is used in similar figurative senses in Rolle, Hilton, Kempe, Pecock, and a range of Wycliffite texts (see *MED* s.v. 'homli', adj. (2)). See also Aers, *Sanctifying Signs*, 157–78.

10 *euen aftur þe biddyng of my fadur*. Along with the following claim that the Jews were told not to believe Christ unless he did the works of the one who sent him, these are the author's substitution for 'ut homines qui sunt christi ecclesia sint beati' (*Dialogus*, 2/2–3). Again, this is at least in part an effort to keep Reson in character as Christ.

11–12 John 10: 37.

12–73 Here the author, like Wyclif, uses a model of the three estates (lords, clergy, and commons) as the basis for an extended exposition on failings in the proper administration of contemporary society (here called 'my churche', or for Wyclif, 'my church militant', 'meam militantem ecclesiam', *Dialogus*, 2/3–4). Criticism of the behaviour of individual estates (whether according to a threefold division or a larger number of more finely differentiated occupations in the world) is a commonplace of estates satire: on this tradition see Mann, *Medieval Estates Satire*. On three-estate models in *Piers Plowman* and other late medieval English works, see Cole, 'Trifunctionality and the Tree of Charity'. Probably the most famous late medieval English example of a sermon addressing the estates in turn, one found in many lollard manuscripts, is Thomas Wimbledon's 1388 sermon: for an edition see Owen, 'Thomas Wimbledon's Sermon'. Other Wycliffite writings in which the three estates are a central expository tool include *Omnis Plantacio,* the related tract *Fundamentum aliud* (Hudson, *Works of a Lollard Preacher*, 2–153, and cf. Matthew 362–96) and 'On the Seven Deadly Sins' (Arnold 119–67)

12–13 *lordis, prestis, and comyns*. This list of the three estates, preceding the exposition of the proper role of each in turn, is added by the author. In addition, clerics come first in Wyclif's version (*Dialogus*, 2/4), followed by lords (*Dialogus*, 2/12) then 'vulgares' (*Dialogus*, 2/20)—an ordering the author will conform with later on; see RG 35, 41. While it is more usual for lords to come first, Wimbledon too (though without comment) places the clergy first throughout his sermon (see previous note).

13–14 The claim that lords are the vicars of God is not uncontroversial: consider, for example, the opening of *Omnis Plantacio* and the related tract *Fundamentum Aliud*, where lords are designated as the vicars of God, clerics as the vicars of Christ, and their respective proper activities in the world designated with this in mind: lords should punish and reward, clerics should teach and preach (2/1–5/11, and see Wyclif's treatment of the same topic, *Tractatus de officio regis*, ed. Pollard and Sayle, 121/32–122/1). Readers of Wyclif's *Dialogus* were apparently aware of this demarcation of roles: Vienna, Österreichische Nationalbibliothek MS 3930 includes at this point the annotation 'sacerdos vicarius christi, dominus vicarius divinitatis' (*Dialogus*, 2/13 apparatus).

17–32 *For oft tymes . . . passe not þat.* This extended explanation of the precise circumstances under which a priest may receive his livelihood from those he instructs has been added by the translator, omitting a shorter explanation of how the clergy should live on tithes and be grateful to the Lord (or lord) who provides them (*Dialogus*, 2/7–11). A similar provision appears in the seventh article of the *37 Concl.* (12/9–16)– though the *37 Concl.* author seems more interested in his three corollaries about how support may be withdrawn from clergy who fail to perform their duties (13/8–18/13).

37 *þise two sistris.* Here the author begins a loose yet extended allegory according to which the estates become sisters; later at RG 68–9, 71, and 79–80 he develops his allegory by calling the three sisters the three parts of Christ's spouse, the body of the Church, among whom there should be harmonious agreement. This shift illustrates the author's predilection for personification and allegory, but also his stress on interdependence in place of Wyclif's hierarchies (Wyclif had distinguished superior or inferior parts of the body of the Church rather than designating them as sisters, e.g. *Dialogus*, 3/3–4, 3/8, 3/11).

40 *And þus.* The beginning of chapter 2 in Wyclif's *Dialogus* (though note that the chapter divisions are questionable: see Thomson [408], 270 n. 23). The author seems to stick close to Wyclif's words at the beginning of each chapter, then diverge as he sees fit, then leap forward to the beginning of a new chapter. Late in the dialogue, in the divergences after his leaps forward, the author will begin to knit together material from adjoining chapters in a more complex way (see e.g. RG 210–37 and n.). But if his practice of beginning anew at the opening of each chapter remains consistent, then the chapter divisions in the translator's copy of Wyclif's *Dialogus* might be presumed to correspond with the printed edition until RG 297–306 (see note below).

46–57 *For bi couetise . . . puple and me.* Again (as at RG 17–32) the author substitutes a description of how priests should avoid covetous behaviour for Wyclif's less pastorally oriented description of how clerics should behave (*Dialogus*, 3/18–4/2).

51–4 Gen. 3: 10–11.

60–2 *But . . . charite.* An admonition, substituted for Wyclif's justification of the power of temporal lords (*Dialogus*, 4/6–7).

63–8 *And þis . . . leid abouen.* This emphasis on the worthiness and value of the commons and their eventual reward has been added.

68–9, 71 *sistris . . . spouse.* See RG 37 n.

74 The rest of Wyclif's chapter 2 (*Dialogus*, 4/16–5/11), an extended explanation of how the body of the Church is arranged, is omitted. Wyclif's chapter 3 corresponds to *And for I . . .*

79–80 See RG 37 n. Here the sisters (cf. RG 37, 68–9, 71) replace Wyclif's reference to the Church as mother (*Dialogus*, 5/17).

80–3 *If presthod . . . her state* This retrospective explanation for why the clergy are discussed before lords, rather than the reverse as is usual in treatments of the three estates, has been added by the author, in place of a warning about how ignorance leads to rebellion (*Dialogus*, 5/22–6/3).

84–9 Num. 18: 20–1. The following two biblical quotations repeat this ruling in almost the same words: see RG 97–101 and n., RG 104–6 and n.

89–95 A loose paraphrase of the rest of Wyclif's chapter 3 (*Dialogus*, 6/14–7/10). Wyclif is not so concerned with the mutual responsibilities of clergy and lords. Instead he elaborates on why the papal court, itself mired in heresy, is not qualified to pronounce on the heresy of others.

90–1 *þe bokis ben commyn to men.* It seems rather tendentious, or at the least wishful thinking, to claim that the kinds of possession proper to the clergy are common knowledge thanks to the ready availability of the Bible and its correct interpretation on this point.

94 *resoun at domesdaye.* Probably an allusion to 'redde racionem', Luke 16: 2, and also to reason as designation for God—possibly to Wimbledon's sermon (see RG 12–73 n.) as well. While Wyclif censures knights who consent to the sins of the clergy by failing to prevent them (*Dialogus*, 7/1–4), he does not mention 'domesdaye', either here or where RG later refers to it repeatedly (see RG 112, 273, 285, 287, and though without mentioning the word, at the conclusion of the dialogue, 378–83).

96 *þe secounde witnesse.* Wyclif's chapter 4 begins.

97–101 Deut. 18: 1–2.

101–2 This is the dialogue's first reference to human as opposed to divine authority; the author will conclude his dialogue with a version of Wyclif's systematic exposition on the subject (the 'foure answeris to spechis' and their explanation: see RG 357–75 and n.)

103 *þe þridde lawe.* The author jumps to the start of Wyclif's chapter 5 here.

104–6 Ezek. 44: 28.

106–8 *And noo . . . þe feende.* Paraphrases *Dialogus*, 10/1–9. The author abandons the rest of chapter 5 in favour of the excursus that follows (RG 108–99), then picks up chapter 6 (RG 200).

108–99 *And to conferme . . . Amen.* An extended interpolation that does not appear in Wyclif's *Dialogus*. See Introduction, pp. l–li.

118–42 *And no Cristen man . . . obedience done to tyrauntis.* While it is common for Wycliffite writings to enjoin obedience to secular rulers even when those rulers are unjust, pointing out by way of restraint that secular rulers in turn have obligations to those who serve them (see JR 994–6 and n.), Wycliffites sometimes insist, as here, that the only possible obedience to a ruler who requires one to act contrary to Christ is a resistive obedience, or refusal (see JR 943–58 and n.). Typically the second sort of resistive obedience applies to the ecclesiastical hierarchy rather than to secular rulers, though the author does not specify this here except in RG 137's reference to a 'false prelat'. There is a similar exchange between Arundel and Thorpe in the *Testimony of William Thorpe*, 46/747–49/840. See also *37 Concl.*, 47/17–50/13.

120 *new ordris.* That is, the fraternal orders, founded or reformulated out of older groups from the early thirteenth century on. For much more extensive comment on friars, see JR, as well as the *Upland Series*: Wyclif's *Dialogus* does not seem especially concerned with friars.

127 *triuauntis.* This is a term frequently used by Wycliffites to translate 'trutannos' or 'discolos' ('tyrants'): see Somerset, *Clerical Discourse*, 3 n. 1.

137–8 *iche man may suppose or knowe.* This terminology anticipates the description drawn from Wyclif's *Dialogus* of the four answers to speeches (see RG 357–75 and n.)—the passage from the *Dialogus* with which the translation ends, and perhaps the author's main motivation in choosing to adapt the *Dialogus*.

141 *kny3t of God.* See RG 13–14 and n.

145–61 *O Iesu . . . longe trespasse.* The author addresses Christ directly here, abandoning his attempts to keep Reson in character as Christ (see RG 7 n.). The shift to direct address moves the author, though temporarily, into the more personal, affect-laden mode of devotional texts that aim to prepare their readers for death. For a study of this genre and its affiliates see Appleford, 'Learning to Die'.

168–9 Christ responds to criticisms by the Pharisees of his or the apostles' eating and drinking habits at Matt. 12: 1–8, 15: 1–20, Mark 2: 23–7, 7: 1–23, Luke 5: 30–9, 6: 1–5, 7: 34–5.

168 *oure hooly abbot.* See also RG 171, 183, 187, 197. On Christ as abbot see JR 336 n.

172–83 Christ provides instruction on praying the Pater Noster at Matt. 6: 9–13, Luke 11: 1–4. lollard and non-lollard writers alike in late medieval England saw the Pater Noster as the basis of all prayer and the best of prayers. Treatises on prayer advising on its use, commentaries, and devotional works structured in whole or in part around the Pater Noster abound: for an introductory survey see Gillespie, ''Thy will be done'. Lollards place unusual emphasis on how right living itself is a form of prayer (see RG 180–3, and cf. 'De Precacionibus Sacris', Arnold 219–29, esp. 219–20). And lollard commentaries on the Pater Noster stress their distinctive beliefs and their polemical contentions in place of a wide range of other possible content. For lollard commentaries on the Pater Noster see Arnold 93–7 (item 2 in R) and 98–110, Matthew 198–202, as well as the more polemical 'Seven Heresies', Arnold 441–6 (item 4 in R).

182 *hungri to ȝerne aftur ritwisnesse*. A reference to the fourth of Matthew's eight beatitudes in the opening of the Sermon on the Mount: see Matt. 5: 6, and cf. Luke 6: 21.

195–6 *brouȝt in customes bi þe feend*: 'customs brought in by the devil'.

200 *Siþ þre witnessis*. Here the author returns to working closely with Wyclif's *Dialogus*. The first sentence gives a prospectus of RG 200–63, the remaining portion of Reson's long opening speech, which draws on chapters 6 and 7 of the *Dialogus*: the three witnesses are the quotations from Mark, Matthew, and Timothy. RG 200–37 is loosely based on *Dialogus*, chapter 6, though it draws the quotation from Peter from chapter 7. From this point forward, after the interpolated passage from RG 108–99, efforts to recast Wyclif's third-person references to Christ are abandoned.

205–8 Mark 10: 42–4.

210–37 *þis word of Crist . . . lesse value*. This passage has been substituted for the rest of Wyclif's chapter (12/2–22), and its use of the quotation from Mark it draws from the *Dialogus* has a different emphasis. Wyclif is concerned to show that Christ by his example encourages his apostles and vicars to reject high status in the world in favour of Christ's example of humility and patience. Thus prelates of the Church and the pope are heretics and followers of Antichrist, and so are the temporal lords who consent to their activity. The author of RG, on the other hand, again has a pastoral emphasis that especially condemns covetousness, this time enabled by a distinction between human law and divine law. He builds his exposition on Peter's injunction to priests to feed their flock, complaining that priests nowadays ignore this injunction, instead relying on 'mennes lawis of lesse value', the decretals of the pope (he draws here on the end of Wyclif's chapter 7, 14/13–21), and loving the world and worldly goods.

213–16 1 Pet 5: 2–3.

238 *And ȝitt*. The author skips to the opening of Wyclif's *Dialogus*, chapter 7.

242–4 Matt. 8: 20.

244–5 This summary replaces Wyclif's quotation and exposition of 2 Cor. 8: 9 and Prov. 30: 8, as well as an intervening complaint that friars blaspheme by claiming they beg following Christ's example.

245–7 The comparison of merchants to foxes and lords to birds is the translator's.

249–50 1 Tim. 6: 8. Paul's first letter to Timothy is traditionally read as a source of advice for the qualifications and proper conduct of bishops, as well as a range of other pastoral topics.

250–63 *Here biddiþ . . . hour of deþ*. This interpretative passage is substituted for the remainder of Wyclif's chapter 7. The author focuses on how the covetous behaviour of contemporary bishops is 'aȝeynes Crist and þe state of treue bischops', as explained by Paul to Timothy, ending with a brief nautical comparison that (once again slipping momentarily into the 'learn to die' mode; see RG 145–61 and n.) enjoins 'Cristen men' to live in preparation for death. Wyclif instead reiterates that the pope is a heretic then moves on to an exposition of 1 Pet. 5: 2 (used by the author at the end of the previous chapter): see *Dialogus*, 14/4–21 and RG 210–37 n.

255 *chosen vessells*. See Acts 9: 15.

264–71 *I haue herd þee . . . lawes of þe pope*. The author jumps to the opening of Wyclif's chapter 8. This is a close summary of the first speech made by Wyclif's Mendacium, *Dialogus*, 15/1–18.

272–6 Rather than accusing his opponent of mixing truth with falsehood, as Veritas accuses Mendacium in Wyclif's *Dialogus*, 15/19–20, Reson gives an ethical imperative for speaking truth that helps to bolster his authority and credibility. This alteration helps to maintain the dialogue's characterization: it might be seen as odd for Gabbyng to speak even some truth. More importantly, as we have seen, when a disputant in a dialogue speaks on behalf or the status or quality that he represents, the result is typically to establish his authority in argument (Introduction, p. xv). This is why the author goes on to weigh 'reson' against truth here (*And so . . . aȝens reson* RG 274–6). The weighing of 'reson' that begins here and concludes with its measuring against 'autorite' below (RG 293–7 and n.) anticipates the dialogue's conclusion. So does the mention of 'domesdaye' added here by the author (see RG 94 n. for more examples).

276–81 *þe furst slowen . . . gret kyndenesse*. Leaps to the start of Wyclif's chapter 9, and draws on *Dialogus*, 17/2–10.

281–93 *And as . . . for euermore*. Returns to chapter 8 and gives a fairly close paraphrase of *Dialogus*, 15/25–16/10 and 16/14–17, though the author's explanation of 'tyme wiþouten end aftur domesday' and 'state of innocentis' expand markedly on Wyclif's cryptic 'ut patet de statu innocencie et statu glorie' (*Dialogus*, 16/7–8).

293–7 Like Veritas in *Dialogus*, 16/27–9, though in different terms, Reson here tells Gabbyng why his argument is unacceptable, in the process giving readers grounds to reject it on the grounds of both authority and reason. See above, RG 272–6 n., and below, RG 305 and n., 329–38 and n.

297–306 *And as anentis . . . acceptid here*. Here the author leaps forward to a passage part way through Wyclif's *Dialogus* chapter 9, 18/17, and summarizes its contents closely to 19/5. This is the first occasion where a leap forward in Wyclif's *Dialogus* made by the author of RG does not correspond to a chapter division in the text edited by Pollard, and it may indicate that the author was working from a text with different chapter divisions (see also RG 40 n.).

305 *reson wiþ Goddis lawe* Reason and Scripture are very frequently cited as a pair in Wycliffite writings as the necessary grounds for any legitimate argument. See JR 76 n. and Somerset, *Clerical Discourse*, 180–3. See also below, RG 311–19.

307–10 *Hit semiþ . . . fewe eritikis*. This succinct rendition of Mendacium's argument (*Dialogus*, 19/14–21) highlights Wyclif's concern with defining legitimate and illegitimate grounds for argumentation.

311–12, 316–19 *þese wordis . . . to hem. . . . And it nys . . . of his lawe*. A close paraphrase of *Dialogus*, 19/22–4, 20/8–11, though in between Wyclif, unlike the author, does not supply the precise wording of a pithy counter-argument.

313–16 This recommended reply draws on *Dialogus*, 20/14–18, though without citing Augustine as Wyclif does.

321–9 The author skips over the discussion of saints and their fallibility in Wyclif's chapter 10, *Dialogus,* 20/26–21/11—there is a closer analogue to the chapter 10 passage in JR 265–325. Instead, the author draws on chapter 11, *Dialogus*, 22/10–29.

327–8 *two popis*. As in Wyclif's *Dialogus* chapter 11, 22/13, this is a reference to the Papal Schism (on which see JR 185–6 and n.).

327–8 *if two popis diffyneden contraries, God mote falle to hem boþe*: 'if two popes determined contraries (i.e. made opposing definitive pronouncements), then God would have to agree with both of them' (that is, God would have to assent to granting both contraries as true, a logical absurdity). Contraries, in everyday speech, are opposites, or opposing claims. In the technical sense, contraries and contradictories are not the same: drawing on Aristotle's *De Interpretatione*, especially chapters 6 and 7 (see *Aristotle's Categories and On Interpretation*, trans. Ackrill, part of the elementary logic curriculum at Oxford, Wyclif and his contemporaries defined 'contraries' as opposed propositions that while they cannot both be true, might both be false (for example, 'every man is running' and 'no man is running', both false if some men are running), while 'contradictories' are opposed propositions only one of which can be true (for example, 'every man is running' and 'not every man is running'). Either the technical or the looser sense of 'contrary' may obtain here.

329–38 This first attempt at a systematic explanation of what mental attitudes are appropriate towards what sorts of statements, and on what grounds, draws briefly on chapter 10 of Wyclif's *Dialogus*, 20/23–6 (cf. RG 338). The rest of this passage is the author's own formulation, though it also draws on *Dialogus*, 21/22–9, a passage that foregrounds conformity to Scripture without commenting on reason. However, the weighing of conformity with reason and Scripture in the search for truth, and the withholding of confirmation or denial for matters that may not be proven in this way, are consistent with Wyclif's and Wycliffite statements elsewhere. These are, for example, explained more fully in Wyclif's *Dialogus*, chapter 12, 24/6–22, a passage the author works with closely (cf. RG 357–75 and n).

338 *And as anentis witnesse . . .* Here the author leaps to the start of Wyclif's chapter 11, *Dialogus*, 21/12.

340 Eccl. 1: 15.

341–2 Dan. 13: 2–63. The story of Susanna had considerable popular currency in medieval England. See e.g. the *Pistel of Swete Susan*, a verse rendition in the Vernon manuscript: *Minor Poems of the Vernon Manuscript*, ed.Furnivall, 626–36. For similar usage of this story by Wycliffites elsewhere see Matthew 74/34; *Lanterne of Liȝt* 113/11.

342–3 3 Kings 18: 15–40.

343–6 *And as anentis . . . last deed* condenses *Dialogus*, 22/4–10. The author then omits Wyclif's complaint about papal authority and papal elections, *Dialogus*, 22/10–25, before picking up the final sentence of Wyclif's chapter 11, *Dialogus*, 22/25–9; cf. RG 346–8 *Bi þis colour . . . loue of truthe.*

349–53 Gabbyng's objection is a condensed version of Mendacium's at the start of Wyclif's chapter 12, *Dialogus*, 23/1–14, with the difference that Mendacium points beyond papal authority to the spectre of civil unrest (23/13–14), while Gabbyng claims Reson's proposal would lead to a complete breakdown of any human belief (RG 352–3).

354–7 *þou farest . . . mankynd*e The biblical anecdote about 'gabbyng' by the 'fend' breaks down any straightforward characterization of Reson's interlocutor as either 'Gabbyng' or 'þe fende' (cf. RG 4, and see also RG 7 n.). On the other hand, it allows the author to substitute a familiar biblical story (cf. Gen. 3: 1–6) for Wyclif's corresponding barrage of academic terminology: 'Video quod a patre mendacii didicisti distincciones et equivocaciones subterfugere, et inconveniencia saltem tibi apparencia concludere videaris' (*Dialogus*, 23/15–17).

357–63, 363–75 This is a close translation of part of Wyclif's chapter 12, *Dialogus*, 24/6–22 and 24/25–25/1. The author skips Wyclif's sideswipe at contemporary teaching in logic: 'Ideo debemus catholice relinquere famosum puerile principium quod omnis proposicio proposita sit concedenda, neganda, vel dubitanda' (*Dialogus*, 24/22–5), and slightly expands the discussion of how these recommended attitudes apply to the question of our own and others' salvation. For a comparative examination of several such instructive passages in Wycliffite writings see Somerset, *Clerical Discourse*, 205–8; see also JR 282 n., FS 153–6 n.

375–82 *And þus. . .* This peroration provides a thematic connection to the discussion of the seven works of mercy that appears next in R (see Introduction, p. xxxiv).

376–7 James 5: 20. James suggests that anyone who turns a sinner from the error of his ways can save that sinner's soul. The author interprets this reproof as a charitable act, although James does not explicitly label it as such. For a conceptual link similar to the one in the conclusion of this dialogue, between charity, correction of the faults of others, and the works of mercy for which every person will be held accountable at their death and the Last Judgement, see JR 803–24. See also RG 381–2 n., below, on the seven spiritual works of mercy (among which reproof of sinners is typically listed).

378–82 Matt. 25: 31–46 is Matthew's full account of the Last Judgement; for Christ's address to the wicked who shall be damned because they did not do the works of mercy see Matt. 25: 41–6. The biblical passage is paraphrased and expanded here rather than translated precisely: Matthew does not distinguish 'bodily' and 'gostly' works of mercy, for example (see following note).

381–2 *seuen warkes of mercy . . . bodily ne gostly* The seven works of mercy are often regarded as a guide to behaviour in the world in accordance with charity. For Wycliffites they are a programme of charitable pastoral life to which the laity can aspire, and of complaint against clergy who fail to perform them. The seven bodily (or corporal) works of mercy are feeding the hungry, giving drink to the thirsty, clothing the naked, giving housing to the homeless, visiting the sick, visiting those in prison, and burying the dead. The first six are listed repeatedly in Matthew's account of the Last Judgement at Matt. 25: 31–46; the seventh is drawn from Tobit (Tob. 2). The seven 'gostly' (or spiritual) works of mercy are teaching the ignorant, counselling others to the way to heaven, chastising the sinful, comforting those fearful of God's mercy, forgiving those who have wronged you, patience, and prayer. The ordering and interpretation of the spiritual works, even more than the corporal works, varies considerably: this list is drawn from the Wycliffite commentary on the seven bodily and spiritual works of mercy as edited by Arnold 168–82—the same treatise (though Arnold's edition is based on another manuscript) that follows RG. For a standard late medieval exposition see the *Fasciculus Morum*, 528–9; for another Wycliffite commentary see Matthew, 13–18.

382–3 *Man if þu wilt do þeis dedis seuen þu schalt haue þe blis of heuen, etc.* The 'etc.' suggests that this was a familiar tag of the kind quoted repeatedly in pastoral manuals and sermons. The verse does not appear in *NewIMEV*, however.

DIALOGUE BETWEEN A CLERK AND A KNIGHT

1–2 On the social standing, training, and anticipated mode of debate implied in this description of the status of each participant, see the further development in CK 4–8, 19–28, 30–2, 33–44, 260–4, 282–8, 419–22, as well as the Introduction, pp. liii–liv.

4–11, 12–19 The opening exchange neatly sets up the Clerk's and Knight's opposing claims. The Clerk speaks for papal supremacy: he asserts that the temporal (or secular) hierarchy should be governed by holy Church, and that any temporal interference with spiritual (or ecclesiastical) governance and possessions is contrary to God's law. While the Knight does not deny that the pope does have a legitimate sphere of influence (see also CK 87–107 and n., where he states his position more fully), his concern is that the pope and clergy are attempting to encroach on the temporal sphere and reduce the king's power. Wyclif, and Wycliffites, are typically less temperate on the subject of papal power than the Knight, though this is at least partly because they are usually engaged in polemic rather than ecclesiology: thus they criticize papal corruption rather than describing papal jurisdiction in the abstract. For brief, historical introductions to the issues and arguments the Clerk and Knight will debate, see Watt, 'Spiritual and Temporal Powers', and Black, 'Church and State'. On Wyclif's own political thought see the introductory article and recommended further reading by Stephen Lahey in the *Stanford Encyclopedia of Philosophy*, <http://plato.stanford.edu/entries/wyclif-political/> accessed 1 Nov. 2006. The Clerk's position is typically hierocratic: he subordinates temporal to spiritual power, yet does not mean so much to imply that the church should take over the day-to-day governance of kingdoms, as that kings ought to regard the pope as their superior and on some occasions obey his orders. Like many royalist anti-hierocrats, the Knight does not attempt to argue the opposite—that the pope is subordinate to kings and emperors—but rather that the pope has only a distinct, limited sphere of influence, over spiritual matters.

48–9 *þe pope es Cristes vikere here on erþ, and his powere es oneliche of God.* The papal title 'vicar of Christ', in use from the fifth century until the present day, might seem a neutral designation, yet arguments over the vicariate of the pope as opposed to that of the king are highly volatile, as will transpire (see CK 52–4, 55–8, 65–7, 162–6, and nn.; cf. Trevisa, *Dialogus*, 5/3–11/3). Typically such arguments dispute who rules vicariously in place of whom (the pope as vicar of Peter? of Christ? of God? the king as vicar of Christ?), who confers that vicariate (Christ? God? the pope in his role as vicar?), whether all, or only some, of the capacities of the ruler are given to the vicar (does the pope have *plenitudo potestatis*, that is, full ultimate authority over matters temporal as well as spiritual?), and what mode of election and what conduct validate the vicariate and its continuation. For the development of these claims and their implications see Ullmann, *The Growth of Papal Government*; Wilks, *The Problem of Sovereignty in the Later Middle Ages*; Watt, *Theory of Papal Monarchy*; Pennington, *Pope and Bishops*; Tierney, *Foundations*. Wycliffite writings more usually dispute the vicarious powers of lords or knights as opposed to priests or prelates; cf. RG 13–14 and n.

50–2 Exod. 18: 19, 32: 27. The 'emperoures law' is normally the term for Roman civil law, yet of course Justinian does not cite the example of Moses. On the tendency to describe papal power in imperial terms, and drawing on Roman civil law, see Watt, *Theory of Papal Monarchy*, 86–8. The most likely reason for the Clerk's incongruous citation (arguably an afterthought appended to the previous sentence, but it fits there even less well) would seem to be that it prepares the way for the Knight's rebuttal that England has never been subject to the emperor's law (see below, CK 149–52, and cf. Trevisa, *Dialogus*, 3/1, Arnold 326/16–327/27). In using this line of argument the Knight also follows Wyclif: see e.g. *De Potestate Pape*, 226/34–228/13; see also Tatnall, 'John Wyclif and Ecclesia Anglicana'.

52–4 In canon law, as here, the pope is compared with Moses to show that he has full temporal and spiritual power (D. 33 c. 6).

55–8 Jer. 1: 10.

63 Matt. 5: 17. Biblically based arguments that refer to the Old Testament frequently turn on the question of whether anything in Christ's precepts might be said to supersede or cancel out what the old law says; on such occasions this passage is usually what justifies the retention of Old Testament precepts alongside the New.

65–7 Matt. 16: 18–19. This passage is a favourite for papal supremacists, who typically claim the pope is Peter's successor and contemporary proponent of the power conferred by Christ on Peter (cf. CK 48–9 n., and see Tierney, *Foundations*, 23–32).

79–87 Num. 22: 21–35, 2 Pet. 2: 15–16. The Knight equates the clergy with Balaam and secular lords with Balaam's ass, who repeatedly refuses Balaam's urging to take the route the angel of God forbids, then finally with

God's help reproaches Balaam. Bede cites the passage to justify lay instruction of the clergy in his commentary on 2 Peter; his commentary is quoted in the *Decretum* among arguments for when and how laymen can reprove the clergy (C. 2 q. 7 c. 31). The example is popular in fifteenth-century English writings: see *The Life of St Norbert by John Capgrave O.E.S.A. (1393–1464)*, ed. Smetana, 26/139. Balaam is also given credit for the first prophecy of Christ's incarnation: se e.g. *A Critical Edition of John Lydgate's Life of our Lady*, ed. Lauritis, 588/25–9; *The Three Kings of Cologne*, ed. Horstmann, 4/4–30. And he is used, citing Jude 1: 11, as an example of covetousness: see *A Fourteenth-Century English Biblical Version*, ed. Paues, 219/41–4; *Dives and Pauper* i. ii. 262/1–263/26.

87–107 The Knight asserts that however comprehensive it may be, Church power properly covers only a spiritual jurisdiction confined to a narrow scope of pastoral activities. For a similar set of arguments see Trevisa, *Dialogus*, esp. 11/4–19/8 Cf. the Clerk's rebuttal and redefinition of the Knight's terms at CK 365–73. 'Spiritualte' is similarly disputed, at the incitement of Wrath, in *Piers Plowman* B 5.145–51 (possessioners vs. friars) and C 6.118–27 (friars vs. prelates, called Beggars and Barons).

95 *seuen dedes of merci*. See RG 381–2 n.

107–8 *a man schall be for he will noȝt come to hem atte first somounynge*: 'a man shall be excommunicated because he will not come to them at the first summons'.

107–17 Corruption in the Church's administration of penance is a frequent Wycliffite complaint—although equally it is often acknowledged that confession in itself may have some validity, and the efficacy of confession to God (with or without accompanying confession to a priest) is often urged. See *Middle English Rosarium*, Cambridge, Gonville and Caius College MS 354/581 f. 23, Matthew 181/1–182/15, 186/14–34; *37 Concl.*, 18/14–22/24; JR 528–9 and n., JR 550–85 and nn., FS 188–98 and nn.

116–17 Mary Magdalene is commonly used as the type of a deeply sinful person who has been saved by thorough repentance: the gospel basis is Luke 7: 47–50. See, for example, the *Fasciculus Morum*, e.g. 124/15–25, and for a Wycliffite example, *37 Concl.*, 20/5–7; in both cases she is listed with Peter and Paul.

118–20 1 Cor. 4: 1.

120–3 Christ instructs the apostles that whoever would be first among them should be the minister and servant of the others at Matt. 20: 25–8 and Luke 22: 24–7. 'In spiritualte' is the author's additional stipulation.

127–30 The 'charter' of the donation of Constantine referred to here is a document forged in the eighth century in which it is recorded that Constantine conferred on Sylvester imperial power, dignity, emblems, the

Lateran palace, and rulership over Rome and even the cities and towns of the whole Western hemisphere. The full text is available online at The Latin Library, <http://www.thelatinlibrary.com/donation.html>, accessed 12 October 2006. The document makes a perilous defence for clerical possession, for if the Church acquired temporal power and goods through Constantine, then it can be asserted (as in the Knight's reply, CK 139–57) that Constantine acted against God's wishes, for God neither confers nor endorses temporal possession by the clergy. Constantine's supposed donation was widely criticized in late medieval English writings: see e.g. Gower, *CA* 2.3187–3496; *Piers Plowman* B 15.557–67/C 17.220–51; Matthew 377/28–381/32.

155–7 *aȝaine Goddes will and moni lawes of diuers popes es about to supplant and benyme oure kinge real power þat es ȝeuene to him be God himself*: 'against God's will and many laws of various popes, [the pope] is working to supplant and take away our king's royal power given to him by God himself'.

161–2 The Knight is cynical (or his papal clerks are) about reasons why cardinals might find themselves at odds with the pope. Yet the circumstances under which cardinals might overrule or depose a heretical or tyrannical pope, even if that pope may draw his authority from God, had been and still were the subject of prolonged theoretical debate—as well as practical application, most immediately for this writer perhaps to the Papal Schism (on which see JR 153 n.), though the issue had also been of acute concern in the early fourteenth-century conflicts between Boniface VIII, the Colonna cardinals, and Philip IV of France, in which accusations of heresy and tyranny had been made. On these conflicts see *Boniface VIII en Procès*, ed. Coste.

162–6 The Knight's defence of his assertion that the king's power is conferred on him directly by God rather than (as hierocratic thinkers would have it) through the pope's mediation is rather perfunctory, perhaps because by the time of writing kings do not routinely seek legitimation from popes. His vague references are probably to 1 Kings 8: 5–22 and D. 96 c. 6.

176–8 *and was bicause þat þan was holi chirch noȝt so born doune, and her power wiþstonde, as it has bene now longe tyme*: 'and this was because holy Church was not then so oppressed, and its power resisted, as it has been now for a long time'.

197–9 *þe þrid dele o þe land es in her handes, and bene waxen worldliche lordes þat þe comone popil es greteli anentisid þerbi*: 'a third of the land is in their hands, and they have become worldly lords, with the result that the common people are greatly depleted by this'. The estimate that the Church owns one-third of the land in England also appears in the record of the 1380 parliament in which proposals for the poll tax were presented:

the Commons replied that since the clergy 'occupie la tierce partie del roialme', the laity would consent to raise two-thirds of the required levy if the clergy took responsibility for one-third. (*PROME* Richard II, 1380 November, art. 13).

201–7 On the arguments that the Knight opposes here, in favour of clerical possession on the grounds that church goods are inalienable and against it on the grounds that the Church ought to return to apostolic poverty, see further CK 253–9 and n., 213–18 and n.

210–13 Arguments that profess to inform the king about contemporary conditions and the ways that they contravene the right order of things hinge on the assertion (hinted at several times in this dialogue, as in each of the others, esp. JR 990 and n., FS 285–300 and n., RG 118–42 and n.) that proper information obliges its secular recipients to act. If they do not, they will become participants by consent in the activities they know of but do not prevent.

213–18 There are many Wycliffite arguments made on the grounds that the Knight so briefly lists here for why the clergy ought not to be involved in secular affairs. For those that complain, as here, that clerics usurp secular lordship and possessions when they ought to live in apostolic poverty, see *37 Concl.*, 1/1–2/12; Matthew 235/31–237/8, 376/22–379/24; *Tractatus de Regibus*, 12/25–15/31. For complaints about clerical service to lords see below, CK 279–88 and n.

225–9 In response to the Clerk's extension of pastoral care to cover supervision of temporal affairs (see CK 126–32), the Knight insists that the laity, most especially the king, are responsible for supervising and reforming the clergy's behaviour. The secular ruler is bound to defend and protect the Church, a precept mentioned repeatedly in canon law (see e.g. D. 63 c. 3, 27, 33, and see the oath required of bishops and dependents of the pope, on which many secular coronation oaths in Europe were modelled, in the *Liber Extra*, X 2.24.4; see also Kantorowicz, 'Inalienability: A Note on Canonical Practice', esp. 492 n. 26). However, the author also suggests that the secular ruler is obliged to 'ȝeue straite rekynynge' not only for his own actions, but those of the Church. Canon law, on the other hand, quoting Gelasius's famous letter on the separation of spiritual and temporal powers and subordination of the temporal to the spiritual, 'Duo sunt', assigned the responsibility of rendering an account for the souls under their care to the spiritual power (D. 96 c. 10).

253–9 For canon law against the alienation (that is, the transfer of ownership) of Church possessions see the Decretals of Gregory IX, X 3.13.1–13. In addition, Boniface VIII's papal bull *Clericos laicos* of 1296 (available online at the Internet Medieval Sourcebook, <http: //www.fordham.edu/halsall/source/b8-clericos.html>) forbade the clergy to cede any property to secular power under any circumstances without papal approval: this bull seems to be the Knight's target later, at CK 394–406. For more details on why church possession was controversial see CK 365–73 n.

272–8 See D. 32 c. 5, 6, and cf. D. 81 c. 15. Cf. Matthew 435/9–30; *37 Concl.*, 125/14–128/8.

279–88 See also the Wycliffite complaints about clerics neglecting pastoral duties for secular lordship listed at CK 213–18 n. For complaints about clerics who take secular office in the service of lords, see 'Twelve Conclusions' in *SEWW*, 26/62–72; *37 Concl.*, 2/13–4/5; Matthew 13/10–20, 22/11–24/11, 242/5–19. The gospel basis for decrying the service of two masters may be found at Matt. 6: 24, Luke 16: 13. The Knight's vaguer references to Paul and canon law may refer to 2 Tim. 2: 4 (frequently adduced in such contexts), perhaps to 1 Cor. 6: 4, and to D. 88 c. 4, 14, and C. 21 q. 3 c. 4.

312–13 *borell clerk*. 'Borell' refers to a type of cloth typically worn by lay persons; the term is used metonymically to describe lay persons, generally of low degree and little education. Other 'borell' men or clerks may be found in Chaucer, *Prologue of the Monk's Tale* 7.3145; *Prologue of the Franklin's Tale* 5.716; *Summoner's Tale* 3.1872; Gower, *CA* prol.52; *Piers Plowman* B 10.292; Hoccleve, *Regiment of Princes*, ed. Blyth, 1439. The combination of a word used to describe laymen and their typical characteristics with 'clerk', normally applied to clerics and associated with the book-learning they are thought to possess, blurs lay and ecclesiastic status in such a way that the precise standing of the person being described is obscured, and the conventional equation between clerical status and education destabilized: 'borell clerk' could designate an ill-educated cleric, or an educated layman, or an ill-educated layman with clerical pretensions. Cf. CK 343–8.

317–18 Christ instructs his apostles or disciples to teach and preach at Matt. 10: 7, 28: 19–20; Mark 3: 14, 12, 16: 14–20 esp. 15; Luke 9: 2, 6, 10; John 10.

323–5 Rom. 13: 1–4. For CK's author, *her power es noȝt bot of God*: 'their power is from God alone'. For Paul in Rom. 13: 1, there is no power except from God, a broader claim.

329–30, 334–5 Luke 22: 32.

335–7 Christ had promised before his crucifixion that the faith would not fail (see previous note), but between his execution and resurrection the apostles all lost faith; therefore during that period the faith was preserved in Mary alone. Cf. *37 Concl.*, 73/14–74/8, where laymen and humble priests are said to be like Mary in this respect. For a survey of the origins and uses of this claim from the eleventh to the seventeenth centuries see Congar, 'Incidence ecclésiologique d'un thème de dévotion mariale'.

338 ff. *þou saist þat holi chirche* . . . For an earlier edition of a selection from this dialogue, starting here and continuing to the end, see *SEWW* 131–4.

352–3 Wycliffites tend to prefer—or ostentatiously to claim to prefer—argument based on Scripture. But on occasion, as here, they meet their opponents on their own ground by citing canon law. *37 Concl.*, probably the Wycliffite text that cites canon law most extensively, explains that the laws of the pope are good as far as they accord with Scripture and reason; the difficulty is that so often they do not, and thus harm the church (44/15–47/16).

356–7 *bot vndernymmynge of þat, þat*: 'but only in criticism of the fact that'.

363–5 English ecclesiastics as much as secular officials seem to have thought it crucial to insist upon their allegiance to the king and present themselves as his supporters, however much contortion this might require. For an example of such contortion see the competition for most faithful allegiance in the exchange between Jack Upland, Friar Daw, and Upland's Rejoinder in the *Upland series*, esp. *JU* 62/180, *FDR* 90/561–76, *UR* 110/270–5.

365–73 The Clerk asserts separate 'spiritual' and 'temporal' jurisdictions in a rather different sense than the Knight's (cf. CK 87–107 and n.): he defines 'spiritual' as referring not to the Church's responsibilities for teaching, preaching, and administering the sacraments, but to the Church's material possessions. While the Knight's previous usage is restricted and prescriptive, the Clerk's usage is restricted and descriptive: here 'spiritual' is a near-synonym for 'ecclesiastical' and refers specifically to Church possessions. On a usage similar to the Clerk's and its role in disputes over taxation of Church possession, see Swanson, *Church and Society in Late Medieval England*, 111–12. On canon law forbidding the alienation (transfer of ownership) of church possessions, see CK 253–9 n.

386 *amortaise*. Land or goods are amortized, or alienated into mortmain, when their ownership is transferred to a corporation: the corporation of greatest concern here, and in the Statute of Mortmain of 1279 which attempted to prohibit the practice, is the Church. The problem is that since a corporation does not die, the property will hence be held in perpetuity unless its ownership is transferred again—and canon law forbids any such transfer of Church property (see CK 203–7 n.). On the administration of the Statute of Mortmain in England see Raban, *Mortmain Legislation and the English Church*. Wycliffites disapprove strongly of amortization: see e.g. *37 Concl.*, 92/4–94/3, 97/3–5, 111/19, Arnold 307/6–36.

419–22 Note the self-consciously literary play at the end of the dialogue (CK 464–5), where the Knight himself uses just the kind of ending he says the Clerk resorts to when reason fails him.

436–7 Rom. 13: 1–4; cf. CK 323–5.

438–45 The argument about the two swords has its basis in Luke 22: 38. For a very helpful introduction to and survey of the arguments of papal and anti-papal theorists using this passage see Watt, 'Spiritual and Temporal Powers'. Typically one sword is taken to symbolize temporal and the other spiritual jurisdiction; at issue are the questions whether Peter may exercise temporal as well as spiritual power; whether even if not, he still retains some ultimate control over temporal power; and whether Peter's capacities or lack of them have any bearing on the pope's jurisdiction.

448–52 Matt. 26: 52, John 18: 10.

452–4 Eph. 6: 17.

455–6 Rom. 13: 1–4; cf. CK 323–5, 436–7.

GLOSSARY

The Glossary is selective, designed to provide a guide for students with some previous exposure to Chaucer, with particular attention to the specialized or technical usage of common words. Only the forms and the meanings of words that seem likely to cause difficulty are included: no attempt is made to provide a full inventory either of forms or of meanings. Thus, if a word is sometimes used in its fully modern sense, sometimes in a less familiar sense, only the unfamiliar sense may be included. The directive *see note* refers the reader to the Explanatory Notes for the first line reference given (unless otherwise specified).

Line references employ the abbreviations for the titles of the dialogues used throughout this volume (JR, FS, RG, CK). The first few instances of any given headword are listed; as a result, the preponderance of examples of frequently occurring words are drawn from JR. The most common spelling in the text where a word first occurs (for many but not all words, JR) is generally used as the headword. To aid the reader in finding the relevant entry, cross-references from variant spellings are as full as possible. All later spellings that might give difficulty are recorded under the main headword.

Only actual forms found in the text are listed, never hypothetical uninflected forms. Emended forms are marked with an asterisk. Standard grammatical abbreviations are employed. For nouns, only the singular form is included, except where the plural has a special sense or spelling that may cause trouble, or where the singular never occurs. For verbs where the infinitive occurs, only the infinitive and any spellings or forms that might give difficulty are listed; however, line references may incorporate instances and phrases using forms other than the infinitive where this may elucidate meaning and usage. For verbs where the infinitive does not occur, a full list of forms is included, and all variant spellings are gathered under the most frequently occurring spelling of the first form to be listed. In either case, verb forms are listed in the order *inf.*, *(1, 2, 3) sg. pr. ind.*, *(1, 2, 3) pl. pr. ind.*, *(1, 2, 3) sg. pr. subj.*, *(1, 2, 3) pl. pr. subj.*, *imp. sg.*, *imp. pl. pr. p.*, *(1, 2, 3) sg. pa. ind.*, *(1, 2, 3) pl. pa. ind.*, *(1, 2, 3) sg. pa. subj.*, *(1, 2, 3) pl. pa. subj.*, *pa. p.*, *ppl. adj.* Person is not always specified in the plural and subjunctive. Verbal nouns are given separate entries.

The following conventions are used in alphabetizing premodern spellings. Variation of i/y is included under i, though not where y is used consonantally as in modern English. J at the beginning of a word is very rare and is alphabetized under I. Past participles with an i-prefix are listed alphabetically under the verb from which they are derived, though crossreferences also appear amidst the entries for 'i'. Yogh (ȝ) follows g and thorn (þ) follows t. The scribes usually use v for initial v and u, and u within words for both v and u: in the Glossary, these spellings are sorted and alphabetized according to modern usage.

A

a *see* **haue, a** *v. inf.*
a-beggynge *see* **o(n)** *prep.*
abhomynable *adj.* abominable, unsuitable as human behaviour, repellent FS 181
ab(i)l(e) *adj.* apt, qualified, competent, capable CK 137, 139, ~ *of connynge* knowledgeable CK 27
abil(e) *v. inf.* make suitable JR 222, 227
abite, abute *n.* habit JR 30, 31, 184, etc.
abot *n.* abbot JR 366
aboue(n) *adj.* raised above, superior to CK 9, 56, 70, etc.
abou(ȝ)te *prep.* about, concerning JR 674, 757, 758, etc.
about(e) *adv.* as *adj.* *ben* ~ *to make þat* are in the process of bringing it about that FS 18, ~ . . . *to* plotting to, working to CK 16, 156, 164, etc.
abrege *v. inf.* diminish CK 17, 164, 358, etc.
abusiones *n. pl.* abuses CK 404

accept(ed) *ppl. adj.* ~ *to* acceptable to JR 735, RG 132
accident *n.* (1) a variable property or characteristic of a thing, as opposed to its more essential and invariable 'substance' JR 929 (*see note*) Polemical references often, as here, pun on the less technical senses of the term: (2) a fortuitous happening, (3) a pathological change, (4) a specious explanation (see *MED*).
accidentaliche *adv.* incidentally JR 596
accusiþ *v. 3 sg. pr. ind.* convicts, condemns JR 135
acordauntlyche *adv.* in accordance with FS 247
acorde *n.* harmony, concord RG 72
acorde *v. inf.* ~ *to*, ~ *wiþ* be (or become) in agreement with, reconcile with RG 300
acordynge, acordinge *ppl. adj.* in accordance with FS 5, CK 459
acursid *v. pa. p.* ~ *of* cursed by FS 206
afer *adv.* far off JR 50, 268
affermen *v. 3 pl. pr. ind.* affirm, endorse JR 318
afied *v. 1 sg. pa. subj.* ~ *me in* trusted, put faith in JR 801
aftur *adv.* afterwards, later JR 174, 269, 896
aftur *conj.* ~ *þat* after the time when JR 92
aftur, aftir, efter *prep.* after CK 128, according to JR 702, 792, in accordance with JR 20, 349, 395, etc., ~ (*þat*) according to whether FS 24, 25, ~ *þat* insofar as FS 142, in accord with that CK 226
agayne *see* **aʒe(y)ne, agayne** *adv.*
agene *see* **aʒe(y)n(e), agene** *prep.*
aʒaynes, aʒaines *see* **aʒe(y)n(e)s, aʒeins, aʒenst, aʒaynes, aʒaines** *prep.*
aʒeynbyʒing *pr. p.* ~ *for* redeeming RG 210
aʒe(y)ne, agayne *adv.* again JR 258, 499, RG 281, in return JR 997, 998, *torne* ~ return CK 217
aʒe(y)n(e), agene *prep.* against JR 652, 1003, RG 162, etc.
aʒe(y)n(e)s, aʒeins, aʒenst, aʒaynes, aʒaines *prep.* against JR 74, 197, 285, FS 89, CK 8, etc., contrary to FS 75
aʒen(e)s *conj.* concerning JR 140, 142, 154 (not in *MED*)
aʒeneseiþ *v. 3 sg. pr. ind.* denies JR 545; **aʒeneseyen** *3 pl. pr. ind.* deny JR 387
aʒenstande *v. inf.* oppose, resist JR 950
aʒenward(e) *adv.* on the contrary JR 639, the other way around FS 15
aʒt *see* **awe** *v. 3 sg. pr. ind.*
al(le) *adj. of* ~ *oþere* of all FS 152; ~ *þing* everything FS 4, 41, 45, etc.; ~ *þingis* everything (pl. with sg. sense) FS 39, 54, 55, etc.; ~ *o(o)ne* (*wiþ*) entirely the same (as) FS 31, 128, 129
al *adv.* entirely ~ *only*, ~ *onli* only JR 54, 274, 826, etc.
al *conj.* ~ *be I* even though I am CK 30, ~ *be it þat* even though FS 32, 40, 65, etc., ~ *if see* **al (ʒ)if** *conj.*, *þouʒ* ~ *see* **þouʒ** *conj.*
alege *v. inf.* give as evidence, claim, allege RG 125, CK 134; **aleggen** *3 pl. pr. ind.* JR 924, FS 257 (*see also* **allegeaunce** *n.*)
algatis *adv.* in every way JR 277, 987, FS 282, etc.
al (ʒ)if *conj.* even if JR 23-4, 285, 463, 508, etc.
alyue *adj.* alive FS 172
alkemie *n.* alchemy JR 83
allegeaunce *n.* claim, allegation CK 154
almasful, almesful *adj.* generous (in giving alms) FS 283, 286
almes(s) *n. pl.* alms, monetary support JR 729, 730, 744, etc., *in* ~ by way of charity, from alms CK 204, 266
almes(s)(e)-dede *n.* act of giving alms FS 249, 276, 277
almiʒthi *adj.* almighty JR 363
als *adv.* also CK 247
als *conj.* as JR 220, CK 10, 38, etc.,
amend(e) *v. inf.* ameliorate, rectify RG 146; *refl. inf.* ~ *him of his synne* repent CK 106
amendyng *vbl. n.* improvement RG 24
amys(se) *adv.* wrongly JR 110, 711, 816
amonge *prep.* among *knowe hem* ~ *hemself* distinguish them JR 655
amonge *adv.* in many places, again and again JR 506 (it is also possible that **amonge** is prepositional and its object is missing)
amortaise *v. inf.* alienate in mortmain (*see note*) CK 386

an *conj.* and RG 7
and *conj.* if RG 52
anem(p)(s)te(s), anentis *prep.* (*as*) ~ as concerns, against JR 725, 759, 764, RG 281, etc.
anentisid *v. pa. p.* weakened, depleted CK 199
anoon *conj.* ~ *as* as soon as FS 116, 122
answeren *v. 3 pl. pr. ind.* ~ *togeder*, correspond in kind JR 796
answerynge *ppl. adj.* ~ *to hym*, in accordance with it FS 26
antecrist *n.* Antichrist, ~ *clerke(s)* clerk(s) of Antichrist JR 999, 1030
apis *n. gen.* ape's JR 875; *n. pl.* apes JR 897
apostasie *n.* apostasy, abandonment of faith JR 824
apostata, apostita *n.* abandoner of the faith JR 642, 783
apreue *v. inf.* approve, endorse FS 4
approued *ppl. adj.* ~ *of* approved by FS 63
araied *ppl. adj.* dressed, arrayed CK 24
arowes *n. pl.* arrows JR 131
arunt(e) *v. inf.* revile, scold RG 190, 302 (not in *MED*; *see OED*)
asaie *v. imp.* test, try out JR 84; **asseyed** *v. 3 sg. pa. ind.* RG 355
aschameþ *v. 3 pl. pr. ind.* ~ *of* are ashamed by FS 295
aschaping *vbl. n.* ~ *fro* getting away safely from, success in avoiding JR 130
askyng *vbl. n.* request RG 115, **axingis** *pl.* questions JR 1023
askiþ *see* **ax(e)** *v. inf.*
asoyled *see* **assoile** *v. inf.*
asoiling *vbl. n.* absolution JR 568
assoile *v. inf.* absolve CK 112, 431; **asoyled** *pa. p.* solved, answered JR 694
asseyed *see* **asaie** *v. imp.*
atte *prep.* with JR 7
atteynte *v. pa. p.* ~ *in* convicted of FS 99
attones *adv.* at the same time CK 286
auditours *n. pl.* listeners, audience members RG 132
auter *n. brede of þe* ~ the Eucharist JR 924
autorite *n.* authority JR 137, 139, 141, etc.
auaile *v. inf.* be useful, benefit, help CK 115
auansid *v. pa. p.* promoted, appointed to a benefice CK 293
auaunsid *ppl. adj.* endowed with benefices or promotions, elevated in the social hierarchy CK 24
avoydide *v. 1 sg. pa. ind.* put away FS 16
awe *v. 3 sg. pr. ind.* ought (modal *v.*, sometimes *impers.*, expressing obligation) RG 118; **ouȝt, aȝt** *3 sg. pr. ind.* ought RG 291, CK 159, etc.; **aȝtest** *2 sg. pr. ind.* ought CK 375; **aȝt, owen** *3 pl. pr. ind.* ought RG 134, CK 48, 194; **owen** *impers. pr. ind.* ought RG 61
aweye *adv. as predicate* gone, elsewhere, absent (*see MED* s.v. 'awei', adv. 9) JR 825
awen, awne *adj.* own CK 136, 355
ax(e) *v. inf.* ask for, require JR 330, 572, 819, etc.; **askiþ** *3 sg. pr. ind.* requires RG 151, 153
axingis *see* **askyng** *vbl. n.*
ay(e) *adv.* always RG 117, 151, 182

B

bacbitynge *n.* slander JR 486
bad *see* **biddeþ, biddiþ** *v. 3 sg. pr. ind.*
bagged *ppl. adj.* bag-using (*see note*); swollen, bulging (*see MED* s.v. 'baggen', v.(1) b) JR 54, 829, 830
bayle, baile *n.* baillif, one with delegated administrative authority over a lord's affairs CK 289, 292
bate *n.* strife, discord JR 632
be, bi *prep.* by JR 1, 4, 36, 496, etc., about, concerning RG 2, with respect to, according to RG 19, 214, 224, etc., through RG 294, ~ *lijf/lyif* and ~ *word* through living example and through verbal teaching RG 45-6, 212
bede, beden *see* **biddeþ, biddiþ** *v. 3 sg. pr. ind.*
beding *vbl. n.* praying (with beads) JR 1013 (*see also* **biddeþ, biddiþ** *v. 3 sg. pr. ind.*, and **biddyng, bidding(e)** *vbl. n.*)
before *conj.* ~ *(þat)* before JR 77, 168, 298, etc.
beggerie *n.* practice of begging JR 786, 829

begyleþ *v. 3 sg. pr. ind.* fools, beguiles RG 323; **begiled** *pa. p.* RG 326
begiling *vbl. n.* trickery, beguiling RG 147
behalfe *n. on Goddes* ~ on God's side, in accord with God's will JR 313
beleeue *v. inf.* believe RG 331
bele(e)ue *n. see* **bile(e)ue, bele(e)ue** *n.*
beldyng *vbl. n.* building, construction JR 745
beneiþe *adv.* beneath JR 33
benym(e) *v. inf.* take away from CK 156, 158, 257, etc.
berd(e) *n.* beard FS 43, 63, 65
bere *v. inf.* sustain, support RG 31, ~ . . . *companye* accompany JR 989, ~ *hem on hand* accuse (someone) CK 208, 263, ~ *hem vp* support them RG 261-2, ~ *vp* elevate JR 802, ~ *vpon hem* display JR 488; **born** *pa. p.* carried, borne ~ *doune* brought low, oppressed CK 177, 412
berkyng *vbl. n.* barking JR 178
besides, byside, bisidis *prep.* in addition to JR 414, FS 268, along with JR 506, apart from JR 834
betene *v. inf.* beat CK 57; **bett** *3 sg. pa. ind.* CK 81
betokeneþ, bitokneþ *v. 3 sg. pr. ind.* signify JR 35, 588, 603, CK 455, etc.; **betokene(n)** *3 pl. pr. ind.* symbolize JR 31, 34; **betokned** *pa. p.* CK 89
better *comp. adv. he miȝt* ~ *do* it would be better for him to do JR 528
better *n. for þe* ~ for the better (thing) JR 960
betuix, bytwixe, bitwixe *prep.* between JR 626, 775, FS 2, 128, 264
beupere *n.* father (used to address priest) OR peer, companion JR 1002
bi *see* **be, bi** *prep.*
bi *see* **big(g)e, bi** *v. inf.*
biddeþ, biddiþ *v. 3 sg. pr. ind.* asks, orders (with clause), orders to, asks to (with *inf.*), asks for (with *n.*) JR 1, 335, 410, etc.; **bidden** *3 pl. pr. ind.* JR 916; **bidde** *3 sg. pr. subj.* JR 378; **biddyng(e), bidding(e)** *pr. p.* ~ . . . *mercy* asking . . . for mercy FS 184, 186, 187, etc.; **bad** *1 sg. pa. ind.* RG 10; **bad** *3 sg. pa. ind.* JR 845, 876, CK 97; **bede** *3 sg. pa. subj.* FS 273; **beden** *pa. p.* ~ *of* asked by RG 21; **biden** *pa. p.* prayed CK 334
biddyng, bidding(e) *vbl. n.* directive JR 101, 832, 837, etc.
bifore *adv.* first JR 757
bifore *pref.* ~* *honour* give precedence to FS 6 (not in *MED*; *see note*); ~ *deliberacioun* premeditation FS 68 (not in *MED*)
bifore *prep.* before, *was* ~ *ȝow* was held before you FS 2; before FS 70, 80
big(g)e, bi *v. inf.* buy FS 301, CK 397, 439
biggers *n.* beggars FS 223
biggynge, bigginge *vbl. n.* begging FS 217, 218
bygynne *v. inf. al to* ~ to be begun all over again JR 117
bilawes *n. pl.* bylaws JR 774
bile(e)ue, bele(e)ue *n.* belief, creed JR 936, 1030, FS 4 (*see note*), RG 116, 175, etc., *Crist* ~ belief in Christ FS 35, *of* (*þe*) ~ of faith FS 39, 42
bynde *v. inf.* obligate, bind CK 103; **bynde** *3 pl. pr. ind.* ~ *not* are not binding JR 695; **bounden** *pa. p.* CK 66, 226
biried *v. pa. p.* buried JR 26, 638
byside, bisidis *see* **besides, byside, bisidis** *prep.*
bisie *adj.* ~ *to* eager to JR 310
bisi(e) *v. refl. inf.* concern himself/herself/themselves (with) JR 757, etc.
bisied *ppl. adj.* preoccupied JR 851
bisili, bisily *adv.* assiduously JR 1012, RG 56, 61
bisines(se) *n.* occupation, eagerness, concern JR 89, 130, 309, etc.
bitoke *v. 3 sg. pa. ind.* entrusted to, gave CK 97
bitokneþ *see* **betokeneþ, bitokneþ** *v. 3 sg. pr. ind.*
bytwixe, bitwixe *see* **betuix, bytwixe, bitwixe** *prep.*
blaberiþ *v. 3 sg. pr. ind.* blabbers JR 953
blackenes *n.* blackness JR 686
blasfeme *n.* blasphemy JR 50; **blasfemes** *n. pl.* blasphemies JR 207, 235, 506, blasphemers JR 45, 208, 915
bleckeþ *v. 3 sg. pr. ind.* blackens JR 578
blemyche *v. inf.* harm JR 50
blesse *n.* bliss FS 147

blinden *v. 3 pl. pr. ind.* make obscure JR 768
blyndest *superl. adj.* blindest, most blinkered JR 231
blowing *n.* ~ *of name* boasting JR 245
bodili, bodely, bodelich(e), bodily, bodilyche *adj.* physical, material (often as opposed to **gostili, gostily, goostly(che)**) JR 13, 29, 739, 974, etc., FS 138
bonde *n.* pledge, commitment *take in his* ~ pledged CK 228
bo(u)ndis *n. pl.* bounds, boundaries RG 60, 83
borell *adj.* lay, unlearned (*see note*) CK 312, 344, 347
born *see* **bere** *v. inf.*
bost *n.* boasting JR 614
bot *see* **but, bot** *conj.*
boþe *adv.* also, too JR 475, 477, 485, etc.
bounden *see* **bynde** *v. inf.*
boundis *see* **bo(u)ndis** *n. pl.*
bowe *v. inf.* ~ *from* bend from, turn aside from JR 277, FS 76–7
brekynge *vbl. n.* breaking FS 219
brent *v. pa. p.* burnt JR 197, 400
breþeren *n. pl.* brothers, brethren JR 166, 644, 711, etc.
briddis *n. pl.* birds RG 243
bryngiþ *v. 3 sg. pr. ind.* ~ *to* leads to FS 35, 36
brolles *n. pl.* offspring JR 408
but, bot *conj.* only JR 92, 105, 324; *conj.* unless JR 122, 523; *conj.* except RG 118; (*no*) ~ *if conj.* unless JR 215, 470, 628, RG 174, etc.; ~ *for conj.* were it not for, except because FS 99, 132; *no more* ~ . . . nothing more than . . . FS 208; ~ *of* nothing but FS 84

C

caas *n.* situation JR 107, *in* ~ *þat* in a situation where JR 758
caccheþ *v. 3 sg. pr. ind.* drives, urges, ~ . . . *to councel* enjoins to take advice JR 60
cakest *v. 2 sg. pr. ind.* excrete JR 409
cam, camen *see* **com(m(e)** *v. inf.*
can *see* **kunne** *v. inf.*
cap(i)teynes *n. pl.* captains JR 160, 710
cardenal(l)es *n. pl.* cardinals JR 230, 232
cardenal *adj.* principal JR 419
care(y)n(e) *n.* corpse JR 10, 23
carpen *v. 3 pl. pr. ind.* speak, chatter JR 474
cast *v. inf.* ~ *for** plot to attain JR 104; **casten** *3 pl. pr. ind.* plot JR 77
castes *n. pl.* plots, tricks JR 920
cause *n.* reason JR 184, 216, 218, etc., argument, example RG 209
cautel *n.* trick, deceit JR 375
certaine *n.* a certain sum of money CK 109
certe(y)n, certaine, certayne *adj.* sure, convinced JR 113, 127, *in* ~ sure, convinced FS 245, *in* ~ *as emphatic* indeed CK 178, 183, 322
certen *adv.* indeed JR 91
certes, certis *adv.* certainly JR 101, 368, 416, etc.
chafer *v. inf.* buy and sell JR 1013
chaffer *n.* merchandise JR 1014
chaieris *n. pl.* chairs JR 100
chalengiþ *v. 3 pl. pr. ind.* lay claim to JR 914
changaunt *adj.* variable JR 681
chanoun *n.* canon (usually Augustinian canon) RG 165; (more usually *pl.*) **chanoun(u)s** *n. pl.* JR 145, 158, 889, etc.
chapilen *n.* clergyman who assists member of clergy of higher rank in performing his duties JR 93
chapitre *n.* the members of a religious order, convent, convent, etc., typically when acting as an administrative or legislative body JR 99
charge *v. inf.* burden JR 521, etc., consider important JR 634 etc.; **chargeþe** *3 sg. pr. ind.* commands CK 323; **charge** *3 sg. pr. subj.* consider important JR 250; **chargid** *3 sg. pa. ind.* appointed CK 143
charge *n.* obligation, responsibility FS 289, CK 231, 237, ~ *of* burden with respect to RG 166
chargyng *vbl. n. þer* ~ the burden they bring JR 456
charteris *n. pl.* charters JR 1025
checiþ *see* **chese** *v. inf.*
cheef *adj.* chief, principal RG 301
chese *v. inf.* choose JR 523, 741, FS 4; **checiþ** *3 sg. pr. ind.* JR 96; **chese** *3 sg. pa. ind.* RG 150; **ches** *3 pl. pa. ind.* JR

986; **chosen** *pa. p.* JR 79; *3 pl. pa. subj.* JR 237
chesing, chesyng *vbl. n.* choice JR 249, ~ *of men* men's choice JR 248
chirche, kirke *n.* church JR 4, 6, 66, 1003, etc.
chois(e) *n.* choice JR 740, 882
chosen *see* **chese** *v. inf.*
cite *n.* city FS 251
claþid *v. pa. p.* clothed JR 32
clede *v. pa. p.* dressed JR 602
clene *adj.* pure JR 734, 775, 849, ~ *be hemself* unaltered, unadulterated JR 772
clenely, cleneli *adv.* purely JR 858, 864
clennes *n.* purity JR 32, 605, 692, etc.
clepiþ *v. 3 sg. pr. ind.* calls JR 26, 242; **clepen, clepyn, clepes** *pl. pr. ind.* call JR 342, 1002, RG 4, CK 161; **cleped** *3 pl. pa. ind.* called RG 18; **clepid** *pa. p.* called JR 100, 341, 430, etc.
clereli(che) *adv.* clearly JR 322, purely JR 860
clergi(e), clergy *n.* (1) clergy (the status in the world) CK 7, 9, 15, etc.; **clergie** *n. gen. þe* ~ *hondes* the hands of the clergy CK 394-5; (2) learning RG 216, CK 22, 25 (often a given usage is deliberately ambiguous between these two semantic fields)
cleue *v. 3 pl. pr. subj.* ~ *to* be devoted/obedient to JR 62
closed *v. pa. p.* enclosed JR 923
closter *n.* cloister JR 659
clouted *ppl. adj.* patched, palliated, mistakenly emended JR 331, 332, 784, etc.
cloutes *n. pl.* patches JR 337
clouen *v. pa. p.* split, divided JR 185, 186
clumben *v. pa. p.* ~ *þerover* climbed over JR 424
coynte *adj.* elaborately contrived JR 736
collectis *n.* collections (of alms) FS 261
colourid *v. pa. p.* ~ *wiþ* given the false appearance of FS 339
colour(e) *n.* feigned appearance FS 312, argument (sometimes with implication of speciousness) RG 167, 346, CK 203, etc.; **colores** *n. pl.* colours (of habit: implying the heraldic sense and the symbolism that this would imply: see *MED* s.v. 'colour', n. 2a) JR 591
comaund *v. inf.* make commands CK 61
com(m(e)) *v. inf.* come JR 129, RG 38, etc; **come(n)** *3 pl. pr. ind.* come JR 691, ~ . . . *to* measure up to (not in *MED*, but see s.v. 'comen', v. 4a) JR 278, ~ . . . *þerto* attain to that, achieve that JR 794; **com(e)** *3 sg. pr. subj.* come JR 122, 143, 542; **come(n)** *3 pl. pr. subj.* come JR 62, 298, 648; **cam** *3 sg. pa. ind.*, came JR 122; **come** *3 sg. pa. ind.* came FS 239, 248, RG 209; **com(e(n))** came *3 pl. pa. ind.* JR 121, 136, 151, 448, etc.; **camen** *3 pl. pa. ind.* JR 154; **com** *3 sg. pa. subj.* came JR 625; **comen** *3 pl. pa. subj.*, came JR 127; **commen** *pa. p.* come RG 260
comense *v. inf.* be granted privileges as master or doctor, lecture (see *MED* s.v. 'commencen', v. 3a) JR 53, etc.
comensing(e) *vbl. n.* becoming master of arts JR 86, 99*
cominalte *see* **comunte, cominalte** *n.*
comoun *adj.* ~ *profit* common or public good RG 30, ~ *seel* shared, official, and communally binding seal (*see note*) JR 1012, 1016, 1022, etc.
comoune *v. inf.* associate, share, deal FS 311
comounli *adv.* often JR 577, 768, 838
comunte, cominalte *n.* community FS 289, 297
con *see* **kunne** *v. inf.*
concel *v. inf.* counsel JR 828
conceleþ *v. 3 pl. pr. ind.* conceal CK 245
concense *n.* consent JR 990
conferme *v. inf.* confirm RG 108, *3 sg. pr. subj.* RG 305
confermed *ppl. adj.* ~ *in* confirmed in JR 591, ~ *of* confirmed by JR 183, 618, RG 196
confermed *ppl. adj.* ~ *to* obedient to, in conformity with JR 249, 569, 945
confermyng *vbl. n.* confirmation RG 221
confessed, confessid *ppl. adj., often as vbl. n.* (person who has) confessed (usually discussed in relation to a confessor) JR 532, 535, 574
confessiþ *v. 3 sg. pr. ind.* affirms JR 760
connen *see* **kunne** *v. inf.*
connynge *see* **cunnynge, connynge** *vbl. n.*
conseyue *v. inf.* learn, comprehend JR 212
contenyd *v. pa. p.* contained RG 173

contynue(l)lyche *adv.* continually FS 157, 168, 170
contrari(e) *adj.* contrary JR 101, 389, 946, etc.,
contrari(e) *adv.* contrary JR 942
contrari(e) *n.* opposite JR 295, 411, RG 48, etc. (*see* RG 327–8 n.), *to* ~ the other way JR 309
contrarien *v. 3 pl. pr. ind.* speak/act/be contrary to JR 71, 90, 351, etc., ~ *togeder* are contrary to one another JR 490
contrarious(e) *adj.* contrary, in opposition FS 34, RG 71
contrariouste *n.* state of being contrary (to God) JR 488
copis *n. pl.* cloaks JR 692
corsedli *adv.* damnably JR 525
corsid *ppl. adj.* accursed, damnable CK 409
corsynge *vbl. n.* excommunication CK 106
cost *n. of litel* ~ requiring little expense or labour JR 1023
costi *adj.* valuable, costly JR 738
cote *n.* tunic, outer garment CK 439
councel *see* **counse(i)l, councel** *n.*
counfort *v. inf.* ~ . . . *to fiȝt* encourage/incite . . . to fight JR 989; **counforted, counfortid,** *pa. p.* comforted, encouraged JR 687, RG 155
counse(i)l, councel *n.* advice JR 60, RG 176, council CK 183; **counseyles(is)** *n. pl. Cristis* ~ Christ's special precepts FS 200, 212
countrollore *n.* keeper of counter-roll (for checking accounts), steward in charge of expenditures, any official with similar duties CK 283
couaitise *see* **coue(i)tise, couetyse, couaitise, couoytise** *n.*
coueit(e), coueyt *v. inf.* desire, seek after JR 102, etc.
coueytynge *vbl. n.* desiring FS 219, 324
coue(i)tise, couetyse, couaitise, couoytise *n.* greed, covetousness JR 356, 524, RG 46, etc.
coueitouse *adj.* greedy, covetous RG 289
couenant *n.* ~ *wiþ his wittis* internal resolution JR 574
couent *n.* religious group or order JR 350, 365, 368, etc.
coue(i)tise, couetyse *see* **coue(i)tise, couetyse, couaitise, couoytise** *n.*
couoytise *see* **coue(i)tise, couetyse, couaitise, couoytise** *n.*
cowde *see* **kunne** *v. inf.*
craft *n.* profession, field of expertise JR 52, 56, 834, etc., *it is no* ~ it shows no expertise JR 520, *be þer* ~ using their expertise JR 471; **craftis** *n. pl.* tricks JR 38
creature *n.* created thing JR 863, person RG 131, 174
cressing *n.* increase JR 641
crie, cry *v. inf.* ~ (*him*) *mercy* plead (with him) for mercy FS 195, 197, RG 301; **crien** *3 pl. pr. ind.* ~ *in* proclaim by means of JR 672
crienge, cryynge *vbl. n.* ~ *of mercy* pleading for mercy FS 191, 192
crokeþ *v. 3 sg. pr. ind.* diverges, bends aside JR 248; **croken** *pl. pr. ind.* diverge JR 37
cropon *ppl. adj.* (having) crept JR 11
crowned *v. pa. p.* rewarded, honoured JR 56
cunnynge, connynge *vbl. n.* knowledge, skill FS 14, CK 77, 359, etc.; *ppl. adj.* knowledgeable CK 25, ~(. . .)*of* knowledgeable about CK 22, 35 (*see also* **kunne** *v. inf.*)
cuntres *n. pl.* countries JR 377
curatis, curates *n. pl.* parish priests JR 449, 510, etc.
cure *n.* ~ *of . . . soules* benefice for parish, spiritual responsibility for parishioners CK 280, 288
curteis *adj.* courteous, courtly, gracious RG 184
custumable *adj.* customary, habitual, entrenched RG 55

D

daie *n. in adv. phrases: all* ~ constantly CK 16, *iche* ~ everyday JR 601, *moni* ~ for a long time CK 176, *þis* ~ nowadays JR 950
idampned *v. pa. p.* damned FS 154, 155
dar *v. 3 pl. pr. ind.* dare JR 207
dawen *adv.* down RG 7
declareþ *v. 3 sg. pr. ind.* explains, makes clear JR 8; **declare** *imp.* ~ *hem more* explain them further JR 18

decreeȝ(e), decrees *n. pl.* Gratian's *Decretum*, the rulings contained therein, or more loosely, canon law CK 31, 41, 166, etc.
decretal(l)(e)s *n. pl.* the *Decretals of Gregory IX*, also known as the *Liber Extra*, or more loosely, the rulings it contains RG 217, 234, CK 216
dede *n.* deed, action JR 56, etc. *in* ~ in reality, in action JR 583, FS 26, 317, etc.; **dedus** *n. pl.* JR 700
dede, deed *adj.* dead JR 10, 23, 25, etc.
de(e)d(e)ly(che), dedeli *adj.* mortal, deadly FS 161, 163, 164, 167, 194, etc.
deden *see* **do(ne)** *v. inf.*
dedus *see* **dede** *n.*
deel *n.* mourning JR 11
defau(ȝ)te *n.* deficiency, sin JR 396, 838, RG 141, *in* ~ has failed (in some activity) FS 118
defauteþ *v. 3 sg. pr. ind.* fails (in some activity) FS 119
defouled, defoulid *ppl. adj.* defiled, impure FS 178, 180
degre *n.* (academic) degree JR 121
dele *n.* part, portion CK 197
dele *v. inf.* administer CK 93
delyberacioun *n.* deliberation, thought FS 81, 83, 84, etc.
demen *v. inf.* judge FS 144; **demynge** *pr. p.* judging FS 140
demynge *vbl. n.* judgement FS 136
departis *v. 3 sg. pr. ind.* separates RG 57; **departen** *3 pl. pr. ind.* ~ *to* share with JR 493; **departe** *imp.* separate, go away RG 379; **departid** *1 sg. pa. ind.* ~ *in* divided into RG 12; **departed** *3 pl. pa. ind. . . . to* shared . . . with JR 307; **departid** *pa. p.* ~ *among* shared among FS 267, ~ *from* separated from RG 46
departing *vbl. n.* separation JR 270
depli *adv.* deeply JR 811
deppest *superl. adj.* deepest JR 840
deseyueþ, deseyuen, dessaiueþ *see* **disceyue** *v. inf.*
deseyuyng *vbl. n.* ~ *of þer soule* self-deception JR 1009
desertis *n. pl. wiþouten . . .* ~ without (someone) deserving it FS 108, 141
dette *n.* debt, state of indebtedness FS 276, 281
deuel *n.* devil JR 12, 992
deuys *n. at poynt* ~ exactly, to perfection JR 271
deuocioun *n.* devotion, religious contemplation JR 721, 737
deuorse, diuorse *n.* divorce, separation JR 626, 786
diden *see* **do(ne)** *v. inf.*
diffyneden *v. 3 pl. pa. subj.* determine, decide (*see note*) RG 328
dippe *v. inf.* ~ *in þer habites* saturate their habits with JR 714
disceyue *v. inf.* JR 991; **deseyueþ** *3 sg. pr. ind.* deceives JR 38, 452; **deseyuen** *3 pl. pr. ind.* JR 701; **dessaiueþ** *3 pl. pr. ind.* CK 245; **dissaiue** *3 pl. pr. ind.* CK 208
discensioun *n.* dissent JR 679
discression, discrecioun *n.* discretion JR 972 ~ *of resoun* capacity for reasoned choice FS 69
discriueþ *v. 3 sg. pr. ind.* describes JR 9
discriuynge *vbl. n.* description JR 8
disspende *v. inf.* spend JR 132
dispending *vbl. n.* ~ *of churches* expenditure on churches JR 726
dispendores *n. pl.* stewards, almoners CK 119
dispenses *n. pl. make þer* ~ pay their expenses JR 85
dispensid *v. pa. p.* ~ *wiþ hem* granted them by special dispensation RG 111
dispergeþ *v. 3 sg. pr. ind.* damages JR 57
dispisen *v. inf.* despise JR 466
dispite *n.* ~ *of* contempt for JR 34
dispitiden *v. 3 pl. pa. subj.* engaged in disputation, argued RG 3
disposing *vbl. n.* management, arrangement, disposition RG 226
disputusun *n.* disputation FS 2, 7
dissaites *n. pl.* deceits, deceptions CK 408
dissaiue *see* **disceyue** *v. inf.*
dissolued *v. pa. p.* done away with, dissolved JR 627, 918, 933
distourbelen *v. 3 pl. pr. subj.* ~ *most* most disturb JR 396; **disturbeled** *pa. p.* disturbed JR 851
distried, distroued, distrowed *v. pa. p.* destroyed JR 258, 292, 680
disturbeling *vbl. n.* disturbance JR 533
disturblaunce *n.* disturbance JR 454
diuers(e) *adj.* different JR 151, 848, 849, etc.

diuite *n.* riches (not in *MED*) FS 254
diuorse *see* **deuorse, diuorse** *n.*
docturis, dottouris *n. pl.* learned persons JR 924, *fowre* ~ four evangelists JR 119, 263
do(ne) *v. inf.* do, perform JR 73 etc., act CK 456, ~ *it in dede* by fulfilling it JR 583, ~ *sacrifice* make sacrifice JR 983, *þerwiþ* (. . .) *noȝt to* ~ , *no more to* ~ *þerwiþ* not (somebody's) affair CK 315, 388–9, *as causative*, *see* **hide; dostow** *2 sg. pr. ind.*, do you (**dost** contr. with **þou**) CK 420; **doþ** *3 sg. pr. ind.* ~ *awaie* removes JR 532; **don** *3 pl. pr. ind.*, ~ . . . *inprison* make . . . imprison (causative) JR 920; **doun** *3 pl. pr. ind.* JR 96, 512, 539, etc.; **deden** *3 pl. pa. ind.* JR 128; **diden** *3 pl. pa. ind.*. JR 366, 710; *pa. p.* FS 326; **don(e)** *pa. p.* JR 110, 111, FS 326, etc., ~ (. . .) *to deþ* put to death JR 256, 400; **doun** *pa. p.* JR 536, 551, 603, etc.; **idon** *pa. p.* FS 194
doing, doynge *vbl. n.* action, behaviour JR 878, CK 354, activity, business CK 255, 302; **doynges** *pl.* affairs, business CK 213, 357, conduct CK 245
do(o)m(e) *n.* judgement RG 151, 153, *dai(e) of* ~, *daye o* ~ Last Judgement JR 115, 690, 702, CK 281-2, ~ *place* hall or forum for holding court (*see note*) FS 28, *don* ~ give judgement FS 360
domesday(e), domysday *n.* Last Judgement RG 94, 112, 273, etc.
dottouris *see* **docturis, dottouris** *n.*
doumbenesse *n.* silence JR 471
dowed, dowid *v. 3 sg. pa. ind.* endowed JR 225; *pa. p.* CK 195
dowyng, dowing *vbl. n.* endowment JR 228, RG 322, *hadde* ~ *of* had an endowment from JR 306
drawe *v. inf.* pull RG 124; **drowe** *3 sg. pa. ind.* drew CK 449; **drawyn** *pa. p.* led away RG 43
drecche *v. inf.* destroy spiritually JR 12
dreynte *v. pa. p.* drowned RG 275
drede *v. inf.* ~ *vpon* be concerned about JR 812; **drede** *refl. 1 sg. pr. ind.* ~ *me* fear CK 20, 40
drede *n.* fear JR 201, 873, *it is no* ~ there is no doubt JR 141, 484, *no* ~ no doubt JR 407
drynke *n.* (alcoholic) drink JR 900
dritt *n.* filth, dirt, excrement RG 222
dryueþ *v. 3 sg. pr. ind.* drives, forces JR 515
drounken *ppl. adj.* drunk JR 898
drowe *see* **drawe** *v. inf.*
duelt *see* **dwelliþ** *v. 3 sg. pr. ind.*
durynge *vbl. n.* enduring, remaining FS 172
dwelliþ *v. 3 sg. pr. ind.* remains, abides FS 163; **dwellen** *3 pl. pr. ind.* FS 161; **dwelle** *imp.* ~ *beneþe* stop short of, remain outside RG 331; **duelt** *3 pl. pa. ind.* dwelled JR 180

E

ech(e), iche *pron.* (*as adj.*) each and every, every JR 15, 133, 734, FS 12, etc., (*as n.*) every one JR 1021, FS 267, RG 79, etc.
effecte *n. comeþ aftir in* ~ results, follows FS 139
eft(e) *adv.* again JR 114, 431
efter *see* **aftur, aftir, efter** *prep.*
eftesoones *adv.* again, a second time FS 21
eiȝen, iȝen *n. pl.* eyes JR 756, FS 37, 225, etc.
eir(e) *n.* air JR 450, RG 243
eke *adv.* also JR 431, RG 132
(e)elde *n.* age JR 20, antiquity JR 697, *chaunging of* ~ aging JR 909
ellis *adj.* in addition RG 89
ellis, elles *adv.* else, other(wise) JR 385, 844, 888, etc., *or* ~ or else JR 76, 415, 707, etc.
enclinyng *ppl. adj.* ~ *to* yearning towards, desirous of RG 47
encroche *v. inf.* ~ *to ȝou* appropriate, take CK 378
ende *n.* purpose RG 341
endurid *ppl. adj.* hardened, habituated RG 304
enfecte *adj.* infected, compromised RG 228
enfourmed *v. pa. p.* informed, advised CK 211
englaymed *v. pa. p.* covered with sticky substance, filth, or poison CK 196
ensaumple *v. inf.* provide an example (of) FS 313, 320, 321, etc.
ensa(u)mple, ensaumpil *n.* example FS

218, 309, CK 432, etc., *take* ~ *of hem* follow their example JR 502
entent *n.* intention, purpose JR 813, 815, RG 224, etc., *to þe same* ~ for the same purpose JR 620
eny *see* **ony, oni, eny** *adj.*
equyte *n.* equity, equivalence FS 221
erd(e) *n.* earth (as opposed to heaven or hell) CK 62, 66, 67
ereyne *n.* spider JR 1020
(h)eritage *n.* inheritance, something inheritable RG 86, 98, 101, etc.
eritikis *n. pl.* heretics RG 310
erst *adv.* first, earlier CK 400
ert *v. 2 sg. pr. ind.* are CK 21; **nys, nis, nes** *v. 3 sg. pr. ind.* (**ne** contr. with **ys**) is not RG 316, CK 137, 278, ~ *but* is nothing but FS 184; **were** *v. 3 sg. pa. subj. it* ~ *to* it would be as well to JR 6–7; **iwere** *3 pl. pa. subj.* were JR 128
erþely, erþeli, erþelyche *adj.* earthly, secular, of this world JR 737, 996, FS 254, etc.,
euen(e) *adv.* equally, exactly RG 10, ~ . . . *in þat þat* exactly in as much as JR 668, straight, directly JR 29, *smac(c)hen* ~ *see* **smaccheþ** *v. 3 sg. pr. ind.*
euer(e) *adv.* always JR 305, 895, ~ *more* always FS 163, 173, 174
euerich(e) *adj.* every RG 28, 174, ~ *a* every CK 221
euydence, euydens *n.* evidence RG 363, 365, etc. *is an* ~ *to men* shows men evidence JR 251
excesse *n.* excess, excessiveness JR 125, 359, 735, etc.
excusacions *n. pl.* excuses CK 298
excuseþ *v. 3 sg. pr. ind.* ~ *not* does not excuse JR 892; **excusen** *3 pl. pr. ind.* ~ *not* do not excuse JR 123; **excusid** *3 sg. pa. subj.* ~ *not* would not excuse JR 132; *pa. p.* CK 299
expowne *v. inf.* explain, expound JR 412; **expoune** *pl. pr. ind.* JR 417
expresse *adj.* explicit JR 546
exsposiciones *n. pl.* explanations, expositions CK 447

F

fabellis, fabeles *n. pl.* fictions, JR 140, 726
fadur, fadir, fader *n.* father JR 176, 191, 192, etc., FS 107, etc.; *my* ~ *lawe* my father's law RG 18
fagist *v. 2 sg. pr. ind.* flatter JR 789; **fagen** *3 pl. pr. ind.* ~ . . . *þat* deceive (by claiming) that JR 624; **faged** *1 sg. pa. subj.* flattered JR 801
fagyng *vbl. n.* flattery JR 194
faileþ *v. 3 sg. pr. ind.* is lacking JR 433, 460; **failen** *pl. pr. ind.* JR 438, 440; **failed** *pl. pa. ind.* JR 177; **faylen** *impers. pl. pr. ind.* ~ *me* I lack JR 138; **hym failed** *impers. pa. subj.* he would lack JR 869
faytour *n.* cheat, faker FS 185, 187
fall(e) *v. inf.* (1) fall, descend, decline (often in spiritual senses, i.e. into sin) JR 114, ~ *herfro* fall away from JR 319; *pl. pr. ind.* ~ *fro* fall away from JR 332; **fallen** *pl. pr. ind.* ~ *in*, fall into JR 567, 620, 621; (2) *inf.* ~ *to* side with RG 328; (3) *inf.* happen, befall JR 573, 641, CK 308, (*with dative*) ~ *him*, befall him JR 97; **fallen** *3 pl. pr. ind.* ~ *þes freres* befall the friars JR 646; **falleþ, falliþ** *impers. pr. ind. it* ~ it happens JR 618, 644, 962; (4) **falleþ, falliþ** *impers. pr. ind.* ~ *to* belongs to, pertains to, befits JR 52, 524, 739; **fel(le)** *3 pl. pr. subj.* ~ (*to*) JR 95, 449; (5) **fallen** *3 pl. pr. ind.* start (to do something) JR 99
false *n.* falsehood JR 409
falshed *n.* falsehood RG 323
farest *v. 2 sg. pr. ind.* behave RG 354; **faren** *3 pl. pr. ind.* ~ *as* behave like FS 258
farisee *n.* Pharisee FS 224; **pharesies, pharesees, phariseus, pharises, pharezes, farisees** *n. pl.* JR 70, 72, 73, 100, 398, 440, 538, FS 352, 355
fast *adv.* steadfastly, zealously JR 696
fastre *comp. adv.* more zealously, harder RG 289
fauȝte *n.* deficiency, lack JR 448, fault, lack JR 827, 843, *put* ~ *in* blame JR 333; **fawttes, fauȝtes** *n. pl.* faults JR 148, 806
fauorabil *adj.* ~ *to* biased toward CK 37
fawour *n.* honour JR 201
fawttes *see* **fauȝte** *n.*
fediþ *v. 3 sg. pr. ind.* ~ *of* nourishes JR 756
feile *adj.* many JR 468

feyne *v. inf.* pretend RG 272
feyned, feynid *ppl. adj.* false, pretended RG 195, 342, 373
feynyng *vbl. n.* deception JR 701
feynt(e) *adj.* faint, half-hearted RG 190, 355
felyng(e) *n.* capacity for sensation, feeling JR 139, FS 148
fellenes *n.* cruelty JR 143
fer *adv.* far JR 705, 767
ferforþ *adv.* far FS 287, 294, CK 426, *so* ~ *þat* to such an extent that CK 199
ferþe *see* **fourte, ferþe** *num. ord.*
ferþer *adv.* further JR 577, 621, CK 148
ferthyn *n.* farthing FS 349
fieþ *v. 3 pl. pr. ind.* disparage, refuse JR 635
fifte *num. ord.* fifth JR 766
figur(e), fygure *n.* symbol, prefiguration JR 177, CK 51, *in* ~ as an allegory, more precisely a tropology FS 249
(i)figured *v. pa. p.* symbolised, prefigured JR 171, FS 224, CK 89
fyȝelid *v. pa. p.* defiled, mired RG 192
fiȝt(e) *v. inf.* fight JR 986, 989; **fiȝteþ** *3 sg. pr. ind. chirche þat* ~ *in erþe* church militant (*see note*) JR 196
fiȝtting *vbl. n.* fighting JR 987
fyle *n.* file FS 7
firist *see* **frist, firist** *num. ord.*
first *adv. as* ~ as before, as at first JR 510
fyueþ *num. ord.* fifth RG 96
fle(ȝ)(e) *v. inf.* flee RG 20, 182, 198; *imp.* flee JR 942
fleynge *vbl. n.* fleeing, avoiding FS 76
fleschely *adj.* preoccupied with sins of this world/of the flesh RG 140
floreschon *v. 3 pl. pr. ind.* embellish JR 208
foolis *n. gen.* fool's RG 235; **fo(o)les, fo(o)lis** *n. pl.* fools JR 30, 234, 878, 889, etc.
foli, foly *n.* folly JR 239, 526, 875, etc.; **folies** *n. pl.* follies JR 716
foly *adj.* foolish RG 139, ~ *it is of hem* it is foolish of them JR 590
folily *adv.* foolishly RG 95
foloweþ *v. 3 pl. pr. ind.* ~ *of* follow (as a logical consequence) from CK 405
fonde, fondoun *see* **fo(u)nde** *v. 3 sg. pa. ind.*
foole *adj.* foolish JR 378
for *conj.* for, because, since JR 7, 23, 30, etc.
for *prep.* ~ *to prep. w. inf.* JR 12, 18, 230, etc., ~ *forþe* onward JR 289, *bisied hem* ~ were concerned about JR 738
forbed *v. 1 sg. pr. ind.* forbid RG 44; **forbediþ** *3 sg. pr. ind.* JR 977; **forbet** *3 sg. pa. ind.* CK 121; **forboden** *pa. p.* CK 213, 254, 284, etc.
forbot *n.* interdiction CK 362
fordoþ *v. 3 sg. pr. ind.* does away with JR 787
forfendeþ *v. 3 sg. pr. ind.* forbids JR 89
forȝeten *v. pa. p.* forgotten CK 307
forȝetynge *vbl. n. of* ~ from forgetfulness FS 93
forȝetyngnesse* *n.* forgetfulness FS 89
forȝeuenesse *n.* forgiveness FS 141
forme *adj.* first FS 107
fororrid *ppl. adj.* in garments trimmed with fur (*see MED* s.v. 'furrure', n.) CK 24
forsoþe *adv.* truly FS 20
forþere *adv.* furthermore FS 209
forþerd *v. pa. p.* furthered, advanced, supported CK 426
foulis *n. pl.* fowls, birds RG 247
fo(u)nde *v. 3 sg. pa. ind.* found, discovered JR 232, RG 355; **fondoun, ifounde, founden** *pa. p.* JR 232, 984, FS 284, RG 179
founded *v. pa. p.* ~ *on*, ~ *in* based on JR 58, 76
fourme *n.* model, type, pattern, example RG 214, 216, 231, *in her* ~ according to the model they follow RG 226, *in his* ~ according to his model, i.e. as in Scripture RG 317, *after þe* ~ *of Goddis lawe* as given in the Bible RG 382
fourte, ferþe *num. ord.* fourth JR 190, 429, 659
fowre *num. card.* four JR 27, 119
fre(e) *adj.* free, unconstrained JR 880, RG 136, 169, etc.
freli, freely *adv.* without constraint JR 634, RG 35, 186
frenes *n.* liberty, state of being free of superfluous rules JR 677
freres *n. pl. foure* ~ four orders of friars JR 178, 182
frist, firist *num. ord.* first JR 612, 725
fro *prep.* from, JR 15, 114, 130, etc.,

fru(ȝ)te *n.* product, result JR 91, 456, fruit JR 474
ful *adv.* fully JR 204, 773, very JR 705
fulfille *v. inf.* carry out, obey, act in accordance with FS 201, 206, etc.

G

gabbyng *n.* falsehood, lie RG 4, 356, etc., name of personified disputant embodying falsehood, RG *passim*
gader *see* **geder(e), gader** *v. inf.*
gaf(e) *see* **ȝeef, ȝif, ȝyue, ȝeue(n)** *v.inf.*
galpe *v. inf.* gulp JR 65
gamen *n.* game, i.e., animal(s) sought in hunting (*see note*) JR 450
gates *n. pl. on many* ~ in many ways JR 53
geder(e), gader *v. inf.* encompass, include JR 650, 651, 828, conclude JR 483; **gadered** *pa. p.* ~ *of* collected from JR 88
getyng *vbl. n.* acquisition RG 222
gile *v. inf.* deceive, beguile JR 30, *3 pl. pr. ind.* ~ . . . *of* deceive . . . about JR 923
gilt *v. inf.* ~ *to* sin against CK 21
gladlyer *comp. adv.* more gladly RG 175
glenen *v. 3 pl. pr. ind.* ~ *to hem* scrounge for themselves JR 498
glosatowres *n. pl.* commentators JR 206
glosen *v. 3 pl. pr. ind.* provide glosses for (often with negative connotations, as here) JR 920
glosis *n. pl.* glosses, interpretations JR 320
glotoun *n.* glutton JR 900; **glotouns** *n. gen.* glutton's JR 897; **glotoun(e)s** *n. pl.* gluttons JR 436, 898
godhed *n.* divinity, divine nature RG 14, 19, 277
goiþ, go(o)þ, goinge, goynge *see* **goste** *v. 2 sg. pr. ind.*
go(o)d(e) *adj.* good JR 146, 283, 899
go(o)d(e) *n.* property, money, commodities (commonly *sg.*, where now *pl.* 'goods' would normally be used) CK 366, 367, 368, etc., *þe worldes* ~ worldly goods JR 345, good (part) JR 886; **go(o)de(s), goodis** *n. pl.* goods JR 78, 83, 126, etc., good things, JR 129
gost(e) *n.* ghost, spirit *holi* ~ Holy Spirit JR 380, 532, *of þe* ~ spiritual CK 453
goste *v. 2 sg. pr. ind. þou* ~ *hard to me* you are being hard on me CK 249; **goiþ, go(o)þ** *3 sg. pr. ind. bifore* . . . ~, ~ *bifore* precedes FS 80, 84, 86; **goinge, goynge** *pr. p.* ~ *bifore* preceding FS 97, *in oure forþ* ~ as we proceed CK 43-4
gost(i)li, gosteli(ch(e)), gostily, goostly(che) *adj.* spiritual (often as opposed to **bodili, bodely, bodily, bodilyche**) JR 370, 611, 739, FS 137, etc.
gostili *adv.* ~ *to speike* speaking in the spiritual/allegorical sense JR 13
gouernaile *n.* governance, rule CK 204, 389, 391
grandely *adv.* ?broadly JR 136 (not in *MED*)
graunt(e) *v. inf.* concede, affirm, allow JR 76*, RG 216, etc.; **granten** *v. 3pl. pr. ind.* JR 708
graunt(e) *n.* gift, favour JR 830, RG 270, 298, etc.
gredily *adv.* greedily JR 493
gregeþ *v. 3 pl. pr. ind.* increases JR 42; **gregynge** *pr. p.* increasing FS 185
gresse *n.* grass JR 28
greteli(ch) *adv.* greatly, very much CK 24, 133, 195, etc.
gretnesse *n.* importance JR 213
gret(t)(e) *adj.* important JR 9, 24, 184, etc.; **grettere** *comp.adj.* FS 169; **grettest(e)** *superl. adj.* greatest FS 18, 150, 152, etc.
greueþ *v. 3 sg. pr. ind.* makes heavier (*MED* s.v. 'greven', v. 4); or perhaps 'increases' (*MED* s.v. 'grouen', v. 5) JR 771
greuoslyche *adv.* grievously FS 183; **greuouselokere** *comp. adv.* more grievously FS 188
gr(o)unden *v. refl. 3 pl. pr. ind.* ~ *hem* found their argument JR 156, 300, etc.; **grounde** *3 pl. pr. subj.* ~ *hem* 1015; **gr(o)(u)nded, (i)gr(o)(u)ndid** *pa. p.* founded, given evidential basis JR 321, FS 49, RG 273, ~ *on*, ~ *in* founded on JR 105, 599, etc., ~ *onto* grafted onto JR 526, *see also* **vngrounded** *ppl. adj.*
ground(e) *n.* foundation, basis JR 817, 853, FS 151, 152, etc.
grucchen *v. 3 pl. pr. ind.* complain,

grumble RG 252, **grucched** *3 pl. pa. subj.* JR 285
grucching *vbl. n.* grumbling, complaining RG 144
gulardes *n. gen.* of satirical jesters or buffoons (*see note*) JR 69
gulles *n. pl.* ?gulletfuls JR 65 (not in *MED*)

ȝ

ȝaf(fe), ȝaue *see* **ȝeef, ȝif, ȝyue, ȝeue(n)** *v. inf.*
ȝe *pron. pers. nom. 2 pl.* (in addition to *pl.* usage, appears in place of 'þou' as mark of formality or respect) you CK 123, 130, etc.
ȝee *adv.* yes FS 196
ȝeef, ȝif, ȝyue, ȝeue(n) *v. inf.* give JR 523, 586, FS 331, etc.; **ȝeue** *1 sg. pres. ind.* FS 227; **ȝeueþ** *3 sg. pr. ind.* JR 854; **ȝiueþ** *3 sg. pr. ind.* JR 339, 996; **ȝeffeþ** *3 sg. pres. ind.* JR 532; **ȝeueþ** *3 pl. pr. ind.* JR 240; **ȝeue** *3 sg. pr. subj.* CK 414, 422; **ȝif** *3 sg. pres. subj.* JR 240; **ȝeuynge** *pr. p.* CK 94; **ȝeuen** *3 sg. pa. ind.* JR 184; **ȝaf(fe)** *3 sg. pa. ind.* JR 144, 233, 413, etc.; **ȝaue** *3 sg. pa. ind.* CK 52, 62, 86; **gaf(e)** *3 sg. pa. ind.* CK 54, 88; **ȝeuen(e) ȝyuen, ȝouen** *pa. p.* JR 879, RG 196, etc., (*see also* **ȝouen** *ppl. adj.*; **ȝeue** *pa. p.*) *be* ~ . . . let . . . be given FS 7
ȝe(e)r(e) *n.* year, *ones in þe* ~ once a year JR 547, *bi* ~ annually CK 109, *sg. for pl. with num. card.* RG 8, 292
ȝef *see* **(ȝ)if, ȝef, ȝeue, ȝiue** *conj.*
ȝeffeþ *see* **ȝeef, ȝif, ȝyue, ȝeue(n)** *v. inf.*
ȝeft *n.* gift CK 148; **ȝeftis** *n. pl.* JR 715, 901
ȝelowe *adj.* yellow FS 259
ȝer(e) *see* **ȝe(e)r(e)** *n.*
ȝerne *v. inf.* yearn, desire RG 182
ȝeue *see* **(ȝ)if, ȝef, ȝeue, ȝiue** *conj.*
ȝeuyng(e), ȝyuyng *vbl. n.* giving JR 730, 869, FS 276; *ppl. adj.* RG 18, etc. (*and see* **ȝeef, ȝif, ȝyue, ȝeue(n)** *v. inf.*)
(ȝ)if, ȝef, ȝeue, ȝiue *conj.* if JR 59, 286, CK 45, 157, etc., ~ *þat* if JR 378, 865, 870
ȝif *see* **ȝeef, ȝif, ȝyue, ȝeue(n)** *v. inf.*
ȝifte *n.* gift JR 913; **ȝiftis** *n. pl.* JR 854
ȝildynge *vbl. n.* yielding FS 280
ȝis *adv.* yes CK 126
ȝit(t), ȝut *adv.* yet JR 51, 136, RG 125, etc.
ȝiue *see* **(ȝ)if, ȝef, ȝeue, ȝiue** *conj.*
ȝyuyng *see* **ȝeuyng(e), ȝyuyng** *vbl. n.*
ȝoc *n.* yoke RG 124
ȝollynge *ppl. adj.* yowling, howling FS 238
ȝonge *adj.* young FS 115, 121
ȝouen *ppl. adj.* given RG 90 *see also* **ȝeef, ȝif, ȝyue, ȝeue(n)** *v. inf.*
ȝow(e) *pron. pers. acc. 2 sg.* you JR 943, FS 2, 358, etc.
ȝowþe *n.* youth JR 127
ȝut *see* **ȝit(t), ȝut** *adv.*

H

hald *see* **holde, hoold, hald** *v. inf.*
haliday *n.* holy day, i.e., Sunday or religious holiday RG 29
halow *v. inf.* consecrate, make holy JR 222, 631, etc.; **halwid** *pa. p.* consecrated FS 112
halowing *vbl. n.* consecration JR 222
han *see* **haue, a** *v. inf.*
hangeþ *v. 3 pl. pr. ind.* hang, depend, *in* . . . ~ depend on FS 204
hard *adj.* difficult, troublesome CK 281
hardy *adj.* foolishly bold RG 256
harlot *n.* idle rogue, vagabond JR 338; **harlatis, harlotes** *n. pl.* JR 59, 469
harmeþ *v. 3 sg. pr. ind. to many* ~ it damages many JR 831
harmenge *vbl. n.* ~ *of* damage to JR 153
harneyes *n.* harness, *preuye* ~ genitals FS 134
haue, a *v. inf.* as auxiliary JR 987, ~ *of* receive from JR 470; **haþ** *3 sg. pr. ind.* ~ *hem for* considers them as FS 128; **han** *3 pl. pr. ind.* ~ . . . *to sustene* have wherewithal to sustain JR 507; **naueþ*** *pl. pres. ind.* do not have (**ne** contr. with **haueþ**) FS 70; **hauynge** *pr. p.*. owning FS 30, *pr. p. possessions* ~ owning possessions FS 33
hede *n.* heed JR 301, 659, 913, etc.
hed(e), he(u)ed *n.* head, chief JR 185, 221, 531, 1000, RG 203, 244
heele *n.* heel JR 570
heiȝest *see* **hiȝe** *adj.*
hele *v. inf.* heal JR 520, 521, etc.
hele *n.* health RG 79, 81

helpe *n. ne* ~ *hadde be of* if they had not had the support of JR 399, *in þer* ~ in helping them JR 802

helpe *v. inf.* ~ (*to*) support, contribute to sustaining JR 133, 732; **holpen** *pa. p.* CK 200

helþe *n. soule* ~ salvation RG 227

hem, þaim *pron. pers. 3 pl. acc. and refl.* them, themselves JR 2, 7, etc., CK 7, 10

hemsilf, himsilf *pron. pers. 3 pl. refl. and emphatic* themselves, they themselves JR 185, 488, etc.

henesse *n.* high rank, honour JR 103

herbis *n. pl.* plants FS 300, 305

her(e) *see* **þer(e), her(e), þair** *pron. pers. poss. 3 pl.*

here *n.* ear CK 449

here *v. inf.* attend to JR 274, 275, etc., (*see note*), ~ *of* hear about JR 275

herebi *adv.* by this CK 123

herfor(e) *adv.* therefore, for this JR 273, 574, 578, etc.

herfro *adv.* from this JR 319

heritage *see* **(h)eritage** *n.*

heroffe *adv.* from this JR 678

herto *adv.* to this JR 913

hes *pron. pers. 3 sg. poss.* his JR 350

hest *n.* commandment FS 9, 12, 175, etc., **he(e)stis** *n. pl.* (*ten*) ~ ten commandments FS 46, 47, 49, etc., ~ (*of God*) ten commandments and/or Christ's two commandments (see FS 201–6 n.) FS 9, 14, 114, etc.

heþin *adj.* heathen JR 121

heued *see* **hed(e), he(u)ed** *n.*

heuenelyche *adv.* in a manner befitting heaven FS 229

hide *v. inf. do* ~ have hidden, cause to be hidden JR 769; **hid(d)(e)** *pa. p.* JR 533, ~ *vnto*, reserved to JR 613

hiȝe *v. inf.* raise high JR 723; **hieþ** *3 sg. pr. ind.* JR 51; **hiȝed** *3 sg. pa. subj.* JR 869; *pa. p.* JR 729 *see also* **hiȝed** *ppl. adj.*

hiȝe *adj.* high JR 100, 116, 119, etc.; **hi(e)ȝest(e), heiȝest** *adj. superl.* highest JR 840, FS 53, RG 72, 300, etc.

hiȝed *ppl. adj.* raised high JR 52

hiȝenesse *n.* height JR 700

hil *v. inf. refl.* ~ *hem* cover themselves RG 167

hillynge, hylyng *vbl. n.* clothing, covering RG 250, 252

him, hym *pron. pers. acc. 3 sg.* it (more usually 'him') CK 152, *3 sg. refl.* himself JR 391

himsilf *pron. pers. 3 sg. refl. and emphatic* himself FS 124, etc., itself CK 151, *of* ~ with respect to him RG 54, *to* ~ with respect to himself FS 244

his *pron. pers. poss. 3 sg.* its (more usually 'his') CK 151

hode *n. pl.* hoods (*see note*) JR 451

holde, hoold, hald *v. inf.* hold, keep JR 420, 439, 881, etc., ~ *hir hele* protect her health RG 79; *2 sg. pr. ind. ȝe ne* ~ *noȝt of* you set no store by CK 167; **hold** *3 pl. pr. ind.* ~ *of me* have power by my grant RG 15; **holdin** *3 pl. pr. subj.* JR 886; **held** *3 sg. pa. ind.* JR 159, 883; **holden** *refl. 3 pl. pa. ind.* ~ *hem* consider themselves FS 235; **(i)holde(n)** *pa. p.* (of person) required, obliged JR 853, 995, FS 92, 297, etc. (of obligation, rule, etc.) kept JR 755, 833

holdyng *vbl. n.* ~ *of* maintenance of JR 771

holiche, holly, holli *adv.* completely JR 828, 839, 883, CK 384

holpen *see* **helpe** *v. inf.*

hondreþ *num. card.* hundred CK 233

honestliche *adv.* honestly CK 143

honour *v. inf. see* **bifore** *pref.*

hool *adj.* entire, complete, unshared RG 58

hoomly *adv.* intimately (*see note*) RG 9

hope *v. 1 sg. pr. ind.* ~ *of* hope for JR 112; **hopen** *3 pl. pr. ind.* hope for JR 481

horedam, horedom *n.* whoredom JR 41, 609, 698, etc.

hore *n.* whore JR 776; **hores** *n. pl.* whores JR 697

hou *adv.* how RG 77, 84, 115, etc. *in* ~ *vnclene* in what impure JR 629

howses *n. pl.* houses JR 48, 189, 747

I

iauels *n. pl.* rascals CK 420

jawnes *n.* jaundice FS 258

iche *see* **ech(e), iche** *pron.*

idampned *see under* **dampned**

idon *see* **do(ne)** *v. inf.*
Iew *n.* Jew JR 210
if þat *see* **(ȝ)if, ȝef, ȝeue, ȝiue** *conj.*
ifigured *see* **(i)figured** *v. pa. p.*
ifounde *see* **fo(u)nde** *v. 3 sg. pa. ind.*
igroundid *see* **gr(o)unden** *v. refl. 3 pl. pr. ind.*
iȝen *see* **eiȝen, iȝen** *n. pl.*
iholde *see* **holde, hoold, hald** *v. inf.*
ilke *pron.* same, *þat* ~ that very same person JR 243
imade *see* **make** *v. inf.*
ymages *n. pl.* images JR 756
imarkid *see* **marke** *v. inf.*
imingeled *see under* **mingeled**
in *prep.* on JR 168, 206
inedide *see* **nediþ** *v. impers. 3 sg. pr. ind.*
indicatife *adj.* indicative (mood of verb) FS 24
inobedient *adj.* disobedient JR 411
inow(e), ynoȝe, inouȝ *adv.* enough JR 52, 322, 610, 1005, etc.
inparatif(e) *adj.* imperative (*see note*) FS 10, 24
inpertinent *adj.* not necessary, not essential JR 709
inpossible *adj.* absurd JR 608
inprison *v. inf.* imprison JR 921 *see also* **do(ne)** *v. inf.*
inpungnynge *vbl. n.* ~ *of* (intellectual) assault on, contradiction of JR 195
insensible *adj.* not capable of being sensed JR 269
into *prep.* ~ *þis day* up until today JR 177, ~ *þe confusioun of hem* aiming to confuse/thwart them, FS 61
ypocrisye, ypocrisie, ypocricie *n.* hypocrisy JR 38, 113, 116, 434, 1009, etc.
ypocrite *n.* hypocrite JR 107
ypocrit(e) *adj.* hypocritical JR 608, 769
irekened *see* **rekenes** *v. 2 sg. pr. ind.*
irreligiouse *adj. as n.* irreligious/anti-religious followers (of Antichrist) RG 123, 162
ispende *see* **spende** *v. inf.*
itauȝt *see* **t(h)eche** *v. inf.*
iuge *v. inf.* judge JR 252, 702, RG 5
iugement *n.* judgement JR 211
iuges *n. pl.* judges JR 369
iust *adj.* just JR 961
iusticie *n.* justice JR 422, 662
iustifie *v. inf.* justify JR 111
iustified* *ppl. adj.* vindicated, judged as righteous FS 237
yuel(l), iuel *adj.* evil JR 126, 146, 361, 805, etc.
iweddid *see* **wedded, (i)weddid** *v. pa. p.*
iwere *see* **ert** *v. 2 sg. pr. ind.*

K

kaies *n. pl.* keys CK 65
kep(e) *v. inf.* observe, maintain, hold to JR 441, 548, 549, etc., *to* ~ *me fro* to keep myself away from JR 114, *to* ~ *hem* by/in keeping them JR 863; **kepid** *3 pl. pa. ind.* JR 844; *pa. p.* JR 905
kynd(e) *n.* nature, type JR 1003, *goode of* ~ natural goodness JR 141, *in his* ~ intrinsically JR 459, FS 65, *in* ~ by (their) nature JR 193, 1020, FS 156
kyndeli, kyndely *adv.* naturally JR 953, 954
kyndenesse *n.* kindness RG 279, 281
kyndom *n.* kingdom FS 251
kynrede(n) *n.* kindred JR 40, 608, 698, etc.
kirke *see* **chirche, kirke** *n.*
knawen *see* **knowe** *v. l sg. pr. ind.*
knytt *v. 3 sg. pr. subj.* knit, unite, bind RG 34
knytte *n.* knight JR 202; **kny(ȝ)ttes, knyttis** *n. pl.* knights JR 207, 259, 298, 537, etc.
knowe *v. l sg. pr. ind.* acknowledge JR 112; **knawen** *pa. p.* known CK 129
knowyng(e) *vbl. n.* recognition JR 131, knowledge FS 148, understanding CK 408
knowen *ppl. adj.* recognized JR 269
knoweleche *n.* knowledge *to* ~ *of þe world* for the world to know JR 612
knowleche *v. 3 pl. pr. ind.* acknowledge, affirm FS 180; **knowlechinge** *pr. p.* FS 236
kockis *n. gen.* ~ *crowe* cock's crow, dawn RG 177
kunne *v. inf.* know (how to), understand, be able to RG 76; **can** *1 sg. pres. ind.* CK 39, 414, 426; **can(st)** *2 sg. pr. ind.* CK 38, 263; **can** *3 sg. pr. ind.* CK 424; **can** *3 pl. pr. ind.* JR 83; **con** *3 pl. pr. ind.* CK 345; **can** *2 sg. pres. subj.* CK 349; **conne(n)** *3 pl. pr. subj.* CK 356, FS 294, *ne* ~ *no forþer* do not know

how to proceed CK 421; **couþ** *3 pl. pa. subj.* CK 347; **cowde** *3 pl. pa. subj.* were able to JR 876 (*see also* **cunnynge, connynge** *vbl. n.*)

L

lacked *v. impers. pa. ind. hem* ~ they lacked JR 147

lackynge *vbl. n.* lack, privation FS 146, 159

laft *see* **le(e)ue** *v. inf.*

langid *see* **longeþ** *v. 3 sg. pr. ind.*

lasse *adj.* less FS 206, 211, *þe* ~ all the less JR 650 (*see also* **lesse** *comp. adj.*)

lassiþ, lassen, lassid *see* **lessen** *v. inf.*

last *v. inf.* persist, continue RG 303

lasting *vbl. n.* perseverance JR 588

late *adv.* recently JR 96, CK 1

late *see* **let** *v. inf.*

lattere *neuere þe* ~ *adv.* neverthless FS 66

led(e) *v. pa. p.* ~ *wit* in the company of, guided by JR 455, ~ *bi himself* self-governed CK 151

leder *n.* leader, ruler CK 51

ledyng *vbl. n.* guidance JR 282

leful *see* **le(ue)ful** *adj.*

legeman *n.* vassal, subject CK 363, 374

lemman *n.* lover, concubine CK 273

lenger(e) *comp. adj.* longer JR 905, FS 169

lepur *n.* leprosy JR 47

lere *v. inf.* learn CK 29

lesing(e) *n.* lie JR 186, 187, 188, etc.; **lesynges, lesing(e)s, liȝes** *n. pl.* JR 54, 55, 56, CK 245

lesse *comp. adj.* lesser JR 288, 631, 670; **leste** *superl. adj.* least FS 19 (*see also* **lasse** *adj.*)

lessen *v. inf.* reduce, diminish, take away (from) CK 17; **lassiþ** *3 sg. pr. ind.* FS 205; **lassen** *3 pl. pr. ind.* FS 303; **lessinge** *pr. p.* diminution CK 358; **lassid** *3 sg. pa. subj.* FS 165; **lessid** *pa. p.* JR 678

let *v. inf.* allow JR 634; **lete** *3 sg. pr. subj.* CK 233; **let** *3 pl. pr. subj.* JR 901; **late, lette** *imp.* CK 460, ~ *telle me* let me be told JR 894; **lete** *3 pl. pa. ind.* JR 149

lett(e) *v. inf.* (with *inf.*) fail, neglect JR 872; (with person(s) or *pers. pron.*) hinder, prevent RG 71, CK 230, ~ *þat þere be no* prevent there from being any FS 298; **lettiþ** *3 sg. pr. ind.* JR 202, 525; **lett** *3 sg. pr. subj.* RG 254; **lettid** *3 pl. pa. ind.* refrained JR 820; *pa. p.* hindered RG 253

lettinge *vbl. n.* hindrance CK 191

lettrid *ppl. adj.* educated CK 19

letturer *n.* learning RG 27

letyn *v. 3 pl. pr. ind.* ~ *hemsilf* consider themselves FS 333

leue *adj.* dear CK 302

leue *see* **lyue, leue** *v. inf.*

leue *v. 3 sg. pr. subj.* grant CK 414, 422, 464

le(e)ue *v. inf.* leave, abandon JR 282, 491, 829, etc., ~ *to* desist from JR 275, 296, 872; **leuynge** *pr. p.* JR 582 (*and see* **le(e)uyng(e)** *vbl. n.*); **laft, lefte** *pa. p.* rejected JR 667, 960

le(ue)ful *adj.* lawful JR 412, 877

leuefully *adv.* lawfully RG 21, 30

leueþ *v. 3 sg. pr. ind.* believes FS 35; **leuen** *3 pl. pr. ind.* believe FS 33

le(e)uyng(e) *vbl. n.* abandoning JR 540, 711, etc.

lewd(e), lewed, lewid *adj.* stupid, uneducated, lay JR 216, 364, 740, 836, etc.

liccherie *n.* lechery, lust CK 278

liche *adj.* like JR 69

lickely *adv.* probably JR 126

licly, licli *adj. is* ~ *to* seems probable to (*see MED* s.v. 'likli', *adj.* 1 a), esp. the first two Wycliffite examples given) JR 477, 818

lyen *v. inf.* lie, tell a falsehood JR 53; **lie** *3 pl. pr. ind.* ~ *in* falsify by means of JR 620

lyfed *see* **lyue, leue** *v. inf.*

lyflode *n.* livelihood, income FS 29, 319

lyft *see* **liȝften** *v. 3 pl. pr. ind.*

liggeþ *v. 3 sg. pr. ind.* ~ *þerinne* is involved JR 213

lyȝeris *n. pl.* liars JR 57

liȝes *see* **lesing(e)** *n.*

liȝften *v. 3 pl. pr. ind.* lift FS 227; **lyft** *3 sg. pa. ind.* lifted FS 225

liȝt *adj.* easy JR 579, 880

liȝtly, lyȝtly, liȝtli *adv.* easily JR 234, 544, 641, etc.

liȝtlier *adv. intens.* more easily JR 864

liȝtt *v. 3 sg. pr. ind.* descends, rests JR 195
liȝttid *v. pa. p.* illuminated JR 637
lijf, liif, lyue *n.* life JR 25, 110, 117, 849, etc., way of life JR 386, *in þis* ~ during life on earth JR 773, 833, 861
lykynge *ppl. adj.* pleasing FS 150
likiþ *v. impers. pr. ind. hem* ~ it is pleasing to them JR 702; **likid** *impers. pa. ind. him* ~ it was pleasing to him CK 402
lymes *n. pl.* limbs, members JR 403
limite *v. inf.* appoint, license JR 571; **lymyt** *pa. p.* assigned RG 59, 83
lymytid *ppl. adj.* ~ *in certeyne* set specific limits (*see MED* s.v. 'limiten', 3a) RG 177
litel, litil *adv.* little JR 285, 308, 860, etc. *be* ~ *and* ~ little by little JR 288, *helpiþ* ~ has little importance to JR 763
litteliþ, littleþ* *v. 3 sg. pr. ind.* diminishes JR 617*, 770
lyue, leue *v. inf.* live RG 63, *but* ~ *as we wolde* but (that we should) live as we wish JR 932; **lyueden** *3 pl. pa. ind.* JR 159; **lyfed** *3 pl. pa. ind.* JR 306
lyue *see* **lijf, liif, lyue** *n.*
lyuyng(e) *vbl. n.* living JR 242, 352, 430, etc., *in his* ~ in his way of life JR 304, *in* ~ in (their) rule or manner of living JR 268, 868
lokiþ *v. 3 sg. pr. ind.* expects JR 98; **looke** *3 sg. pr. subj.* ~ *he wele* let him see to it RG 31; **loke** *1 pl. pr. subj.* examine, attend JR 772; **loke** *imp.* examine, attend JR 394
longeþ *v. 3 sg. pr. ind.* belongs CK 369, 433, ~ *þerto* pertains to it, is associated with it CK 129; **langid** *3 sg. pa. ind.* CK 451
lore *n.* teaching JR 3, 196
lorschip *n.* dominion, lordship, ~ *of* dominion over JR 914
losed *v. pa. p.* loosed, let go JR 157
louyng(e) *vbl. n.* love JR 795, 796, praise, reverence JR 1013
lowtynge* *vbl. n.* ~ *to* worshipping, bowing down to FS 337
lusty *adj.* lustful, desirous RG 232

M

ma(a)d(e)(d), madist *see* **make** *v. inf.*
magnifie *v. 3 pl. pr. ind.* praise, (falsely) esteem as important JR 185, 919
maynte(y)ne *v. inf.* maintain, support JR 515*, 995, FS 222, etc.
mayntenynge *vbl. n.* maintenance, sustenance FS 218
maister(e) *n.* master CK 80, 82, 400, etc., ~ *o diuinite* master in divinity CK 35; **maystres** *n. pl.* masters (of arts) FS 21
maistri(e) *n.* dominance (often associated with force or threats) CK 164, 250, 264, etc.
make *v. inf.* ~ *of deliberacioun* deliberate, decide FS 82, 88; ~ *þer dispenses* pay their expenses JR 85; **make, makiþ** *3 sg. pr. ind.* ~ *hem to trist* makes them trust JR 452; **madist** *2 sg. pa ind.* made JR 794; **ma(a)d(e)(d)** *pa. p.* made JR 226, 905, etc., *was* ~ became FS 16, *ben* ~ *ded* are killed JR 725, ~ *to write it* had it written RG 75; **maked** *pa. p.* JR 426, 775, **ima(a)de** *pa. p.* FS 261, 274, *ȝe ben* ~ there should be prepared for you FS 22
maked *ppl. adj.* made JR 537
makyng(e), making *vbl. n.* construction JR 721, 725, 738, etc.
malis *n.* malice JR 398
mameliþ *v. 3 sg. pr. ind.* mumbles JR 946
ma(u)ndement *n.* JR 792, 844, etc.
maner(e) *n.* way, kind (of) RG 362, 364, 372, etc., custom, habit JR 813, CK 41, 420, *all* ~ every kind of CK 70, 121, 371, *in* ~ after a fashion, so to speak JR 564-5, CK 3, ~ *of* kinds of JR 101, RG 1, *oþer* ~ *vse* another sort of use JR 597, ~ *of lyuynge* way of life JR 241; *þis* ~ *mater* this kind of material JR 5; **manere(s)** *n. pl.* ways, kinds, JR 849, 598, 943, FS 73, RG 241, behaviour, customs JR 134, 389
manhode *n.* manhood, humanity RG 277
mannes *n. gen.* man's, human JR 751, 833, 935, etc.
mansleing *n.* murder JR 632
manslers *n. pl.* murderers JR 405
marchaundis *n. pl.* merchants RG 246
marke *v. inf.* observe JR 944; **imarkid** *pa. p.* marked (by God's grace; *see MED* s.v. 'marken', v.(1) 5) FS 156
mate *v. inf.* defeat (as in chess) JR 728

mater *n.* ~ *of scole* scholastic discourse, topics, or argument JR 706
mawmet *n.* idol FS 337
mede *n.* reward, payment JR 571, 572, 690, etc.
medeful(l)y *adv.* meritoriously JR 582, RG 374
medelen *v. 3 pl. pr. ind.* mix JR 55, 1009
medelid *ppl. adj.* mixed RG 14
medelynge *vbl. n.* mixing JR 146
meden *v. inf.* reward FS 302
medicyne *n.* remedy, medicine JR 523
mekeli, mekely *adv.* meekly JR 112, 810
mell *v. inf.* ~ *o(f)* interfere with CK 9, 72; *refl. inf.* ~ *him (þer)of* CK 18, 313, 316, etc.
mendynge *vbl. n. wiþ þe* ~ *of ȝow* with your amendments, for you to amend FS 358
mene *n.* mediator, means CK 144
mene *v. inf.* mean, *þat es to* ~ in other words, by which is meant CK 442
men(n)e *n.* midpoint between extremes, ~ *of vertu(e)* virtuous mean JR 660, 754
menoures *n. pl.* friars minor, Franciscans JR 157, *frere* ~ JR 687
meri *adj.* merry, happy CK 312
meselrie *n.* leprosy CK 142
mesure, mesour *n.* moderation, measure JR 423, 438, 440, RG 170, etc.
mesurably *adv.* in moderation RG 50
met(t)e *n.* food JR 895, 900, FS 23, *at þe* ~ at meals JR 100, FS 94
meue *v. inf.* persuade, move JR 894, RG 36, 332; **moueþ** *3 sg. pr. ind.* JR 218, 229, 867, etc.; **moued** *3 sg. pa. subj.* JR 215; **moued** *pa. p.* raised CK 13; **meued** *pa. p.* ~ *of* moved/inspired by JR 865
myche, mich(e), muche *adv. in so* ~ to that extent JR 664, *as* ~ *as* as great as if JR 403, ~ *more* all the more FS 55, 303, *to* ~ excessively RG 267, CK 20
michel *n.* ~ *of* the greater part of CK 361
mychelnesse *n.* greatness of amount or size FS 346
mydel *n.* middle JR 392
miȝt *n.* power, capacity, might CK 79, 84, 88, etc.
mikel *adv.* much *in als* ~ *as* as much as CK 220
imingeled *v. pa. p.* mixed up JR 706 (*not in MED, but see MED* s.v. 'mengen', v. *for the most likely derivation*)
ministren *v. inf.* administer JR 579
mynster *n.* monastery or nunnery, church thereof, any church or cathedral JR 730, 731
mischeue *n.* misfortune, wickedness CK 308
misdoers *n. pl.* evil doers CK 325
misleued *v. 3 pl. pa. subj.* erred in belief CK 327
misseoccupie *v. 3 pl. pr. subj.* wrongly occupy CK 265
missespend *v. 3 pl. pr. subj.* wrongly spend CK 266
mysschape *n.* misshapenness JR 611
misturned *ppl. adj.* perverted JR 55
mysvse *v. inf.* misuse JR 902
mo *comp. adj.* more JR 522, 818, ~ *to* two more JR 520
modir *n.* mother, *his/here* ~ *wombe* his/their mother's womb FS 106, 107, 112
mone *n.* money CK 399, 400, etc.
mones *n. pl.* moons JR 173
moni *adj.* many CK 23, 156, 172, etc.
moores *n. pl.* deserts JR 164
more *comp. adj.* greater JR 174, 217, 235, etc., better, more closely JR 251, 373, ~ *in multitude* greater in number JR 317, *in* ~ *and lesse* in greater and lesser cases JR 796
morne(n) *v. 3 pl. pr. ind.* sorrow, mourn JR 685, 689
mornyng *vbl. n.* ~ *of* sorrow for JR 32
mo(o)st *superl. adj.* most *man* ~ *pacient* the most patient of men JR 390, greatest RG 176
mot(e) *v. 3 sg. pr. ind.* must JR 331, 598, etc.; **mute** *3 sg. pr. ind.* RG 302; **moten** *3 pl. pr. ind.* JR 657, RG 56, 239; **mot** *3 pl. pr. ind.* JR 330, 749, etc.; **mut** *3 pl. pr. ind.* JR 85; **muten** *3 pl. pr. ind.* RG 262; **mote** *3 sg. pr. subj.* JR 547, 561
moueþ, moued *see* **meue**
mow(e)n *v. 3 pl. pr. ind.* may, might, are able to/capable of RG 120, 166, etc.; **mow** *1 sg. pr. subj.* CK 26; **mow(e)** *2 sg. pr. subj.* CK 123, 130, 298, etc.; **mowe** *3 sg. pr. subj.* CK 180; **mowe** *3 pl. pr. subj.* FS 294; **miȝt** *1 sg. pa. ind.*

(with present sense) CK 20; *2 sg. pa ind.* CK 58, etc.; **myȝt** *3 sg. pa. ind.* JR 522, **mouȝte**, *3 pl. pa. subj.* JR 887
moweþes *n. pl.* mouths JR 55
muk *n.* money JR 487
mut *see* **mot(e)** *v. 3 sg. pr. ind.*

N

naked *adj.* bare, unadorned JR 267
nakidly *adv.* unconditionally JR 276
name *n.* reputation JR 245, 789, 802
nameli(ch), namelyche *adv.* especially JR 682, FS 342, CK 235
nappiþ *v. 3 sg. pr. ind.* sleeps JR 190
naþeles *adv.* nonetheless JR 24, 285, 347, etc.
naueþ* *see* **haue, a** *v. inf.*
ne *conj.* nor JR 22, 48, 64, etc., *ne(i)þer . . . ~* neither . . . nor JR 299, 738, etc., *adv.* not (often as double negative, for emphasis) JR 41, 57, 132, etc., *~ were* if it were not for JR 445, 785; *see also* **wilt** *v. 2 sg. pr. ind.*; **ert** *v. 2 sg. pr. ind.*; **haue, a** *v. inf.*
nede *n. ~ is* is necessary RG 259, *it is no ~* there is no need JR 511, *~ was, was ~* it was necessary JR 559, RG 266, *as it were ~* according to need FS 267
nedi, nedy *adj.* needy, indigent JR 492, 493, 507
nediþ *v. 3 sg. pr. ind.* requires, obliges JR 247*, RG 299; **nede** *3 pl. pr. ind.* JR 714; **nedid** *pa. p.* JR 235, RG 290
nediþ *v. impers. 3 sg. pr. ind. ȝou ~* it is necessary for you FS 21 *hem ~* it is necessary for them RG 170; **inedide, nedede** *impers. pa. ind. þer beþ ~* it was necessary FS 268, *him ~* was necessary for him CK 398; **nedid** *impers. pa. subj. ~ hem not* it would not be necessary for them JR 64
nede, nedis, nedly *adv.* necessarily (with forms of **moten**) JR 657, FS 247, RG 76, etc.
neiȝbore *n.* neighbour FS 202, 204, 286
neiȝeþ *v. 3 sg. pr. ind.* approaches JR 268; **nyed** *pa. p.* JR 987
neiþer *adv.* not (*see note*) FS 98
ner *prep.* near JR 666
nes *see* **ert** *v. 2 sg. pr. ind.*
neuer *adv. be þer ~ so miche* however much there may be JR 378, *be it ~ so . . .* however . . . it may be JR 736, 737
newe . . . and newe *adv.* continually anew FS 163-4, 168, 173-4, etc.
next *adv.* nearest RG 16, 42
nyed *see* **neiȝeþ** *v. 3 sg. pr. ind.*
ny(ȝe) *adj.* nigh, near JR 281, 554
niȝttes *n. pl.* nights, *on ~* at night JR 713
nill *see* **wilt** *v. 2 sg. pr. ind.*
nys, nis *see* **ert** *v. 2 sg. pr. ind.*
noȝt *see* **no(u)ȝt(h), not** *pron. and* **no(u)ȝt(t)** *adv.*
noie *v. inf.* trouble, injure JR 911
noiþer, nouþer, nouþur *adj.* neither JR 666, RG 94, CK 407
no(o)(n) *adj.* no JR 139, 350, 549, etc.
no(o)n *pron.* none, not one JR 39, 365, 834, etc.
no(o)n-delyberacioun *n.* lack of any deliberation (*see note*) FS 102, 103
norische *v. inf.* nourish JR 511
not *see* **no(u)ȝt(h), not** *pron.*
note *v. 1 pl. pr. subj.* notice, remark JR 267
nouelrie *n.* novelty (usually with negative connotation) RG 308
nouȝ *see* **now(e), nouȝ** *adv.*
no(u)ȝt(t) *adv.* not JR 697, FS 14, 34, etc.
no(u)ȝt(h), not *pron.* nought, nothing JR 376, RG 88, 305, CK 424, *a þing of ~* nothing JR 396
nouþer, nouþur *see* **noiþer, nouþer, nouþur** *adj.*
now(e), nouȝ *adv.* now JR 539, *~ . . . and ~* sometimes . . . and sometimes JR 960

O

o *see* **o(f)(f)** *prep.*, **o(o)(n), on(e)** *num. card.*, **o(n)** *prep.*
obeyschaunce *n.* obedience FS 113
obeie *v. inf.* obey JR 993
obei(e)s(e), obe(i)sche, obeysche *v. inf. ~ to* be obedient to, be subject to JR 373, 423, 939, 941, RG 126, 134
obeysers *n. pl. ~ to* persons obedient to RG 133
oblychyn *v. inf.* bind by vow, *~ to refl.* pledge self to JR 124

occacioun *n.* opportunity, temptation, cause JR 621

o(f)(f), *prep.* of JR 525, CK 9, 35, 41, etc., by JR 121, 183, etc., from JR 63, 82, etc., for JR 112, in JR 247, 446, etc., with JR 855, concerning JR 924, FS 37, *take* . . . ~ take . . . as of JR 139

offendiþ *v. 3 sg. pr. ind.* ~ *in* transgresses against FS 210

office *n.* duty JR 306, 510, CK 100, position JR 524, CK 283, 284, etc., *her* ~ their duties RG 59, CK 239, *in* ~ *with* working for CK 32, ~ *of* . . . position associated with the duty of . . . CK 244; **offises** *n. pl.* positions, tasks associated with them RG 254

oft(e) *adv.* often JR 116, 435, 471, etc., ~ *siþe(s)/siþus* JR 283, 581, 970, FS 80, 81, etc., ~ *tyme(s)* RG 17, 313

ofter *comp. adj.* more often JR 444

oiþer *adj.* either JR 276

old(e)nesse *n.* antiquity, age JR 162, 167

o(o)(n), on(e) *num. card.* one JR 105, 113, 179, 181, 215, 261, 290, 363, etc., *alle* . . . ~ . . . *wiþ* the same as, unified with FS 271, *of* ~ . . . *wiþ* of the same . . . as FS 277; *num. as n.* one (thing) CK 377; *see also* **o(n)** *prep.*, **one** *adv.*

ooned *v. pa. p.* made one, unified JR 679, 683

oonis, ones *adv.* once CK 394, *at* ~ at once, at the same time RG 164

o(n) *prep.* on ~ **beggynge** begging FS 319 (*reduced forms* **a-beggynge** FS 342, **o-beggynge** FS 351), ~ *þis half* on this side of CK 18, in JR 53, 481, 817, etc.

one *adv.* alone FS 345

oneli(ch(e)) *adv.* only CK 49, 92, 337

onone *adv.* right away CK 449

ony, oni, eny *adj.* any FS 49, RG 122, CK 114, etc.

opon, open, opyn *adj.* clear, straightforward, manifest JR 90, 281, 403, etc.

oponli, oponly, openli(ch(e)), opinli, opinly *adv.* openly, clearly JR 348, 406, 432, 492, 556, etc.

optatife *adj.* optative (mood of verb) FS 24

orde(y)ne *v. inf.* arrange, establish JR 21; **wordeyned** *3 sg. pa. ind.* JR 314

ord(e)r(e), ord(o)ur *n.* community under religious rule JR 37, 340, 359, etc., rank, class, or other special group JR 386, 393, *Cristis* ~ community following the proper rule of Christ JR 153, 345, etc., ~ *of beggeris* mendicant order (i.e. one of the orders of friars) FS 343, rule(s) for living pertaining to a special group JR 439, 475, 478, etc., rite, form of religious service JR 58, arrangement or sequence of items, ranking JR 682, 842, *in* ~ *þat* in the degree/ranking that JR 861; **ord(e)ris, ord(e)res** *n. pl.* religious orders JR 39, 170, 174, etc.

ordina(u)nce *n.* prescribed custom, authorized practice JR 36, 550, 906, 935, 936, etc., *at þe* ~ *of* under the guidance of JR 603; *n. pl.* established order, authorized practices JR 580, 582, 934

ostis *n. pl.* (eucharistic) hosts JR 1019

oþer, oþir *adj.* other JR 11, 86, 95, FS 86, etc.

oþer *conj. see* **o(u)þer** *conj.*

oþer(e), oþur *pron.* other, others (frequently with plural sense) JR 168, 204, 299, FS 125, RG 35, etc.

ouer(e), our(e) *prep.* above, more than JR 793, 795, FS 53, 202, 203, CK 131, 304, ~ *þis* in addition JR 335, 383, 555

ouer(e) *adv.* furthermore JR 410; *adv.intens.* ~ *harde* too difficult JR 313, ~ *grett* too great JR 319

ouerlede *v. 2 pl. pr. subj.* oppress CK 447

ou(ȝ)t *adv.* out JR 10, 11, 12, etc. ~ *of houses* outdoors JR 763

ouȝt *pron.* anything RG 302

ouȝt *see* **awe** *v. 3 sg. pr. ind.*

our(e) *see* **ouer(e), oure** *prep.*

our(e)nementis *n.* ornaments JR 722*, 750, 751, etc.

ouþer *adv.* either JR 193

o(u)þer *conj.* or JR 801, either JR 805, 927

oure *pron. pers. poss. 1 pl.* ours JR 385

ow *interj.* oh CK 417

owen *see* **awe** *v. 3 sg. pr. ind.*

P

pacientliche *adv.* patiently CK 75

paied, payde, pay(ȝ)ed *v. pa. p.* satisfied RG 89, CK 33, 155, etc., ~ *of* satisfied with JR 363, RG 250, 252
paynem *adj.* pagan JR 134, 210
parde *interj.* by God! (or more mildly) certainly, indeed CK 126, 136, 149, etc.
parfyt *see* **perfiȝt, parfyt** *adj.*
parische *adj.* parish JR 732
parted *ppl. adj.* separate JR 780
parten *v. refl. 3 pl. pr. ind.* ~ *hem fro* separate themselves from JR 407; **partid** *v. pa. p.* separated JR 786
part(y)(e) *n.* group or individual shares, sides, or parties (two or more, distinguished by status, opinions, etc.) FS 8, RG 13, 16, etc., *on Goddis* ~ on God's side, among God's people RG 103, *þe toþur* ~ the opposing view RG 265, share or division RG 85, 98; **parti(e)s** *n. pl.* (in this case referring to groups) JR 567, 578, 680, RG 191, etc.
parting *vbl. n.* creating of division JR 683
passe *v. inf.* surpass JR 444, ~ *from* leave JR 889, go beyond RG 60, 102, etc.
patrouned *v. pa. p.* ~ *of* given patronage by JR 342
peyne *n.* pain, punishment JR 229, 256, etc., *is to hem no* ~ is not painful for them FS 147, *is* ~ *to him* is painful to him FS 158
peynting *vbl. n.* painting JR 756
peyriþ *v. 3 sg. pr. ind.* becomes worse JR 267
peysibilliche *adv.* peacefully, without interference CK 180
penytaunsers *n. pl.* confessors RG 190
pepel, pepul *see* **pupel, pepel, pepul, popel, pupil, puple, pupul** *n. pl.*
perel *n.* danger JR 6, 195, *n.* as *adj. it is* ~ it is dangerous JR 244; **pereles, perellis** *n. pl.* JR 66, 131
per(e)louse *adj.* dangerous JR 852, ~ *on speche* dangerous to say JR 543
perfeccioun *n. for his* ~ in order to live as perfectly (*see* **perfiȝt, parfyt** *adj.*) as possible for him RG 23
perfiȝt, parfyt *adj.* perfect (in sense of spiritual perfection) JR 181, 385, FS 333
perpetue *v. inf.* forever continue in JR 589
personel *adj.* personal FS 121
persouns *n. pl.* parsons JR 1016
pes *n.* peace CK 179
Peter *interj.* 'by St Peter!' CK 12, 326
pharesies, pharesees, phariseus, pharises, pharezes *see* **farisee** *n.*
pinche, pynche *v. inf.* ~ *at* criticize JR 22, 68
pynt *n.* pint JR 898
pistel *n.* epistle, letter CK 275
places *n. pl.* religious houses or foundations JR 629, 630, *cf.* JR 633, 639 and note
plantes *n. pl.* foundations, institutions *sett* ~ establish institutions or foundations CK 58
plees *n. pl.* pleas, petitions, legal proceedings FS 301
pleyn *adj.* clear, unambiguous, unmistakeable RG 202
plente *n.* ample supply FS 298
plenteuouslyche *adv. most* ~ in greatest plenty, in most luxury FS 296
poynt(e) *n.* particular JR 561, CK 164, article, item in a list RG 323, *at* ~ *deuys* exactly, to perfection JR 271, *in* ~ *to* at the point of, about to CK 415; **poyntis** *n. pl.* constituent parts, items in a list, principles JR 102, 327, 358, etc.
poluten *v. 3 pl. pr. ind.* pollute, desecrate JR 630; **polute** *pa. p.* JR 633
pondrede *v. pa. p.* considered JR 207
popel *see* **pupel, pepel, pepul, popel, pupil, puple, pupul** *n. pl.*
popis *n. gen.* of the pope JR 172, *n. pl.* JR 222
porpos *n.* purpose JR 129
po(s)cessio(u)n, possessio(u)n *n.* all worldly and/or spiritual goods possessed by an individual or group, inheritance RG 87, 100, 105, etc.
postles *n. pl.* apostles RG 169
pounde(s) *n. pl.* pounds, money JR 508, 1008
pouert(e) *n.* poverty JR 125, 293, 344, etc.
power *n. is of* ~ is powerful, has power FS 286, 287
practiffe *adj.* practical (knowledge) JR 84
prechour(e)s, prechouris *n. pl.* preachers (refers either to the preaching friars or Dominicans, whose activities are criticized, or to the

preferred 'God's preachers', who preach as God had directed) JR 157, 158, 163, 465, etc., FS 27
predicacions *n. pl.* sermons, preaching CK 238
preeris *see* **preier** *n.*
preie *v. inf.* pray, pray to, request JR 749; **preiynge** *pr. p.* requesting (you) FS 3
preier *n.* prayer JR 761, 767; **preeris** *n. pl.* JR 769
pre(y)se, preise *v. inf. for to* ~ praiseworthy JR 280, 765, 772, *most schuld* ~ *þe freres* the friars should value most JR 724; **preised** *pa. p.* ~ *of* praised by JR 852
preistis *n. pl.* priests JR 1017
prelate *n.* prelate, bishop, person of high ecclesiastical rank (usually derogatory in Wycliffite writings) JR 944, 953, 962, etc.
prented *v. pa. p.* imprinted RG 335
prese *see* **pre(y)se, preise** *v. inf.*
presounen *see* **prisoune** *v. 3 pl. pr. ind.*
preueie, preuey *see* **priue(y), preueie, preuey** *adj.*
preueþ *v. 3 pl. pr. ind.* give evidence, prove FS 32
prikkynge *pr. p.* pricking CK 85; **prikid** *v. 3 sg. pa. ind.* pricked, pierced CK 81
prime *n.* (1) one of the hours (or offices) of the daily liturgy, divine office, or breviary, recited at around 6 am; (2) the time of day at which Prime is recited RG 178
principallich *adv.* especially, above all CK 221
princyples *n. pl.* axioms, fundamental knowledge FS 21
priour *n.* leader of a monastery, house of mendicants, house of canons, or a group of such houses JR 365, 378, 381
prisoune *v. 3 pl. pr. ind.* imprison JR 919; **presounen** *3 pl. pr. ind.* JR 644; **priso(u)ned** *v. pa. p.* JR 784, 918; *see also* **inprison** *v. inf.*
prisonyng *vbl. n.* imprisoning JR 711
pryuacioun *n.* lack, condition of being without FS 152
priue(y), preueie, preuey *adj.* private, secret JR 86, 150, 576, 613, etc.
priuely *adv.* secretly JR 495
priuilage *n.* privilege, reserved right JR 901
processe *n. be* ~ *of tyme* through the passage of time JR 269
procuryng *vbl. n. be* ~ *of* at the instigation of JR 257
profetes *see* **profit(e)** *n.*
profi(ʒ)t(e), profete, prophete *v. inf.* ~ . . . (*to*) profit, benefit JR 242, 346, 746, 899, etc.
profit(e) *n. to* ~ *of* for the benefit of JR 458, *it were* ~ *to* it would benefit JR 565, ~ *to* for the benefit of JR 816; **profetes** *n. pl.* profits, benefits JR 505
propred, proprid *ppl. adj.* ~ *to* reserved to, assigned to JR 915, RG 72
propur *adv.* as an individual or private possession JR 353
publiche *v. inf.* make public JR 3
punysche *v. inf.* punish JR 781
punisching *vbl. n.* ~ *of* punishment of JR 142
pupel, pepel, pepul, popel, pupil, puple, pupul *n. pl.* people JR 38, 85, 433, 462, etc.
pupplican *n.* publican, gatherer of taxes or tolls FS 234
pure *adj.* unqualified, simple FS 276
purpur *adj.* purple JR 602
pursue *v. inf.* persecute, harass JR 982
puruey *v. inf.* provide, make purveyance for RG 220; **purueying** *pr. p.* RG 214
put(te) *v. inf.* put ~ *aba(c)k* reject JR 419, 797, ~ (. . . *inne*) establish JR 293, 914, ~ *in* give to JR 741, put on the line, risk JR 937, ~ *into* direct towards FS 232 ~ *to* add to JR 335, ~ *vp* sheathe CK 450, ~ *vpon/in/on* ascribe to JR 352, 359, 1024
putrie *n.* adultery (here, metaphorical) JR 787

Q

quick *adj.* alive FS 123
quoynte *adj.* deceptively ingenious, sophistical JR 949

R

ratelid *v. pa. p.* ~ *out* glibly and rapidly said RG 264
raþer(e) *comp. adv.* earlier, ~ *þanne* earlier than, before FS 143, 144

raveyne *n.* robbery, pursuit of prey *in* ~ *of* by plundering from, by preying on FS 238
rauysching, rauisching *vbl.n.* seizing JR 975, 1007
real(e) *adj.* royal, regal CK 157, 165, 375
rede *v. 3 sg. pr. subj.* read the mass JR 96
redress *v. inf.* put right, reform CK 225
redy *adj.* ~ . . . *to* prepared for JR 131
redusid *v. pa. p.* 'reduced', analysed (*see note*) FS 25
regalte *n.* regality CK 384
regne *v. inf.* rule, reign JR 149, RG 95
reguler *adj.* (1) belonging to a religious order, (2) marked by uniformity of action, procedure, or occurrence (see *OED* s.v. 'regular', adj, 3a, earliest example 1594) JR 405 (yet probably puns on first meaning)
reherstes *v. 2 sg. pa. ind.* report, run through, mention JR 721; **rehersed** *pa. p.* JR 179, 694
rekenes *v. 2 sg. pr. ind.* enumerate JR 649; **(i)rekened, reknid** *pa. p.* counted up, included in the account FS 335, CK 354
reknynge *vbl. n.* account CK 227
religio(u)n *n.* a particular system of faith and worship (*OED*), the practice of that system's observance JR 359, 605, 707, etc., *Cristis* ~ the system of faith and worship that truly follows Christ JR 57, 62, 328, etc.; **religiouns** *n. pl. priuate* ~ religious orders JR 152, 673
religious *adj. as n. pl.* members of religious orders FS 200, *priuat* ~ FS 356, 357
reme *see* **re(w)me** *n.*
remeuyd *v. pa. p.* removed, dispelled RG 48
remyssioun *n.* forgiveness, pardon (*see note*) FS 191
renewe *v. inf.* reform, alter JR 260
renne *v. inf.* run JR 63
rennynge *vbl. n.* running FS 130
repente *v. refl. 1 pl. pr. subj.* repent RG 157
repreue, reprefe *v. inf.* reprove, admonish JR 70, 75, 287, CK 80, etc., *for to* ~ reprehensible JR 774; **reproueþ** *3 pl. pr. ind.* reprove FS 19 (possibly, instead, an *imp. pl.*);
reproued *pa. p.* ~ *of* reproved by JR 107, ~ *to* given reproof by FS 182
reproue *n.* reproof, correction JR 811
reproueþ, reproued *see* **repreue, reprefe** *v. inf.*
reprouynge *vbl. n.* reproving, correction JR 814
reso(u)n(e) *n.* (argument based on) logic (*see note*) JR 76, 139, 344, etc., argument JR 436, 592, etc., rule, standard JR 662, (faculty of) reason, reasoning JR 211, FS 69, 84, etc., *in* . . . ~ within reason JR 733
restynge *vbl. n.* place of rest FS 251
reuerse *n. do* (*þe*) ~ do the reverse JR 90, 476
reuerse *v. inf.* be/act contrary to JR 291, 315, etc.
reuersing *ppl. adj.* contrary to JR 622
reule, rewle *n.* rule, mode of governance (for living, as of a religious order) JR 158, 159, 183, etc.
reulid *see* **rewle** *v. inf.*
reuling *vbl. n.* governance JR 667
rewde *adj.* rude, uneducated JR 740
rewle *see* **reule, rewle** *n.*
rewle *v. inf.* rule, govern JR 168; **reuled, reulid, rewled, rulid** *pa. p.* governed JR 662, FS 14, 19, RG 81, etc.
re(w)me *n.* realm, kingdom JR 1008, FS 301, 302, etc.
richesse *n.* wealth, worldly goods FS 338
riȝt *adv. intens.* very CK 30, 41, 184, ~ *as* just as FS 75, 86, 108, etc., ~ *so* just so FS 77, 87, 119, etc.
riȝt *v. inf.* make correct, rectify JR 959
riȝt(e) *n.* rule of conduct JR 35, 525; **rites** JR 674
riȝtwise *adj.* righteous RG 151
riȝtwyssenes, riȝwissenes, ri(ȝ)twisnesse *n.* righteousness JR 277, 867, RG 154, 182, etc.
rites *see* **riȝt(e)** *n.*
roote *v. inf.* rot morally or spiritually (see *MED* s.v. 'roten', v.(1), 2.a) RG 228
ro(o)te *n.* root, point of origin JR 176, FS 304, RG 230; **rotis** *n. pl.* FS 305
rouned *v. pa. p.* whispered JR 539
rounyng *vbl. n.* whispering JR 573
rub(b)ynge *vbl. n.* rubbing FS 42, 63, 65
ruly *adj.* disciplined, law-abiding RG 187

S

sacreþ *v. 3 pl. pr. ind.* consecrate JR 926; **sacred** *3 pl. pa. subj.* consecrated JR 1017

sacared *ppl. adj.* consecrated JR 1019

sacring *vbl. n.* consecration JR 927

sad *adj.* serious, difficult FS 23

sai(e), sayne *see* **sei, sey(e), seyn, sai(e)** *v. inf.*

sample *v. 3 pl. pr. ind.* exemplify (not in *MED*) FS 328; **saumplid** *pa. p.* ~ *of* exemplified by RG 204

sanctifie *v. 3 pl. pr. ind.* honour JR 777

sauter *n.* psalter, book of psalms FS 329

sauer *v. inf.* savour, enjoy RG 296; **sauered** *1 sg. pa. ind.* ~ *as* understood (*see note*) FS 16

scentence *see* **s(c)entence** *n.*

schal(l) *v. 1 & 3 sg. pr. ind.* shall (present form with future meaning, usually implying inevitability or obligation) JR 93, 107, etc.; **schalt** *2 sg. pr. ind.* JR 107; **schalltow (schalt** contr. with **þou)** CK 44; **schul(l)** *pl. pr. ind.* JR 176, 177, 258, etc.; **schulen, schulun** *3 pl. pr. ind.* RG 35, 39*, 42, etc.; **sc(h)ul(l)d(e)** *3 sg. pa. ind.* should (past form with present meaning) JR 13, 14, 20, etc.; ~ *be* shall/should be (expressing future, future perfect, or obligation) FS 14, 20, 25, 134, etc.; **schulden** *pl. pa. ind.* JR 2, 8, etc.; **schuldest** *2 sg. pa ind.* JR 947

sc(h)atered *v. pa. p.* scattered, divided JR 502 ~ *aboute* divided among JR 833

schame *v. inf.* ~ *for to speike* be ashamed of speaking JR 18, ~ *to seie* be ashamed to say RG 291; **schame** *imp.* ~ *ȝou of/þou for* shame on you for JR 592, 897

schamefast *adj.* shameful FS 244

schapelarie *n.* scapular, short cloak covering the shoulders JR 693

schapen *v. refl. 3 pl. pr. ind.* ~ *hem to* set themselves to JR 468

scharpe *adj.* sharp, harsh JR 69, 296, 819

scharpeli, scharpely, scharpily, scharpli *adv.* sharply, harshly JR 70, 72, 194, 720

scharpenesse *n.* harshness JR 35

scharping *vbl. n.* sharpening JR 130

schatered *see* **sc(h)atered** *v. pa. p.*

schaunged *v. pa. p.* exchanged, changed JR 44

sched *v. pa. p.* shed, spilt CK 146

schendeþ *v. 3 sg. pr. ind.* harms, disgraces JR 245, 843, 1003

schepe *n. pl.* sheep (metaphor for parishioners) CK 280

schewe(n) *v. inf.* show JR 876, CK 46, etc.

schipp* *n.* ship, boat RG 261

schort(e) *adj.* quickly effected, ready JR 522, short CK 361

schourged *v. pa. p.* scourged FS 330

schrewed *adj.* wicked FS 223

schrewednesse *n.* wickedness FS 222, 338

schrift(e), schrefte *n.* confession JR 544, 545, 553, 577, etc.

schriue *v. inf.* confess (in the sense of hearing confessions) CK 431

schryuen, schriuen *v. pa. p.*, *forms inf. with* 'be' *be* ~ confess JR 547, *es* ~ confesses CK 112

schriuynge *vbl. n.* ~ *of* administering confession to JR 572

scho *pron. pers. nom. 3 sg. fem.* she CK 337

schul(l) *see* **schal(l)** *v. 1 & 3 sg. pres. ind.*

scyences *n. pl.* fields of knowledge FS 13

scyle *see* **skil(l)(e), skylle, scyle** *n.*

sclander *n.* scandal JR 486

sclee *v. inf.* slay FS 105

sclidyng *pr. p.* sliding JR 424

scole *n.* school (usually university), JR 117, 130, *clerkis of* ~ university trained clerics JR 685, *mater of* ~ material pertaining to university teaching JR 706

seche *see* **suche, siche, seche** *adj.*

secheþ *v. 3 sg. pr. ind.* seeks JR 41

seculer *adj.* (1) lay (as opposed to clerical) ~ *men* lay men JR 400, ~ *lordes* non-clerical lords JR 967, 971, 989, etc. (2) of the clergy yet not belonging to a religious order (as opposed to regular) ~ *men* non-regular preachers (*see note*) JR 444, ~ *prestis* non-regular priests JR 369, 412

seculer(i)s, seculeres *n. pl.* secular clergy (*but see note*, *and see* **seculer** *adj.*) JR 106, 409, 451, etc.

seel *n.* seal (for documents) *see* **comoun** *adj.*

se, see(y) *v. inf.* see JR 150, 214, CK 58, etc.; *1 sg. pr. ind.* JR 512; **seeþ** *3 sg. pr. ind.* JR 554; **seene** *pl. pr. ind.* RG 359; **se** *imp.* JR 406; **seen** *pl. pa. ind.* JR 161, 167, etc.; **see** *3 pl. pa. subj.* JR 286; **sene** *pa. p.* CK 23, 113, 130

sei, sey(e), seyn, sai(e) *v. inf.* say JR 31, 106, 235, 526, etc.; **sei** *1 sg. pr. ind.* JR 139; **sei(e)st, saist** *2 sg. pr. ind.* JR 788, 961, etc.; **seiþ, seeþ, saiþ** *3 sg. pr. ind.* JR 40, 633, CK 118, etc.; **sayne** *2 pl. pr. ind.* CK 388; **sey(e)n(e), seien, sayne** *3 pl. pr. ind.* JR 23, 379, 622, etc.; **sei(e)** *2 sg. pr. subj.* JR 518, 882, etc.; **sai** *2 pl. pr. subj.* CK 377; **seide(n)** *3 pl. pa. ind.* JR 162, 167, 181, etc.; **seid(e), said** *pa. p.* JR 194, 210, 443, etc.

seiynge *vbl. n. masses* ~ saying of masses FS 215

seynge *ppl. adj.* seeing, sighted FS 38

sekyng *vbl. n.* seeking, *for* ~ *of* to seek JR 120

self *pronominal adj. þi* ~ you especially, you yourself JR 106; *adj.* same CK 146, 276

semeful *adj.* seemly, appropriate FS 313

semeþ *v. impers. pr. ind. me* ~ it seems to me JR 180

semeþ *v. 3 sg. pr. ind.* ~ *wele* is seemly, is suitable (see *OED* seem, v2, I) CK 160

sendinge *vbl. n.* conveyance, sending FS 279

sensibili *adv.* carnally, unspiritually JR 770

s(c)entence *n.* meaning, statement JR 21, 23, 105, etc.

sent *n.* saint JR 275, 633; **sentis, sentes** *n. pl.* saints 262, 275, 278, etc.

sepulcre(r) *n.* grave JR 26, CK 336

sepulture *n.* burial JR 579

sermonies *n.* ceremonies JR 907

serten *adj.* ~ *of* sure, secure about JR 1014

serueþ *v. 3 sg. pr. ind.* is of service JR 743, ~ *of nouȝth* does no good JR 376

seruice, seruys *n.* service CK 299, *his* ~ service to him JR 307

sette *v. pa. p.* seated JR 98

settes, settis *n. pl.* sects JR 74, 128

settiþ *v. 3 sg. pr. ind.* ~ *dyfferrence* distinguishes FS 127-8

settynge *pr. p.* ~ . . . *bi* accounting as valuable, placing importance upon FS 254

seþ(e)(n) *see* **siþen, seþen, syþen** *conj.*

sewe, sue, swe *v. inf.* follow JR 134, 204, 281, etc.; **sueþ** *3 sg. pr. ind. of it* ~ it follows (logically) from it JR 209; **seue** *3 pl. pr. subj.* JR 358

sewynge, suying *vbl. n.* following JR 144, 406

sicurly *adv.* certainly JR 115

siche *see* **suche, siche, seche** *adj.*

sidis *n. pl.* sides, positions in debate FS 3

sine *n.* sin CK 253

synge *v. inf.* sin *reguler for to* ~ habitual sinners JR 405

syngnes, singnes *n. pl.* signs JR 609, 612, 621

synguler *adj.* belonging to an individual FS 123

sitees *n. pl.* cities JR 51

siþe, siþes, siþus *n. pl.* times JR 72, 283, 468, 581, 970, *see* **oft(e)** *adv.*

siþ *adv.* next RG 200

siþ(e) *conj.* ~ (*þat*) since, because JR 86, 510, 513, etc.

siþen, syþen *adv.* afterward *euer* ~ ever after JR 172, ago *longe* ~ long ago JR 137

siþen, seþen, syþen *conj.* since, because JR 1, 216, 619, etc., afterwards JR 602

syuyl *adj.* civil (*see note*) FS 308

sixpens *n.* sixpence JR 1029

skil(l)(e), skylle, scyle *n.* reason, argument JR 548, 593, 728, 896, RG 300, etc.

skil(l)full *adj.* proper, fitting, appropriate CK 77, 78

skylfully, skilfulli *adv.* appropriately, justly JR 497, CK 293

skrieþ *v. 3 pl. pr. ind.* describe JR 592

sle *v. inf.* slay JR 402, 979, CK 233, etc.; **slowen** *3 pl. pa. ind.* RG 276; **slowe** *3 sg. pa. subj.* slew CK 233; *3 pl. pa. subj.* CK 240

sleyng, sleing *vbl. n.* slaying JR 221, 222, 631, 632

smaccheþ *v. 3 sg. pr. ind.* is tainted with JR 669; *3 pl. pr. ind.* are tainted with JR 672; **smac(c)hen** *3 pl. pr. ind.* ~ *euene* smell like, are suggestive of JR 665, 666

smyten *v. pa. p.* smitten JR 47, 871

snibbe *v. 1 sg. pr. ind.* criticize JR 807
so *adv.* such JR 559, ~ *þat* in such a way that JR 14, 32, 72, etc., ~ *longe* long enough FS 82, ~ *miche as* as much as JR 447, ~ *myche þat* to this extent JR 324
so *adv. intens. if* ~ if JR 274
so *conj.* ~ *þat* provided that JR 852, FS 115
soget *adj.* subject, subordinate CK 150
solempne *adj.* imposing JR 748
somdele *adv.* to a limited extent CK 20
somdele *pron. indef.* some part CK 162
sommes *n.* sums, simple arithmetic FS 11 (*MED* s.v. 'somme', n.(2) 2 includes this sense but does not associate it with the instruction of children)
somounynge *vbl. n.* summons (to appear in ecclesiastical court) CK 108
sondri *adj.* different, separate, various CK 285
sone *adv.* straightaway CK 261
sone *n.* son FS 131, 133, etc.; **sones** *n. pl.* sons, progeny FS 118
sophemesse *n. pl.* sophemes (*see note*) FS 17
sopplaunt *v. inf.* supplant, usurp CK 164
soteler *comp. adj.* ~ *to hym* more clever/cunning for him JR 39
sotilte *n.* subtlety, trickery CK 378
soþ(e) *adj.* true JR 447, 563, 731, etc., *þat þes is* ~ to show this is true JR 481
soþe *n.* truth JR 518, 822
soþely, soþ(e)li *adv.* truly JR 397, 657, 890, etc.
soþenes truth CK 115
souneþ, souniþ *v. 3 sg. pr. ind.* ~ . . . *in* leads toward JR 670, ~ *to* is conducive to RG 30, 92
souen *v. pa. p.* sown, disseminated JR 88
souerayne, soueraine *n.* sovereign, highest ruler CK 60, 64, etc.; **soueréyns** *n. pl.* sovereigns, rulers RG 124
souerayntе, souerainte *n.* sovereignty, supreme leadership CK 389, 391, etc.
sparche* *n.* spark FS 192
spare *v. inf.* hold back, desist JR 200
sparing *vbl. n.* holding back JR 184
speche *n.* discussion JR 199; **spechis** *n. pl.* utterances, statements RG 1, 358
special(l)y, speciali *adv.* especially JR 116, 473, 649, etc.
specked *ppl. adj.* patched, variegated JR 339
spede *v. inf.* do good, benefit JR 910
speike *v. inf.* speak JR 13, 18, 74, etc.
spende *v. inf.* expend, spend ~ *amys* squander FS 174; **ispende** *pa. p.* spent FS 175
spensis *n. pl.* expenditures JR 125
spirituale, spirituele *adj.* (1) religious, devotional, or holy (vs. secular); (2) ecclesiastical (vs. temporal) (often with equivocation between senses: *see also* **spiritualte** *n.*) CK 342, 367, 443
spiritualte *n.* (1) religious, devotional, or holy matters as opposed to secular or mundane; (2) ecclesiastical persons, jurisdiction, or possessions as opposed to temporal (often with equivocation or wordplay between these senses: *see* CK 87–107 n.; *see also* **spirituale, spirituele** *adj.*) CK 91, 92, 123, etc.
spores *n. pl.* spurs CK 81
spoyle *v. inf.* ~ *hem from* deprive them of JR 607; **spoules** *3 sg. pr. ind.* strip, deprive, despoil JR 756
sprite *n.* spirit FS 113, 114
spuynge *vbl. n.* vomit RG 282
staaf *n.* staff JR 254
stab(e)led *v. pa. p.* made firm JR 129, CK 333
stabulnesse *n.* stability JR 588
stanched *v. pa. p.* overcome, restrained JR 1011
standeþ *see* **stonde, stande** *v. inf.*
state *n.* estate, status, position or condition in the world RG 59, 83, 253, etc.
stede *v. pa. p.* situated JR 554
stid *n.* place RG 66
stif(e)ly *adv.* immovably JR 426, 977
stynt *v. 1 pl. pr. subj.* stop, cease RG 181
styre, stirre *v. inf.* incite JR 380, FS 314
stiryng, styrynge *vbl. n.* tumult, confusion JR 684, motivation, incitement FS 331, 336
stode *see* **stonde, stande** *v. inf.*
stodie *v. inf.* ~ (*to*), strive to, take pains to JR 2
stok *n.* trunk JR 474
stonde, stande *v. inf.* ~ *afer* remain far removed JR 50, ~ *in* remain in/within

JR 425, 426, etc., ~ *to* support JR 236; **stondiþ, stondeþ, standeþ** *3 sg. pr. ind.* ~ *in* is in JR 6, etc., consists in JR 327, 345, 495, etc., ~ *þerby* remains steadfast in JR 256, ~ (. . .) *wiþ* is consistent with JR 866; *3 pl. pr. ind.* ~ *in* are in JR 402, ~ *wiþ* are compatible with JR 975; **stonde** *v. imp.* ~ . . . *in wille* be steadfast JR 977; **stode** *3 sg. pa. ind.* ~ *in* consisted of JR 981; *3 sg. pa. subj.* were to remain in JR 293
stopped *v. pa. p.* ~ *wiþ* filled with JR 798
straite *see* **strett, streit, straite** *adj.*
straitliche *adv.* strictly CK 323
straunge *adj.* outlandish JR 925
straungen *v. 3 pl. pr. ind.* are estranged or distant JR 704
streccheþ(e) *v. 3 sg. pr. ind.* ~ (. . .) (*to*) covers, extends to CK 92, 149, 210; **streche** *3 sg. pr. subj.* CK 90
strett, streit, straite *adj.* strict, exacting RG 197, CK 227, overstrict, harsh JR 967
stryue *v. 3 pl. pr. ind.* argue JR 155, 696; **stryuen** *3 pl. pr. ind.* JR 698; **strof** *v. pl. pa. ind.* JR 697
striuyng *vbl. n.* dispute, argument RG 214
stryues *n. pl.* strifes, disputes JR 178, 694, 699
stronge *adj.* able-bodied FS 217, 220, 223 etc.
suche, siche, seche *adj.* such, the/that kind of RG 29, 30, 333, etc., ~ *manere* this sort of JR 352, ~ *a* just this sort (of) JR 670
sue, sueþ *see* **sewe, sue, swe** *v. inf.*
suying *see* **sewynge, suying** *vbl. n.*
suelowen *v. 3 pl. pr. ind.* swallow JR 636
suffer, suffren, suffrin *v. inf.* allow, permit JR 122, undergo, suffer JR 976; *3 pl. pr. ind.* allow RG 95; **suffering** *pr. p.* allowing JR 978
suffering *vbl. n.* ~ *of* submitting to JR 394, 975, 977
suffrid *ppl. adj.* suffered, undergone RG 144
sugett *n.* subject JR 973; **suggetes** *n. pl.* CK 303, 322, 413, etc.
sumtyme *adv.* once JR 128, sometimes JR 346, 584
sungoun *v. 3 pl. pa. ind.* sang JR 1018
superflu *adj.* superfluous JR 450
suppose, supposon *v. inf.* hypothesize but do not affirm as belief (*see note*) JR 282, 938
suspecte *v. 1 sg. pl. subj.* ~ *we* let us be suspicious of JR 1025
suspecte *ppl. adj.* ~ *of* under suspicion of JR 1030
suspended *v. pa. p.* ~ *from hym* he is excused from (it), JR 94
swaged *v. pa. p.* redeemed, assuaged RG 268
swe *see* **sewe, sue, swe** *v. inf.*
swerde *n.* sword CK 325, 436, 441
swete *n.* following JR 277

T

taȝt *see* **t(h)eche** *v. inf.*
taken *v. refl. 3 pl. pr. ind.* betake themselves to, have recourse to JR 381; **took** *3 sg. pa. ind.* ~ *of* gave FS 255; **take** *pa. p.* apprehended JR 633; **token** *pa. p.* taken CK 280
tale *n.* account, story JR 928, 931, CK 136
tallyages *n. pl.* taxes (esp. but not only on land), forced levies, tribute payments CK 200
t(h)eche *v. inf.* teach JR 877, ~ *forþe* disseminate CK 60; **tauten** *pl. pa. ind.* taught RG 212; **(i)ta(u)ȝt** *pa. p.* taught FS 21, CK 34
techinge *vbl. n.* teaching JR 460, *in* ~ *of it* through its teaching JR 253
tell *v. inf.* ~ . . . *forþe* disseminate CK 97; **telliþ** *3 sg. pr. ind.* reveals, displays JR 671; *pl. pr. ind.* add up *or* recite FS 10; **tellen, telle** *3 pl. pr. ind.* ~ . . . *be/bi* give importance to JR 640, 777; **tolde** *pa. p.* ~ *by in* respected among JR 162
temperal(e), temperall, temparal, temperele *adj.* material, of this present life (as opposed to spiritual or heavenly; *see also* **temperalte** *n.*) JR 83, 492, FS 233, etc.
temperali *adv.* moderately JR 660
temperalte *n.* temporal (vs spiritual) part (of society) CK 5, 152, 202, etc., temporal (i.e. secular) affairs CK 91, 190, 433, etc.; **temperaltes** *n. pl.* temporal affairs CK 366 (*see also*

temperal(e), temperall, temparal, temperele *adj.*)
tendurly *adv.* solicitously JR 781
theche *see* **t(h)eche** *v. inf.*
thrilleris *n. pl.* ? piercers, penetrators (by derivation from the verb 'thirlen'?) (not in *MED*) (*see note*) FS 312
tillid *v. 3 sg. pa. subj.* enticed JR 289
tyme *n.* time *be* ~ in a timely fashion CK 409, *eche* ~ at all times FS 360, *eny* ~ at any time, ever RG 239, *for* ~ according to your seniority (*see note*) FS 21, *for a more* ~ for a longer time JR 911, *fro þe* ~ from the time when RG 260, *in* ~ *whanne*, when FS 92, *in processe of* ~ over time CK 387, 403, *longe* ~ for a long time CK 31, 178, *many* ~ often JR 460, 619, *to þe* ~ *þat* until FS 69, *þat* ~ at that time CK 174, 190
tirantrie *n.* tyranny JR 467
title *n.* evidence of claim, right, or legal ownership JR 186
tyþis *n. pl.* tithes FS 227
to *prep.* for JR 79, 131, 180, etc., to the point of JR 977, until CK 179, ~ *heuenward* toward heaven RG 36, ~ *God ward* toward God CK 188–9, 237
to *adv. intens.* too JR 68, 159, 207, etc.
to *see* **tuo, to, twey(n)** *num. card.* and **tuo, to, twey** *adv.*
tofor(e) *adv.* before, earlier CK 73, 136, 248, etc.
togeder(e), togidre *adv.* together, mutually JR 174, 490, 796, RG 3, etc.
token *see* **taken** *v. refl. 3 pl. pr. ind.*
tokene, tokyn *n.* sign, token RG 194, *in* ~ *þat* as a sign that, in order to show that CK 441
tolde *see* **tell** *v. inf.*
tonge *n. in* ~ using the tongue JR 471
took *see* **taken** *v. refl. 3 pl. pr. ind.*
toþere, toþur *pron.* other JR 267, RG 133, 265; **toþere** *pron. pl.* others FS 350
touchinge *pr. p.* ~ *þat* with reference to the claim that CK 103
trayterouse *adj.* traitorous FS 184, 187
traytour, traitour *n.* betrayer JR 108, 111
trauaile, traue(i)l(e), traueyle *n.* labour JR 31, 479, 688, FS 29, etc.
trauayl(l)e, trauaile, traue(y)l(e) *v. inf.* labour JR 661, FS 229, 291, etc., *schulde we only* ~ we should labour exclusively JR 120
trauaylynge, traue(y)(l)lynge *vbl. n.* labour FS 213, 316, 331
trauaylous *adj.* assiduous, hard-working FS 288
traueyloures *n. pl.* labourers FS 300
tresore *n.* money, funds CK 289, 294
tresorere *n.* treasurer CK 284
trespas(s)(e) *n.* wrongful action JR 653, 784, FS 184, etc.
trespas *v. inf.* do wrong JR 782; **trespausen** *3 pl. pr. ind.* JR 464; **trespassid** *pa. p.* ~ . . . *to* done wrong against FS 183
trewe *adj.* true JR 210, 237
trewly, trewliche *adv.* truly JR 778, CK 188
trewþe, treuþe *n.* truth JR 37, 58, 200, etc.
trist *v. inf.* trust CK 20, ~ *on* put trust in JR 452
tristily *adv.* trustingly JR 297
triuauntis *n. pl.* tyrants (*see note*) RG 127
troufulinges *n. pl.* frivolous stories JR 461
trow(e) *v. inf.* believe (that) JR 246, 248, 264, etc., ~ *to* believe in JR 562, RG 11
trubily *adj.* troublous, turbid, murky JR 428
tuo, to, twey(n) *num. card.* two JR 4, 33, 943, FS 6, etc.
tuo, to, twey *adv.* twice FS 226, ~ *so gode* twice as good JR 899, ~ *so miche* twice as much JR 899
twey(n) *see* **tuo, to, twey(n)** *num. card.*
twey *see* **tuo, to, twey** *adv.*

Þ

þai *pron. pers. nom. 3 pl.* they CK 9, 42, 109, etc.
þaim *see* **hem, þaim** *pron. pers. 3 pl. acc. and refl.*
þair *see* **þer(e), her(e), þair** *pron. pers. poss. 3 pl.*
þan(n)(e), þen(ne) *adv.* then JR 50, 62, 64, 678, RG 116, etc.
þan(n)(e), þen(ne) *conj.* than JR 39, 140, 730, RG 8, etc.

þanke *n.* thanks, favour JR 96
þat, þat þat *rel.* that which, what JR 926, FS 37, 54, 74, etc.; *in ~ ~ adv.* insofar as JR 303, 304, 316, etc.
þeere *adv.* there (unemphatic to introduce modal passive verb) FS 62
þefes *n. pl.* thieves JR 1011
þei *pron. dem. pl.* those (elsewhere it means 'they' as one might expect) FS 154
þenke *v. inf.* consider ~ *wel vpon* consider well JR 509, ~ . . . *on* think about JR 575; **þenken** *3 pl. pr. ind.*, consider JR 52; **þenkyn** *3 pl. pr. ind.* think RG 161; **þenke** *imp.* consider JR 594, ~ *on* consider further JR 658; **þouȝte(n)** *3 pl. pa. ind.* intended JR 147, RG 254
þenkeþ *see* **þink(eþ), þenkeþ** *v. impers. pr. ind.*
þenne *see* **þan(n)(e), þen(ne)** *adv. and conj.*
þer(e), her(e), þair *pron. pers. poss. 3 pl.* their JR 4, 22, 31, 42, CK 7, etc.
þeraftur *adv.* after that, in accordance with that RG 228
þer-aȝeyn *adv.* against that RG 180
þerbi, þerby *adv.* by (means of) that JR 30*, 256, RG 2, etc.
þer(e) *rel.* where JR 799, RG 273
þerfore *adv.* for that JR 663, 778, 782, etc.
þerof *adv.* from that JR 122, RG 231, CK 14, etc.
þerto *adv.* to that JR 215, 406, 794, etc., as well as that JR 363
þerwiþ *adv.* with that, within that JR 441, RG 194, 267
þes *pron. dem. sg.* this FS 249
þeues *n. pl.* thieves JR 1003, FS 218
þicke *adv.* thickly JR 190
þickelier *comp. adj.* more densely JR 444
þilk(e) *pron. dem. sg.* that same FS 89, 109, 126, *pron. dem. pl.* those FS 16, 34, 112, etc.
þink(eþ), þenkeþ *v. impers. pr. ind.* seems *me* ~ it seems to me JR 68, 117, 212, etc., *it ~ me* it seems to me JR 142
þis *pron. dem. pl.* these JR 134, 152, 351, etc.
þisilf *pron. pers. 2 sg. refl.* yourself FS 203
þo *def. art.* the RG 21 (not in *MED*, but see *LALME*: mainly Northern, but see LP Bed 4708, Nfk 4646, Sal 4218)
þof *see* **þouȝ, þof** *conj.*
þorȝe, þor(o)uȝ, þorow *prep.* through JR 244, RG 42, RG 53, CK 277, etc., ~ *kynde* by nature FS 117, *þer* ~ by that means RG 124
þouȝ, þof *conj.* although JR 585, ~ *al* although RG 152, ~ (*þat*) *it were so þat* despite the fact that CK 138, 147, 331
þouȝt *n.* thought JR 608, *hadden her ~ on* were intent on JR 307
þouȝte(n) *see* **þenke** *v. inf.*
þre(e) *num. card.* three JR 30, 33, 327, etc.
þred(e), þrid(d)(e) *num. ord.* third JR 189, 223, 427, 668, 759, 1001, etc.
þries *adv.* three times JR 44, 600
þristiþ *v. 3 sg. pr. ind.* thirsts RG 189
þritty *num. card.* thirty RG 8

U

vaken *see* **wake** *v. inf.*
vnabel, vnable *adj.* unsuitable, incapable JR 235, ~ *to* unsuited to FS 181
vnauysed *ppl. adj.* thoughtless, unconsidered FS 42
vncerteyne *adj.* wavering, uncertain, transitory RG 336
vnchaungeable *adj.* immutable RG 115
vnclene *adj.* impure JR 629
vndelyberacioun *n.* lack of deliberation FS 96
vndernym *v. inf.* criticize CK 80
vndernymmynge *vbl. n.* criticism CK 357
vnderstonde *v. inf.* understand CK 313, *es to* ~ means, is interpreted CK 104; **vnderstonde** *v. pa. p.* meant CK 55
vndorne *n.* (1) one of the hours (or offices) of the daily liturgy, divine office, or breviary, recited at around 9 am, more commonly known as Terce; (2) the time of day at which Terce is recited; (3) can also refer to midday or late afternoon (see *MED* s.v. 'undern', n.) RG 178
vndur, vnder *prep.* guaranteed by (*see note*) JR 1012, 1022, 1028, subordinate to CK 72, 73, 204, etc.

vngrounded ppl. adj. without basis JR 968
vnkynde *adj.* unkind, unnatural, ungrateful RG 280
vnkyndely *adv.* unnaturally JR 371
vnleful *adj.* unlawful JR 385
vnriȝtfull *adj.* unjust CK 84
vnriȝtfullich *adv.* unjustly CK 81
vnskilfull *adj.* incapable of reasoning CK 87
vntrewe *adj.* unfaithful JR 202, FS 179
vpon *prep.* out of JR 812
vse *n.* custom JR 549, 598, 932, *Salusbiri(e)* ~ Sarum ritual JR 933, 959
vse *v. inf.* practise JR 834, 866, CK 110
vsing *vbl. n.* use, wearing JR 587
vtward *adj.* outward, visible RG 163
varien *v. 3 pl. pr. ind.* ~ *fro* diverge from JR 416, ~ *in* are divergent in JR 1022; **variden** *3 pl. pa. ind.* diverged (from Christ's way) JR 272
variing *vbl. n.* ~ *of* variation in JR 912
veyn(e) *adj.* useless FS 17, 64
vencuscheþ *v. 3 sg. pr. ind.* vanquishes FS 5
vengabel *adj.* inclined to revenge JR 396
venge *v. refl. inf.* ~ *hem* revenge themselves JR 357
vengeaunce, veniaunce *n.* ~ *of* revenge against JR 816, punishment CK 277
venymyd *v. pa. p.* poisoned RG 230
venym(e) *n.* poison JR 103, 472, 886, etc, ~ *of soule* poison to the soul JR 668
uereylyche *adv.* indeed, in fact, truly FS 82
verrey, verrai *adj.* true FS 36, 37, CK 239
verrylykere *comp. adv.* more truly FS 356
vertu(e) *n.* power JR 231, 586, *be* ~ *of* because of JR 379, ~ *of* power from JR 622, *be þe* ~ *þerof* as a result of its power JR 625; **vertues** *n. pl. in* ~ established in virtue, virtuous JR 591
vertues *adj.* virtuous JR 17
vessells *n. pl.* vessels, emissaries (*see note*) RG 255
vicarie, vicary, viker(e) *n.* vicar, one who holds power in place of another JR 205, 209, 227, etc.
vyne *n.* wine JR 898
voidede *v. 3 pl. pa. subj.* got rid of, annihilated JR 1018
vouchesaaf *v. inf.* consent, grant RG 187

W

wake *v. inf.* stay awake, be vigilant RG 56; **vaken** *v. 3 pl. pr. ind.* JR 356
wakyng(e), wakinge *vbl. n.* awakening in the night (for prayer) FS 224, RG 164, 171
wandred *ppl. adj.* wandering, in exile JR 753
wan(n)(e) *conj.* when JR 74, 80, 96, etc., ~ *þat* when JR 468
wantiþ *v. impers. pr. ind. hym* ~, he lacks JR 24; **wanten** *3 pl. pr. subj.* lack RG 65
wantyng *vbl. n.* lack RG 27
wappid *ppl. adj.* wrapped JR 11
war(e) *adj.* aware, informed, wary JR 1, 581, 825, etc.
ware *see* **weþer, ware, wher** *interrog. conj.*
warkes *n. pl.* works, actions RG 381
wast *n.* waste JR 610, *in* ~ as *adv.* wastefully JR 78
wat *rel.* ~ *þat* whatever JR 499, ~ *man or woman* whatever man or woman JR 624
waxen *v. pa. p.* grown CK 198
wedded, (i)weddid *v. pa. p.* married JR 834, FS 256
wedded *ppl. adj.* ~ *wiþ* bound fast to (e.g. by vow) JR 313, 581
wedding, weddynge *vbl. n.* joining, binding (e.g. by vow) JR 43, 616, 770, etc.
wede *n.* weed FS 299
wederkoc *n.* weathervane JR 803
wele *adv.* well *þat it* ~ *be* that all may be well CK 414, 422, 464, (as intensifier) ~ *more* much greater CK 279
welle *see* **wyl, wil(le), welle** *n.*
wendeþ *v. 3 sg. pr. ind.* goes JR 10; **went** *pa. p. was* ~ had gone JR 367
weneþ *v. 3 pl. pr. ind.* think, suppose CK 113; **wenynge** *pr. p.* CK 144
went *see* **wendeþ** *v. 3 sg. pr. ind.*
werchen *see* **wirch(e), worche** *v. inf.*
were *interrog. conj.* where JR 414, 876
were *n.* state of doubt, uncertainty, anxiety CK 14

were *see* **ert** *v. 2 sg. pr. ind.*
were *v. inf.* wear JR 339, **weriþ** *3 sg. pr. ind. as it* ~ insofar as it wears it JR 713
werkday *n.* work day, i.e. weekday RG 28
werk(e) *n.* labour, work JR 457, etc., accomplishment or artefact resulting from labours RG 68, CK 290
wers(e) *comp. adj.* worse JR 459, 712, 1020
werst *superl. adj.* worst JR 1010
wete *see* **wite, wete, wiȝt, wit(t)** *v. inf.*
weþer, wheþur *adv.* or *particle* introducing a direct question (no Modern English equivalent) JR 264, RG 110, 148
weþer, ware, wher *interrog. conj.* whether JR 369, 394, 583, 706, 772, 808, etc.
weye *n.* way, path JR 118, 289, FS 75, etc.; **weies, weyes** *n. pl. many* ~ as *adv.* in many ways JR 77, 460
what *coord. conj.* ~ *be* ___ *and* ___ both by ____ and ____ (*see MED* s.v. 'what', 3b) CK 411
wheche *see* **wiche, wheche** *rel.*
wher *see* **weþer, ware, wher** *interrog. conj.*
wherbi *rel.* by means of which CK 350
wherin *rel.* (with ellipsis of antecedent) that within which RG 244
whiȝtnesse *n.* whiteness JR 692
whiles *adv.* whilst RG 158, CK 187
whitt *adj.* white JR 601
w(h)oso *pron. rel.* whoever JR 443, FS 205, 207, 210, etc.; *pron. indef.* JR 289
wy *interrog. conj.* why JR 214, 633
wiche, wheche *rel.* which JR 415, 496, RG 4, etc.
wiȝt *see* **wite, wete, wiȝt, wit(t)** *v. inf.*
wyl, wil(le), welle *n.* will JR 952, 954, *in* (. . .) ~ *to* intending to FS 183, 190, 193; *wiþ(outen) good* ~ *to* with(out) the good intention of FS 186, 189; ~ *of him* his (faculty of) will FS 83
wile *n.* while *litel* ~ a little while JR 1026; **wiles** *n. pl. be þer* ~, alternately, in their turns JR 4
wilful *adj.* willing, deliberate RG 154, ~ *to forȝyue* willing to forgive RG 184
wilfu(l)ly *adv.* willingly, deliberately, by one's own free will RG 137, 186, 215
willi *adv.* willingly, freely JR 551
wilt *v. 2 sg. pr. ind.* want to, wish to JR 85, 91, 1010, etc.; **nill** *2 sg. pr. ind.* do not want to (**ne** contr. with **will**) CK 265; **wol(l)en, wolun** *3 pl. pr. ind.* want to JR 999, RG 111, etc.; **wole** *3 sg. pr. subj.* may wish JR 783; **wold** *3 sg. pa. ind.* (with present sense) wish to CK 108; *3 pl. pa. ind.* (with present sense) wish to CK 109; **wolde** *3 pl. pa. ind.* wanted to JR 441; **wolde** *1 sg. pa. subj.* want(ed) to, wish(ed) JR 111, 113, 127, etc.; *3 sg. pa. subj. God* ~, ~ *God*, would that God (would grant) JR 47, 128, 699; *1 pl. pa. subj.* JR 497
wynne *n.* wine JR 927
wynne *v. inf.* earn JR 462, ~ *hem* gain for themselves RG 221, ~ *hem to heuen* earn their way to heaven RG 223
wynnyng(e) *vbl. n.* profit JR 474, 479, 481, etc., *cause of* ~ for the goal of profit JR 484
wirch(e), worche *v. inf.* work, do JR 815, CK 289, 295; **werchen** *1 pl. pr. ind. þat we* ~, what we do JR 804; **wurching** *pr. p.* working, acting, doing RG 180
wirchyng, wurchyng *vbl. n.* labours, deeds RG 151, behaviour, actions RG 226
wise *n.* way JR 481, 978, 1027, *none oþer* ~, *adv.* in no other way CK 40
wit *see* **wiþ, wit** *prep.*
wite, wete, wiȝt, wit(t) *v. inf.* know JR 8, 555, 1010, RG 201, 218, etc.; **wot(e)** *1 sg. pr. ind.* JR 115, 120, 123, etc.; **wost(e)** *2 sg. pr. ind.* CK 48, 340, 355, etc.; **witen** *pl. pr. ind.* CK 169; **witte** *imp.* JR 703; **wist(e)** *3 sg. pa. ind.* JR 811, CK 273
witnesse *n.* testimony, evidence JR 138, 317, RG 339, etc.
witnesse *v. inf.* testify to, assert JR 1016, RG 309
witnessynge *pr. p.* taking as testimony/proof FS 12
witouten *prep.* without RG 377
witt(e) *n.* meaning, understanding RG 90, 312, *upon þe same* ~ by the same token, according to the same understanding JR 587; capacity for understanding JR 636, 840, 869, etc.
witt(e) *see* **wite, wete, wiȝt, wit(t)** *v. inf.*

witty *adj. al* ~ all-knowing JR 363
wiþ, wit *prep.* with JR 316, 455, etc., against JR 1
wiþal *prep.* with RG 167
wiþdrawinge *vbl. n.* ~ *of þer prechynge*, their withholding of preaching JR 482
wiþholdiþ constrains, restrains, holds back FS 330
wiþou(ȝ)te(n) *adv.* outside, out of JR 61, 65, from JR 65; *adj.* without JR 45, 194, 346, etc.
wiþouȝteforþe, *adv.* outwardly JR 628
wiþsaid *v. pa. p.* denied CK 47
wiþstonde *v. inf.* resist, stand against CK 71, 84, 212, etc.
wiþstondinge *vbl. n.* resistance CK 360
woke *n.* week FS 226
wold(e), wole, wol(l)en, wolun *see* **wilt** *v. 2 sg. pr. ind.*
wo(u)nder *n.* marvel JR 1002 *I haue . . .* ~ I am surprised, I marvel (in disbelief) CK 4, *it es* (. . .) ~ it is surprising/hard to believe CK 71, 154, 370, etc., *it semeþ* ~ it seems amazing JR 221 (predicative uses without article are listed here as *n.* rather than *adj.*, following *MED*)
wonderful *adj.* causing wonder or awe JR 247
wonderfullich *adv.* in a manner hard to credit CK 320
wondreþ *v. impers. pr. ind. me* ~ *þat* I marvel that CK 133, 348
wondringe *pr. p.* ~ *of* marvelling at FS 60
wone *v. inf.* dwell, remain RG 199; **wonyng** *pr. p. for þer* ~ because they were living JR 164
wonyng *ppl. adj.* dwelling RG 65
woo *n.* woe JR 73
worche *see* **wirch(e), worche** *v. inf.*
word *n.* utterance, statement RG 211, 217
wordeyned *see* **orde(y)ne** *v. inf.*
wordelynesse *n.* attachment to things of this world JR 286
wordely, wordeli *see* **wor(l)dely, worldli(ch(e)), worliche** *adj.*
worderes *n. pl.* warders JR 375
world(e) *n.* secular life, life in this world (as opposed to the afterlife or a spiritual life) JR 15, 26, 97, etc., *of þe* ~, worldly JR 30, 92, 103, etc., *to þe* ~ to persons in secular life in this world JR 245, 399, 505, etc., with respect to worldly things RG 232; **worldes** *n. gen.* worldly JR 474, *of þe* ~ *good*, of worldly goods JR 345
wor(l)dely, worldli(ch(e)), worliche *adj.* secular, in this world (*see* **world(e)** *n.*) JR 15, 159, 285, 995, CK 125, etc.
worschipe *v. inf.* honour JR 200
worschipe, wurschip *n.* honour JR 92, RG 44, 65, etc., *to* ~ *of him* for his honour/worship JR 815
worþe *adj.* worth, *noþing* ~, *not* ~ of no value JR 372, 568, worthwhile JR 538
worþi *adj.* wealthy JR 225, deserved, fitting *it were . . .* ~ *þat* it is fitting that CK 163
woso *see* **w(h)oso** *pron. rel.*
wot(e) *see* **wite, wete, wiȝt, wit(t)** *v. inf.*
wounder *see* **wo(u)nder** *n.*
wreþ *n.* anger *þe sones of* ~ the sons of anger FS 118
writen *ppl. adj.* written FS 2
wronges *n. pl. þer* ~ wrongs done to them JR 395
wroþe *adj.* angry CK 40, 261, 345
wurchyng, wurching *see* **wirch(e), worche** *v. inf. and* **wirchyng, wurchyng** *vbl. n.*
wurschip *see* **worschipe, wurschip** *n.*

INDEX OF BIBLICAL REFERENCES

All biblical quotations, references, and allusions in the text of the dialogues and in the Explanatory Notes are included here. The text is cited wherever the bible is quoted there, even if imprecisely; for vaguer references (e.g., 'in þe gospell in dyuers places' CK 214) only the note is cited.

GENERAL INDEX

All references in the text of the dialogues to places, named individuals, their writings or the writings in which they are named, canon law (under 'canon law citations'), and anonymous works (under their titles) are included here. Names used as examples without specific reference (e.g., 'nether Ieffe ne Ion' JR 299) are not included. Standard modern versions of names are provided (e.g., 'pseudo-Hildegard' rather than 'Hildagar', JR 1005), but these are in all cases stripped of titles such as 'saint' or 'lord'. Pseudonymous works are alphabetized under the names of their supposed authors. Crossreferences are provided wherever original spellings or versions of names are alphabetically distant or difficult to recognize from the modern equivalent. The Explanatory Notes are cited wherever they provide further details, but are not fully indexed here. Biblical names and designations (e.g. 'þe wise man', FS 103–4) are included and crossreferenced, but for quotations please consult the Index of Biblical References.